I0523309

Herbert Maxwell

Studies in the topography of Galloway;

Being a list of nearly 4000 names of places, with remarks on their origin and meaning, and an introductory essay

Herbert Maxwell

Studies in the topography of Galloway;
Being a list of nearly 4000 names of places, with remarks on their origin and meaning, and an introductory essay

ISBN/EAN: 9783337810047

Printed in Europe, USA, Canada, Australia, Japan

Cover: Foto ©ninafisch / pixelio.de

More available books at **www.hansebooks.com**

STUDIES

IN THE

TOPOGRAPHY OF GALLOWAY

BEING A LIST OF

*NEARLY 4000 NAMES OF PLACES WITH REMARKS
ON THEIR ORIGIN AND MEANING, AND
AN INTRODUCTORY ESSAY*

BY

SIR HERBERT EUSTACE MAXWELL, Bart.

OF MONREITH

M.P., F.S.A., F.S.A. SCOT., F.L.S., ETC.

*" Disce, docendus adhuc quæ censet amiculus, ut si
Cæcus iter monstrare velit."*　　HORACE, *Epist.* i. 17. 3.

EDINBURGH: DAVID DOUGLAS

MDCCCLXXXVII.

𝕿𝖍𝖎𝖘 𝕰𝖘𝖘𝖆𝖞 𝖎𝖘 𝕯𝖊𝖉𝖎𝖈𝖆𝖙𝖊𝖉

TO THE

COUNTESS OF GALLOWAY

BY HER PERMISSION.

CONTENTS.

PREFACE.

THE collection of materials for the following pages was suggested some years ago by the perusal of an early edition of Dr. Joyce's *Irish Names of Places*. The identity apparent between many of the local names sifted and interpreted by that learned writer and those of Galloway, seemed to point to the possibility of some advance being achieved by the classification and comparison of all the names in that province. To any student who may in future approach the task more fully equipped with that knowledge of Celtic literature in which the present writer confesses him-self—*in limine*—sadly imperfect, it may at least be serviceable to find nearly four thousand names of places alphabetically arranged. The agitated course of politics during the twelve months commencing in August 1885 (involving three elections for the county of Wigtown), and almost incessant parliamentary and official work subsequently, have interfered considerably with the attention due to the revisal of proofs, and I gratefully record my sense of the patience shown by Mr. David Douglas in conducting the work through the press. To Mr. Carrick Moore of Corswall, also, to whom I was permitted to submit the proofs, and to whom many valued suggestions are owed, I wish to offer my sincere thanks.

MONREITH, *May 7th,* 1887.

AUTHORITIES QUOTED.

ABBREVIATIONS.	TITLES.
Agnew, . .	A History of the Hereditary Sheriffs of Galloway, by Sir Andrew Agnew, Bart, M.P. Edinburgh, 1864.
Armstrong,	The History of Liddesdale, Eskdale, Ewesdale, Wauchopedale, and the Debateable Land, by Robert Bruce Armstrong. Part I. from the twelfth century to 1530. 4to, Edinburgh, MDCCCLXXXIII.
Barnbarroch, .	Correspondence of Sir Patrick Waus of Barnbarroch, Knight, 1540-1597. Edited by Robert Vans Agnew, F.S.A. Scot. 8vo, Edinburgh, 1882.
Brev. Aberd., .	Breviarium Aberdonense; republished in facsimile for the Bannatyne Club. 2 vols. 4to, Edinburgh, 1852.
Buchanan, .	Travels in the Western Hebrides from 1782 to 1790.
Celt. Scot., .	Celtic Scotland, a History of Ancient Alban, by William F. Skene, LL.D. 3 vols. 8vo, Edinburgh, 1876-80.
Coll. A.G.A.A.,	Historical and Archæological Collections of Ayrshire and Galloway.
Cormac, . .	Sanas Cormaic (in "Three Irish Glossaries," ed. W. S[tokes], London, 1862).
Corm. Tran., .	Cormac's Glossary, translated by J. O'Donovan, ed. W. Stokes. Calcutta, 1868.
Crauf. MS., .	A MS. History of the Macdoualls of Garthland (written *circ.* 1750), by Mr. Craufurd, in the possession of Henry Macdouall of Garthland, Esq.
Cuninghame, .	Cuninghame, topographised by Timothy Pont, A.M., 1604-1608, with continuations and illustrative notices by the late James Dobie of Crummock, F.S.A. Scot., edited by his son, John Shedden Dobie. 4to, Glasgow, 1876.
Eccles. Antiq.,	Ecclesiastical Antiquities of Down, Connor, and Dromore, consisting of a taxation of those dioceses, compiled in the year MCCCVI., with notes and illustrations by the Rev. William Reeves, M.B., M.R.I.A. 4to, Dublin, 1847.
Eg., . .	Egerton MS. in British Museum.
Fél., . .	Félire des Oengus, the Calendar of Oengus. Dublin, 1880.
Four Masters, .	Annals of the Kingdom of Ireland, by the Four Masters. Edited by John O'Donovan, LL.D. 7 vols. 4to, Dublin, 1856.
Hy Fiachrach,	The Genealogies, Tribes, and Customs of the Hy Fiachrach. Edited by John O'Donovan. 4to, Dublin, 1844.

ABBREVIATIONS.	TITLES.
Hy Many,	The Tribes and Customs of the Hy Many, commonly called O'Kelly's Country, with a Translation and Notes, by John O'Donovan. 4to, Dublin, 1843.
Inq. ad Cap.,	Inquisitionum ad Capellam Domini Regis Retornatarum quae in publicis archivis Scotiae adhuc servantur Abbrevatio. In this reference are included various names extracted from the Rotuli Scotiæ and some other public records.
Ir. Gl.,	Irish Glosses, ed. Whitley Stokes. Dublin, 1860.
Ir. Hist. & Arch.	The Journal of the Irish Historical and Archæological Association of Ireland. Dublin.
Jamieson,	Dictionary of the Scottish Language. New edition, 8vo, Edinburgh, 1877.
Joyce,	The Origin and History of Irish Names of Places, by P. W. Joyce, LL.D., etc. 2 vols. 8vo, 5th edition, Dublin, 1883.
Kal. Scot. Saints,	Kalendars of the Scottish Saints, with personal notices of those of Alba, Laudonia, and Strathclyde, by Alexander Penrose Forbes, D.C.L. 4to, Edinburgh, 1872.
Lluyd,	Archaeologia Britannica, giving some account additional to what has already been published of the Languages, Histories, and Customs of the original inhabitants of Great Britain, from collections and observations in travels through Wales, Cornwal, Bas-Bretagne, Ireland, and Scotland. By Edward Lluyd, M.A. of Jesus College, Keeper of the Ashmolean Museum, Oxford. Vol. I. Glossography. Folio, Oxford, 1707. The second volume was never published.
LU,	Leabhar na h-Uidri. Ed. Dublin, 1870.
Lucas,	Studies in Nidderdale, by Joseph Lucas. 8vo, London, N.D. (1885).
Macalpine,	A Pronouncing Gaelic Dictionary, to which is prefixed a concise but most comprehensive Gaelic Grammar, by Neil Macalpine. Edited by John Mackenzie, 1847. Eighth edition, 8vo, Edinburgh, 1881.
Macfarlane MS.,	Manuscript of 17th century in Advocates' Library, Edinburgh, printed in Appendix to Symson's Galloway.
Maclellan,	*Gallovidiae Descriptio ; Joanne Maclellano Autore.* Printed with Pont's Maps in Blaeu's Geography.
M'Kerlie,	History of the Lands and their Owners in Galloway. 5 vols. 8vo, Edinburgh, 1870-79.
Mactaggart,	Scottish Gallovidian Encyclopædia, by John Mactaggart. 8vo, London, 1824.
Muircheartach,	The circuit of Ireland, by Muircheartach MacNeill, prince of Aileach. Edited, etc., by John O'Donovan. 4to, Dublin, 184 .
O'Dav.,	O'Davoren's Glossary (in Stokes' "Three Irish Glossaries").

ABBREVIATIONS.	TITLES.

O'Don. Topogr., The Topographical Poems of John O'Dubhagain and Giolla Na Naomh O'Huidrin. Edited, etc., by John O'Donovan, LL.D., M.R.I.A. 8vo, Dublin, 1862.

O'Reilly, . . Edward O'Reilly's Irish-English Dictionary. A new edition. Dublin, 1864.

P., . . . Timothy Pont's Maps of Galloway, in *Geographiae Blaviana volumine sexto, quo Liber* xii. xiii., *Europae continentur.* Folio, Amsterdam, 1662 (the survey was executed about 1604).

Pict. Scot. Chron., Chronicles of the Picts, Chronicles of the Scots, and other Early Memorials of Scottish History. Edited by William F. Skene, LL.D. Edinburgh, 1867.

Pitcairn, . . Criminal Trials in Scotland, from A.D. 1488 to A.D. 1624, compiled from the Original Records and MSS., with Historical Notes and Illustrations. By Robert Pitcairn, 4 vols., 1829-33 (Bannatyne Club).

Proc. Soc. An. Scot. Proceedings of the Society of Antiquaries of Scotland. 4to, Edinburgh.

Reeves, . . The Life of St. Columba, Founder of Hy; written by Adamnan, ninth Abbot of that Monastery. Edited by William Reeves, D.D. 4to, Dublin, 1857.

Rhys, Lectures on Welsh Philology, by John Rhys, M.A. 2d edition. 8vo, London, 1879.

Shaw, . . History of the Province of Moray, by the Rev. Lachlan Shaw. 4to, Elgin, 1827.

Sibbald MS., . Manuscript of 17th century in Advocates' Library, Edinburgh, printed in Appendix to Symson's Galloway.

Skeat, An Etymological Dictionary of the English Language, by the Rev. Walter Skeat, etc. etc. 4to, Oxford, 1882.

Symson, . . A large Description of Galloway, by Andrew Symson, minister of Kirkinner, MDCLXXXIV., with an Appendix containing original papers from the Sibbald and Macfarlane MSS. 8vo, Edinburgh, MDCCCXXIII.

Windisch, . Irische Texte mit Wörterbuch von Ernest Windisch. 8vo, Leipzig, 1880.

W. P. MS., . MS. Rentals of Whithorn Priory Lands, 1550-85.

KEY TO ABBREVIATIONS AND SYMBOLS.

A.S. = Anglo-Saxon, or Old Northern English.

B. = Breton, the Brythonic dialect spoken by the Celtic population of Brittany.

BR. SC. = Broad, or Lowland Scotch, especially the dialect of Galloway and Nithsdale.

C. = Cornish, the Brythonic dialect formerly spoken by the natives of Cornwall.

DAN. = Modern Danish.

DU. = Modern Dutch.

E. = Modern English.

ERSE = The Goidhelic dialect now spoken in parts of Ireland.

F. = Modern French.

G. = Modern German.

GAEL. = Gaelic, the Goidhelic dialect now spoken by the Scottish Highlanders.

GK. = Classical Greek.

GOTH. = Gothic.

ICEL. = Icelandic, the Scandinavian speech of the natives of Iceland, which represents most nearly, of all modern Scandinavian dialects, the Old Norse spoken by the Norse and Danish marauders of the eight and ninth centuries.

LAT. = Classical Latin.

LOW LAT. = Low or Mediæval Latin.

LITH. = Lithuanian, a Slavonic branch of Aryan speech.

M. = Manx, the Goidhelic dialect now spoken by the natives of the Isle of Man.

M.E. = Middle English, from about A.D. 1200 to A.D. 1500.

M.H.G. = Middle High German, or the speech of Mediæval Germany proper, as distinguished from that of other districts of Teutonic speech.

O. ERSE = The Goidhelic language of the earliest Welsh inscriptions previous to the sixth century, and of the earliest Irish MSS. and inscriptions.

O.F. = Old French (of Burguy, Cotgrave, or Roquefort).

O.H.G. = Old High German, or the language of Germany proper previous to the twelfth century.

o.w. = Old Welsh, from the sixth century, when the difference between Brythonic and Goidhelic speech appears to have been first established in Britain, down to the Reformation.

RUSS. = Modern Russian.

SKT. = Sanskrit.

SWED. = Modern Swedish.

W. = Modern Welsh, the Brythonic dialect of the Celtic population of Wales, from the fifteenth century.

Cf. = 'compare.'

q.v. = 'quod vide,' *i.e.* which see.

's.c.' following the name of the parish = sea-coast, *i.e.* that the place is on the coast, where the names are generally of a well-defined class.

s.v. = 'sub verbo,' *i.e.* under the word. Thus [p. 92], "*Skeat, s.v. Well* (2)."

— (minus mark) = 'derived from.' Thus [p. 52, under Altaggart], "O. ERSE *sacard* – LAT. *sacerdos*," signifying that *sacard* is a direct loan from the Latin.

+ (plus mark) = 'cognate with, related to, springing from a common root, but not derived from.' Thus [p. 52, under Altibrair, "*Brathair*, a brother, W. *brawd*, C. *bredar* + A.S. *bróthor* + ICEL. *brodir* + GOTH. *bróthar* + O.H.G. *pruoder* + RUSS. *brat'* + LAT. *frater* + GK. φράτηρ + SKT. *bhrátri* – √BHAR, to bear," signifying that the Celtic, Anglo-Saxon, Icelandic, Gothic, Old High German, Russian, Latin, Greek, and Sanskrit, though not derived one from the other, are related by common origin from the Aryan root BHAR.

√ = an Aryan root up to, but not beyond which, it is possible to trace a word. Thus [p. 79, under Barnolas], "LAT. *sol*, the sun – √SWAR, to glow," signifying that *sol* and the cognate words in other languages are traceable to the Aryan root SWAR.

Variant forms, from old charters and other sources, are printed in parentheses immediately after the names of places in the Glossary.

The parish or parishes in which a name occurs are mentioned in inverted commas after the variant forms.

The derivation (real or supposed) follows in italics, accompanied, when necessary, by the approximate English pronunciation in brackets ; thus, "*Achadh* [aha], a field.'

ERRATA.

PAGE

42. Line 13, *for* " Lucopibia " *read* " Loucopibia " (the Latin equivalent of which is Lucopibia).

103. Line 19, omit from " *Carn* " to " possibly," inclusive.

114. Under " CHALLOCHMUNN " *for* " [tyallach] " *read* " [tullach]," and after " church " insert " Eileanmunde (*i.e.* St. Munde's Isle) a parish in Argyllshire ; also."

117. " CLAUCHREM," and p. 118 " CLAUCHTREM," should come after " CLAUCHLOUDON," on p. 120.

118. " CLAWBELLY " should come after " CLAUNCH," on p. 120.

123. Under " CLOAK HILL," *for* " Carsphairn " *read* " Colvend."

130. Under " CRAIGEAZLE," *for* " Inch " *read* " ' Kells.' A hill of 1550 feet."

186. *For* " GALL MOSS OF DIRNEAUK," *read* " GALL MOSS OF DIRNEARK."

227. Under " KNOCKNAW " delete from " or " to " kiln " inclusive, and " Auchenhay and."

227. *For* " KNOCKNAMOOR " *read* " KNOCKNAMOON," and delete all after " Minigaff."

STUDIES

TOPOGRAPHY OF GALLOWAY.

" Names and technical terms are always a difficulty to translators, especially if the original language be very different in sound and genus from that of the translation. There is, however, an additional difficulty in Irish. In the first place, we have to deal, not with one language, but with several ; for between the language of some Irish tracts and the present spoken language there is an interval of from one thousand to twelve hundred years, during which the Irish language has been constantly undergoing changes. In the second place, as there was no great classical period, the orthography has never been fixed, so that there is often considerable difference in the spelling of the same name in different manuscripts even of the same age."—DR. SULLIVAN, Preface to Introduction to O'Curry's *Irish Lectures*, p. 13.

IT may be doubted if any literary subject which could be selected is more charged with difficulty, more fertile in controversy, more darkened with reckless speculation than that with which the writer of the following pages has attempted to deal.

The names of places, conferred by a people speaking a language which has been for centuries superseded by one of a totally different construction and grammar, and who have left behind them not a vestige of literature, present a problem from which the most ardent scholar might turn back in hopelessness of any approach being made to its solution.

When it is considered how widely Celtic words, rendered phonetically into English letters, differ from their original

A

orthography, how much their present form depends upon the pronunciation of certain dialects many centuries ago—dialects which, both in consonant and vowel sound, and in syllabic stress, are known to have been progressively changing; when it is remembered, in addition, that, like pebbles in a flowing stream, words used by successive generations are rounded and polished often out of all likeness to their original form, it will not be easy to underrate the difficulty which confronts the student in an attempt to deal with everyday speech and living words.

But how vastly is that difficulty enhanced when the words to be dealt with are literally dead words—ghosts and skeletons of ideas, originally suggested by physical features or incidents which have long since been altered, or of which all record has been forgotten ; or commemorative of personages whose last resting-places have been obliterated as completely as their deeds and virtues.

Yet it is precisely in that last condition that the stimulus lies to attempt assistance in a solution of the problem. To peer back into the shadowy past, to fill in some of the details of the landscape, with the main outlines of which we are familiar, which surrounded the primitive inhabitants of our native land; to identify the animals, the trees, and herbs, the minerals which occupied their attention and sustained their lives; to trace the scenes of conflict, of merry-making, of pagan and Christian worship, is a motive as natural as any which causes history to be written.

Names cannot be invented for places. No mere combination of sounds can be contrived to designate hill or dale, river or lake; nor have they been named, as children now are by their parents, according to fancy, interest, or family custom; but they received their appellations, as men and women did in former times, from some distinctive characteristic, from a definite event, or from the name of some individual who identified himself with them. We may be sure that every place-name, however unintelligible to us, was originally as pregnant of meaning as such names as Albert Gate, Virginia, or Cape of Good Hope.

Although many of the place-names of Galloway have been worn down beyond all recognition, yet there are others, in not a few of which the meaning is as clear as that of the inscription on a well-preserved coin; while a third class consist of those which may be identified by their similarity to names in other Celtic districts, the original forms of which have been enshrined in early manuscripts.

1. In dealing with those in the first·class, the utmost that can be done with them is to record them in their present form, together with the earliest variations of spelling. Such names as Caitans, Crogo, Malzie, Cutcloy, Luce, Merrick, Rispain, Rotchell, Bladenoch, Tintum, Syllodioch, Caugh, and many others, may receive at some future day light in which their meanings may be read, but at present they must be classed as unintelligible; it is even impossible to declare in what speech they are framed. The Gaels were not the aboriginal inhabitants of the land of Alba. It may be assumed with something approaching certainty that they were preceded by a small-boned, long-skulled, dark-haired race, speaking a dialect of Iverian, a language which survives in the Basque Province, and which cannot as yet be assigned to any known family of speech. This people, we may believe, were not overcome, extirpated, or absorbed without a prolonged and intermittent struggle. The invaders would adopt and per-petuate some of the names which they found attached to rivers, hills, or woods, and hand them down to us intermingled with their own nomenclature. Cormac has preserved in his glossary two words which he says belonged to the speech of the Firbolg, or dark-haired race in Ireland, namely, *fern*, good ; and *ond*, a stone. But others may very well be supposed to survive in

the names of places. Skene remarks : " The Basque word for water is *Ur*, and analogy would lead us to recognise it in the rivers called Oure, Urr, Ure, Urie, Orrin, and Ore."[1]

Pre-Celtic inhabitants.

Professor Rhys has summed up all that is known of this pre-Celtic race in such clear and concise terms that I am tempted to quote liberally from his work :—

" It is by no means probable that the Celtic immigrants into these islands found them without inhabitants, or that they arrived in sufficient force to exterminate them. Consequently it may be supposed that in the course of ages the conquered races adopted the language of the invading race, but not without introducing some of their own idioms. The question, then, is, who these pre-Celtic islanders were, and whether the Celtic languages still have non-Aryan traits which may be ascribed to their influence. In answer to the first of these questions, it has been supposed that the people whom the Celts found here must have been of Iberian origin, and nearly akin with the ancient inhabitants of Aquitania and the Basques of modern times. In support of this may be mentioned the testimony of Tacitus in his *Agricola*, where, in default of other sources of information, he bases his statements on the racial differences which betrayed themselves in the personal appearance of the British populations of his day. Among other things, he there fixes on the Silures as being Iberians. The whole chapter is worth reproducing, however cruel it may seem to disturb the dreams of those who take it for granted that when the Romans got to know this island it was inhabited by one homogeneous and unmixed race, to which they continue to give the unmeaning name of Ancient Britons :—

"' Who were the first inhabitants of Britain, whether indigenous or immigrant, is a question involved in the obscurity usual among barbarians. Their temperament of body is various, whence deductions are formed of their various origin.

---

[1] *Celtic Scotland*, i. 216.

Thus the ruddy hair and large limbs of the Caledonians point out a German derivation; the swarthy complexion and curled hair of the Silures, together with their situation opposite Spain, render it probable that a colony of the ancient Iberi possessed themselves of that territory. They who are nearest Gaul resemble the inhabitants of that country, whether from the duration of hereditary influence, or whether it be that when lands jut forward in opposite directions, climate gives the same condition of body to the inhabitants of both. On a general survey, however, it appears probable that the Gauls originally took possession of the neighbouring coast. The sacred rites and superstitions of those people are discernible among the Britons. The languages of the two nations do not greatly differ. The same audacity in provoking danger, and irresolution in facing it when present, is observable in both. The Britons, however, display more ferocity, not being yet softened by a long peace; for it appears from history that the Gauls were once renowned in war, till, losing their valour with their liberty, languor and indolence entered amongst them. The same change has also taken place among those of the Britons who have been long subdued; but the rest continue such as the Gauls formerly were.' (Bohn's translation of *Tacitus.*)

" Accordingly, some of the non-Aryan traits of Welsh and Irish may be expected to admit of being explained by means of Basque. Unfortunately, however, that language is not found to assist us so readily as one could have wished, as it is only known in a comparatively late form." [1]

The author then proceeds, on the supposition that the consonant *p* had no place in the alphabet of Goidhelic speech, to indicate certain districts where the occurrence of that consonant in place-names suggests that they were occupied by a pre-Celtic race, who have left this trace of their vocabulary.

[1] *Lectures on Welsh Philology*, by John Rhys, M.A., etc. etc., 2d Edition, London, 1879, pp. 178-180.

Among these he mentions Lucopibia, a town of the Novantæ, supposed to have stood near Luce Bay in Wigtonshire.

Without following this somewhat slender clue further, it would appear that in some of these unintelligible names are echoed the accents of a race of whom every other trace that may be recognised has long since passed away; but we must remember the natural tendency in a people using names of which they know not the meaning to assimilate them to some word of a similar sound in their own language expressive of a distinct idea. Thus the Celtic successors of the primitive people must have acted under the same influence as the English speakers who followed them, and, adopting certain words and names from their predecessors, have recast them in their own tongue with a totally different significance.

A few instances in modern times will suffice to explain this process.

Spurious etymologies. There is a small loch in Glasserton parish, on the shoulder of Barhullion Fell, which bears the name of Lochanhour. Owing to comparatively recent drainage it is liable in summer to become completely dry, reappearing with the autumn rains. The first time I heard its name was in my boyhood. I was shooting round its shore when the keeper mentioned its name. He added: "It means *loch-in-an-hour*, for an hour's rain fills it." This may have come to be the idea associated with the name in the minds of the present generation, or it may, more probably, have been devised by the keeper on the spot; at all events, it remained fixed in my own mind as the original meaning till I began to inquire deeper into these things. Then it became evident that the name was much older than the present depleted state of the lakelet; that the real name is *lochán odhar* [owr], the grey tarn, named probably from a huge mass of grey glaciated rock lying along the northern shore.

Again, there is a hill in Inch parish called Auld Taggart. Mactaggart has become a common surname in Galloway, and doubtless the country people now connect the name with an aged individual who bore it. But on the opposite side of the river Luce, within a few hundred yards of Auld Taggart, is a stream called Altaggart, that is, *Allt-t-sagairt* [altaggart],[1] the priest's glen or stream ; and the name has been transferred with modification to the hill opposite.

A familiar instance is that of the Phœnix Park in Dublin, which owes its present form to a corruption of *fionn uisc* [finn isk], the clear water. "It was originally the name of the beautiful and perfectly transparent spring well near the Phœnix Pillar, situated just outside the wall of the vice-regal grounds behind the gate lodge, and which is the head of the stream that supplies the pond near the Zoological Gardens. To complete the illusion, the Earl of Chesterfield, in the year 1745, erected a pillar near the well, with the figure of a phœnix rising from its ashes on the top of it, and most Dublin people now believe that the Park received its name from this pillar. The change from *fionn uisg'* to phœnix is not peculiar to Dublin, for the river Finisk, which joins the Blackwater below Cappoquin, is called Phœnix by Smith in his history of Waterford." [2]

The name of the beautiful demesne of Shambelly, close to New Abbey, in the stewartry of Kirkcudbright, is sadly garbled from the original Celtic. *Sean baile* [shan bally] is a term applied to many places, with the signification "old homestead or building." In Shinvalley in Penninghame, Shanvolley in Kirkcowan, as well as Shanvalley and Shanavally in Ireland, is preserved the aspirated form *sean bhaile* [shan vally].

This kind of attempt to impose a fictitious meaning upon names of places has been connived at by those who ought to know better. Charles Mackay, writing in Bentley's *Miscellany* for 1839, makes fun of the guessing school of etymology.

---

[1] The intrusive *t* eclipses and silences the *s*.
[2] Joyce's *Irish Names of Places*, vol. i. p. 42.

"Teddington," he says, " is a small place, chiefly remarkable for the first and last lock upon the Thames in aid of navigation. Etymologists found a very satisfactory explanation of the name of this village, and plumed themselves mightily on their cleverness. The tides flow up no farther than Teddington, and therefore, said they, the derivation of the word is obvious —'Tide-ending-town, from whence by abbreviation and corruption Tide-ing-ton—Teddington.'

" This was all very satisfactory, there was not a word to be said against it.

" Unluckily, however, Mr. Lysons, one of your men of dates and figures, one of those people whose provoking exactitude so often upsets theories, discovered that the original name of the place was not Teddington, but Totyngton. After this the etymologists had nothing to say for themselves—'a plain tale put them down,' unless, like the French philosopher in similar circumstances, they consoled themselves with the reflection that it was very unbecoming in a fact to rise up in opposition to their theory."

Nor is this all that tends to lead the inquirer off the true scent. A secondary process has set in since Broad Scots has ceased to be regarded as the language of educated persons. The Ordnance Surveyors in more than one instance seem to have attempted to make genteel and orthodox names which sounded in their ears like Broad Scotch, and therefore a vulgar *patois*. Here is an example. The Old Water is the name given in the Ordnance Survey Maps to a tributary of the Cluden in Irongray parish. This is the English rendering of that which sounds like "Auld Water," but which is in truth a hybrid name for the stream, namely, Gaelic *allt*, a glen or stream, and English *water*. *Allt* itself is a word which has travelled very far from its original root-meaning. Connected originally with Latin *altus* (high), it signified a height or cliff, but the meaning slid thence to the vale or glen between the heights, and finally into the stream within the vale.[1]

Another example is Gleniron in New Luce, where, however, the modern form, although the result of Anglicising what was supposed to be Broad Scots, has not concealed what may have been the original sense. The name appears in Pont's map as Klonairn, which sufficiently closely represents the Irish *cluain iairn*, meadow of the iron.

2. The second class is that into which names may be thrown, of the meaning of which there can be no reasonable doubt from the completeness with which the old Erse or mediæval Gaelic has been preserved. Such are Barglass (*barr glas*), the green top; Craigbernoch (*creag béarnach*), the cloven crag; Drummuckloch (*druim muclach*), the swine's ridge, or ridge of the swine pasture; Inchbane (*innis bán*), the white isle, or river pasture; Auchabrick (*achadh breac*), the speckled or variegated field; Knockdawn (*cnoc don*), the brown hill; and countless others. Yet these names have been in daily use for generations by persons, not one in ten thousand of whom had the slightest apprehension of their significance, nor cared to inquire into the origin of what they received as convenient, ready-made appellations. Unaltered Celtic names.

3. Finally, there is a large class which have to be very carefully dealt with, not without a prospect of discovering much, if not all, of their meaning. It consists of those names which have been rendered into English letters in phonetic imitation of the Erse or Gaelic originals, but widely differing in appearance from them, owing to the different value of letters in the two languages. It must be recollected that, short of an elaborate and laborious system of sound-signs or palæotype, such as that brought to so great perfection by Mr. Sweet, Mr. Ellis, and Mr. Melville Bell, which requires a degree of study and delicate attention that few ordinary readers have time to give, no alphabet suffices to indicate, except in a rough and Altered Celtic names.

---

[1] See under " Aldergowan " in the Glossary.

ready way, the niceties of oral sound.   The syllables in brackets, which follow the Erse words in the Glossary, forming the main part of this work, can be regarded only as a most imperfect mode of indicating the pronunciation of the original —valuable, if at all, chiefly in showing the contracting and elisive effect of the aspirate and eclipse upon consonants. But even that degree of precision cannot be claimed for the present forms of most of the Celtic place-names in Galloway. Some of them retain the form in which they were originally cast by clerks engrossing deeds containing names in the Gaelic vernacular never before reduced to writing.   Thus in Culquhirk (pronounced Culhwirk) is retained the Old Northern English *quh*, now represented by *wh*; in Challoch the softened sound remains of *t* followed by a diphthong, the original word being *tealach* [tyallagh], a forge.   This softening process is carried even further in the English *ration, nation, portion,* etc.

In others the present spelling is a further corruption of the earliest written forms, due to subsequent change in the pronunciation, or by the growth of a fictitious meaning.   A clear example of this change may be seen in the name Loch Hempton in Mochrum parish, which has assumed such a familiar Anglo-Saxon countenance as would probably exclude it from a list of names of Celtic origin, were it not that Pont, writing about a quarter of a century after Gaelic is believed to have ceased to be spoken in Galloway, spells it Dyrhympen.   Now, whatever the suffix *-hympen* may represent, *dyr* is the Old Celtic *dobhar, dur,* water, and bespeaks for Dyrhympen an origin anterior to the Anglo-Saxon occupation of the province.   Were it not for this, how plausible, seeing that Hempton Loch is within a stone-throw of the old Castle of Mochrum, would have been the suggestion that it was the loch of the *hame-town* (Hampton) or homestead.

Not to travel more than half a mile from this moorland lake, we may take the modern name of a similar piece of water,

Loch Wayoch, which, assuming it to be Erse, might very fairly represent *loch bheithach* [vayagh], which is very likely the true etymology, the meaning being the loch of the birchwood. But Pont calls it Loch Chrauochy, which points to an alternative origin of a similar meaning, *i.e. loch chraebhach* [hravagh], lake of the wood, or of the trees. Lastly, not to multiply instances of a very numerous class, taking the name of another lake, Lochan of Vice, in the parish of Tungland, appears in Pont's map in a form which, although it does not explain the meaning, at least shows that the present form is a corruption, for it is there written Loch Voyis, and in the Sibbald MS. of the seventeenth century it is rendered Loch Vuy.

It is clear from what has been said, that, had we nothing to rely upon but forms in Latin or English manuscripts from the twelfth century onwards, valuable and suggestive as many of these are, we should at most have little more than rude repre- sentations of the sound of Celtic names rendered in English letters by scribes, who probably, in many cases, did not under- stand the Erse language, or, at all events, could not write it. Further, it has to be borne in mind, especially by south-country readers, that in these early transcripts of Celtic names, the value of the English letters is not that of these letters in Modern, but in Middle English, of which the pronunciation was pro- bably much the same as in Lothian Broad Scots. *Ch* and *gh* are guttural spirants as in Broad Scots *loch, rough ;* although at the beginning of names, such as Challoch or Chipper (repre- senting Erse *tea* and *tio*), and in the solitary instance of Curchie- hill, in the middle of a name, *ch* is sounded as in English *church.* Pont uses *ch* where in modern use a simple aspirate is sounded, as in Barhapple, but in doing so he was probably faithful to the pronunciation of his day, when the sound of the aspirated *c* of *barr chapul,* hill of the horses, had not been further softened.

In Broad Scots, as in Old and Middle English, the *r* is trilled even when followed by a consonant or coming at the end of a word. This is an assistance in arriving at the Celtic original, which would be lost if the *r* receives no more than its value in Modern English. Thus a boy educated at Eton would speak of Bahwinnock, Bahveunohan, Barrūh, Caanfaw, Caansmaw, instead of the true pronunciation Barwinnock, Barvernoghan, Barraer, Cairnfore, Cairnsmore. Fortunately, at the time when these names were first written in English deeds, the *r* was fully trilled, and, even if the people of Galloway were now to adopt the silent *r*, it would not disappear from its important place in the names.

There are also certain vowel-sounds, such as the broad *a* and the Scots *u*, without attention to which it is not possible to arrive at the original pronunciation.

Absence of vernacular Celtic literature in Scotland. The copious Goidhelic literature of Erin or Ireland, of which many originals and many transcripts have been preserved to our day, has but a meagre counterpart in the vernacular of Alba or Scotland.

The Pictish Chronicle, which Mr. Skene assigns to the tenth century, was, in his opinion, compiled by the monks of Brechin.

The marginal entries in *The Book of Deer*, dating from the eleventh and twelfth centuries, are in the vernacular Gaelic of Alba, while the text of the Gospels which form the book itself offers evidence from which "there seems nothing improbable in concluding that it may have been written by a native scribe of Alba in the ninth century."[1]

No other manuscripts have as yet been claimed as the work of Alban writers. The fires of the Reformation burned so fiercely and so long in Scotland as to have consumed to all appearance every other fragment of the literature which we may assume to have been stored in the numerous ecclesiastical houses of the north.

---

[1] *The Book of Deer*, p. xxiii. Edited for the Spalding Club by John Stuart, LL.D. 4to, Edinburgh, 1869.

It might seem, therefore, to be as hopeless to attempt to reduce Galloway names to their original form as if we supposed France to have been overrun by English, her literature destroyed, her language forgotten, and English adopted as the vernacular. French names, written down phonetically by English lawyers of the present day, whom we must suppose, to maintain the parallel, utterly ignorant of the French language, would then present pleasing problems to the etymologist. From Bawdoe, Rewong, Reeshlew, Shattleroe Potyae, Shoveenie, to reconstruct Bordeaux, Rouen, Richelieu, Chatellerault, Poitiers, and Chauvigny, would be as difficult, and to some seem as ridiculous, as to expand Macherally into *Machair Amhalghaidh*, or reduce Shambelly to *sean baile*.

But, propitiously to my present task, there are innumerable places in Ireland bearing the same names as places in Galloway and other Goidhelic districts of Scotland. The primary forms of many of these Irish names have been preserved in the early annals, poems, and other manuscripts. They have been well sifted and identified by such masterly writers as Reeves, O'Donovan, Joyce, and others, were it not for whose labours it would have been wellnigh hopeless for the writer of these pages to attempt his undertaking.

Many place-names in Ireland synonymous with those in Galloway.

When, for example, Macherally in Kirkmaiden (locally pronounced Macherowly), is found to have its equivalent in Magherally, a parish in Ireland ; and when such an accomplished Celtic scholar as Dr. Reeves assigns as the interpretation of the latter place *machair Amhalghaidh* [Owlhay], Aulay's field, it is surely not assuming too much that the Wigtonshire name has the same meaning, especially when we find Macaulays still living in the immediate vicinity. Terally, in the same parish, may with equal safety be equated with Tirawley in Mayo, and construed *tir Amhalghaidh*, Aulay's land. But how vain would have been all endeavour, in the absence of the Irish parallels, to have restored the redundant consonants which are the pride of ancient and the stumbling-block of modern glotto-logists.

Proper names sometimes have assumed a Latinised form. Thus Devorgilla, grand-daughter of Uchtred, Lord of Galloway, and wife of John Baliol, the foundress of Baliol College and Sweetheart Abbey, bore a name which was written in Erse *Derbhforgaill*, in which the *bh* sounds as the Latin *v*.

The ancient languages of Galloway. Dismissing as unattainable all record of the speech of the pre-Celtic inhabitants of Galloway, it may be well to recapitulate briefly the conclusions which the researches of Rhys, Skene, Stokes, and other students tend to establish.

" The Celtic languages still spoken are Welsh, Breton, and Gaelic in Ireland, the Highlands of Scotland, and the Isle of Man. Among the dead ones are Old Cornish, Pictish, and Gaulish. Of these, Cornish, which ceased to be spoken only in the latter part of the last century, has left us a considerable amount of literature, while the Pictish words extant may be counted on one's fingers. The old Gauls have left behind them a number of monuments, from which, together with other sources, a fair number of their names, and a few other specimens of their vocabulary, have been collected—-enough, in fact, to assign them to their proper place in the Celtic family."[1]

So far as the British Isles are concerned, the Celtic tongue divides itself into two main families : the Goidhelic or Gaelic, embracing the dialects of Erse or Irish, Scottish Gaelic, and Manx ; the Brythonic or Welsh, those of Welsh, Cornish, and Breton, and, according to Professor Rhys, possibly Pictish. Until recently it has been argued that the Goidhelic speech represented that of the first invading force of Continental Celts who occupied Britain, ousting the aboriginal Iverian race, and who were themselves subsequently dispossessed of part of their territory, including the greater part of England, Wales, and what is now known as Scotland, as far north as Alclyde or

---

[1] *Lectures on Welsh Philology*, p. 15.

Dumbarton. The second wave of invasion was supposed to consist of a Celtic people, speaking a different dialect, namely, the Brythonic, Cymric, or Welsh race, who were ranked as part of the Gaulish population of the Continent. But Professor Rhys[1] leans to the opinion that there is no such dividing line to be drawn. Far from disputing the existence of two distinct branches of Celtic speech in Britain, the Goidhelic and Brythonic, he inclines to the opinion that the classification of the entire Celtic family into Goidhelic and Gallo-British branches is erroneous, and supports the view which presents "two branches, whereof the one embraces the Celts of the Continent, and the other those of the islands."

The close resemblance between Old Cornish and Breton speech he accounts for by the regurgitation which undoubtedly took place between the population of the south-west of England and the north-west of France, a process which has its parallel in the emigration of the Scots of northern Ireland to Alban (now Scotland) in the fifth century.

For the practical purposes of the present inquiry we may be content with the certainty that two distinct branches of Celtic speech did exist in North Britain at the time when most of the place-names in Galloway were conferred. If the Picts of Galloway spoke the Pictish language, it appears, from the evidence of these names, to have belonged to the Goidhelic or Gaelic rather than to the Brythonic or Welsh branch, which prevailed in the adjacent territory of Alclyde; indeed, the close resemblance borne by our local names to those of Ulster almost compel the assumption that the Picts of Galloway and the Scots of Dalriada spoke a common tongue. To borrow a simile from geology, the *facies* of the fossils in either district is so similar as to cause them to be assigned to the same formation. The colophon to the Gospels in the *Book of Deer* "is identical," says Mr. Whitley Stokes, "with the oldest Irish glosses in Zeuss's *Grammatica Celtica*."

Goidhelic names.

---

[1] *Lectures on Welsh Philology,* p. 22.

It must be remembered, too, that Erse or Gaelic continued to be spoken in Galloway until the closing years of the sixteenth century. If there had been any organic difference between the Gaelic of Galloway and that of the Highlands, it could scarcely have failed to have been noticed by contemporary writers, but both are spoken of in common as *Ersche*. No doubt there are names in the Province whose present form would bear being assigned to a Brythonic origin, but with these I have not ventured to deal, any more than with those of even more obscure origin. It is left to writers better acquainted with the Welsh speech to trace that language in such words as Peneilly, Pinminnoch, Penwhirn, Pinwherry, Cutreoch, Cutcloy, Manwhill, in which it is quite possible the Welsh *pen*, a head, *coed*, a wood, and *maen*, a stone, may be preserved.

The contact of the Province of Galloway with the Brythonic district of Alclyde, and the alternate warfare and alliance between the tribes inhabiting the two districts, would no doubt lead us to expect an admixture, to some extent, of Welsh names in the topography of Galloway. But having regard to the want of knowledge of the extinct Pictish speech, if indeed it was spoken by the Picts of Galloway, it is safer to refrain from speculation on names with a seemingly Welsh appearance.

The bulk of the names appear referable to a Goidhelic origin. These may have been conferred at any period from the first occupation of Galloway by the Gaels down to the time when Gaelic ceased to be the vernacular of the province. To the first of these limits it is difficult to assign an approximate date. If, as Professor Rhys suggests, the Pictish dialect belonged to the Brythonic rather than to the Goidhelic branch, then we naturally turn to the conquest of Galloway by Alpin, the last king of Scottish Dalriada,[1] in the eighth century, and it might be supposed that his followers who settled there originated the

---

[1] Occisus est in Gallowathia postquam eam penitus destruxit et devastavit. —*Chronicle of the Picts and Scots.*

Goidhelic names. But Professor Rhys assigns approximately
the divergence of Brythonic speech from Goidhelic to the sixth
century, being supported in that view by the fact that the early
Welsh inscriptions are so Goidhelic in form as to have been long
and strenuously claimed by Irish archæologists as evidence of the
occupation of Wales by Irish Gaels. "It would be needless,"
he adds, "to dwell on the fact that it is by no means certain
that the change of qv into p took place at the same time everywhere on Brythonic ground from the Clyde to the Loire."

If the Pictish inhabitants of the remote shores of Galloway
were Brythonic Celts, they would rather lag behind than precede
their kindred in Alclyde, Cumberland, and Wales, in yielding
to the new pronunciation ; consequently, taking the sixth century as the central period of the formation of Welsh speech,
little time would intervene before their province was overrun by
Alpin's Gaels, and their speech discontinued. It seems reasonable, therefore, to suppose that Brythonic speech was never the
vernacular of Galloway, that a dialect of Gaelic or Erse was
spoken from the first advent of the Celts down to the time when
it was superseded by Northern English.

The latter limitation may safely be applied to the lowland
districts at an earlier period than to the hills, when the ancient
tongue would continue to be spoken in the glens long after it
had ceased on the plains. Thus we find a much larger admixture of Teutonic names in such parishes as Sorbie, Kirkinner,
Kirkbean, and Colvend, than in the hill and moorland tracts
of Dalry, Carsphairn, Kirkcowan, and New Luce.

But even these data leave great vagueness as to the antiquity Antiquity of
place-names.
of our Celtic names of places. To go no further back than the
fourth century, when St. Ninian began the conversion of the
Galwegian Picts, Gaelic names may have been conferred at any
time between that and the sixteenth century, or a space of 1200
years. Most names of hills, rivers, cliffs, and other permanent
and striking landscape features may most probably be assigned

to the earlier moiety of that period, while those of houses and fields would be gradually conferred as the country became settled up and cultivated.

Next in number to the Gaelic names come those of Teutonic origin, framed in the Old Northern English or Northumbrian language, a dialect of Anglo-Saxon. That this was spoken, if not by any large number of the people, at all events by the clerics, we have recently received very conclusive evidence. The fragments of two Runic inscriptions upon carved crosses were discovered, one in 1885, in the ruins of the Priory Church at Whithorn, the other in 1886, under a mass of cliff debris in St. Ninian's Cave, in the adjacent parish of Glasserton. Professor Stephens assigns these Runes approximately to the sixth century.

The first-named cross had received severe handling to shape it into the conventional type of modern headstone. The greater part of the inscription, which had been cut on the edge of the stone and round the circular head, had been tooled off; the runes which remain are equivalent to the following:—

T * L F E R þ S.

Professor Stephens of Copenhagen is of opinion that the lost letter after T is I, which would, if restored, give a name which is not uncommon, viz., Tilferþ (meaning good-peace). It occurs in the oldest documents variously written Tilfriþ, Tilfrið, Tilfrith, Tilferd, Tilferð, and Tilferþ. It is probably the name of the man in whose memory the stone was erected, and the formula appears, from analogy, to have run somewhat in this way—

" (*This stane æfter*) Tilferþ s(*ette*)."

Of the inscription on the other cross also unhappily only a fragment remains. In this case, however, the damage has not been wanton, but accidental. Among the interesting discoveries recently made in St. Ninian's Cave, and since the publication of its first exploration,[1] was that of a cross richly carved with an intricate design of interlaced Celtic character. The lower part of the carved face was occupied by a tablet, the greater portion of which had been broken off by the fall of a huge mass of rock from the cliff above. The inscription appears to have been in one line only, of which the final word remains, reading equivalent to

WROTE,

i.e. wrought, worked, made. "Thus," writes Professor Stephens, "some such common formula, in stave-rime, as—

(*Æfter Warinæ Wulfstan*) wrote.

Consequently both ristings are in old north English, Northumbrian, most likely of the sixth century."

Besides these two inscriptions only four others referable to such an early date are known to me as having been identified in Wigtonshire, and they afford no clue to the spoken language of the district, being in Latin; one on a cross near Whithorn, one on a slab in the pavement of St. Ninian's Cave, and two in the old churchyard of Kirkmadrine. But there may be others in the Stewartry, and it is almost certain that the diligent inquiry now being made into such matters in the district will result in bringing to light more. ·

To this Anglo-Saxon or Early Northern English dialect are to be assigned most of the words ending in *-et* (such as Aiket, Blaiket, Birket), a syllable which represents the A.S. *wudu*, a wood; in *rig*, A.S. *hric*, a back or ridge (corresponding in sense to Erse *druim*, Welsh *cefn*), such as Brannet Rig, Eldrig, etc.; in *ton*, A.S. *tún*, an enclosure, a dwelling, Br. Scots *toun*, cognate with Erse *dún*, Welsh *din*.

But there are other names of Teutonic form not directly referable to Anglo-Saxon, but framed in Middle Northern English. Thus Tod Rig and Toddly, the ridge and the "lea," or field of

Middle Northern English.

---

[1] *Proceedings of Soc. Scott. Antiq.*, vol. vii., New Series, p. 83. *Collections Ayr and Galloway Arch. Assoc.*, vol. v. p. 1.

the fox, contain the word *tod*, fox, which is of Scandinavian origin, borrowed by Northern English speakers directly from that source, and unknown in Anglo-Saxon. Such names must be considered some centuries younger than the other Teutonic forms.

Lastly, there is the Scandinavian element to deal with. The Norsemen began in the eighth century to be the terror of the Celtic and aboriginal tribes inhabiting Scotland and Ireland. They formed settlements, and occupied fertile districts on the seaboard at various points of our coast. Ignorance of their language, which is most nearly represented by the Icelandic speech of the present day, debars the present writer from venturing far towards the solution of those names in Galloway which seem to be referable to this people. But several are clearly capable of explanation by comparison with Icelandic forms, and it is hoped that attention may be paid by some capable student to the names in the list ending in *-wick* and *-by*.

To sum up the data available for the present inquiry, it seems probable that we have—

First, a number of names surviving from aboriginal Iverian speech, incapable at present of any solution, and probably greatly altered in form by Celtic tongues, and subsequent reduction into English writing. These may be referred to a period anterior to the Christian era.

Second, the bulk of the names in the district framed in the Goidhelic branch of Celtic, a dialect of which was probably spoken by the Cruithne or Picts of Galloway from, say, the second century down to the sixteenth, but the majority of which probably date from the first ten centuries of that large space of time.

Third, a limited number—to identify which no attempt has hitherto been made—of names in the Brythonic branch of Celtic, imported from the neighbouring Province of Strathclyde in the interval between the sixth century, when St. Kentigern reconverted the Galloway Picts to Christianity, and the eleventh, when Brythonic speech had probably died out in Central Scotland.

Fourth, names in Anglo-Saxon or Old Northern English, which are not likely to have been established earlier than the sixth or later than the ninth century.

Fifth, those in the Scandinavian tongue, proceeding from the marauders of the eighth and two following centuries ; and

Sixth, names in Middle English or Broad Scots, not older than the thirteenth century.

Of course besides these there are a considerable number, but not so large as might be supposed, of what may be called modern names, both in Broad Scots and English, but the meaning of these is readily ascertained.

Place-names may be arranged in two classes—Simple and Compound. Erse or Gaelic names of the first class consist either of a substantive indicative of some natural feature— as Clone (*cluain*, a meadow), Drum (*druim*, a ridge), Blair (*blár*, a plain)—or of an adjectival derivative from the name of some animal, plant, mineral, or natural feature which distinguished the locality, as Brockloch, a place of badgers (*broclach*, badgery) ; Clauchrie, a stony place (*clacharach* or *cloichreach*, stony) ; Gannoch or Genoch, a sandy place (*gaineach* or *gainmheach*, sandy). Such names almost invariably have the stress on the first syllable.

Names of the second class consist of a substantive, generally, according to Celtic construction, occupying the first place, and a qualitative, either an adjective in the nominative, or a noun in the oblique case, with or without the definite article. Thus Blairbuy represents *blár*, a field, and *buidhe*, yellow (the *d* being silenced by the aspirate). Auchenshinnoch is little altered from the original *achadh*, a field (the *d* silent as before), *an sionaich*, of the fox (*s* before a diphthong, of which the first vowel is *e* or *a*, is sounded like our *sh*), or *achadh na sionach*, field of the foxes.

In many names the article is omitted, as in Balgown, from *baile*, the ground or house, *gobhain* (*bh* sounds *v* or *w*), of the smith; and often the place of qualitative is occupied by the name of an individual, as in Balmurrie, *i.e. baile*, the ground or house, *Muireadhaich* (Murragh), of Murray. In these compounds the stress will generally be found on the first syllable of the qualitative; so, although we speak of Tànnoch, which is *tamhnach* [tawnagh], a word for a meadow not found in modern Gaelic, with the stress on the first syllable, it is transferred in Tannyflùx (*i.e. tamhnach fliuch*, wet meadow) to the last as the qualitative. By observing the incidence of the stress in local pronunciation of names, valuable assistance is derived in arriving at a conclusion as to their original form. For example, in a name like Cùllendeugh or Cùllendoch, it might be inferred that the syllable *deuch* or *doch* represents the adjective *dubh* [dooh], black or dark, and that the meaning was *cuileann dubh*, the dark holly-tree. But the incidence of the stress on the first syllable points to its being a simple name, *cuileanach*, a place of hollies—an adjectival form from *cuileann*. The *d* has been inserted in these two names in Girthon, Kirkmabreck, and New Abbey parishes; while in Balmaghie it remains, as Cullenoch, in nearly its original form.

This rule is very constant, even where the name becomes much corrupted and disguised. There are two places called Inshanks,—one in Kirkcowan, the other in Kirkmaiden. It is a corruption of *uinnsean* [inshan], the ash-trees; and the stress remains to this day on the first syllable, though it might be expected to travel to the second when the meaning of the word was so completely lost, and when it assumed such a misleading form.

The position of the stress as indicative of simple and compound names is not peculiar to Celtic speech. In Teutonic languages the qualitative is placed first. Thus, Whìthorn = A.S. *hwit œrn*, the white house, retains the stress on the adjective ; Stòneykirk = Steenie's or St. Stephen's church, on the qualitative proper name. In both of these names the change according to rule from the narrow *a* or *e* sound to the round *o* may be noticed.

Sometimes, for no particular apparent reason, the usual order in Erse compounds is reversed, and the qualitative is placed first. Instances of these exceptional cases are Aùchness, *i.e. each innis*, the horse pasture ; Dùloch, *i.e. dubh loch*, the black lake ; Càmelon and Càmling, *i.e. cam linn*, the crooked pool ; but in every case the stress follows the qualitative syllable. Compare its position in Lincòm, *i.e. linn cam*, the crooked pool, the exact equivalent of Càmling.

In the language of the Irish Celts—which is referred to throughout as Erse—the stress is said to have been laid on the latter part of the simple words of more than one syllable, whereas in the dialect of the Scottish Gael it is supposed to have moved forward towards the beginning. This causes names of places in Ireland to have been somewhat differently Anglicised from the same names in Scotland. For example, *suidheachàn* [seehan], a little seat, a residence, becomes Seeghane in Dublin and Seehanes in Cork, appearing in Galloway as Sheuchan, with the stress on the first syllable.

A somewhat unusual example of the Irish stress remains in Knockàn, the name of a field in Kirkinner, *i.e. cnocán*, diminutive of *cnoc*, a hill. The farm of which it is a part bears the name of Little Hills, which is a translation of the Celtic. According to the usual position of the stress in Gallovidian speech, this name would have become Knòckan, like Knòckans in Minnigaff and Lòchans in Inch, but for some unknown reason the local population have handed down the Irish pronunciation, and not the Scottish. In like manner Mahàar in Kirkcolm, representing the Erse *machair*, has the stress on the last syllable, while Màcher in Inch, and all the many names beginning with this word, have the stress on the first.

    In compound names the prefix is usually easily identified. Of hill names *druim* and *cnoc* rival each other in frequency. The low glaciated "sow-back" ridges, so characteristic of the undulating plain districts, are appropriately denominated "drums"—the Erse *druim* being closely cognate with the Latin *dorsum*, a back.[1] *Cnoc*, of which the initial hard *c*, formerly sounded, has become silent, expresses a more isolated circular or precipitous eminence. Upwards of two hundred and twenty hills in Galloway rejoice in the prefix *Knock;* and it may be remarked that their distribution, though apparently capricious, must have depended on circumstances which can only now be surmised. The parishes of Stoneykirk and Sorby are not unlike in natural features. Both consist of undulating lowland, yet the former seems to have been inhabited more persistently by a Gaelic-speaking race than the latter; for, whereas in Stoneykirk there are twenty-six names beginning with *Knock*, in Sorby there is not one.

Next in frequency among hill-names comes *barr*, which means the top of anything. *Sliabh*, pronounced Slieve in Irish, becomes Slew in Scottish names. In Scotland the meaning also varies, signifying a moorland rather than a hill or mountain, as it does in Ireland. *Meall*, a hill, and *maol*, bald (a bald hill or headland) are difficult to distinguish from each other in Anglicised names, but both are common in the Province, the former generally forming the prefix Mill, the latter Mull.

Beann and *Beannán* are easily recognised in the syllables Ben and Bennan; *cruach*, a stack-like hill, as Croach, etc.; *mullach, learg, leargaidh, leacán, sron, ceann, muine, gob*, are of

---

[1] It is worthy of notice that of the many hundred names in Galloway beginning with *Drum*, Pont notes only a very few. There can be no doubt that the names existed in his day, but he seems to have disregarded those that were not also the name of a house or farm. *Cefn*, the Welsh equivalent of *druim*, a back or ridge, is preserved in several names in the Brythonic district of Strathclyde. Thus Giffen, in North Ayrshire, is a ridge which forms a sharply defined feature descried for many miles in the flat landscape around it.

frequent occurrence, while *ros, roine, teanga,* and *rudha* indicate points of land or headlands.

In the prolific Celtic root *carr,* a stone, may be traced *carraic* and *creag* (the former referring exclusively to sea-cliffs), Anglicised with little change as Carrick and Craig. *Carn* also, a word existing in all Celtic dialects, is from the same root. It means primarily a heap of stones, and generally is limited to the heap over a grave ; but sometimes it means a hill. *Clach* or *cloch, léac* or *liag,* present themselves with little disguise. The latter (becoming *leck* or *lick*), with the literal meaning of a flag or flat stone, often signifies a burial-place, from the flat stones used in making cists ; while the former bears a variety of meanings, from the simple one of " a stone," through all the various objects for which stones were employed, either as memorials, tombstones, worshipping stones (as in Clachanarrie), foundation stones of huts, Christian churches, etc.

Flat lands, fields, and enclosures are prefixes by such *Fields and plains.* familiar words as *achadh,* meaning arable land ; *faithche,* a " green," whence our Broad Scotch "fey"; *blár,* a plain ; *mach,* also a plain, becoming Mye or May, and its derivative *machair,* which in modern Gaelic is limited in meaning to flat land bordering on the sea, but which formerly had a more general application. *Tamhnach,* mentioned above as a word unknown to modern Highlanders, appears as a prefix in numerous places throughout the Province, and means a wet mowing meadow.

The commonest prefix denoting water, whether as a stream *Water.* or as a pool, is the Celtic *pol.* It may be recognised in names beginning Pol, Pal, Pil, Pul, Phil, Phal, Fil, Fal, Fauld, and even Pen and Pin. The obsolete Celtic *dohhar, dur,* gives the initial syllables Dar, Der, Dir, so common in the hilly and moorland districts ; while *allt,* which bears the original meaning of " a height," has come, as shown in the Glossary, to mean a glen or stream, in which sense it is usually found in Galloway.[1] *Linn*

----

[1] See under " Aldergowan."

signifies a pool in a river, and *tiobar*, a well, assumes the forms *tibber* and *chipper*.

Dwellings.   Habitations and strongholds are indicated by the prefixes Dun, Car, Bal or Bally, Ty, Bo, from the Erse *dún*, and *cathair*, a fort; *baile*, literally a townland, but the meaning of which became transferred to the house on the land; *teach*, gen. *tighe*, a house, and *both*, a hut. But *cathair* [caer] is readily confused with *ceathramhaidh* [carrou], a land-quarter, which the process of phonetic decay has reduced to a single syllable; indeed, in the absence of old written forms, it is difficult to identify *cathair* as a prefix in more than two or three Galloway names.

Another syllable which is hard to assign to one of three or four words is that which appears as the prefix Cal, Cul, or Kil. *Cul*, a back (in respect of position); *cuil*, a corner; *coill*, a wood, and *cill*, a cell or chapel, all melt indiscriminately into one of these forms, and it is by local characteristics or history that they must be referred to their proper signification. In this way it is safe to translate Culmore *coill mór*, the great wood, for a large part of that farm is flat land containing innumerable trunks and roots of oak-trees; Kildarroch is probably *coill darach*, the oak wood, though it may stand for *cuil darach*, the corner of the oaks, or *cul darach*, the hill-back of the oaks. But in almost every case where Kil antecedes a proper name it is safe to assume that the name is not older than the sixth century, and that the name signifies the *cille* or cell of an early saint. Such names are Kilmorie, Kildonan, Kilcormack.

Qualitative suffixes.   Difficult as the task sometimes proves to unravel the first part of compound place-names, it is simplicity itself compared with that involved in the solution of suffixes, which are usually the qualitative of the first word. Not only has the usual effect of the invariable tendency to economise labour in pronunciation to be considered, a tendency which leads, as a rule, to the abbreviation of the original form, but the peculiar liability to aspiration which marks the Celtic consonants *b, c, d, f, g, m, p, s, t.* The aspirate, which in Erse literature is indicated by a dot over the letter, appears in written Gaelic as *h* following the aspirated consonant. Its effect upon *d, f, s,* and *t* is to silence them, or to reduce them to a slight *h* or *y* sound; *bh* and *mh* are sounded like *v* or *w,* and in some cases become almost silent, as in *dubh* [dooh], black ; *Amhalghadh* [Owlhay], Aulay; while *ph* has much the same value as in English.

The difficulty of recovering the consonant silenced by the aspirate is well shown in the name Barnolas, a hill in Tungland parish. It is only by comparison with the names Barsoles, Barsolis, and Barsolus (the latter of which names is actually written by Pont *Barolis*), that it becomes apparent that the original form was *Barr an sholais,* the beacon-hill; the initial *s,* being aspirated in the oblique case, has left no trace in the Anglicised orthography.

Ch and *gh* in Erse have the same value of guttural spirants as they have in Broad Scots. They are often represented in modern forms of place-names by *h,* as in Barhapple (Pont's *Barchapil*), *i.e. barr chapul,* hill of the horses. When *ch,* pronounced as in English *church,* occurs in a name of Celtic origin, it is perfectly certain that the original consonant was not *c* or *ch,* but a dental followed by a diphthong. Thus Challoch stands for *tealach,* and Chipper for *tiobar.*

The letter *h* has no organic existence in the Celtic alphabets, therefore, when it occurs at the beginning of a syllable, it either marks the alteration of a lost consonant by aspiration, or is redundant, marking, in some cases, the accent of the tone syllable.[1] The student's first business, then, is to determine what consonant, if any, has disappeared; aided by analogy of other forms of the word, in names either in the locality under consideration, or in other Celtic districts, he will arrive at the correct solution in many more cases than might at first seem possible.

---

[1] Rhys's *Lectures on Welsh Philology,* p. 262.

Another process which results in disguising the meaning of Celtic compounds is that known to Irish grammarians as *eclipsis*, in respect of which Professor Rhys's language deserves attention. "There is nothing," he says,[1] "in eclipses which may be regarded as peculiar to the Celtic languages; but I will only cite from other languages just a sufficient number of analogous instances to indicate some of the quarters where more may be found. You may have wondered how such English words as the following, now pronounced *dumm, lamm, clime*, came to be written *dumb, lamb, climb*. The answer of course is, that the *b* in them was formerly pronounced, and that this is merely another case of spelling lagging behind the pronunciation—*litera scripta manet*. To this class of words may be added the modern *woodbine*, which at an earlier stage of the language was written *wudubínd*; and, to come down to our own day, all of you have heard London called *Lunnun*. Beyond the Tweed this and more of the kind may be considered classic: witness the following stanza from Burns's 'Five Carlins':—

> ' " Then neist came in a sodger youth,
>   And spak wi' modest grace,
>   *An'* he wad gae to *Lon'on* town
>   If sae their pleasure was."

Here may also be mentioned that there are German dialects which habitually use *kinner, wunner, wennen, unner, brannwin,* for the book forms *kinder, wunder, wenden, unter, branntwein.* Similarly in Old Norse *bann* and *lann* are found for *band* and *land,* not to mention the common reduction of *nð* into *nn,* as in *finna,* 'to find'; *annarr,* 'other' (German, *ander*); *munnr,* 'mouth' (German, *mund*), and the like."

But our difficulty in dealing with this process in Anglicised forms of Galloway names is that "*litera scripta* non *manet.*" The names never were written in the original Erse; all that

---

[1] *Op. cit.* p. 55.

remain are letters to represent the sound of the names in the fifteenth, sixteenth, or seventeenth centuries. So in Dunman and Lagniemawn we are led by the analogy of Dunnaman and Dunmany in Ireland to supply the eclipsed *b* in *dún m-beann* (the *m* which eclipses the *b* being the residuum of *nam*, the genitive plural of the definite article), the fortress of the peaks or gables, and by that of Cornaman in Cavan, and Eilean-nam-ban in Iona, to supply it in *lag na m-ban*, the hollow of the women, and thus arrive at the meaning.

In the most ancient instances of eclipse, dating, in all probability, from a time before Celtic speech was written, the eclipsed and silent consonant does not appear even in the earliest spellings. Thus *mna*, the genitive singular of *ban*, a woman, stands for *m-bana*. The initial *k* of knock, the common name for a hill, is still retained in our writings, for although it is now silent, it is pronounced in the Gaelic *cnoc*, and struck the ears of those who first committed local names to writing, in addition to which the similarity to the English *knock*, a blow, would tend to the identity of spelling in the two words.

The consonants most liable to disappear by eclipse are—

b	eclipsed by	*m*
c, d, and *g*	„	*n*
s	„	*t.*

The latter case is frequently the cause of obscurity, as in the names Baltier and Knocktaggart, which stand for *baile t-sair*, western townland, *cnoc t-sagairt*, the priest's hill.

The use of the definite article and its preservation in com- The article. pound place-names is uncertain. Sometimes it remains complete, as in Ilan-na-guy, *oiléan na gaethe*, island of the wind; sometimes it is reduced to a single vowel, as in Knockiebae, *cnoc na beith*, hill of the birches; sometimes to a single consonant, as in Arndarroch, *ard na darach*, height of the oaks, where it eclipses the preceding consonant; often it is absent altogether, as in Barhullion, *barr chuileann*, hill of hollies.

The employment of the English definite article before some names in Galloway has been the subject of speculation. It has been suggested that its presence denotes that the name which it precedes is a simple word in the original Celtic, expressive of some natural or artificial feature, without qualitative. Thus we hear country people talk of the Derry, the Airlour, the Knock, the Larroch, the Lochans, the Barr, etc.; but never of the Monreith, the Barlae, the Knockcrosh, the Glenhowl. It seems to me, however, that its use depends upon the position of the stress. Names accénted on the first syllable or mono-syllabic names are those which take the definite article. I cannot recall a single instance of a name accented on the second or following syllable which is ever used with the definite article. The stress in compound place-names is nearly always found, as has been pointed out, on the first syllable of the qualitative, or, in an uncompounded name, on the first syllable of that name. Several compounds may be mentioned before which the article is commonly used, as the Dhuloch, the Dowies, the Glaisters, but in all these the qualitative, contrary to the usual custom, precedes the substantive; and in Teutonic compounds, as the Eldrig, the article is again found in use. It appears then, that it is used merely for euphony, a certain difficulty, having to be overcome in commencing a name with the stress syllable.

Animals—whether domestic or of the chase—give, as might be expected, names to many places. *Gabhar* or *gobhar* [gower] is limited in meaning among the Irish and Highlanders to the goat; but in early times it was equally used for the horse. Cormac gives *gabur*, a goat, and *gobur*, a horse; and in the many names in Galloway which contain this word it is im-possible to say with certainty which animal is referred to. Where the aspirated form is preserved, as in Auchengower, Craignegowrie (*creag na goïbhre*), Inchnagour, etc., it may be surmised that the name is more recent than the use of *gobur* for a horse; but names like Blairnagobber and Barngaber point to the earlier form, without the aspirate, of which the sense is ambiguous.

The commonest names of the horse are *éch* and *capul*, appearing in Auchness (*ech inis*), Barneight (*barr n-ech*), etc.; and in Craignagapple, Fannygapple (*faithche na-gcapul*); the aspirated form giving names like Barhapple and Port Whapple. *Lair*, a mare, gen. *laira*, comes to us in Auchenlarie (*achadh na laira*), Garthlearie, Craiglarie, etc., and *searrach* [sharragh], a foal, in Balsarroch and Barsherry.

Cattle are indicated by the words *bo*, as in Darnimow (*dobhar na-mbo*); *croch*, cattle, as in Dirnow, formerly Dyrnagrow (*dobhar na croch*); *mart*, an ox, as in Ardnimord (*ard na na-mart*); *laoch*, a calf, as in Ballochalee (*bealach na laoch*).

Sheep are usually designated *caera*, forming part of many names, *e.g.* Drumacarie, Culgary, Lumagary.

The pig seems to have been the favourite eponymus among domestic animals, numerous places retaining *muc* and *muclach* in their names, such as Culmick, Clachanamuck, Muclach, Drummuclach. Other names for swine are *torc*, a boar, preserved in Glenturk; *arc* or *orc* a pig or other large animal, in Craiggork; *banbh* [banniv], a young pig, in Auchnabony.

The commonest designation for a dog in Irish is *cu*, gen. *con*, but it is not to be recognised in names in this district, unless Carrickcone and Port Mona, both in Kirkmaiden, may be taken as compounds of *con*, the latter being called by Pont Port-na-mony-a-Koane, which may be a contraction of *port na monadh a' con*, port of the moor of the dog. The dog was so indispensable and highly-prized an animal among Celtic races, who were dependent, to a large extent, upon the chase for their subsistence; it appears so frequently in their earliest literature, and bears so important a part in tradition, that we must suppose it to have borne another name in Galloway.

Accordingly we find many names containing *madadh* [maddy], which is another name for a dog; although some of them may refer to wolves, which bore, among other names, that of *madadh fael.* Drummoddie, Claymoddie, Craigmoddie, Dalvadie, etc., may therefore be held to be designated either from dogs or wolves.

It can hardly be supposed that animals so hurtful, and, at the same time, so plentiful as wolves were during the early and Middle Ages, can have been exterminated without leaving their name associated with some of their haunts; yet it is not easy to identify in the names of places in the district any of the usual words meaning " wolf " in Erse, namely, *fael*, *bréach*, or *mac-tire.* It is possible that the latter word is preserved in Drummatier, and *bréach* may survive in some of the numerous names ending in *brake* or *breck*, though these syllables may be generally assumed to refer to the surface of the land, *i.e. bréc*, brindled or variegated.

The wolf's near relative, the fox, must always have been plentiful, for we frequently find the common name for him, *sionach* [shinnagh], distinguishing natural features; as Blairshinnoch, Auchenshinnoch, Inchshannoch—the latter place having the alternative name in the present day of Foxes' Rattle.[1] The older form of the word, *sindach*, is retained in Craigshindie and Craigsundie. It is well to remember, however, that some of these appellations may have been taken from the names of men, who, after the fashion of most barbarous or semi-civilised races, appropriate or receive the names of animals, in virtue sometimes of personal qualities, sometimes from an assumed cognisance. Auchenshinnoch may thus be either the field of the fox or Sionach's field. In Ireland, a numerous family of Sionachs assumed the name of Fox in obedience to the proscriptive laws which compelled them to relinquish their Celtic appellation, and by the latter name their descendants are still

---

[1] *Rattle*, a mass of fallen *débris* at the foot of a cliff.

known.[1] It is, of course, impossible at the present day to decide whether such place-names derive from the animal or from the individual who was called after the animal.

Another wild animal, which is, however, wellnigh extinct in Galloway now, is the eponymus of a large number of places, namely, the badger, whose name *broc*, is the same in Celtic and Anglo-Saxon speech. This beast was a favourite article of diet; to the present day badger hams are considered a delicacy in parts of Ireland; consequently it is not surprising to find many places bearing the names of Brockloch (*broclach*, a badger warren), Cairnbrock, Killbrocks (*coill broc*, badger wood), and so on.

Eilte, gen. *eilidh*, a hind, is probably the origin of Kilhilt (*coill eilte*), wood of the hinds, Craignelder, and other names; *dorán*, an otter, of Puldowran and Aldowran; *cat*, the wild-cat,[2] of Drumwhat, Alwhat, Cairn-na-gath.

En, a bird, may be recognised in Barnean, Dernain, Knock- nain; *iolare* [illery], the eagle, in Benyellary; *fitheach* [feeach], the raven, in Craigenveoch; *seobhag* [shog], the hawk, in Garn-shog; *faeilán*, the sea-gull, in Derwhillan; *coileach*, a cock (probably a heathcock or grouse), in Craigenholly.

Birds.

Fish are commemorated in Lochanscadden and Culscadden, from *sgadán*, a herring; in Lochenbreck and Altibrick, from *bréc*, a trout; in Lanebreddan, from *bradán*, a salmon; frogs in Lingloskin and Darloskine, from *losgán*, a frog; and even the insect world seems to have given names to Barnshangan, Dernashangan, and many other places, from *scangán* [shangan], an ant. The latter name, however, meaning literally the

Fish, reptiles, and insects.

---

[1] Dr. John Stuart mentions the application of an equivalent soubriquet in English-speaking times:—"One of the monks who bore the body of St. Cuthbert to the grave was guilty, says Reginald, of hiding a cheese from his brethren, and was believed for a time to have been changed into a fox, whence his descendants were named *Tod*, 'quod vulpiculam sonat.'"—*Book of Deer*, cvi.

[2] The domestic cat was probably unknown in North Britain in Celtic times.

slender or wee fellow, may very likely have been the name of individuals.

Vegetation. Woods, trees, and plants, naturally present themselves in all countries as distinctive features of locality; accordingly our place-names contain a vivid portraiture of the primitive vegetation of the land. *Coill*, a wood, appears both as a prefix, as in Culmore, *coill mór*, the great wood, and as a suffix, as in Glenwhillie, *gleann choille*, the glen of the wood. The Scots pine is plentiful in our bogs, and was freely used in the construction of crannogs or lake-dwellings; it is therefore somewhat strange that the only place which seems to have taken its name from that tree is Loch Goosey, in Kells parish, from *guithseach* [geusagh], a pine.

Probably the most important tree, and not the least common, was the oak, which accounts for the innumerable places named from *dair, dara, darach*, an oak, such as Auchendarroch, Drumdarrochy, Kildarroch; while *doire* [dirrie], meaning a wood generally, but also specially an oak wood, gives Derry, Blairderry, etc. Both these words, however, in composition are difficult to distinguish in Anglicised names from the form assumed by *dearg*, red.

Beith [bey], the birch seems to have been as common as the oak, and may frequently be recognised in the syllable -bay or -bae, as in Polbae, Falbae, Knockiebay, or aspirated *bheith* [vey], as in Auchenvey; and the adjectival form *beithach* [bayoch], a place of birches, yields Beoch. Other trees are *fuinnsean, uinnsean*, or *uinnseóg* [inshan, inshog], the ash, as in Inshanks, Drumnaminshog; *fearn*, the alder, as in Balfern, Drumfarnachan; *cuillean*, the holly, as in Barhullion, Collin Island; from whence comes *cuilleanach*, a place of hollies, giving Cullenoch and Cullendoch; *sailcach* [sallagh], the willow, giving Barsalloch; *coll*, a hazel, Barquhill, and the more modern form *caldtun*, Caldons; *leamh* [lav] the elm, as in Lavach, or combined with *coill*, as in Barluell (*barr leamh-*

chuill [lavwhill], hill-top of the elm wood). There is also an alternative form *sleamh,* or *sleamhán* [slav, slavan], which remains in Craigslouan (*creag sleamhan,* crag of the elms). *Sceithóg* [skeog], the hawthorn, comes often in such names as Skeog, Drumskeog, Auchenskeoch. Humbler vegetation sufficed to distinguish Barnernie, from *airne,* a sloe-bush ; Drangan and Cardryne, from *droiccheann* or *droineann,* the black thorn ; Smirle, from *smeur, smeurlach,* a bramble; Auchendolly, from *dealg* [dallug] a thorn ; Auchengilshie, Tarwilkie, Knockgulsha from *giolc,* the rush ; Freuch, from *fraoch,* heather ; Drumrannie, from *raineach,* fern.

Offices and occupations are largely represented; *e.g. ri,* a king or chief, as in Ardrie ; Grennan, being *greanán,* the chief residence where he dwelt; *bard,* a rhymer, in Dirvaird and Barnboard ; *gobha* [gow], gen. *gobhan* [gown], a smith, in Balgown ; Challoch, from *tealach,* the smith's forge, and Drumacardy, from *cearda* [carda], also a forge or workshop. *Grésach,* a cobbler or embroiderer, is retained in Balgracie (*baile gresaich,* the cobbler's house); while mills were plentiful, as shown by the many names containing *muilean,* as Drummullin, four times in Wigtonshire alone, Dernemullie, and so on. Offices and trades.

The advent of Christianity introduced a new element. Words descriptive of ecclesiastical offices or rites were adapted from the Latin to suit Celtic lips. *Sacart* or *sagart,* the priest (from Lat. *sacerdos*), built himself a *cill,* a cell or chapel (Lat. *cella*); so to this day Altaggart (*allt shagairt,* the priest's stream) flows past the site of Kilfeather (*cill Pheaduir,* Peter's cell). *Easpug,* a bishop (Lat. *episcopus*), *abb,* an abbot, *cléreg,* a cleric, *manach,* a monk (*monachus*), *brathair* [braar], a friar, *cailleach,* a nun (this last not being a borrowed word), all have their memories perpetuated in Gillespie, Balnab, Portaclearys, Kermanachan, Altibrair, and Portencalzie. The Celtic *cill* passed insensibly into the old Northern English *kirk* (A.-S. *circce,* E. *church*). So we find such names as Kirkpatrick written indifferently Kil- Christian nomenclature.

patrick and Kirkpatrick, in both of which forms the Celtic construction, with the qualitative last, is retained.   The low Latin *capella*, a chapel, passed into the Erse *caipeal*, and survives not only in names like Chapelrossan and Barcaple, but as in alternative forms like Chapelheron or Chipperheron, in which *caipeal*, a chapel, and *tiobar*, a well, seem to compete which shall commemorate St. Kieran.

Celtic hagiology is as slippery a subject as Celtic etymology, but there are many early dedications which cannot be mistaken. The name of the earliest evangelist of Galloway, St. Ninian, appears in many places, as Ninian, Ringan, and Dingan.   The great missionary of the rival church of Ireland, Columba, has left his name ineffaceably stamped in the name Kirkcolm— a parish which, as early as Edward Second's reign, was pronounced as now, Kircum.[1]   In the same parish, Killiemacuddican probably represents an endearing appellation after St. Cuthbert (*cille ma Cudacain*), whose name appears with more propriety in the written form of Kirkcudbright, though even there the pronunciation goes far to disguise it—Kirkcoobrie.   St. Peter, St. Fillan, St. Martin, St. Mary, St. Winnock, St. Bricius, St. Kennera, and a host of minor personages, are commemorated in Kilfeather, Kilfillan, Kirkmadrine, Kilmorie, Kirkgunzeon, Kirkmabreck, Kirkinner, and other ecclesiastical sites.

The name of the Saviour himself seems to be preserved in Clachaneasy (*clachan Iosa*) and Kirkchrist, while the lurid light of an earlier and more savage faith lingers round Beltane Hill   Clachanarrie, the stones of worship, may denote a pagan monument where the converted Gael bowed to the new religion, whose priests knew how to take a right advantage of the habits of devotion associated with certain localities.

As the symbol of the new faith grew to be a familiar landmark in the eyes of the people, the cross became a fre-

[1] See Kirkcolm in Glossary.

quent component in local names, as is testified by names like Craigencrosh, Balnacross, Crosherie, and, in one place at least, Clayshant (*clach scant*, the holy stone), the Latin *sanctus* preserves, in Celtic dress, very much of its original appearance.

The surface of the land was designated *garbh* [garriv], rough, or *carrach*, with the same meaning, in Garvilland or Knockenharrie ; *min* [meen] or *reidh* [ray], smooth, as Barmeen, Drumrae. Hills were *mór*, great, or *beag*, little, as Drummore, Drumbeg. When land grew light-coloured grass it would be apt to be described as *bán,* white, like Drumbain, *fionn* [fiun], white, like Blairfin, or *buidhe* [bwee], yellow, like Drumbuie ; when heather grew dark upon it, *don*, brown, would give the name Drumdon ; and when peat or bog gave it a still darker hue, it would come to be known as *dubh* [dooh], like Drumdow. Green pasture is spoken of as *glas*, green, as in Barglas, while grey cliffs, or land strewn with boulders, is *liath* [lee], grey, as Craiginlee, or *riabhach* [reeagh], grey, as Drumreoch. *Odhar* [owr] is another word signifying grey, which appears in many names, such as Drumours. Redness from any cause, whether from peculiar vegetation, red soil, or, in some cases, from bloodshed, is expressed by one of three words, namely, *dearg*, giving Baryerrock and Barjarg ; *ruadh* [roo], in Teroye and Tannieroach, or *corcor, corcorach*, in Barncorkrie. Dappled or variegated places are called *bréc* or *ceannfhionn* [cannon], as Knockbreak and Knockcannon.

In short, every possible characteristic, whether of position, size, shape, colour, vegetation, consistency, every well-known variety of animals fed or hunted on the land, all customs religious or otherwise, all occupations or handicrafts, as well as names of individuals, readily lent themselves as definitions of locality, and were applied by the early inhabitants in precisely the same simple, practical, and occasionally imaginative way, as is practised by people of the present day.

From the time of Ptolemy nearly twelve hundred years

Early topo-
graphers of
Galloway.
elapsed from which we glean nothing, except incidentally, of the topography of Galloway.

About the year 1250 Matthew Paris compiled his *Abbreviatio Chronicorum*,[1] in which he gives an interesting map of Great Britain,[2] the whole of Scotland, in accordance with the error prevalent among geographers from the days of Ptolemy, being represented as deflected to the east, Galloway occupying the north-west extremity; the province (*Galeweia*) is placed north of the river making Clydesdale (*fluvius faciens Cludesdale*), and it contains no names of places.

Next in order of antiquity is a map[3] which hung until the middle of the eighteenth century in the Bodleian Library, and to which Mr. Cosmo Innes assigned a date earlier than A.D. 1330. It contains Great Britain and part of Ireland. Galloway is here treated in greater detail; in common with the whole island from Kent to Caithness, it is sparsely sprinkled with quaint red-roofed houses. The following names of places are given :—

candida casa	(Whithorn).
mons crefel	(Criffel).
fluv. dee	(R. Dee).
loghdone	(Loch Doon).
f. loghenawe	(probably Lochnaw, for although placed N.E. of the Dee, it is near the head of Loch Ryan, which is represented as running east and west).

Then we have a map from the MS. of John Hardyng,[4] author of the *Rhyming Chronicle*, who was employed by Henry VI. for various political purposes in Scotland, A.D. 1437-1460. In

---

[1] Cott. MSS., British Museum, Jul. D. vii. fol. 50, B.

[2] Reproduced in the *National Manuscripts of Scotland*, vol. II., plate vᴬ.

[3] *Ibid.* vol. III., plate ii.

[4] *Hardyng's Chronicle*; Selden MSS. B. 10 (3356), Bodleian Library. This map is reproduced in the *National Manuscripts of Scotland*, vol. II. plate lxviii.

Galway (Galloway) appear the names Kirkubrigh, Treve (Threave), and Sulway (Solway).

Besides these there exists a report upon the Western Marches of Scotland, prepared probably by an English official between the years 1563 and 1566.[1] The first portion of the MS. has disappeared; it begins in a most tantalising way in the middle of a description of the coast of Galloway, and an estimate of the force required to seize and hold it. Wigston (Wigtown), Cardines, Crukilton, Kirkcowbright, and other places are described with the utmost minuteness, and the views are carefully drawn and vividly coloured. The name of the writer and artist is not preserved.

Towards the close of the century a complete and laborious survey of the province was for the first time undertaken. No one who has made a study, however limited, of the topography of Galloway, can fail to pay a tribute of praise to the memory of Timothy Pont. The labour involved in the production of his maps and writings would have been meritorious even had he been able to command modern appliances of survey and locomotion. But when it is remembered that Scotland in the sixteenth and seventeenth centuries was traversed by few roads, and was in a condition varying between civil war and constant social disturbance, one cannot but marvel at the patience with which he prosecuted his task, and the completeness to which he brought it, and, at the same time, feel regret that he did not live to see his work in the hands of the public.

Timothy Pont was the eldest son of Mr. Robert Pont, a minister of the Church of Scotland immediately after the

----

[1] Cott. MSS., British Museum; *Titus*, c. xii. fol. 76 to 87. This document has been printed in the *History of Liddesdale, Eskdale, Ewesdale, Wauchopedale, and the Debateable Land*, by R. B. Armstrong (Edinburgh, 1883), Part I., App. p. cvi. The coloured drawings of Cardiness (Cruggleton ?) Castle, Kirkcudbright, Carlaverock Castle, and Annan, are beautifully executed in facsimile.

Reformation.　He and his brother Zachary matriculated in St. Leonard's College, St. Andrews, in 1579-80, and graduated in 1583-84.　In 1574 Timothy's father, who was Provost of Trinity College, Edinburgh, granted him, while still a schoolboy, a charter of the church lands of Strathmartin and of Pentempler. Timothy was appointed minister of Dunnett, in Caithness, in 1600, and notices of him as parson of that parish are found down to the year 1610.　He seems, however, to have travelled in person over the greater part of Scotland, including the Isles, and to have collected a vast amount of material, topographical, historic, and antiquarian.　His death must have taken place between 1610 and 1614, in which latter year Mr. William Smith was in occupation of the benefice of Dunnett, but, minute as are the circumstantial details of many ignoble lives and deaths in all periods of our history, Timothy Pont's energetic soul passed away without record, and no man knows where his bones were laid.

But a noble monument was reared to his memory by his own hands.　His maps and papers passed into the hands of Robert Gordon of Straloch, geographer and antiquary, "second son of Sir John Gordon of Pitlurg, who was directed by Charles I. to aid the Blaeus of Amsterdam with such information as the writings of Pont afforded, to further their project of publishing an atlas of Scotland in their great work of an Atlas of the World, which they undertook in 1655."[1]

Fifty years or thereby after his death the results of Pont's labours were given to the world in Blaeu's magnificent Atlas, wherein, enshrined in time-mellowed vellum, is stored a mass of information such as has rarely been committed to the hands of a single publisher.　Four maps are devoted to Galloway, one containing the whole Province, another the Sheriffdom of Wigton, a third the western half of the Stewartry of Kirkcudbright, and a fourth showing the eastern half.　They are

---

[1] Pont's *Cuninghame Topographised*, Introd., p. viii.

accompanied by an extract from Camden descriptive of the Province, and also by au article from the pen of Mr. John Maclellan, a translation of which is given in the Appendix.

Many of the names contain misprints; others, owing to the maps having been engraved in Amsterdam, have received a Dutch complexion, which may be recognised in variations such as Boirlant for Bordland (or Boreland, as it is now written); nevertheless, making every allowance for this, as well as for the arbitrariness of the spelling of the period, the value of Pont's rendering of the names as they sounded in his ears in 1600 and the ten succeeding years, cannot be exaggerated in relation to an attempt to interpret them.

The vernacular of Galloway is said to have continued Erse or Gaelic until about the time of the geographer's birth. He probably encountered it still lingering in the wild districts of the Glenkens, Glentrool, and the moorland districts of Wigtonshire, and even if he were ignorant of it at the commencement of his work, his incumbency of the Highland parish of Dunnett must have given him a familiarity with its sound and sense. In his "Alphabett" of places in Cuninghame, he interprets many Gaelic names, consequently his rendering of place-names in Galloway is infinitely more valuable than if they had been written down by a scribe ignorant of the speech in which they are framed. But though we accept gratefully their written forms of names, the greatest care must be exercised in accepting the etymologies of early writers. There seems to be a fascination in the pursuit of the idea conveyed in a local name, which, from the earliest times, has prevailed to lead sober-minded historians into rash speculations. Even the earnest Pont waxes almost waggish in his glee at having hit upon a connection between Ptolemy's Lucopibia and Whithorn: " Neirunto this (Vigtoune) Ptolemee placed the city Leucophibia, therafter the episcopall seat of St. Ninian, wich Beda calleth Candida Casa, and wee now in this same sense Whithorne. Quhat say you then if Ptolemee, after his maner, translated that name in Greeke λευκα οικιδια, that is, Whitt-houses (instead quhereof the transcribers have thruste upone us Leucophibia), wich the picts termed Candida Casa."[1]

It is perhaps hardly necessary to remark that Ptolemy wrote three centuries before Ninian built his Candida Casa. The name doubtless expressed the appearance of the first stone-and-lime building in these parts, as distinguished from struc-tures of dry stone, wood, or wattle. Among the crofters of the West Highlands at this day the distinction is well under-stood between a " black house " of dry stone and thatch, and a " white house " of stone and mortar with slate roof. Further, Ptolemy did not write Leucophibia, but Lucopibia, and as the locality he assigned to this place is extremely vague, it is much more probable that the name contains the original form of the name now written "Luce."

Another instance of wild identification of places is given by Peter Heylin, who in his *Cosmography* (London, 1669) speaks of " the *Novantes*, containing *Galloway, Carrick, Kyle*, and *Cun-ningham*. Principal places of the which were *Lucopibia*, now *Whithern*, and *Berigonium*, now *Bargenie*" (Lib. i. 285). Having rendered Ptolemy's Rerigonium into Berigonium, and found Bargeny to correspond to the sound of the erroneous rendering, he unhesitatingly identified one with the other.

In the seventeenth century several topographical treatises on Galloway were compiled. Of these there survive the follow-ing :—*Description of the Stewartrie of Kircudbright*,[2] *Description of the Parish of Kirkpatrick Durham*,[3] *Description of the Parish of Minygaff*,[4] *Description of the Shcriffdom of Wigtoun*, by Sir Andrew Agnew of Lochnaw, and David Dunbar of Baildon ;[5]

---

[1] Pont's ms., Advocates' Library, 33. 2. 27, No. 14.
[2] Sibbald mss., Advocates' Library, Jac. v. 1. 4.
[3] Macfarlane mss., vol. i. p. 510 ; Advocates' Library, Jac. v. 4. 19.
[4] *Ibid.* vol. i. p. 517 ; Advocates' Library, Jac. v. 4. 19.
[5] Sibbald mss., Advocates' Library, Jac. v. 1. 4.

Further Account anent Galloway, by Dr. Archbald.[1]   These tracts are printed in the Appendix to Symson's *Description of Galloway*.[2]

It is to be understood that no more is claimed for the The present work is tentative. following pages than to be a contribution to the study of the local names of Galloway.   Difficulties, in themselves most forbidding, and almost sufficient to stop even an accomplished Celtic scholar on the threshold, might well have deterred an humble student such as the present writer.   But it seemed to him that some portion of what has been done for Ireland by the labours of O'Donovan, Reeves, Joyce, and others, may some day be accomplished for Scotland; and if the collection and systematic arrangement of names, and their collation with those conferred in Ireland by a people speaking the same language and leading similar lives, should prove an assistance to those who in future may undertake the work with higher qualifications for success, then it may be that the labour connected with the task has not been altogether wasted.

Most of the names in the Glossary will be found in the Ordnance Survey maps, but many which the surveyors have omitted have been copied from estate maps in private hands. My grateful thanks are due to those who have kindly assisted me in the search for these names, which are in danger of being lost sight of; and I will thankfully receive any further contributions of names not recorded in these pages.   Other names I have received orally, which do not appear in any maps or documents which I have seen.   Some of them are interesting: Scrabba, for example, the name of two strips of pasture, one in Mochrum, the other in Glasserton parish, is the Erse *scrath bo* [scrawbo], cows'-grass, and corresponds with Scrabo in Ireland.

---

[1] Sibbald MSS., Advocates' Library, W. 5. 17.   This Tract refers almost exclusively to the natural history of the district.

[2] *A Large Description of Galloway*, by Andrew Symson, Minister of Kirkinner, MDCLXXXIV., with an Appendix containing Original Papers from the Sibbald and Macfarlane MSS.   Edinburgh, 1823.

The supposed derivations and meanings are, of course, with very few exceptions, stated tentatively.   Where the sense and origin are very doubtful, a note of interrogation [?] follows the Celtic words; the explanations in these cases are intended purely as suggestions.   Dr. Joyce's work on the *Origin and History of Irish Names of Places* has been constantly referred to, as being the most complete study on topographical nomenclature known to me.   The *Irische Texte, mit Wörterbuch* of Professor Windisch, has been relied on for Old Erse forms, while Dr. Reeves's monumental work, *Adamnan's Life of St. Columba,* and Dr. O'Donovan's *Annals of the Four Masters* have been found a perfect treasure-house of learned information.

An attempt has been made to show the origin and connection of many of the words entering into our topography, and their connection with other branches of Aryan speech. In this I have relied mainly on Professor Skeat's *Etymological Dictionary of the English Language,* while Dr. Jamieson's well-known *Dictionary of the Scottish Language* is freely quoted in explanation of many Lowland or Broad Scots words applied to features of land, although the advance of Comparative Etymology since the days of the last-named writer has rendered his derivations almost useless.

AN TÍR-CHUNNTAS GALLGAIDHEL

AN TÍR-CHUNNTAS GALLGAIDHEL

(THE TOPOGRAPHY OF GALLOWAY).

ACHIE HILL (*P.* Achy). 'Kells.' *Achadh* [aha], a field ; translated *campulus* by *Adamnan*. *Pont* explains *achadh*, as "ane Irich vord signifies a folde or a crofte of land gained out of a vyld ground of before vnmanured."—*Cuninghame*, p. 50. Origin uncertain, but possibly connected with Lat. *ager*, a field. It is liable to confusion in compound names with *ath*, *atha* [ah, aha], a ford. *Cf.* AUCHIE ; also Agha, a parish in Carlow, and many names beginning with Ach, Auch, Agh, Augh, Auchie, and Aghy, in both Scotland and Ireland.

ACQUAINTANCE HILL. 'Carsphairn.' *Cf.* QUANTAN'S HILL.

ADDERHALL. 'Penninghame.' *Eadar ghabhal* [?] [howl], between the forks. *Cf.* Addergoole, Adderagool, Addrigoole, Adrigole, Edergole, and Edergoole in various parts of Ireland, *i.e. eadar gabhal* [adder gowl], between the (prongs of a) fork (of a river, roads, etc.); or perhaps like Adderwal in Donegal (*eadar bhaile*, mid-town), in which sense *see* BALMINNOCH. *Joyce*, i. 529, ii. 444.

AGGISTON.   ' Sorbie.'

AIKET HILL (*Inq. ad Cap.* 1550, Aikhead). 'Urr.' A.S. *ác wudu*, oak wood. A.S. *ác* gives BR. SC. *aik*, and (by change of long *a* according to rule into *oo*), M.E. *oke, ook*, E. *oak* + DU. *eik* + ICEL. *eik* + DAN. *eeg, eg* + SWED. *ek* + G. *eiche*, from Teut. type *aika* (*Skeat*, s. v. oak). A.S. *wudu* (whence M.E. *wode, wde*, E. wood, BR. SC. *wud*) + ICEL. *viðr*, a tree, wood + DAN. and SWED. *ved* + M.H.G. *wite*, O.H.G. *witu* + ERSE and GAEL. *fiodh* + W. *gwydd*. *Skeat* suggests original sense was "twig," mass of twigs, bush, connected with E. *withy* — √*wi*, to twine.

AIKEY BUSH (*P.* Oakybuss, Akybuss). 'Balmaclellan.' Aiken bush, oak wood. The second syllable *-ey* is the remains of the suffix *-en ;* BR. SC. *aiken* (*Jamieson*), A.S. *ácen* (*Bosworth*), of or belonging to the oak.

AIKIEHEAD. 'Penninghame.' BR. SC. *aiken head*, hill of oaks.

AIKIE SLACK. 'Colvend.' BR. SC. *aiken slack,* oak hollow. "*Slak, slack, slake,* an opening in the higher part of a hill, where it becomes less steep, and forms a sort of pass."— *Jamieson.* A.S. *sleac,* slack, slow; M.E. *slak,* E. *slack*+ICEL. *slakr*+SWED and DAN. *slak*+PROV. G. *schlack,* slack+M.H.G. *slach,* O.H.G. *slah.* All from a TEUT. base *slaka,* slack. The idea of slack used topographically seems to be intermission, relaxation, where the hill "leaves off" being steep, or where the effort in climbing is "slackened."

AIMEY HILL.   'Kirkcowan.'

AIRD (*Inq. ad Cap.* 1623, Aird; 1668, Aird). 'Inch.' *Ard,* high, a height. The same in ERSE, GAEL., C., and M.+LAT. *arduus.*

AÍRDRIE. 'Kirkbean.' *See under* ARDRIE.

AIRDS (*Inq. ad Cap.* 1576, Airdis; *P.* Airds). 'Girthon,' 'Kells,' 'Rerwick,' 'Troqueer.' The heights. *See* AIRD, to which E. plural has been added.

AÌRIE. 'Balmaghie,' 'Kells.' *Airidh* [airie], a shieling, a hill-pasture. "*Airghe,* a place for summer grazing in the mountains."—*Lluyd.* This word does not seem to have survived in Irish place-names, but in the *Martyrology of Donegal* it is preserved in several, as *Airidh Locha Con,* the shieling or pasture of Loch Conn; *Airidh fotha,* the long or far shieling; *Airiud bainne, Ariud-Brosca, Airidh-indaich, Ariudh-muill,* etc.

AIRIEBÈNNAN. 'Kells.' *Airidh* [airie] *beannain,* shieling or pasture of the hill; dim. of *beann,* or *airidh bennan,* shieling of the calves; "*bendan (bennán?)*", *O'Dav.* p. 57. *See under* BENNAN.

AIRIEGLÀSSEN (*Inq. ad Cap.* 1698, Whytharriglassen *vel* Whyte-darriglassen). 'Kirkcowan.' *Airidh* [airie] *glasán* [?], green hill-pasture. The terminal *án* is often added without a diminutive signification. *Lluyd* gives *glasuaine,* green, as equivalent to *glas.* "Some nouns ending in *an* and *og* do not always express diminutive ideas."—*O'Donovan.*

 The meaning may also be *airidh glaisín,* hill-pasture or shieling of the streamlet (*cf.* Ardglushin in Cavan, the height of the streamlet); or again, Glasan's shieling, from a man's name. Glasan and Glaisin from *glas,* green, are mentioned by *O'Donovan* as one of the numerous names of men formed from adjectives denoting colour (*Topographical Poems,* p. 55).

AIRIEHÀSSAN (*P.* Aryhassen). 'Kirkinner.' *Airidh chasain* [?] [hassan], shieling of the pathway. A farm on the old pack-horse track from Mochrum to Wigton. *Cf.* BALHASIE,

CULQUHASEN; also Cassan in Fermanagh, Cussan in Kilkenny, Cossaun in Galway, Ardnagassan in Donegal, Ardnagassane in Tipperary, etc. GAEL. *casan*, a path, perhaps akin to E. *causeway*, in which mistaken etymology has introduced *wa;* formerly *causey* (*Milton*, P.L., x. 415, and *causé* Barbour's *Bruce*, ed. *Skeat*, xviii. 128, 140)—O.F. *caucie* (F. *chaussée*, SPAN. *calzada*)—LOW LAT. *calciata* (*calciata via*), a causeway—LAT. *calx*.

AIRIEHÈMMING (*Inq. ad Cap.* 1628, Areheman; *P.* Aryhaman; *Inq. ad Cap.* 1650, Aricheman; 1663, Arihemmane). 'Old Luce.' *Cf.* AREEMING.

AIRIELÌCK (*P.* Airluick). 'Mochrum.' *Airidh léc* or *lic*, shieling of the flat stones (or tombs). Flags used to be quarried here, a wall of which was found encircling a crannog or lakedwelling in the moss, which was excavated in 1884.—*Coll. A.G.A.A.*, vol. v. p. 114; O. ERSE *lec*, ERSE *leac* [lack], *lic* [lick], *liag* [leeg], GAEL. *leac*, W. *lhechen* + LAT. *lapis* + GK. λίθος. For gen. plur. *léc*, *cf.* "O étrochta léc lógmar."—*Fis Adamnáin* (from *Lebor Brec*) 18, l. 30, *Windisch*, p. 182; but in the *Lebor na hUidre* the same passage is given, " O etrochta léac logmar," showing the alternative form.

AIRIELÌG (*Inq. ad Cap.* 1692, Arielig; 1667, Arilig; *P.* Ariluig, Erluganair, Arylaganair). 'Kirkcowan.' *Airidh luig*, shieling of the hollow, or of the loch. *Loch*, gen. *locha* or *luig*. "*Luig*, the gen. of *loch*, *An luig*, of the lake."—*Lluyd*. Arylaganair looks like *airidh luig an air*, shieling of the hollow of slaughter, or of the ploughing.

AIRIEÒLLAND (*Inq. ad Cap.* 1668, Ardowland; *P.* Aryoullan; *Symson*, Ariullan; *Inq. ad Cap.* 1697, Arioland; *Inq. ad Cap.* 1628, Areulanes). 'Mochrum,' 'Old Luce,' 'Stoneykirk.'

AIRIEQUHÌLLART [*pron.* Airiewhillart], (*P.* Arychollart; *Inq. ad Cap.* 1664, Airiquhillart). 'Mochrum.' *Airidh abhalghoirt* [?] [airy oulart], shieling of the apple-garden. *Cf.* Ballywhollart in Down, Ballinoulart in Wexford and King's County, Oulart in Wexford, and Knockullard in Carlow. O. ERSE *aball*, *uball*, ERSE *abhal*, GAEL. *ubhall* + W. *afal*, B. *aval* + ICEL. *epli* + DU. *appel* + O. FRIES. *appel* + A.S. *æple æppel* (whence M.E. *appel*, *appil*, E. *apple*) + SWED. *äple*, *äpple* + DAN. *æble* + O.H.G. *aphol*, G. *apfel* + RUSS. *jabloko* + LITH. *obulys*.

AÌRIES (*W. P.* MSS. Areiss; *P.* Aryes, Aries; *Inq. ad Cap.* 1568, Airie; 1625, Airie). 'Kirkcolm,' 'Kirkinner.' *Aros*, a house, a dwelling. "*Aras*, a room, a house."—*Lluyd*. This word does not appear in Irish names.

AÌRLESS (*P.* Airlyis). 'Kirkinner.'

AÌRLOUR (*P.* Arlair; *Inq. ad Cap.* 1684, Aulare *vel* Airlare). 'Mochrum.' *Urlár* [?], a floor; hence a flat piece of land. *Cf.* Urlar in Sligo and Urlaur in Mayo.

AÌRY HILL (*P.* Ary). 'Rerwick.' *See under* AIRIE.

AÌRYLAND (*Inq. ad Cap.* 1605, Arilane; *P.* Arylane). 'Kelton.' *Airidh leathan* [airie lahan], broad hill-pasture. *Leathan* 'is often shortened to *lane*, especially in the north (of Ireland): as in Gortlane, near Cushendall, in Antrim, Lislane in Derry and Tyrone.'—*Joyce*, ii. 418. *See under* AUCHLANE.

AKEWHAN FORD (on the Dee).

ALCHERRY CLEUGH. 'Carsphairn.' The prefix appears to be *aill*, a cliff, or perhaps *allt*, a glen or stream. *See under* CLEUGH.

ALDERGÒWAN. 'Colvend.' *Allt an gobhan* [gown or gowen], the smith's glen. In primitive times the smith or worker in metals occupied an important office, and the word *gobha* [gow] gen. sing. *gobhan, gobha, gabond*, enters into innumerable place-names in Scotland and Ireland; O. ERSE *goba*, O. W. *gob*, W. *gof*, C. and B. *gof*. O. ERSE *alt*, "cliff or height," *ab altitudine* (*Corm. Transl.*, p. 56) ; GAEL. "*allt*, a river with precipitous banks ; a river, a brook."—*Macalpine*. In Galloway and Ulster, it nearly always means a glen, or the stream that runs within the glen. The change of meaning has been progressive, from the height to the valley between the heights, thence to the stream in the valley. There are many words meaning "hill" that come to mean "hollow," and *vice versa*.

ALDÒURAN. 'Leswalt.' *Allt dóran*, glen of the otters, otterburn. *Cf.* POLDOWRAN, PULDORES. *Dóran = dobharan* [doveran, doran], the water-animal ; ERSE *dobharchú*, the water-dog, W. *dyfrgi*, C. *dourghi*, B. *durki*, M̃ *dûr*. The idea is the same in Celtic and Teutonic languages. Thus *otter* — A.S. *otor* + DU. *otter* + ICEL. *otr* + DAN. *odder* + SWED. *utter* + G. *otter* + RUSS. *vuidra* + LITH. *udra* + GK. ὕδρα, a water-snake. The common Teutonic type is *utra*, answering to Aryan *udra*, standing for orig. *wadra ;* it is closely related to *water*. The sense is 'water-animal.' (*Skeat*.)

ALHÀNG (a hill 2100 ft.) (*P.* Aldhing). 'Carsphairn.' *Faill*, or *aill*, a cliff or precipice. Usually *faill* in the south of Ireland becomes *fhaill* [ail] in the north. *Cf.* O. ERSE *ail*, a stone.

ALGÒWER STRAND 'Girthon.' *Allt*, or *aill gabhar* [gower], the glen or cliff of the goats. *Cf.* Allagower in Dublin county). "*Strand*, a rivulet."—*Jamieson.* A.S. *strand*, a margin. *Gabhar* or *gobhar*, a goat, gen. *goibhre*, O. ERSE *gabar*, a horse or goat + W. *gafar* + C. *gauvr* + B. *gauvr* + LAT. *caper.* The word was originally applied both to the horse and the goat. *Cormac* gives *gabur*, a goat, *gobur*, a horse. In Colgan's Life of St. Aidus *Loch-gabhra* is translated *Stagnum-equi.* In mod. Gael. *gobhar* means a she-goat as distinct from *boc*, a he-goat. In this case, and many others, owing to the wild, rugged ground, and to the fact that wild goats exist in considerable numbers still, the name may be safely assumed as having been given in reference to goats rather than to horses.

ALLANBÀNK. 'Buittle.'

ALLANBÀY. 'Minigaff.' *Aill an beith* [bey], cliff of the birch-tree, or *eilean beith*, island or river-meadow of the birches. *Beith* or *beth*, W. *beduen.* B. *bezo, bedho* + LAT. *betula.*

ALLAN'S CROSS. 'Rerwick.'

ALLANDÒO. 'Leswalt.' *Eilean dubh* [allan doov or doo], black isle. O. ERSE *oilén*, ERSE *oiléan*, GAEL. *eilean* + A.S. *igland* (whence M.E. *iland, ylond*) + DU. *eiland* + ICEL. *eyland*, G. *eiland*, etc. Means primarily an island, but, like *innis* (BR. SC. *inch*, and *isle*), is often applied to pasture beside water. Neither *oiléan* nor E. *island* are at all related, except in sense, to E. *isle* — LAT. *insula. Dubh* is a very common word in composition, assuming the various forms of *duff, doo, dow, dhu, dew, dee*, etc. It is used both as prefix and suffix. W. *du.* C. *diu*, B. *deia.*

ALLANÈASY. 'Leswalt.' There is an island of the same name on the West Highland coast, on which are remains of a chapel, and which bears the sense of *eilean Iosa* [eesa], isle of Jesus. *Cf.* CLACHANEASY.

ALLANGÌBBON (an island in the Ken). 'Dalry.' *Eilean*, an island.

ALLEN HEAD. 'Kirkmaiden,' 'Whithorn.' *Aillean* [?], the cliffs. *See under* ALHANG.

ALMORNESS [*pron.* Àmmerness]. 'Buittle.'

ALMANACK HILL. ' Inch.' *Allt manach* [?], the glen of the monks. Close by is Auld Taggart, *q.v.* ERSE, C., and B. *manach*, W. *mynach*—LAT. *monachus* (whence A.S. *munec*, E. *monk*)+GK. μοναχὸς, solitary, deriv. of μόνος, alone. Difficult to distinguish, in some names, from *meadhonach* [minnach].

ALRÀITH. ' Carsphairn.' *Aill raith* [?], cliff of the fort. *See under* WRAITH.

ALT, The. ' Glasserton,' ' Kirkinner.' *Allt*, a height. The primitive meaning seems to have been retained in each of these places. *See under* ALDERGOWAN.

ALTÀDOCH BURN.   ' Kirkmaiden.'

ALTÀGGART BURN (*P.* Alt. Taggart). ' New Luce.' *Allt shágairt* [haggart], the priest's glen. O. ERSE *sacard* (*Cormac,* sacart) — LAT. *sacerdos* (lit. " a presenter of holy offerings "), from LAT. *base* SAC, which, being nasalised, gives *sancire*, to establish, confirm, of which past part. *sanctus* gives F. *saint,* E. *saint.* In this word the *s* in composition often disappears (as in this name) by aspiration, or is eclipsed by *t*, as in BARTAGGART. *Cf.* Carrickataggart, in Donegal, and many other names in Ireland.

ALTAIN. ' Kirkmaiden.' *Alltán*, a little glen or streamlet; dim. of *allt*.

ALT GLEN, The. ' Mochrum.' *Allt*, a glen; the pleonastic name of the glen at Alticry.

ALTIBÈASTIE (*P.* Alaveisty). ' Kells.' *Allt a' biasta* (gen. of *beist*), glen of the beast, or of the serpent. *Cormac, béist*=LAT. *bestia ;* W. *bwyst* (in *bwyst-fil*). *Pont's* writing shows the aspirated form of genitive, *bheiste.* *Cf.* BALLOCHABEASTIE ; also Altnapaste in Ireland, Knocknabeast in Roscommon, Lisnapaste in Donegal and Mayo, Tobernapeastia in Kilkenny.

ALTIBRÀIR. ' New Luce.' *Allt a' brathair* [braar], the friar's glen. Close to Kilfeather and Altaggart, *Cf.* PORTBRIAR : also, in Cork county, Garranabraher. *Brathair,* a brother, hence a friar, W. *brawd,* plur. *brodyr,* C. *bredar*+A.S. *bróthor,* whence M.E. *brother* + ICEL. *brodir* + GOTH. *bróthar* + O.H.G. *pruoder*+RUSS. *brat'*+LAT. *frater*+GK. φρατήρ+SKT. *bhrâtri* — √BHAR, to bear.

ALTIBRÌCK STRAND. ' Kells.' *Allt na breac* [brack], stream of the trouts. *Breac,* a trout=*bréc,* spotted ; the spotted fish.

ALTICRỲ (*Inq. ad Cap.* 1582, Alticray; *P.* Aldchry). ' Mochrum.'

ALTIGÒUKIE (*P.* Altigobraide). ' New Luce.'

ALTIVOLIE. ' Stoneykirk.' *Allt na bhuaile* [voolie], glen or stream of the cattle fold. *Cf.* Ballyvooley in Antrim, etc. *Buaile*, deriv. of *bo*, a cow. " The term *booley* was not confined to the mountainous districts, for in some parts of Ireland it was applied to any place where cattle were fed or milked, or which was set apart for dairy purposes."—*Joyce*, i. 229.

ALTIWHÀT. ' Girthon.' *Allt na chat*, glen of the wild cats. *See under* ALWHAT.

ÀLTON (*Inq. ad Cap.* 1629, Auldtoun; 1630, Auldtoune; 1636, Altoun; *P.* Esschonne, from *easdn*, dim. of *eas* [ass], a cascade). ' Kirkmaiden.' *Alltdn*, a streamlet, dim. of *allt*, *see* ALTAIN.

ALTÒGUE [*pron.* Alchogue], (*Inq. ad Cap.* 1697, St. John's Croft, *adjacens* Culgroat, *vocata* Altileog; 1636, Crofta Sancti Johannis *adjacens vocata* Altichoge; *P.* Aldtewick). ' Stoneykirk.' *Alltog*, dim. of *allt*.

ALWHÀNNIE (a hill, 1200 ft.). ' Carsphairn.' *Aill*, a cliff, perhaps *fheannogh*, of the carrion crows, like Mullanavannog in Monaghan. *Cf.* BARWHANNIE.

ALWHÀT (a hill, 1937 ft.). ' Carsphairn.' *Aill chatt* [haat], cliff of the wild cats. *Cat* (GAEL. and ERSE), a word of unknown origin, exists in many languages; DU. *kat* + ICEL. *köttr* + DAN. *kat* + SWED. *katt* + O.H.G. *kater, chazzá* + G. *kater, katze* + W. *cath* + BRET. *caz* + LATE LAT. *catus* + RUSS. *kot', koshka* + ARAB. *qitt* + TURK. *kedi.* + A.S. *cat, catt.* (*Skeat.*) *Cf.* DRUMWHAT, CAIRN-NA-GATH; *also* Roscat in Carlow, and other places in Ireland.

ALWHÌBBIE. ' Stoneykirk.' *Allt*, a stream or glen.

ALWHÌLLAN. ' Kells.' *Aill chuileainn* [hwillan], cliff of the holly bush. *Cuileann*, W. *celyn, celin*, B. *kelen*. In the E. *holly* the final *n* (retained in SC. *hollin*) has been dropped; M.E. *holyn* — A.S. *holen* (this M.E. form produces *holm oak* (*quercus ilicifolius*), the holly-leaved oak) + DU. *hulst* + G. *hülse*, holly + F. *houx*; perhaps the base KUL, HUL is connected with LAT. *culmen*, a peak (*culmus*, a stalk), from the pointed leaves. (*Skeat*).

ANABÀGLISH (*P.* Ennabaguish). ' Mochrum.' *Eanach bogluasgach* or *bogghluiseachd*, the floating bog or morass; a sufficiently close description of the place. *Cf.* Annaghbeg, in Ireland, and many other places in that country with names beginning Annagh, Anna, and Anny. *Eanach*, a moor, a marsh (*O'Reilly*) ; *bogghluiseachd*, floating, moving (*O'Reilly*) ; GAEL. *bogluasgach* ; waving, floating, softly moving (*Macalpine*). Deriv. of *bog*, soft ; *bogach*, a bog. *See under* BOGUE.

ÀNNAT HILL. ' Kirkinner.' *Annoid* [annud], a church. This is on the farm of Kirkland of Longcastle, which accounts for the name.

ÀNNATLAND (near Sweetheart Abbey). ' New Abbey.' Church land. *See under* ANNAT HILL.

ANSTOOL (*P.* Amstel).   ' Balmaghie.'

ÀNWOTH (*Inq.ad Cap.* 1575, Anuecht). (A parish in the Stewartry.)

APPLEBIE (*Inq. ad Cap.* 1598, Aplebie ; *W. P.* MS. Apilbie ; *P.* Apleby). ' Glasserton.'

ARBÌGLAND (*P.* Arbiggland ; *Sibbald* MS. Arbiglam). ' Kirkbean.'

ÀRBRACK (*Inq. ad Cap.* 1625, Arbrok ; *W. P.* MS. Arbrok ; *P.* Arbrock). ' Whithorn.'

ARDÀCHIE (*Inq. ad Cap.* 1633, Ardachir *vel* Aldachie). ' Kirkcowan.' *Ard achadh* [aha], high field. *Cf.* Ardagh and Ardaghy, commonly in Ireland, written by the Annalists *Ardachadh*. *See under* ACHIE *and* AIRD.

ARDNIMÒRD (*Inq. ad Cap.* 1614, Ardnamoird ; 1692, Ardenmort ; 1627, Ardinmorde ; *P.* Arynamoirt). ' Kirkcowan.' *Ard na mart*, height of the oxen, or (if *Pont's* spelling be the original), *airidh na mart*, hill-pasture of the oxen. *Cf.* Stranamort in Cavan, and Cahernamart (the old name of Westport) in Mayo.

ARDOCH (*P.* Airdoch). ' Dalry.' *See under* ARDACHIE. The old name of Craufurdland, in Kilmarnock parish, was Ardach, of which *Pont* says, " Aaird-dach, or Ard-daach, as some interpret it ; a heigh plott, or daach, of land layand vpone a know."—*Cuninghame*, p. 55.

ÀRDRIE. ' Kirkcolm.' *Ard righ*, height of the king or chief (*see under* AUCHENRÈE), or perhaps *ard reidh* [ray], high plain, smooth height. " *Reidh* is usually applied to a mountain flat, or a coarse, moory, level piece of ground among hills."—*Joyce*, i. 427. B. *reiz. Cf.* AIRDRIE. *See under* AUCHENREE.

ÀRDWALL (*P.* Ardwel, Ardwell). ' Anwoth,' ' Borgue,' ' New Abbey.' *Ard gall* [?], the stranger's height, or height of the standing stones. The change from *g* to *w* is according to rule.

ARDWELL.   ' Kirkcolm,' ' Stoneykirk.'
See under ARDWALL.

ARÈEMING (*Inq. ad Cap.* 1604, Arreimein; *Macfarlane* MS., Àriming). 'Kirkpatrick Durham.' *Cf.* AIRIEHEMMING.

ARGRÙSK, ISLE OF (in the Dee). 'Minigaff.'

ÀRKLAND (*Inq. ad Cap.* 1604, Arkland; *P.* Arckland). 'Girthon.'

ARMANÌLLIE. 'Balmaclellan.

ARNDÀRROCH (*P.* Arndarrag, Arndarrach). 'Dalry.' *Ard na darach*, height of the oaks. O. ERSE *dair*, gen. *daro, dara, darach,* GAEL. *darach,* W. *derw,* C. *dar,* B. *derven*+GOTH. *triu*, gen. *triwis,* a tree + SWED. *trä* + DAN. *træ* + ICEL. *tré,* timber+A.S. *treó,* a tree (whence E. *tree*). All from TEUT. type *trewa,* a tree + RUSS. *drevo,* a tree + GK. δρῦς, an oak, δόρυ, a spear shaft + SKT. *dru, dáru,* wood. (*Skeat,* s.v. Tree.)

ARNGRÈNNAN (*Inq. ad Cap.* 1604, Argranane; *P.* Ardgrenen). 'Tungland.' *Ard an grianain* [greenan], the height of the castle. *See under* GRENNAN.

ARNMÀNNOCH (*P.* Ardmannoch, Armaunoch). 'Kirkgunzeon.' *Ard na manach*, height of the monks. Close by is a ruined church. *See under* ALMANACK.

ÀRROW (*Inq. ad Cap.* 1600, Arrow; *P.* Arrow; *W. P.* MS. Arrow). 'Glasserton.' *Arbha* [?] (arva, arwa, arroo), corn. *Cf.* ARVIE and ERVIE, also Clonarrow in King's Co., and Derryarrow in Queen's County.

ÀRTFIELD (*P.* Artfell). 'Old Luce.'

ÀRVIE. (*P.* Aruy, Erby, Errby). 'Kirkcolm,' 'Parton.' *See under* ARROW.

ASIIIEFÀNE. 'Minigaff.'

ASS OF THE GILL (a ravine on the Cree, about a mile above Newton-Stewart). 'Minigaff.' A compound of three languages. GAEL. *eas* [ass], a cascade, SCAND. *gil,* a ravine. First came the Celt, who spoke of it as *eas,* then the Norse invader who called it *gil,* finally English speech united the two by interposing preposition and article.

AUCHABRÌCK. 'Kirkmaiden.' *Achadh bréc* [aha breck], dappled, brindled field. A common epithet of variegated, brindled land (*see* FLECKEDLAND). O. ERSE *bréc,* ERSE and GAEL. *breac,* W. *brech, brith,* formerly *bricta* (*Rhys,* p. 62), B. *briz*+ICEL. *freknur,* pl. freckles + SWED. *fräkne,* a freckle + DAN. *fregne* + E. *freckle, freckly* + GK. περκνός, spotted + SKT. *priçni.*

AUCHENCÀIRN (*Inq. ad Cap.* 1575, Auchincairne; *P.* Achincairn). 'Rerwick.' *Achadh an cairn*, field of the cairn. "I went . . . to Aghakern, or the field of the cairn, a village so called from a cairn near."—*Letter from Bishop Pococke to his sister*, A.D. 1760. O. ERSE *curnd carn*, *curd*, a heap of stones, especially over a grave. GAEL., ERSE, W., M., C., B. *carn*. The root-sense seems to be "stone," not "heap;" probably from a root *car*, whence *carraig*, *creag*, a cliff or rock, *carrach*, rocky (*cara* i. *clocha*, O'Dav., p. 63), B. *karrek*, a rock in the sea, ERSE *ceart*, a pebble, E. *chert*. The genitive of *carn* is now *chuirn*, but the old genitive was *cairnd* or *chairnd* : "Doberat cloich cach fir leo do chur chairnd."—*Leabhar na h-Uidre*, p. 86ᵇ, 40.

AUCHENCLÒY (*Inq. ad Cap.* 1543, Auchincloye; *P.* Achincloy). 'Girthon,' 'Stoneykirk.' *Achadh na cloiche*, field of the stone. Many townlands in Ireland bear the name of Aghnacloy. *Cf.* Auchencloich in Kilbirnie parish, Ayrshire, translated by *Pont*, "Ye fold of stones, or stoney fold."—*Cuninghame*, p. 48.

AUCHENDÀRROCH (*P.* Assindarroch). 'Inch.' *Achadh na darach*, field of the oaks, oakfield. *Cf.* Auchendarroch iu Ayrshire, and Aghindarroch in Tyrone. *See under* ARNDARROCH.

AUCHENDÒLLY (*P.* Achindoly). 'Crossmichael.' *Achadh na dtulach* [?], field of the hillocks, or *achadh na dealg* [dallig], field of the thorns. *Cf.* AUCHENTALLCCH and CLAUCHEN-DOLLY, and, in Antrim, Ballynadolly.

AUCHENFÀD. 'Rerwick,' 'Troqueer.' *Achadh fada*, long or far field. "*Fad, fada*, long, tall."—*O'Reilly.*

ÀUCHENFRÀNCO (*P.* Achinfranco). 'Loch Rutton.' *Achadh an Francaich*, the Frenchman's field. *Cf.* FRANGO HILL, also, in Iona, Port na bhfrancach. ERSE *Francuch*, W. *Frennig*, C. *Vrinkak*.+O.H.G. *franko*, a Frank, a free man. "The origin of the name *Frank* is obscure."—*Skeat.*

AUCHENFLÒWER (*P.* Ach-na-flowir). 'Kirkcudbright.' Perhaps to be compared to Flowerhill in Sligo, which is a semi-translation of *cnoc an lobhair* [lour], the leper's or sick man's hill. *Cf.* DRUMFLOWER. *See under* BARLURE.

AUCHENGÀLIE (*P.* Achingailluy).   'Mochrum.'

AUCHENGÀSHELL. 'Twynholm.' *Achadh an gcaiseail* [aha an gashell], field of the stone fort (castle). ERSE *caiseal*, W. *castell*, C. *castal*+A.S. *castel*+LAT. *castellum*, dim. of *castrum*, a camp.

AUCHENGÌLSHIE (now called Gilshie Feys). 'Kirkinner.'

Achadhán giolchach [ahaan gilhya], rushy field. *Cf.* KNOCK-
GILSIE, KNOCKGULSHA, CASSENGILSHIE, TARWILKIE. "*Giolc,*
a reed or cane."—*Lluyd.* In Southern Ireland *giolc* means
broom, and also sometimes in the North ; *e.g.* Giltagh, in
Fermanagh, which is called "Giltagh or Broomhill" in the
Grand Jury Map of Devenish.—*Joyce,* ii. 335.

AUCHENGÌBBERT (*P.* Achingibbert). 'Urr.' *Achadh an tiobair,*
field of the well. (*See under* AUCHENTIBBERT.) *Tobar* or
tiobar, a well, often appears as *chipper, kibber,* or *kipper,* in
compound as well as in simple place-names ; *e.g.* KIBBERTIE
KITE WELL, CHIPPERMORE, CARRICK KIBBERTIE.

AUCHENGOÒL. 'Rerwick.' *Achadh na gabhal* [gowl] ; literally
the field of the fork (as the dividing of streams), (*gabhal,*
furca, *Ir. Gl.*) ; but in MOD. GAEL. *gabhall* means "a portion
of land done by cattle in ploughing."—*Macalpine.* *O'Clery*
also gives *gabhail,* i. *creach,* plunder. *See under* ADDERHALL.

AUCHENGÒWER. 'Kirkcolm.' *Achadh na gobhar* [aha na gowr],
field of the goats. *See under* ALGOWER.

AUCHENGRÀY. 'New Abbey.' *Achadh na gréaich* [?], field of the
level moor or high flat. *See under* IRONGRAY. Auchengree,
in Dalry parish, Ayrshire, written Achin-gray by *Pont,* is
rendered *Achadh na criadh,* clay field, by his editor, *Dobie.*
(*Cuninghame,* p. 48.)

AUCHENHÀY (*Inq. ad Cap.* 1604, Auchinhey ; MS. 1527, Auchin-
hay ; *P.* Achinhae). 'Borgue,' 'Colvend,' 'Kirkpatrick Durham.' *Achadh na haithe* [aha na haye], field of the kiln.
Aith [āh] a kiln for drying corn. "It is generally found in
the end of names, joined with *na,* the gen. fem. of the
article, followed by *h,* by which it is distinguished from *ath,*
a ford, which takes *an* in the genitive."—*Joyce,* i. 377. *Cf.*
Annahaia and Annahaigh in Monaghan and Armagh, Bally-
nahaha and Ballynahaia in Limerick ; Lisnahay in Antrim,
Gortnahey in Londonderry, and Auchnahay in Antrim, etc.

AUCHENHÌLL. 'Colvend.' *Achadh an chuill* [aha an hill], field of
the hazel bush. O. ERSE *collde* ("*coll,* corylus," *Ir. Gl.*), W.
coll (*Rhys*), C. *goluidhen,* B. *keluedhen,* GAEL. *calltun* + LAT.
corylus (*cosulus*) + DAN. and SWED. *hassel* + ICEL. *hasl* + A.S.
hœsel, whence M.E. *hasel* and E. *hazel.* Hazel-nuts, in prehistoric times, formed an important article of human diet.
When Barhapple Loch, in Old Luce, was drained, a very
large crannog or lake-dwelling was exposed, the lee shore of

the lake (N.E., according to the prevailing S.W. wind) was found strewn with immense quantities of broken nut-shells. *See under* INCH.

AUCHENÌNNES (*Charter* 1696, Auchinfines). 'Urr.' An island in the Water of Urr. *Achadh an inis* (dative case), field in the island.

AUCHENLÀRIE (*P.* Achinlary). 'Anwoth.' *Achadh na laira*, field of the mare. ERSE *larach*, O. ERSE *lair* (*Ir. Gl.* 294), GAEL. *lair*.

AUCHENLÈCK (*P.* Achinlick). 'Minigaff.' *Achadh na léc* [lack], field of the tombs (lit. flat stones). *See under* AIRIELICK. *Cf.* AUCHLEACH.

AUCHENLÒSH (MS. 1527, Auchinlosh). 'Colvend.' *Achadh na lus* [?], field of herbs. *Lus*, porrum (*i.e.* a leek), *Ir. Gl.* 810; W. *llys*, C. *lysûan*, B. *luzauan*. *Cf.* Auchinloss, in Ayrshire.

AUCHENLOY.   'Glasserton.'

AUCHENMÀLG (*P.* Achinmalg). 'Old Luce.'

AUCHENRÈE. 'Port Patrick.' *Achadh an righ* [ree], the king's field. O. ERSE *rí*, gen. *rig*, W. *rhûy*, O.W. *rhi*, C. *rûy*, B. *rue*, plur. *rounet*+LAT. *rex*, gen. *regis*+GOTH. *reiks*+SKT. *rájan*. *Ri* or *righ*, translated king, "is often," says O'Donovan (*Hy Many*, 64 *note*), "applied to a petty chief of one barony."

AUCHENRÈOCH. 'Urr.' *Achadhan riabhach* [ahaan reeugh], little grey field. "*Riabhach*, brindled, tabby, grey."—*O'Reilly*.

AUCHENRÒCHER (*Inq. ad Cap.* 1661, Ardcrocher [*i.e.* hangman's hill]; *P.* Acchrocchyrr). 'Inch.' *Achadh an crochadhair* [croghar], the hangman's field. Deriv. of *croch*, lit. a cross, the gallows. *Cf.* Ardnagroghery in Cork, Knockcrogherie in Connaught, etc.

AUCHENSHEEN (*Inq. ad Cap.* 1604, Auchinschine; *P.* Auchimsheem). 'Colvend.' *Achadh na sion* (?), [aha na sheen], field of the foxgloves. For the gen. plur. of this word, which takes its name from *sith*, a fairy (GAEL. *lus-nam-ban-sith*, plant of the fairies), *cf.* "Is dath sion and cech grúad," *Tochmarc Etaine*, p. 132, l. 25 (*Windisch*). In Irish names the *s* is generally eclipsed by *t*, thus Gortatean in Antrim (*gort a t-sian*), Mullantine and Drumanteane in Armagh; Carrickateane in Cavan, etc. The foxglove seems indelibly connected in the popular mind with fairies, for although the E. word is not, as has been erroneously alleged, from "folk's glove," but from A.S. *foxes glofa* (*cf.* NORW. *revhandskje*, from *rev*, a fox); it goes also by the name of "fairy-fingers." Perhaps *achadh an sidheain* [sheean], the field of the fairies' palace. *Cf.* Aghintain in Tyrone (in which *s* is eclipsed by *t*). *Sidhean* [sheean] gives names to many places in Ireland, Sheean, Shean, Sheaun, Sheehaun. *Joyce*, i. 187, and ii. 329. *Cf.* Fairy Knowes.

AUCHENSHÌNNOCH. 'Dalry.' *Achadh na sionnach* [aha na shinnagh], field of the foxes. O. ERSE *sinnach, sindach;* ERSE and GAEL. *sionnach. Cf.* BLAIRSHINNOCH, INSHANNOCH, KIRSHINNOCH, CRAIGSHUNDIE, BENSHINNIE, CRAIGSHINNIE, TODDLY, etc.; and, in Ireland, Aghnashannagh, Monashinnagh, Coolnashinnagh in Tipperary, and Coolnashinny in Cavan, etc.

AUCHENSKEÒCH (*Inq. ad Cap.* 1604, Auchinskeoche; 1605, Auchinskeaucht; M.S. 1527, Auchinskeauch; *P.* Achinskioch). 'Colvend.' *Achadh na sceithióg* [skeyoge], field of the hawthorns. · *Cf.* in Ireland, Aghnaskeagh and Aghnaskew, etc., and Auchenskeith in Dalry parish, Ayrshire. *See under* SKEOG.

AUCHENTÀLLACH. 'Twynholm.' *Achadh an tealaich* [tyallagh], field of the forge. *See under* CHALLOCH.

AUCHENTÌBBERT (*P.* Achyntybert). 'Port Patrick.' *Achadh an tiprat* or *tiobraid* [tibbred], field of the well. *Cf.* WELLFIELD and AUCHENGIBBERT; also Auchintibber in Ayrshire, Aghintober and Aghatubrid in Ireland. *See under* TIBBERT.

AUCHENVÈAN (*Inq. ad Cap.* 1646, Auchinvea; 1656, Auchinvain). 'Inch.' Probably the same as Auchenvey, *q.v.*

AUCHENVÈY (*Inq. ad Cap.* 1607, Auchinvay). 'Parton.' *Achadh an bheith* [ahanvey], field of birch tree. *See under* ALLANBAY.

AUCHESS. 'Kirkcowan.

AÙCHIE. 'Inch.' *Achadh* [aha], a field. *See under* ACHIE.

AÙCHIE GLEN. 'Kirkmaiden.' *See under* AUCHIE.

AUCHLÀNE. 'Kelton.' *Achadh leathan* [lahan, lane], broad field. *Cf.* Auchleand. O. ERSE *lethan*, W. *llydán*, C. and B. *ledan*, GAEL. *leathan* + LAT. *latus.*

AUCHLÀNNOCHIE. 'Minigaff.'

AUCHLÈACH [*pron.* lee-ach], (*Inq. ad Cap.* 1543, Auchsleoch). 'Stoneykirk.' 'Kirkcolm' (*twice*). *See under* AUCHENLECK.

AUCHLEÀND [*pron.* Aghlyaun], (*P.* Achleaun).   'Wigtown.'
Achadh leathan [aha lahan], broad field.   *See under* AUCHLANE.

AUCHMÀNISTER or AUCHENMÀNISTER.   'Old Luce.'   *Achadh an
mainisdir*, the field of the monastery, close to the Abbey of
Luce.   *Cf.* Aghmanister, in Abbeymahon parish, Cork ;
Drummanister, etc.   From LAT. *monasterium* (whence E. *minster*,
not akin to *minister*) — GK. μοναστήριον — μοναστής, dwelling
alone — μονάζειν — μονός.   *See under* ALMANACK HILL.

AUCHMÀNTLE (*P.* Achmantil).   'Inch.'

AUCHNABÒNY.   'Rerwick.'   *Achadh na banbh* [bonniv], field of
the young pigs ; swine pasture.   *Banb*, a pig (*Cormac*) ;   W.
banw.   *Cf.* Drumbonniff in Down, Drumbanniv in Clare,
Drumbannow in Cavan, etc.

AUCHNÀSSY (*P.* Achtasy).   'Kirkcolm.'

AUCHNÈEL (*Inq. ad Cap.* 1668, Auchmaneil ; *P.* Achneil).   'Les-
walt.'   *Achadh Niaill*, Neil's field.   *Auchmaneil*, from the
Rolls, indicates the patronymic.   *Pont* interprets Ardneill in
Ayrshire as " Neel's knope."   (*Cuninghame*, p. 56.)

AUCHNÈIGHT [*pron.* Aughneagh], (*Inq. ad Cap.* 1610, Auchnaucht).
'Kirkmaiden.'   *Achadh n-ech*, field of the horses.

AÙCHNESS or ACHNESS   (*P.* Achnish).   'Glasserton,' 'Kirkmaiden,'   'Mochrum.'   *Each inis*, horse pasture.   The same
word as Aughinish and Aughnish in various parts of Ireland,
which the *Four Masters* write *Each-Inis* (*inis* meaning a water-
side pasture as well as an island ; *see* INCH).   O. ERSE *ech* +
LAT. *equus* + GK. ἵππος + A.S. *eoh* + SKT. *acva.*

AUCHNIEBÙT.   'Kells.'   *Achadh na boc* [?], field of the he-goats.
Boc + B. and W. *bwch*, a buck ; C. *byk, boch*, a he-goat + A.S. *bucca*
(whence M.E. *bukke*, E. *buck*) + DU. *bok*, a he-goat + ICEL. *bukkr*,
a he-goat + O.H.G. *poch*, a he-goat, a buck + SKT. *bukka*, a goat.

AUCHNÒTTEROCH (*Inq. ad Cap.* 1616, Auchoteroch ; 1668, Auch-
nostroch ; *P.* Atnottroch).   'Leswalt.'   *Achadh in óchtarach*
[ahanoghteragh] upper field ;   O. ERSE *úachtarach*, adj. from s.
úachtar, óchtar ;   ERSE and GAEL. *úachdar*, W. *uch, uched, uchel*,
high, *uchder, uchdra*, height ;   C. *ehwal* ;   B. *uhel*, high.

AUCHRÀE (*P.* Achre).   'Dalry.'   *Achadh reidh* [ray], smooth field.

AUCHRÈOCH [*pron.* ree-agh], (*P.* Achreoch).   'Balmaclellan.'
Achadh riabhach [reeagh], grey field.   *Cf.* AUCHENREOCH ; also
Aghareagh in Ireland.

AUCHTÈN. 'Port Patrick.'

AUCHTRIEVÀNE (from estate-map of Cuil). 'Kirkmabreck.' *Uachdarachd bhàn* [vane], white upper land. *See under* AUCH-NOTTEROCH.

AULDBRECK (*Inq. ad Cap.* 1620, Olbreck. *P.* Ulbreck. *W. P.* MSS. Olbrek). 'Whithorn.' *Allt breac,* trout stream. *See under* ALTIBRICK.

AULD HILL. 'Penninghame' (*twice*). *Allt,* a height. *See under* ALDERGOWAN.

AULD TÀGGART. 'Inch.' *Allt shagairt,* the priest's glen (the aspirate silences the *s*). *See under* ALTAGGART.

AULD WIFE'S GRAVE. 'Inch.'

AWHÌRK (*Inq. ad Cap.* 1637, Auchork; 1543, Aquhork; *P.* Acchork). 'Stoneykirk.' *Achadh a' cheorce* [?] [hurkya], oatfield. *See under* BARNKIRK.

BÀCHLA. 'Kirkmaiden.' "*Bachlach,* mann mit einem stocke (*bachall*)" (*Windisch*), man with a stick. "A herdsman, a rustic."—*O'Reilly.* From *bachall,* a staff, especially a crozier; W. *bagl*—LAT. *baculus.* *Cf.* Moyvoughey, in Westmeath, written by the *Four Masters Magh-bhachla,* the field of the crozier. *Bachlach* was probably used to designate a rock in the same way as *buachail,* a boy, in Ireland. *See under* BOWHILL.

BACK DRUM [M.S. 1527, Backlauch, (*i.e.* back law, or hill)]. 'Kirkmabreck.' English prefix to GAEL. *druim,* a ridge. *See under* DRUM.

BAD'S KNOWE. 'Kirkpatrick Durham.'

BAIL FELL. 'Colvend.' *See under* BELTONHILL.

BÀILIE HILL. 'Stoneykirk.' "*Baillie,* meaning doubtful, perhaps a court or enclosure."—*Jamieson.* MOD. GAEL. *baile* [bally], a town or village, also a farm ; *aig baile,* at home.

Baile, a measure of land, a holding, a townland. "As an existing element, it is the most prevalent of all local terms in Ireland, there being 6400 townlands, or above a tenth of the sum total, into whose names this word enters as an element." —*Reeves.*

It receives the gloss *locus* in the *Book of Armagh,* Cormac's *Glossary,* and the *Book of Lecan,* also Cormac gives *baile* as the equivalent of *rath ;* hence it appears to have been originally

applied specially to the dwelling-place and house, then generally to the land. The old form was *bale:* " In bale athera-
su frim-sa dul it chomdail, ragatsa."—*Serglige Conculaind*, 39.

" Mr. O'Donovan, in his edition of the *Battle of Magh Lena*,
gives probably the oldest view of these land divisions over all
Ireland, as it is attributed to the same Finntan who is said to
have preserved the record of the ancient mythic colonisation
of Ireland."—*Skene, Cell. Scot.* iii. 154.

The poem, of which two or three stanzas here follow, is
well worth the study of any one interested in the subject—

1

How many Trichas in noble Erinn,
How many half-Trichas to accord,
How many Bailes in linked array,
How many doth each Baile sustain.

2

How many Bailes and Tricha-ceds,
In Erinn the abundant in wealth,
I say unto thee—an assertion with sense—
I defy all the learned to confute it.

4

Ten Bailes in each Tricha-ced,
And twenty Bailes (*thirty in all*), it is no falsehood ;
Though small their number to us appears,
Their extent forms a noble country (*crich*).]

5

A Baile sustains three hundred cows,
With twelve Seisrichs—it is no lie ;
Four full herds may therein roam,
With no cow of either touching the other.

*   *   *   *   *

11

Twenty Bailes, too, and five hundred,
And five thousand (*5520 in all*), it is no falsehood,
Since I have taken to divide them
To the number of Bailes in Erinn.

" The word *baile*, which now means a village, town and
townland, is frequently used in the Irish annals to denote the
residence of a chieftain, a castle, or military station, as in the
following example in the *Four Masters*, at the year 1560 :—
" *Do chóidh ar bhárr an bhaile, agus ro fhuaccair go riabhe an
caislén ar a chumus ;*" i.e. " he went up to the top of the *baile*,
and proclaimed that the castle was in his power." It seems
to be derived from the same source as the Greek πόλις, the
Latin *villa*, and the French *ville*."—*Hy Fiachrach*, 210, *note*.

BAILIEWHÌRR (*Inq. ad Cap.* 1600, Balzequhir; *W. P.* MSS. Ballequhir; *Galloway Estate Map,* Balzeuchar; *P.* Balwhyr). 'Whithorn.' The *z* in the variant forms represents a *y* sound, not a sibilant.

BÀINLOCH or BEINLOCH. 'Colvend.'

BALÀNNAN (*Inq. ad Cap.* 1604, Ballannane). 'Tungland.'

BALCÀRRY (*Inq. ad Cap.* 1628, Balcarrie *vel* Ballincarrie; *P.* Barkery). 'Old Luce.' *Baile caithre* [?] [carey], house or land of the standing stones.

BALCÀRY. *Cf.* BALCARRY. 'Rerwick.'

BALCRÀIG (*P.* Balkraig, *W. P.* MSS. Balcreg). 'Glasserton.' *Baile creige,* house or townland of the crag. *Cf.* BALGREGGAN; also, in Ireland, Ballynacragga, Ballynacraig, Ballynacraigy, Ballynacregga, and Ballynacregg.

BALCRÈY. 'Whithorn.'

BALCÙLLENDOCH. 'Penninghame.' *Baile cuileannach* [cullenägh], townland of the holly wood. *See under* CULLENDOCH.

BALDOÒN (*P.* Baldun). 'Wigtown.' *Baile duine,* townland of the fort. There is a large fort here. *Dún,* a fort; W. *din,* a hill-fort; GAEL. *dun* + A.S. *tún,* a fort, enclosure, town, whence, by transferred sense, E. *down,* a hill, from a hill being usually chosen for a stronghold; and also adv. and prep. *down,* a contraction of M.E. *a-down* = A.S. *of dúne,* off the hill (*Skeat*). *Cf.* Ballindoon, in Ireland.

BALENSACK. 'Borgue.'

BALFÈRN (*Inq. ad Cap.* 1608, Balfairne; *P.* Balfairn). 'Kirkgunzeon.' *Baile fearn,* townland of the alders. O. ERSE *fernóg* (*Ir. Gl.* 558), ERSE and GAEL. *fearn, fearnog,* W. *gwern,* B. and C. *guern.*

BALGÈRRAN. 'Crossmichael.'

BALGÒWN (*Inq. ad Cap.* 1600, Bellingowyne; *P.* Balgawin). 'Kirkcolm,' 'Kirkmaiden.' *Baile gobhan* [gown], the smith's house or townland. *See under* ALDERGOWAN. *Cf.* Ballygowan, Ballygow, Ballingowan, frequently in Ireland.

BALGRÀCIE (*P.* Balgresy). 'Leswalt.' Formerly Larbrax Greesie. *See* LARBRAX. *Baile greusach* [gressegh], the cobbler's house. GAEL. *greusach,* a shoemaker — O. ERSE *gréss, greas,* "any arti-

ficial work in the execution of which trade or art is required."
—*O'Don. Suppl.* "*Gréis*, needlework, embroidery, fine clothes,
furniture."—*O'Reilly.*   GAEL. *greas*, embroidery.

BALGRÈDDAN (*P.* Balgreddan ; *Inq. ad Cap.* 1604, Balgredden ;
MS. 1527, Balgredane). 'Kirkcudbright.'

BALGRÈGGAN. 'Stoneykirk.' *Baile gcreigain* [?] [greggan], house
of the little crag. *Cf.* BALCRAIG.

BALHÀSIE.   'Kirkmabreck.'

BALÌG. 'Rerwick.' *Baile luig*, townland of the hollow. (*See
under* LAG.) *Cf.* Ballinlig, Ballinlug, Ballinluig, Ballylig,
and Ballylug, common townland names in Ireland.

BALKÀIL (*P.* Balkel). 'Old Luce.' *Baile caol* [?] [keel], narrow
townland. *Cf.* Ballykeel in Ireland. *See under* CARSKEEL.

BALKÈLLY.   'Kirkmaiden.'

BALKÈRR (*Inq. ad Cap.* 1600, Balker). 'Inch.'

BALLÀIRD (*P.* Balard). 'Kirkinner.' *Baile ard*, high house or
townland. *Cf.* Ballard, in Ireland.

BALLANCÒLLANTIE (*P.* Bhellanheullanduy). 'Old Luce.' *See under*
BALCULLENDOCH.

BALLINCLÀUCH (the old name of Glenluce village). 'Old Luce.'
Baile na cloch, town of the stones, stone town. *Cf.* Ballina-
clogh, Ballyclogh, Ballyclohy, Ballynaclogh, and Ballynacloghy,
frequent names in Ireland.

BALLINGÀIR.   'Dalry.'

BALLINGÈAR (*Inq. ad Cap.* 1571, Ballingae). 'Kells.'

BÀLLOCH (a valley between Barncorkrie and Cairn Fell). 'Kirkmaiden.' *Bealach* [ballagh], a pass, a road, a gap. *Fág-a-
bealach* [faugh-a-ballagh], clear the road ! is the slogan of the
Connaught Rangers. As a prefix *bealach* and *beul atha* [bel-
aha], ford mouth, are often indistinguishable in composition.
Cf. LOCH VALLEY.

BALLOCHABÀRGIN.   'Inch.'

BALLOCHABEÀSTIE (the name of a gateway on the farm of Culroy).
'Old Luce.' *Bealach á biasta*, pass of the beast. *See under*
ALTIBEASTIE.

BALLOCHADÈE. 'Kirkcowan.' *Beul atha duibh* [belahadee]. mouth
of the black ford. O. ERSE *bél*, ERSE *béal*, *beul*, "a mouth, an

orifice, a hole."—*O'Reilly.* *See under* ALLANDOO and CARSNAW.

BALLOCHADÒON. 'Inch.' *Bealach a' duin* or *beul atha duin*, the road, pass, or ford-mouth of the fort. *Cf.* Bealach-duin (*Four Masters*, 770, 778, 855, etc.).

BALLOCHAHÈATHERY. 'Old Luce.'

BALLOCHALÈE. 'Stoneykirk.' *Bealach na laegh* [lea], pass of the calves. *Laegh* generally becomes *lee* in composition, "and the articled terminations *-nalee* and *-nalea* are of frequent occurrence. Ballinalee, in Longford and Sligo, is properly written in Irish *Bel-atha-na-laegh*, the ford-mouth of the calves."— *Joyce*, i. 470. *Cf.* Clonleigh, *i.e.* *Cluain-laegh* (*Four Masters*, 1480). W. *llo*, C. *leaugh*, B. *lue*, GAEL. *laoch*.

BALLOCHANÀMOUR or BALLOCHANÀRMOUR. 'Kirkmabreck.' *Bealach an amuir*, pass of the trough or hollow place. "*Ammor, amor*, a trough." *Corm. Tran.* p. 15. *Cf.* LAGANAMOUR, and in Ireland, Lugannamer and Leganamer in Leitrim, Bohammer in Dublin, Glenannummer in King's County, and Glennanammer in Roscommon.

BALLOCHANÒUR. 'Kirkmabreck.'

BALLOCHARÒDY. 'Kirkcolm.'

BALLOCHGÙNION. 'Kirkmaiden.'

BALLOCHJÀRGON. 'Old Luce.' *Bealach deargán* [dyargan], red pass or road; or perhaps *bealach Deargain*, Dergan's pass. The initial *d* before a diphthong passes into English *j* in composition.

BALLOCHMÝRE. 'Penninghame.'

BALLOCH o' KÌP. 'Kirkcolm.' *Bealach a' cip* [kip], the pass or road of the tree trunk. *Cf.* Knockakip, in Clare County, spoken of by the *Four Masters* (1573) as "*mullach cnuic beoil an chip*," *i.e.* top of the hill of Belankip (*beul an chip*, ford mouth of the tree trunk). O. ERSE *cep*, a post, a block + LAT. *cippus*.

BALLOCHRÀE. 'Kirkcowan.' *Bealach reidh* [ray], smooth pass.

BALLYFÈRRY. 'Inch.' *Baile foithre* [?] [bally fihra], townland of the copse. *See under* WHERRY CROFT.

BALLYMÈLLAN. 'Mochrum.' *Baile muilcain* [meulan], mill house or townland. O. ERSE *muilend* (retaining *d* from LAT. *molendinum*), W. *melyn*, C. *belin, melin*, B. *mul, melin*. The F. *mill*,

(properly *miln*, as in BR. SC.) is descended from LAT. *molina*
√MAR, to grind.

BALMACLÈLLAN (*P.* Ballmacklellann).   A parish in the Stewartry.
Baile Maclellan, Maclellan's land or house.   Named from
John Maclellan, who, "in February 1466, obtained a charter
from King James III. of the lands and village."—*M'Kerlie.*

BALMACRÀIL.   'Kirkmabreck.'

BALMÀE (*P.* Balme).   'Kirkcudbright.'

BALMAGHÌE [*pron.* Magee], (*P.* Balmagy).   A parish in the
Stewartry.   MacGhie's land.

BALMÀNGAN (*P.* Balmangan).   'Rerwick.'

BALMÈG (*Inq. ad Cap.* 1698, Tarhouse in Air (*vel* Tarhirismore)
aliter vocata Balmeg, both the first names being misreadings
of Torhousemuir).   'Wigtown.'   *Baile mbeag* [meg], little
house.   *Cf.* Balbeg, in Ayrshire.   *Cf.* "*mil m-bec,*" little beast,
Compert Conculaind, L. U. 5.   "*In miol m-becc,*" little beast, *Eg.*
(*Windisch*, 139).   O. ERSE *bec, becc,* ERSE *beag* + W. *bach,
bychan,* C. *bian, bihan,* B. *bihan*; perhaps akin to GK. βαιος,
LAT. *ve-* in composition, and possibly E. *wee*, though *Skeat*
gives the latter as being a form of *way.*

BALMÈSH (*Inq. ad Cap.* 1633, Balmasche; 1668, Balmass; *P.* Bal-
mess).   'Old Luce.'

BALMÌNNOCH (*P.* Balmeanach; *Inq. ad Cap.* 1625, Balmanocht).
'Kirkcowan.'   *Baile meadhonach* [minnagh], mid-house or
townland.   *Cf.* Ballymena in Antrim, and Ballymenagh in
other parts of Ireland.   *Meadhonach* — O. ERSE *medón* + A.S.
mid, midde + ICEL. *miðr* + SWED. and DAN. *mid* - (in composition) + GOTH. *midja* + O.H.G. *mitti* + LAT. *medius* + GK. μέσος,
Æolic μέσσος (= μεθ.γος) + SKT. *mádhya.*   All from an
adjectival base, MADYA, root unknown.   (*Skeat.*)

BALMÙRRIE (*Inq. ad Cap.* 1628, Balmurran; *P.* Balmoory).
'New Luce.'   *Baile Muireadhaich* [Murragh], Murray's house.
No fewer than sixty-nine personages of this name are men-
tioned in the *Annals of the Four Masters*, the earliest being
Muireadhach Tireach, who, in A.D. 326, is said to have
expelled Colla Uais, king of Ireland, into Alba (Scotland)
with three hundred followers.   *Cf.* Ballymurry, seat of the
O'Murry's, in Roscommon.

BALNÀB (*P.* Balnab; *W. P.* MSS. Balnab).   'Inch,' 'Whithorn.'
Baile an abadh [abba] or *an aib*, the abbot's house.   Near

Saulseat and Whithorn Priories. In the former case it is referred to in *Inq. ad Cap.* 1600, as an appanage of Glenluce Abbey: "*alia domus vulgo vocata* the Abbot of Glenluce's Skaithouse." *Abb* — LAT. *abbas*, abbot — SYRIAC *abba*, father. *Cf.* Ballinab, in Waterford.

BALNACRÒSS or BARNCRÒSH (*P.* Barncrosches, Barncroshes). 'Tungland.' *Baile na crois*, house of the cross. GAEL. *croich*, gallows, *croch*, to hang, *crois*, a cross; W. *crog*, a cross, *crwg*, a crook, *crogi*, to hang ; C. *croiss*, B. *croas*, ERSE *croch*, a gallows, *cros*, a cross + LAT. *crux*. (*Skeat, s.v.* Crook.) *Cf.* Ballynacross, in Ireland.

BALNÈIL (*P.* Balneel). 'New Luce.' *Baile Niaill*, Niel's house. *Cf.* AUCHNEEL, DRUMNEIL, etc.

BALQUHÌRRIE [*pron.* whirrie], (*Inq. ad Cap.* 1616, Balquhirrie ; 1661, Ballquhirre ; *P.* Balwhyrry). 'Kirkcolm.' *Baile choire* [?] [hurrie], place of the glen. *Coire*, lit. a caldron, hence a place resembling a caldron, a dell; *see under* CORRA POOL. Perhaps more likely *baile fhoithre* [hwihra], land or house of the copsewood. *See under* BALLYFERRY, WHERRY CROFT.

BALRÀGGAN.   'Minigaff.'

BALSÀRROCH (*P.* Balsyrnoch ; *Inq. ad Cap.* 1624, Balseroch). 'Kirkcolm.' *Baile sairach* or *sairthach* [sairagh] [?], eastern place ; apparently a derivative from O. ERSE *sair*, east (*Windisch*), as *iarthach* or *iarach*, from *iar*, west. *Oir, thoir, soir*, are all forms of the word occurring in old Irish MSS., as well as the derivative form *oirthear* [urher]. Perhaps *baile searrach* [sharragh], townland of the foals. *See under* BARSHERRY. *Cf.* Balsarroch in Ayrshire.

BALSCÀLLOCH (*Inq. ad Cap.* 1600, Balstalloch ; *P.* Barskalloch). 'Kirkcolm.' *Baile sceilig*, place of the rock. *Cf.* The Skelligs, two rocks off the coast of Kerry which give the name to Ballinskelligs, which is another form of Balscalloch. "*Sceilig*, a rock."—*O'Reilly.* "*Scillic*, a splinter of stone."— *Cormac.* "*Sceillic*, a sea rock."—*O'Donovan* (in notes on *Four Masters*). W. *skol.* *See under* SCAUR.

BALSHÈRE. 'Kirkmaiden.' *Baile star* [shear], west house or place. *Cf.* Clonshire, *cluain star*, a meadow west of Adare in Limerick. *Iar* [eer], *star* [sheer], both O. ERSE forms signifying "west." *Joyce* (ii. 451) says the primary meaning is "hinder" or "posterior" + SKT. *avara*, posterior. *Whitley Stokes* suggests this as the origin of *Eriu* (which we now

write *Erin*, from the gen. *'Erenn*), Ireland, of which the old
Celtic form seems to have been *Everis* or *Iveris*. See his
Three Irish Glossaries, p. lxiii., note. Derivative forms *iarach*,
iarthach [eeragh], and *siarach*, for which see BLAWWEARY,
BARSHERRY, etc. *Cf.* BALTIER and BALSHERE.

BALSIER [*pron.* seer], (*P.* Balsyir). 'Sorbie.' *See under* BAL-
SHERE.

BALSMITH (*W. P.* MSS., Balsmythe). 'Whithorn.' Probably either
a semi-translation of BALGOWN (*q.v.*), or a mediæval appellation from a person named Smith to distinguish it from
BALNAB, close by.

BALTÈRSAN. 'Penninghame.' *Baile tarsuinn*, the house athwart, or at the crossing. ERSE *trasnu, tarsna*. *Cf.* CRAIG-
TARSON, CRAIGTERSAN ; and, in Ireland, Ballytarsna, Bally-
tarsnay, Ballytrasna, Ballintrasna, Baltrasna.

BALTIÈR (*P.* Bantyre; *W. P.* MSS. Balteyre). 'Sorbie.' *Baile tíar*
[tear], west house. *See under* BALSIER. *Tíar* = *t-síar, t-íar*,
westward.

> " Atat ar in dorus tíar insinnait hi funend grían
>   Graig n-gabor n-glas, brec a mong, is araile corcordend."
>
> *Sergigle Conculaind*, 33, 18.

BALTÒRRENS. 'Kirkcowan.' *Baile torrain*, house or place of the
hillock. KNOWE VILLAGE, in the same parish is the Scotch
equivalent. *Cf.*, however, Ballytoran, in Tipperary, *baile
teórrann*, the town of the boundary, and Knocktoran in
Limerick.

BALÙNTON.   ' Minigaff.'

BALYÈTT (*P.* Balyett).   ' Inch.'

BÀLZIELAND [*pron.* Bailie-land (the *z* has a *y* sound)], (*Inq. ad
Cap.* 1661, Balyelland M'Kellie ; 1610, Balzelland M'Kellie).
'Kirkmaiden.' The old name of Logan. *See under* BAILIE
HILL.

BANDOLIER SLUNK (a gulley on the sea-coast). 'Stoneykirk.'
"*Slunk*, a slough, a quagmire."—*Jamieson*. The word is
applied in Galloway as equiv. of *slouch*, a gulley on the sea-
coast. ERSE *slochd, sloc*. *See under* SLOCK.

BANKBEN, a hill of 800 ft. (*P.* Banck). 'Twynholm.'

BAR or BARR, in many parishes, generally with the definite article
prefixed, and often with pleonastic " Hill " or " Fell " added.
Barr, the top of anything, hence a hill + A.S. *bær, bare*, bare +

ICEL. *berr*, bare, naked, O.H.G. *par*, G. *bar*+LITH. *basus*, bare-footed+SKT. *bhás*, to shine; applied hence to a hill in the same way as *maol*, bald (*see* MEAUL).

BARÀLLAN. 'Wigtown.' *Barr dhallain* [allain] [?], hill-top of the standing stone. *Cf.* Pairc an dhallain, in Cork. Or perhaps *barr Alain*, Alan's hill-top.

BARBÀE (*P.* the same). 'Borgue,' 'Kirkcowan,' 'Stoneykirk.' *Barr beith* [bey], hill of birches. *Cf.* BARBETH and BARBAY. *See under* ALLANBAY.

BARBÀIN. 'Kirkpatrick Durham.' *Barr bán* [bane], white top.

BARBÈGS. 'Port Patrick.' *Barr beag* [beg], little hill.

BARBÈTH (*Inq. ad Cap.* 1616, Barbeth ('Kirkcolm'); *P.* Barbetth ('Kirkcolm')). 'Kirkcolm,' 'New Abbey.' *Barr beithach* [beyach], birchen hill, adjective from *beith*; or possibly from the substantive *beith* (*see* BARBAE), by restoration of the silent *th*, as in *ráth* or *ráith*. (*See* WRAITHS.)

BARBÈY. 'Urr.' *See under* BARBAE.

BARBÙCHANY (*P.* the same; *Inq. ad Cap.* 1685, Barbuchannan). 'Port Patrick.' *Barr bothanach* [bohannagh] [?], hill of the booths or huts; adj. from *bothan*. *Bothán*, casa (*Ir. Gl.* 120), dimin. of *both*, a hut. *See under* BOW.

BARBÙIE. 'Kirkpatrick Irongray.' *Barr buidhe* [buie, bwee], yellow-top. O. ERSE *bude, buide* + LAT. *badius*. An extremely common qualitative of place-names.

BARBÙNNY (*Inq. ad Cap.* 1610, Barbundie; *P.* Barbunduy). 'Kirkcowan.' *Barr buin duibh* [?] [doo], hill of the black bottom, or *bun dubh*, black stumps. *Bun*, the antithesis of *barr*; as in GAEL. "*cha'n fhàg e bun na barr*," he will leave neither bottom nor top (root nor branch)—*Macalpine*; and the Irish, "*gan bhun, gan bharr*," without head or tail. "*Bun*, root, stock, bottom."—*O'Reilly.* W. *bon*, a root; GAEL. *bonn*, the sole of the foot, a foundation, the bottom + DU. *boden* + ICEL. *boln* + DAN. *bund* + SWED. *bolten* + O.H.G. *podam* + G. *boden* + LAT. *fundus* + GK. πυθμήν + SKT. *budhna*, depth. *Cf.* Bunduff, in Donegal, which, however, does not mean "black bottom," but "end of the river Duff."

BARBÙSH. 'Troqueer.'

BARCÀPLE (*P.* Barkapil). 'Tungland.' *Barr caipeail*, hill-top of the chapel. *See under* CHAPELROSSAN.

BARCHÀIN.   ' Kelton.'

BARCHÈSKIE.   'Rerwick.'   *Barr deasgadh* or *deisceart* [?], southern
   hill-top.   O. ERSE. *des-cert*—*dess*, the right hand, or south,
   from the south being on the *right* of a person facing the east;
   ERSE and GAEL. *deas* + W. *dehen* + LAT. *dexter* + GK. δεξιός
   SKT. *dakshina*, on the right + O.H.G. *zëso*, on the right +
   GOTH. *taihswa* + RUSS. *desnitza*, the right hand.   *Cf.* SKT.
   daksha, clever, dexterous.   Or possibly *barr sescinn*, hill-top
   of the marsh.   *Sescenn* gives names to many places in Ireland,
   e.g. Sheskin and Seskin, Seskinrea and Ballinteskin.   Deriv.
   from *siosg*, a sedge.   *Cf.* Ballinteskin, in Leinster.   *Cf.* BAR-
   TASKIE and BARHASKINE.

BARCHÈSNIE.   ' Balmaghie.'

BARCHÈSSIE.   'Penninghame.'   *See under* BARCHESKIE.

BARCHLÝ (*Inq. ad Cap.* 1625, Barincla).   'Kirkcowan.'   *Barr
   cladh* [claa], hill-top of the mounds, or graves.   *See under* CLY.

BARCLAY (*Inq. ad Cap.* 1608, Barclay).   ' 'Rerwick.'   *See*
   BARCHLY.

BARCLÒSII (*P.* Barclossh).   'Kirkgunzeon.'   *Barr clais* [clash],
   hill-top of the trench, pit, or grave.   O. ERSE *class*, a word
   which *Joyce* says is extremely common in the south of Ireland,
   but seldom met with in the north.   It is, however, of frequent occurrence in Galloway.   *Cf.* CLASHMURRAY.

BARCLÒY (*P.* Barcloy).   'Colvend,' 'Kells.'   *Barr cloiche*, hill-top
   of the stone.   *See under* AUCHENCLOY.

BARCLÝ (*P.* Barchly).   'Kirkgunzeon.'   *See under* BARCHLY.

BARDÀRROCH (*P.* Bardarach).   'Kirkpatrick Durham,' 'Minigaff.'
   Barr darach, hill-top of the oaks.   *See under* ARNDARROCH.

BARDÈNNOCH, a hill of 1081 feet (*P.* Bardannoch).   'Carsphairn.'

BARDÒNACHIE.   'Kirkcowan.'   *Barr Donnachaidh* [Donnaghy],
   Duncan's hill-top.   The Erse form of this ancient name is
   Donnchadh.

BARDRÈSTAN (*Inq. ad Cap.* 1601, Bardrestoune; 1607, Bardestane).
   'Urr.'   *Barr Druist*, Drest's or Drostan's hill-top.   "In the
   Liber Hymnorum, or Book of Hymns of the Ancient Church
   of Ireland, edited by Rev. Dr. J. H. Todd, there is a hymn or
   prayer of St. Mugint, and the scholiast in the preface narrates
   the following tradition : 'Mugint made this prayer in Futerna

(Whithorn). The cause was this : Finnen of Magh Bile went to Mugint for instruction, and Rioc and Talmach, and several others with him. Drust was king of Bretan then, and had a daughter, viz., Drusticc was her name, and he gave her to Mugint to be taught to read.' . . . Dr. Todd considers . . . that the Drust of the legend is one of these two Drusts who reigned from 523 to 528. . . . This Drust is therefore clearly connected with Galloway ; and we thus learn that when two kings appear in the Pictish Chronicle as reigning together, one of them is probably king of the Picts of Galloway."—*Celt. Scot.* i. 135. King Drust is thus referred to in a poem quoted by O'Clery in his *Martyrology of Donegal* :—

> " Truist, king of the free bay on the strand,
>   Had one perfect daughter
>   Dustric, she was for every good deed renowned."
>
> *Liber Hymnorum*, p. 117.

Stuart (*Sculptured Stones*, vol. i. p. 31) mentions Trusty's Hill as one of the Boreland Hills in Anwoth parish, but it does not appear to be given in the Ordnance map. *Cf.* TROSTAN, BARTROSTAN. Some of these places may take their names from Drostan, the disciple of St. Columba, who accompanied him in his voyage to Scotland. Drum parish, in Roscommon, was formerly called Druim Drestan.

BARDRÌSTAN. 'Kirkmabreck.' *See under* BARDRESTAN.

BARDRÒCHWOOD (*P.* Bardrochat). 'Minigaff.' *Barr droicheaid* [droghed], hill-top of the bridge (nothing to do with " wood "). An immense number of places in Ireland and Scotland are named from bridges, *e.g.* Drogheda in Ireland, *i.e. droichead atha* [drohed-aha], the bridge of the ford ; and in Galloway *cf.* Droch Head, Kildrochat, Drumdrochat, etc. O. ERSE *drochet, droichet.*

BARÈAN (*P.* Barren). 'Colvend.' *Bairghin* [bareen], a cake. " A piece of land approaching a circular shape is sometimes called *bairghin.* The complete word is exhibited in Barreen, in Kildare."—*Joyce* ii. 56. O. ERSE *bargen.* W. B. and C. *bara,* bread + A.S. *bread* + DU. *brood* + ICEL. *brauð.* *Skeat* quotes *Fick's* suggestion of a connection with root of E. *brew* (from the fermentation of bread in baking)—A.S. *breówen* + O.H.G. *prúwan* + G. *brauen* + ICEL. *brugga* + SWED. *brygga* — √ BHRU, to brew ; BHUR, to boil.

BARÈND. 'Balmaghie,' 'Parton,' 'Rerwick.' *See under* BAREAN.

BARÈND BAR. ' Colvend.' *See under* BAREAN.

BARENESS.   Scand. *berr nes*, bare headland. ' Colvend.'

BARÈWING (*P.* Ewinstoun). ' Balmaclellan.' *Barr Iain*, John's or Ewen's hill-top.

BARFÀDDEN. ' Dalry.' *Barr feadain* [fadden], hill-top of the streamlet ; or perhaps *barr Fadain*, Fadan's, or the long man's hill-top, a man's name (now written Fadzean), deriv. from *fada*, long ; or *barr Phaidin*, the hill top of Paidin, or little Patrick. *Feadán*, a streamlet, is a deriv. of *fead* [fad], a pipe, tube, or whistle, " whence, in a secondary sense, it comes to be applied to those little brooks whose channels are narrow and deep like a tube."—*Joyce*, i. 458. *Cf.* Faddan, Feddan, Fiddan, Fiddane, etc., in Ireland.

BARFÀLLS. ' Penninghame.' The " faulds " (folds or enclosures) of Barr.

BARFÌLL (*P.* Barfill). ' Old Luce,' ' Urr.' *Barr phuill* [fill], hill of the hole, pool, or water of any sort. ERSE and GAEL. *poll*, gen. *puill*, *phuill*, a hole, pit, mire, bog, pond, pool, and even a stream (occurring most frequently in the latter sense in Galloway place-names) ; W. *pwll*, C. *pol*, M. *poyl*, B. *poull* + LAT. *palus*, a marsh, + GK. πηλός, mud. From the Celtic comes A.S. *pól* and G. *pfuhl*, from the former of which M.E. *pol*, *pool*, E. *pool*.

BARFLÀWEN.   ' Kirkcowan.'

BARFRÀGGAN. ' Kelton.' *Barr fraechan* [?], hill of the blaeberries or whortleberries. From this plant are named Frehans, Freahanes, and Freffhanes in Ireland ; Lyrenafreaghaun in Limerick, Kilnafrehan in Waterford (same meaning as Hurtwood, near Leith Hill in Surrey), Kylefreaghane in Tipperary, Binnafreaghan in Tyrone. GAEL. *fraochag*, deriv. of *fraoch*, heather.

BARGÀLY [*pron.* Bargawly], (*P.* Bargaly; *Macfarlane* MS. Burgally). ' Minigaff.' *Borg Amhalghaidh* [owlhay] [?], Aulay's house. " *Brug*, *brúgh* : a palace, a grand house or building ; a royal residence ; a town, a borough ; a fortified place "—*O'Reilly*. " *Borg*, a village."—*Idem.* *See under* BORGUE and MACHERALLY.

BARGÀTTON (*Inq. ad Cap.* 1637, Bargaltoun; *P.* Bargatoun). ' Balmaghie.'

BARGÈSKIN. ' Balmaclellan.' *See under* BARCHESKIE.

BARGLÀSS (*P.* Barglash). 'Kirkinner.' *Barr glas,* green hill. "*Glas* is commonly translated green, and this is its usual acceptation, for we find.it often applied to express the green of grass or foliage. But the word was also used to designate a greyish or bluish green, or rather a greyish blue, a shade of colour having in it little or none of what we should call green. For instance *glas* was often applied to a greyish blue eye, and also to the colour of the water-wagtail. In its topographical application, however, it must generally be understood to mean grass-green."—*Joyce,* ii. 281. W. B. and C. *glas.* "*Glas,* green, verdant, pale, wan, poor."—*O'Reilly.* Prob. akin to LAT. *glaucus,* bluish—GK. γλαυκός, gleaming, silvery, bluish.

BARGRÈNNAN. 'Minigaff.' *Barr grianain* [greenan], hill of the house or palace. *See under* GRENNAN.

BARGRÙG (*P.* Bargrugg). 'Kirkgunzeon.' *Barr gruaig* [?], hill top of the grass. *Gruag,* hair, "by a natural extension of meaning is applied to long *hair-like* grass growing in a marshy or sedgy place. Hence we have in various parts of Ireland Grogach, Grogey, Grogan, Groggan, Grogeen, and Gruig, all signifying sedge—a place producing long sedgy grass."—*Joyce,* ii. 339.

BARHÀMMER. 'Parton.' Close by is a place called Camer, of which *hammer* seems to be the aspirated form.

BARHAPPLE (*Inq. ad Cap.* 1610, Barquhapple; 1624, Barquhapill). 'Kirkcowan.' 'Old Luce.' *Barr chapaill,* hill-top of the horse. *Cf.* PORT WHAPPLE. Perhaps sometimes *barr chapeail,* from the late Latin *capella.* The next hill to Barhapple in Kirkcowan, is called Chapel Hill. ERSE and GAEL. *capall,* a horse (in some places limited in sense to a mare), W. *ceffyl*+LAT. *caballus* (whence ITAL. *cavallo,* F. *cheval*)+GK. καβάλλος, a horse+RUSS. *kobuila,* a mare+ICEL. *kapall,* a horse.

BARHÀRROW (*Inq. ad Cap.* 1599, Barharrow). 'Borgue.' *Barr charrach* [harragh], rough hill-top. *Carrach,* stony, rough — *car, cara,* a stone, or *gharbh* [harriv, harve], rough. *Cf.* Bargarriff, in Ireland.

BARHÀRRY. 'Balmaclellan.' 'Kirkcowan.' *See under* BAR-HARROW.

BARHÀSKINE (*P.* Barchaisken). 'Old Luce.' *Cf.* Barcheskie.

BARHÀSTRY. 'Buittle.'

BARHÌNNIGANS. 'Balmaclellan.' *Barr Fhionnagain* [hinnigan], Finnigan's hill. A man's name, formed from *fionn* (O. ERSE *finn, find*), white.

BARHÒISE [*pron.* Barhoshe], (*Inq. ad Cap.* 1609, Barquhoyis). 'Kirkcowan.' 'Minigaff.' This name is the same as Barcosh, in Dalry parish, Ayrshire, written by *Pont* Barquhoise. *Cuninghame*, p. 83.

BARHÒLM (*P.* Barhoom). 'Kirkmabreck.'

BARHÙLLION (*P.* Baryillen). 'Glasserton.' *Barr chuileann* [hwillan], hill-top of the hollies. *See under* ALWHILLAN. *Cf.* Bohullion (*both chuillinn*, hut of the holly), in Donegal.

BARJÀRG. 'Kirkinner.' *Barr dearg* [dyarg], red hill. *See under* BARYERROCK.

BARLÀE (*P.* Barle; MS. 1527, Barley). 'Kirkcowan.' 'Kirkinner.' 'Penninghame.' *Barr llath* [lec], grey hill-top, or *laegh* [lay], hill-top of the calves. *See under* BALLOCHALEE.

BARLÀMACHAN.   'Penninghame.'

BARLÀUCHLIN (*P.* Barlachlan). 'Penninghame.' *Barr Lochlinn,* Lauchlan's hill-top. *Lochlainn,* lord of Corca-Modhruaidh, is mentioned by the *Four Masters* as dying in 983, and another of the name, the son of Macleachlainn, was slain, 1023. The origin of this name may have been *Lochlannoch,* a Norseman. The names O'Loughlin and MacLauchlan are still common.

BARLÀY (*P.* Barley). 'Balmaclellan.' 'Colvend.' 'Girthon.' *See under* BARLAE.

BARLÈDZIEW [*pron.* Barleddy], (*Inq. ad Cap.* 1620, Barladzew; *IV. P.* MS., Bardlodzew). 'Sorbie.'

BARLÈACH [*pron.* Barlee-ach]. 'New Luce.' *Barr liag,* hill-top of the flat stones, or tombs. *See under* AUCHLEACH and AIRIELICK.

BARLÈNNAN (*P.* Barlenan). 'Kirkcowan.'

BARLÒCCO (*Inq. ad Cap.* 1508, Barloko; *P.* Barlocco). 'Borgue.'

BARLÒCHAN (*P.* Barlochenn). 'Buittle.' *Barr lochain,* hill-top of the lakelet.

BARLÒCKHART (*P.* Barlockhart). 'Old Luce.'

BARLÒKE. 'Borgue.' *Cf.* BARLOCCO and BARLUKA.

BARLÙE.   'Balmaghie.'

BARLÙELL. 'Old Luce.' *Barr leamh chuill* [lavhwill, loughil], hill of the elm wood. *Cf.* Laughil, Loughill, Laghil and Cloonlaughil in Ireland. ERSE *leamh,* usually *leamhán* [lavaun] in the south of Ireland, and *sleamhán* [slavan] in the north. W. *llwyf, llwyfan,* B. *uloch.*

BARLÙITH.   ' Urr.'

BARLÙKA. 'Twynholm.' *Cf.* BARLOCCO and BARLOKE.

BARLÙRE (*P.* Barlune—*misprint*). 'New Luce.' *Barr lobhair* [?] [louer], hill of the leper, or infirm person. O. ERSE *lobor*, *lobur*, infirmus, debilis (*Zeuss*, 781), ERSE and GAEL. *lobhar* + LAT. *lepra*, leprosy + GK. λέπρα, leprosy — GK. λέπρος, scaly, scabby — GK. λέπος, a scale — λέπειν, to peel + RUSS. *lupiti*, to peel + LITH. *lupti*, to scale. ,

BARLÝKE.   ' Kirkcowan.'

BARMAGÀCHAN (*P.* Barmakgachin). 'Borgue.' *Barr mic Eochagain*, M'Geachan's hill. The Irish form is Macgeoghegan. *Cf.* Ballymagautry, in Down, formerly Balimacgehan.

BARMÀRK (*P.* Barmarck).   ' Balmaclellan.'

BARMÀIN. 'Old Luce.' *Barr meadhon* [men], middle hill. *See under* BALMINNOCH for *meadhonach*, of which this is the simpler form. It appears in Irish names such as Inishmaan, Inishmeane, Inishmaine, Kilmain, etc.

BARMÈAL [*pron.* Barmale], (*Charter* 1586 Ballmiell; *P.* Barmeill; *W. P.* MSS. Barmaill). 'Glasserton.' *Barr mdel*, bald or bare hill-top; *see under* MEAUL. *Cf.* BENMEAL.

BARMÈEN. 'Kirkcowan.' *Barr min* [meen], smooth hill; *cf.* Barmeen in Antrim.

BARMÒFFITY (*Inq. ad Cap.*, 1604, Barmoffate). 'Kirkpatrick Durham.'

BARMÒRE (*P.* Barmoir). 'Kirkcowan,' 'Minigaff.' *Barr mór*, great hill-top. ERSE *mór* + W. *mawr*, C. and B. *maur, vaur, vear*.

BARMÒRROW.   ' Balmaclellan.'

BARMÙLLIN. 'Kirkinner.' *Barr muileain*, mill hill. *See under* BALLYMELLAN.

BARNÀER (*P* Barnawyr). 'Old Luce.' *Barr an air*, hill-top of the ploughing, or of the slaughter. *Ar*, ploughing, and *dr*, slaughter, are indistinguishable in composition. "O.W. *air*, W. *aer*, a battle = *agr*- of the same origin as the Greek ἄγρα, a catching, hunting, the chase."—*Rhys*, p. 64. "W. *ar*, ploughed land + ERSE *arathar*, a plough + GK. ἀρόω, I plough + LAT. *aro* + GOTH. *arjan*, to plough + E. *to ear, earth*, that which is *eared* or ploughed."—*Rhys*, p. 92.

BARNAGÈE. 'Glasserton.' *Bearna gaoithe* [barnageeha], gap of the wind. *Cf.* Barnageeha in Mayo; written in the *Annals Bearna-na-gaoithe (Four Masters*, 1590). *See under* CURGHIE.

BARNAMÒN. 'Stoneykirk.' *Barr na mban* [man], the hill-top of the women. *Cf.* LIGNAMAN; also, in Cavan and Leitrim, Cornaman [i.e. *cor na mban*]. O. ERSE *ben*, gen. *mná*, W. *buu*, C. *banen.*

BARNÀUGH.   ' Portpatrick.'

BARNBÀRROCH (*Inq. ad Cap.* 1560, Barnbaroch; *Sibbald* MS. Barinbaro; *P.* Barnbarraugh Castle, Barbarraugh). ' Colvend,' ' Kirkinner.'

BARNBÀUCHLE. 'Loch Rutton.' *Barr an buachail* [?] hill-top of the herdsman, or standing stone. *Buachail*, a boy or cowherd; from *bo*, a cow. *See under* BOWHILL. But compare *Bearna baeghail*, the gap of danger, " used in the Irish Annals to denote a perilous pass where the chief usually placed guards to prevent his enemies from making irruptions into his territory. The Irish to this day use the saying, '*tá sé a m-beárna an bhaoghail,*' *i.e.* 'he is in the gap of danger,' when they see a man in danger of being ruined. For a beautiful description of what the Irish and Highlanders called ' a gap of danger ' in the Highlands of Scotland, the reader is referred to *Waverley*, by Sir Walter Scott, vol. i. c. 15."— *Hy Fiachrach*, 211, note.

BARNBOARD (*Inq. ad Cap.* 1599, Barnebard). 'Balmaghie.' *Barr na bard*, hill-top of the rhymers. This name appears to be taken from the gen. plu., like Derrybard, in Tyrone. Generally the aspirated gen. sing. appears, as in DIRVAIRD (*q.v.*), Gortavard in Donegal, Aghaward in Roscommon, Glenaward in Meath, Ballyward in Down, Tyrone, and Wicklow. When the gen. plu. appears, the *b* is generally eclipsed by *m*, thus Aghnamard (i.e. *achadh na mbard*), Latnamard (i.e. *leacht na mbard*), both in Monaghan, etc. etc. W. *bardd*, ERSE and GAEL. *bard*, C. *bardh*, B. *barz;* a Celtic word which has been borrowed by E. speakers.

BARNCÀLZIE. ' Kirkpatrick Durham.' *Barr na cailleaich*, the hill-top of the nun, or old woman. O. ERSE *caillech*, a nun, an old woman (*Windisch*), ERSE and GAEL. *cailleach*, with the same alternative meaning. Deriv. unknown; that from *caille*, a veil, being suspicious. *See under* CRAIGENCALLIE.

BARNCÀUCHLAN.   ' Minigaff.'

BARNCLEÙGH. 'Kirkpatrick Irongray.'

BARNCÒRKRIE. 'Kirkmaiden.' *Barr an corcoraichdh* [corkeragh], hill-top of the ruddiness, or (plur.) *barran chorcrai*, ruddy hill-tops. There is a mass of ruddy granite exposed here, where the cliff abuts on a bay called PORTENCORKRIE, *q.v.* O. ERSE *corcur* (subst.), *corcra* (adj.), W. *porfor*, ERSE *corcar*, GAEL. *corcur* + M.E. *purpre* (whence E. *purple*, by substitution of *l* for *r*, as in *marble* for M.E. *marbre*, and in *Molly, Dolly*, for Mary, Dorothy (*Skeat*) + LAT. *purpura* = GK. πορφύρα, the purplefish ; πορφύρεος, the orig. sense of which, " as an epithet of the sea, seems to have been 'troubled' or 'raging,' hence dark, and lastly purple. Hence the etymology is from the Gk. πορφύρειν, to grow dark, used of the surging sea, a reduplicated form of φύρειν, to mix up, to mingle, orig. to stir violently √ — BHUR, to move about quickly, whence SKT. *buranya*, to be active, LAT. *furere*, to rage. A.S. *purpur*, is borrowed directly from Latin."—*Skeat, s.v.* Purple. The interchange of *p* and *c* is according to well-known rules.

BARNCRÒSH (*P.* Barncrossches, Barncroshes). 'Tungland.' *See* BALNACROSS.

BARNÈAN (*P.* Barneen). 'Old Luce.' *Barr n-én* [nane], hill-top of the birds. *Cf.* Ardnaneane in Limerick. O. ERSE and ERSE *én*, GAEL. *eun*, W. *edn*, C. *edhyn*, B. *eddn, ezn.*

BARNECÀLLAGH. 'Old Luce.' *See under* BARNCALZIE.

BARNECÒNAHIE. 'Old Luce.' *Barr na' ceannaiche* [kennaghie], hill-top of the merchants or pedlars. This word appears in several Irish names, *e.g.* Bellanaganny, in Meath, which the *Four Masters* (anno 1482) call *Ath-na-gceannaigheadh*, the ford of the pedlars. *Cf.* also Annagannihy in Cork. O. ERSE *cennaige*, a buyer; ERSE *ceannaighe* or *ceannaidhe ;* GAEL. *ceannaiche.*

BARNÈIGHT (*P.* Barnacht). 'Kirkcowan.' *Barr n-ech*, hill of the horses. *See under* AUCHNESS.

BARNÈRNIE [*pron.* Barnairney], (*P.* Barneirny). 'Kirkcowan.' *Barr n-airne* [airnie], hill-top of the sloes. *Cf.* Killarney, three times in Ireland, Magherarny, Clonarny, and Mullarney.

BARNÈSS (*P.* Barness). 'Kirkinner.' *Barr n-easa*, hill-top of the torrent. It is upon the Bladnoch river.

BARNEYCLÈARY. 'Old Luce.' *Barr na' clérech*, hill of the clergy. *Cf.* CLARY and CLARY PARK, and PORTACLEARYS. Also, in

Ireland, Farrancleary, in Cork, Ballynaglerach, in Clare, Tipperary, and Waterford. This word (—LAT. *clericus*) appears in old Irish Texts, "*Clerich hEreun.*"—*Fiacc's Hymn*, i. 6 (A.D. 540); also in *Fis Adamnáin*, 31 (date variously estimated from A.D. 800 to 1000). C. *cloireg*, B. *cloarec*.

BARNEY HILL.   'Kirkcowan.'

BARNFAULD (from estate-map of Cuil).   'Kirkmabreck.'

BARNEYWÀTER. 'Girthon.' *Béarna uachdar*, upper gap or pass. *Uachdar* is corrupted into *water* in some Irish names, *e.g.*, Clowater in Carlow, *cloch uachdar*. *See under* AUCH-NOTTEROCH.   O. ERSE *berna*, a cleft; GAEL. *bearn*, a small gap, a fissure.

BARNFOÒT.   'Girthon.'

BARNGÀBER. 'Borgue.' *Barr na gabar*, hill of the goats; the old unaspirated form of *gabhar*. *See under* ALGOWER.

BARNGÒUF.   'Crossmichael.'

BARNHÌLLIE (*Macfarlane* MS., Barnkylie).   'Balmaclellan.' *Barr na choille* (hillie), hill-top of the wood. The sixteenth century form, Barnkylie, shows the original unaspirated genitive *coille*. ERSE *coill*, GK. ὕλη, LAT. *silua*. Root unknown, and the connection of LAT. and GK. not established.

BARNHÒURIE (*Inq. ad Cap.* 1560, Barnchwry; 1602, Barnhowrie). 'Colvend.' *Barr n-huidhre* [?] [hoorie], hill-top of the dun cow, gen. of *odhar*. "*Odhar* [owr] is often applied to a cow; and several places have derived their names from legendary cows with this designation."—*Joyce*, ii. 287. *Cf.* Monahoora in Down, Loughnaheery and Essnaheery in Tyrone. The celebrated MS. *Lebór na h-Uidre*, the book of the brown cow, is said to have been named from the skin of the animal that covered it.

BÀRNIE HILL. 'Penninghame.' *Béarna*, a gap, a pass. *See under* BARNEYWATER.

BARNIGHLÈA.   'Kirkcowan.'

BARNKÌRK (*P.* Barnkerk). '*Barr na coirce* [kirkya], hill-top of the oats. *Cf.* BARNKÌRKY, CULQUHIRK, and in Ireland Lissacurkia, twice in Roscommon, Farranacurky in Fermanagh. *Coirce*, oats + W. *ceirch*, B. *kerch*, C. *kerh*, perhaps from √GAR, to grind, whence LAT. *granum* + GK. γῦρις, meal, + RUSS. *zerno*, corn. + ICEL., DAN., and SWED. *korn* + A.S. *corn* (E. *corn*) + GOTH. *kaurn* + G. *korn*. Possibly this word is *barr na circe* [kirky], hill-top of the heath-fowl, from *cearc*, a hen; thus, Castlekirk on Lough Corrib is called *Caislen-na-circe* by the *Four Masters.*

BARNKÌRKY. ‘Girthon.’ *See under* BARNKIRK.

BARNÒLAS. ‘Tungland.’ *Barr an sholais* [ōlas], hill-top of the light or the beacon. *Cf.* BARSOLUS (*P.* Barolis), BARSOLES, BARSOLIS, BARNSOUL. Also, in Ireland, Ardsollus in Clare, Drumnasole in Antrim, Rossolus in Monaghan, and several places name Assolas and Athsollis, *atha solais*, the ford of the light, from a light being shown to guide people over the ford. Lights were shown in old times as beacons on hill-tops. A striking picture of a Red Indian signalling with a light on a hill-top was exhibited in a gallery of American and Colonial pictures in London in 1886. The primitive mode of obtaining fire by friction was practised until comparatively recent times in some parts of Scotland. “When a contagious disease enters among cattle, the fire is extinguished in some villages round. Then they force fire with a wheel, or by rubbing a piece of dry wood upon another, and therewith burn juniper in the stalls of the cattle, that the smoke may purify the air about them. . . . This done, the fires in the houses are rekindled from the forced fire. All this I have seen done.”—*Shaw*, p. 290. O. ERSE *sollus* (adj.) bright, prob. akin to LAT. *sol*, the sun, — √SWAR, to glow.

BARNS, THE. ‘Whithorn.’

BARNSÀLLIE (*Inq. ad Cap.* 1668. Barnsullye; *P.* Barnsuille). ‘Old Luce.’ *Barr na seilach* [sallagh], hill of the willows. *Cf.* BARSALLOCH, also Ardsallagh in Meath. O. ERSE *sail*, ERSE and GAEL. *sail, seil, saileach*, W. *helyg* (plur.) + LAT. *salix* + GK. ἑλίκη + ICEL. *selja* + SWED. *sälg* + DAN. *selje* + G. *sahlweide* (—O.H.G. *salahá*), whence M.E. *salwe*, E. *sallow, sally*, and BR. SC. *sauch*. The root meaning is the “water-tree,” *cf.* SKT. *sari*, water, *saras*, a pond, *sarasiya*, the lotus, *sarit*, a river, — √SAR, to flow. (*Skeat, s.v.* Sallow.)

BARNSHÀLLOCH. ‘Balmaclellan,’ ‘Kirkpatrick Irongray.’ *Barr na sealg* [?] [shallug], hill of the hunting. *Cf.* Drumnashalloge in Tyrone, Derrynashallog in Monaghan, Ballinashallog in Derry, Drumashellig in Queen’s County, *i.e. druimna-sealg*, etc. O. ERSE *selg*, ERSE and GAEL. *sealg*, the chase.

BARNSHÀNGAN. ‘Stoneykirk.’ *Barr na seangan* [shangan], hill of the ants. ERSE *seangán* [shangaun], an ant, is a derivative of *seang*, slender, O. ERSE *segon* (*Cormac*). The Ulster pronunciation omits the middle intrusive *n*, and is as if written *shaghan*. Pismire Hill, near Louth, is the modern name of *Cnoc-na-seangan*, the hill of the ants (*Four Masters*, A.D. 1148), but it is quite probable that in other instances it may be from a proper name of an individual, *Seangán*, from *seang*, slender. *Cf.* BARNSHANNON, DALSHANGAN; also Auchenshangan, near Ardrossan (*Cunninghame*, p. 49), and Knocknashagan in Donegal and Fermanagh, Knocknaseggane in Armagh, etc.

BARNSHÀNNON (*Inq. ad Cap.* 1668, Barnsangan, *vel* Dalsangand; *P.* Barnshangan). 'New Luce.' *See under* BARSHANGAN.

BARNSLÀDIE. 'Kirkcowan.' *Barr an slaide* [?], hill of the slaughter. O. ERSE *slaide*, to slay, GAEL. *slad*, carnage + ICEL. *slá* + DAN. *slaae* + SWED. *slå* + GOTH. *slahan* + G. *schlagen* (−O.H.G. *slahan*) + A.S. *sleán* (whence M.E. *sleen*, *slee* E. *slay*, *slaughter*) from Teut. base *slah*, to smite.

BARNSHÒT.   'Balmaclellan.'

BARNSÒUL. 'Kirkpatrick Irongray.' *See under* BARNOLAS.

BARNSTÒBRICK (*P.* Barstobberick H.).   'Tungland.'

BARNÙLTOCH (*P.* Barnulte; *Inq. ad Cap.* 1668, Barnulto; 1623, Barmulto). 'Inch.' *Barr an Ultaich*, the Ulsterman's hill. *Cf.* Knockanulty in Clare, Ardultach in Galway, and Ballinulty.

BARNÙNAN.   'Stoneykirk.'

BARNWÀLLS.   'Balmaclellan.'

BARNYÀRD. 'Kirkpatrick Irongray.' *Bearna ard*, the high pass or gap. *See under* BARNEYWATER.

BARNYCLÀGY. 'Penninghame.' *Barr na claigean* [claggan], hill-top of the skulls. "Applied to a round, dry, rocky hill." —*Joyce*, ii. 428. *Cf.* Claggan, Clagan, and Claggan in Ireland. *Claigean* also means in Mod. Gael. an arable field (*Macalpine*).

BARR. 'Loch Rutton,' 'Rerwick.' *See under* BAR.

BARRÀCHAN (*Inq. ad Cap.* 1612, Barqurochane; *P.* Barchracchan). 'Mochrum.' In Renfrewshire a place of the same name is *pron.* Bàrrachan.

BARRACK SLOUCH (*pron.* Sloogh). 'Kirkcolm, s.c.'   GAEL. "*bearradh* [byarra], the brow of a hill, a precipice."—*Mac-*

alpine. " *Slouch* (gutt.), a deep ravine or gully."—*Jamieson.* A name applied to gullies on a rocky coast—GAEL. *slochd*, a den, a pit.

BARRAÈR. ' Penninghame.' *See under* BARNAER.

BARRÈID. ' Penninghame.'

BARREL HILL. ' Inch.'

BARSÀLLOCH (*P.* Barsalloch, Balsallach). ' Penninghame,' ' Mochrum.' *See under* BARNSALLIE. Or *barr salach,* miry hill. It is impossible to distinguish between *salach,* miry, and *seileach,* a willow, in compound names. *Barr* in some districts of the Highlands bears the secondary meaning of " a road." In Lochaber *barr salach* would mean "the miry road," and this possibly may be the sense here.

BARSCÀRROW (MS. 1527, Barskarauch). ' Stoneykirk.' *Barr sceirach,* rocky hill-top. *See under* LOCH SKERROW.

BARSCÒNE. ' Buittle.'

BARSCRÀITH. ' Colvend.' *Barr scratha* or *scrath* [scraa or scrau], hill of the sod or sods. " Scraw, a thin turf, Gall., Dumfr." —*Jamieson.* "Scraws, thin turfs, pared with flaughter spades, to cover houses."—*Mactaggart. Cf.* NOGNIESCRIE, SCRABBA ; also in Ireland, Ahascragh and Ballinescragh.

BARSHÈRRY. ' Balmaclellan.' *Barr searrach* [sharragh], hill-top of the foals. *Cf.* BALSARROCH ; also Aillenasharragh in Clare, Clonsharragh in Wexford, Carrigeensharragh in Tipperary.

BARSKEÒGH (*P.* Barskyoch ; MS. 1527, Barskeauch). ' Buittle,' ' Kells,' ' Penninghame.' *Barr sceithióg* [skeyoge], hill-top of the hawthorns. *See under* AUCHENSKEOCH.

BARSÒLES. ' Buittle,' ' Old Luce.' *See under* BARNOLAS.

BARSOLIS. ' Crossmichael.' *See under* BARNOLAS.

BARSÒLUS (*Inq. ad Cap.* 1629, Barsoullis ; 1623, Barsollis ; *P.* Barolis). ' Inch.' *See under* BARNOLAS.

BARSTÌBLY. ' Tungland.'

BARTÀGGART (*P.* Bartaggart ; MS. 1527, Barnetagart). ' Balmaclellan.' *Barr-t-sagart* [bartaggart], hill-top of the priests. In the MS. of 1527 Barnetagart [*barr na-tsagart*], shows it is the hill of the *priests,* not of the priest. *See under* ALTAGGART.

BARTÀSKIE. ' Kirkcowan.' *See under* BARCHESKIE.

BARTRÒSTAN (*P.* Bartrostan). ' Penninghame.' *See under* BARDRESTAN.

BARVÀLGANS. 'Penninghame.' *Barr Bholgcain* [?] [volgan],
    Bolcan's hill. *Cf.* Bovolcan in Antrim, which *Colgan* writes
    Both Bolcain (Bolcan's hut) ; Drumbulcan, Drumbulcaun, and
    Drumbulgan, in other parts of Ireland ; also Trabolgan in
    Cork harbour, called *Mur Bolcan* in the Book of Rights.—
    (*Joyce*, ii. 22), and Doonbolgan in Roscommon.

BARVÈNNAN (*P.* Baruennan). 'Penninghame.' *Barr bheannain*
    [vennan], top of the hillock. *Beannán,* dim. of *beann,* a hill.
    See under BENAILSA.

BARVÈRNOCHAN (*P.* Barvarranach).   'Kirkinner.'

BARWHÀNNY (*P.* Barwhony). 'Kirkinner.' *Barr bhainne* [?]
    [wanny, vanny], hill of the milk. This is a very doubtful
    suggestion, but the names Tawnawanny in Fermanagh,
    Tullinwannia in Leitrim, Tullinwonny in Fermanagh, and
    Coolavanny in Kerry, are referred by *Joyce,* ii. 206, to this
    origin. ERSE *bainne,* milk, from *bán,* white. *Cf.* MILKING
    HOLES, MILKING LOAN, and MILKY BRAES.

BARWHÀR (*P.* Barwhar). 'Loch Rutton.' *Barr ghar* [?] [haar],
    near hill-top. O. ERSE *gar,* near (*O'Donovan,* Grammar, p. 122),
    ERSE *gar,* ERSE and GAEL. *gearr,* short + W., B., and C. *byr,* short ;
    gar, ger, near (prep.), C. and B. *ber,* short, *hars,* near (prep.).

BARWHILLANTIE (*P.* Barwhillenty). 'Parton.' *Cf.* BALLAN-
    COLLANTIE.

BARWHIL (*Charter* 1586, Barquhulle). 'Girthon,' 'Kirkcowan.' *Barr
    chuill* [hwill], hill of the hazel bush. *See under* AUCHENHILL.

BARWHINNIE. 'Buittle.' *Barr mhuine* [?] [vinnie, winnie], hill-
    top of the brake or thicket (*O'Donovan*). An old word in
    Irish MSS. appearing as a prefix to a great many Irish names.
    See under DALMONEY.

BARWHINNOCK. 'Twynholm.' *See under* BARWINNOCK.

BARWHIRRAN. 'Penninghame.' *Barr chaerthinn* [hirren], hill-top
    .of the rowan trees (*Joyce,* i. 513). *Cf.* Attachoirinn in Iona,
    Drumkeeran in Leitrim, Fermanagh, and other parts of
    Ireland.

BARWICK.   'Dalry.'

BARWINNOCK (*Inq. ad Cap.* 1616, Barvanock; 1620, Barvennag ; *P.*
    Barwannach, *W. P.* MS. Barvannok, Barvennik). 'Glasser-
    ton.' *Barr bhfeannog* [?] [vannog], hill-top of the carrion
    crows. *Cf.* CORBIESTANE and BARWHINNOCK ; in Ireland,
    Mullanavannog in Monaghan, and (without eclipse of *f* by

bh) Toberfinnock in Wexford. Perhaps *barr mheadhonach* [veannagh], middle hill.

BARYÈRROCK (*P.* Balyerrack). 'Kirkinner.' *Barr dhearg* [yerrug], red hill-top. O. ERSE *derc, derg,* red. *Cf.* PORT-YERROCK, and, in Ireland, Lickerrig (*i.e. lic dhearg*), in Galway, Ratherrig (*i.e. rath dhearg*), in Queen's County.

BÀTWELL. 'Kirkmaiden.'

BÀWNHEAD. 'Carsphairn.' A hybrid word *bán* [bawn], lea-land, with E. substantive. A word applied to grass-land from its pale colour. *See under* WHITELEYS.

BÀZARD LANE (a stream). 'New Luce.' *Cf.* BIZZIARD FELL.

BÀZARD HILL. 'New Luce.'

BELGÀVERIE. 'Kirkcowan.' The prefix is obscure; the latter moiety of this name is apparently *aimhreidh* [avrea], *i.e.* not smooth, uneven, from *aimh*, a negative prefix, and *reidh* [ray], smooth. *Cf.* TYDAVERIES, and, in Ireland, Lackavrea, a mountain on Loch Corrib; Ouvry, in Monaghan, formerly Eaverie; Avery, an island on Connemara coast; Owenavrea in Mayo, etc.

BELLERIG. *See under* BELTON HILL. 'Kelton.'

BELLÈW, CRAIG OF. 'Minigaff.' *Beul umha* [bel ooa], cave mouth. *Cf.* BELLOUE, BILEOW. *See,* for various forms of *uamh,* a cave, *Joyce,* i. 438. O. ERSE *úam.*

BELLÒUE CAVE. 'Port Patrick, s.c.' E. *cave,* added pleonastically. *See under* BELLEW.

BELLYMÀCK (*Inq. ad Cap.* 1548, Ballemak). 'Balmaghie.'

BELSHORE. 'Colvend.'

BELT HILL. 'Balmaclellan.' *See under* BELTONHILL.

BELTONHILL (*P.* Beltanhill). 'Terregles.' *Béail teine,* Baal's fire. "*Béalteine,* the first day of May; so called from the fires lighted on that day by the pagan Irish in honour of the god Beal."—*O'Reilly.* "*Belltaine, i. bil tene . i . tene shoinmech . i . dáthene dognitis druidhe triathaircedlu (no cotinchetlaib) móraib combertis na cethrai arthedmannaib cacha bliadna cusnaténdtibsin.*" "*Biltene, i.e.* a goodly fire, *i.e.* two fires which Druids used to make through incantations (or with great incantations), and they used to bring the cattle to those fires against the diseases of each year."—*Cormac,* p. 6. "On the 1st of May they (the Highlanders) offered sacrifice for the preservation of their cattle; and that day was held sacred to Pan or Baal, and was commonly called La Baal-tine, corruptly 'Beltan-day,' *i.e.* the Day of Baal's Fire. Clear remains of that superstition I have been present at when a young boy. Upon Maundy-Thursday the several herds cut staves of service-wood about three feet long, and put two cross-sticks into clefts in one end of the staff. These staves they laid up till the 1st of May. On that day several herds met together,—every one had two eggs and a bannock, or thick cake of oatmeal, crusted over with the yolks of eggs. They raised a pile of dry wood or sticks on a hillock; then they made the *Deas Soil* thrice round the fire, after which they roasted their eggs, and ate them with a part of the bread. The rest of the bread they brought home to be eaten by the family; and having adorned the heads of their staves with wild herbs, they fixed them on the tops, or above the doors of their several cotes; and this they fancied would preserve the cattle from diseases till next May."—*Shaw*, p. 282. *Whitley Stokes*, however, rejects the derivation from Baal; "the root of *Belt-aine* (as I divide the word) is perhaps the same as that of the Lith. *baltas*, white; the *aine* is a termination as in *sechtmaine*, 'week.'" *Cf.* BARNOLAS, KNOCKTINNEL.

BENÀILSA. 'Minigaff.' ERSE *beann*, GAEL. *beinn* (+LAT. *pinna*), a peak, a hill. O. ERSE *benn*, *bend*, "peak, gable, horn" (*O'Donovan*). Not, as often supposed, a form of W. *pen*, the ERSE and GAEL. equiv. of which is *ceann*. "*Beann* is not applied to great mountains so much in Ireland as in Scotland, . . . but as applied to middle and smaller eminences it is used very extensively."—*Joyce*, i. 383.

BENBRÀCK (*P.* Benbrek). 'Carsphairn.' 'Kells' (*thrice*), 'Dalry.' *Beann breac* [brak], spotted, brindled hill. *See under* AUCHABRICK.

BENBÙIE. 'Glasserton.' *Beann buidhe* [buie, bwee], yellow hill. *Cf.* BENWEE. *See under* BARBUIE.

BENDHÙ [*pron.* Bendèw]. 'Kirkmaiden.' *Beann dubh* [ben doo], black hill. *Cf.* Benduff, Bindoo, Binduff, etc., hills in Ireland.

BENDÒO. 'Kirkmaiden, s.c.' *See under* BENDHU.

BENFÀDZEON [*pron.* fadyen]. 'Girthon.' *See under* BARFADDEN.

BENGÀIRN (a hill of 1280 feet). 'Rerwick.' *Beann gcairn* [gairn], hill of the cairn. *See under* AUCHENCAIRN.

BENGHÌE. 'Girthon.' *Beann gaiethe* [geeha or gwee], hill of the wind. *Cf.* WINDY STANDARD, WINDY HILL, etc. *See under* BARNAGEE.

BENGRÀY (a hill of 1175 feet). 'Girthon.' *Beann gréaich* [?], hill of the high flat or moor. *Cf.* KNOCKGRAY. *See under* AUCHENGRAY.

BENÌNNER. 'Carsphairn.'

BENJÀRG (*P.* Benjarg). 'Girthon.' *Beann dearg* [dyarg], red hill.

BENJÒHN (a hill of 1150 feet). 'Anwoth.' *Beann donn* [?], brown hill. O. ERSE *donn, dond*; GAEL. and ERSE *donn*; W. *dwn* + A.S. *dunn* (whence E. *dun*).

BENLÈIGHT. 'New Luce.' *Beann leacht*, hill of the tombs. *See under* LEIGHT.

BÈNLOCH STRAND. 'Carsphairn.'

BENLOCHAN. 'Kirkmaiden.' *Beann lochain*, hill of the lakelet.

BENMÈAL. 'Girthon.' *Beann máel*, bare hill. *Cf.* BARMEAL. *See under* MEAUL.

BENMÌNNOCH (*P.* Binmeanach Hill). 'Minigaff.' *Beann meadhonach* [meanogh], middle Hill. *See under* BALMINNOCH.

BENMÒRE (a hill 1177 feet). 'Minigaff.' *Beann mór*, great hill.

BÈNNAN (*P.* Bennen). Of frequent occurrence; *beanndn* or *beinndn*, dim. of *beann* or *beinn*, but used as an equivalent; for instance there are two hills of the name, one in Kells of 1800 feet, the other in Irongray of 1175 feet.

BENNANBRÀCK. 'Minigaff.' *Beanndn breac*, brindled or spotted hill. *Cf.* BENBRACK.

BENNAVÈOCH [vēēogh]. 'Kirkmaiden.' *Beann na bhfítheach* [vēēagh], hill of the ravens. *Cf.* CRAIGENVEOCH, DUNVEOCH, and in Ireland Mulnaveagh, near Lifford, and Benaneha (where the *f* has disappeared by aspiration), written in Irish *Beann na fheiche*. O. ERSE *fiach*.

BENNÈEVE. 'Balmaclellan.'

BENNIELÒAN. 'Dalry.'

BENNIGUÌNEA. 'Kells.' *Beann gCinniadh* [?] [ginneh], Kenneth's hill. *Cf.* CAIRN KENNAGH, CAIRNKENNY, CAIRN KINNA, RINGUINEA; and in Ireland, Cairnkenny in Tyrone, etc.

BENÒWR. 'Girthon.' *Beann odhar* [owr], grey hill. O. ERSE *odar*, "pale, wan, dun" (*O'Reilly*).

BENRÒACH (*gutt*). 'Minigaff.' *Beann rúadh* [rooh], red hill. O. ERSE *rúad, rhudd*, C. *rydh*, B. *ryudh*. *Cf.* DU. *rood* + ICEL. *rauðr* + DAN. and SWED. *röd* + G. *roth* + GOTH. *rauds* + A.S. *redd* (whence M.E. *reed, rede*, E. *red*) + LAT. *rufus, rutilus*— √RUDII, to redden, whence SKT. *rudhira*, blood, GK. ἐρεύθειν, ἐρυθρός.

BENSHÌNNIE. 'Parton.' *Beann sionach* [shinnagh], hill of the foxes. *See under* AUCHENSHINNOCH.

BÈNTFOOT. 'Kirkgunzeon.' "*Bent.* 1. A coarse kind of grass growing on hilly ground. 2. The coarse grass growing on the sea-shore. 3. The open field, the plain."—*Jamieson.* Here used in the last sense, *i.e.* the foot of the open pasture. "*Bent*, coarse grass on the moors, the grassy moor itself (as opposed to heathery, or ling-covered moors."—*Lucas*, Nidderdale Glossary. O.H.G. *pinuz*, M.H.G. *binez, binz*, G. *binse*, bent grass.

BENTS. 'Minigaff.' *See under* BENTFOOT (1).

BENTÙDOR or BENTÙTHER. 'Rerwick.' *Beann t-súdaire* [toodery], hill of the tanner. ERSE *súdaire*, a tanner (*Joyce*, ii. 116). In this word the interpolated *t* in composition almost always eclipses *s*. *Cf.* KNOCKTOODEN, LAGTUTOR, and in Ireland, Edennatoodry in Tyrone (*eudan a 'tsudaire*, hill-brow of the tanner), Knockatudor in Cavan, Listooder in Down.

BENNÙSKIE (a rock in the tideway). 'Kirkmaiden.' *Beann uisge* [usky], point (of rock) in the water. O. ERSE *usce*, gen. *usci* (*Windisch*), water; ERSE and GAEL. *uisge*; whence E. *whisky*.

BENWÈE. 'Minigaff.' *Beann bhuidhe* [wee]. *See under* BENBUIE. There is more than one hill in Ireland called Benwec.

BENYÈLLARY (a hill 2359 feet), (*P.* Benellury M.). 'Minigaff.' *Beann iolaire* [illery], hill of the eagles. ERSE *iolaire* (whence Slievanilra, *i.e. sliabh an iolaire*, in Clare County) and *iolar* [iller] (whence Coumaniller in Tipperary); W. *eryr*, C. *er* + A.S. *earn*, eagle, E. *erne*, osprey + DU. *aarn* + ICEL. *aurn, ern*. The white-tailed eagle (*Haliaëtus albicilla*) bred until recent years in this region. The last was shot by Lord Ailsa's keepers about the year 1866. In a description of Minigaff, preserved among the Macfarlane MSS., are some interesting notes on the fauna of this very mountain in the 16th century. "In the remote parts of this great mountain are very large Red-deer; and about the top thereof that fine bird called the Mountain Partridge, or, by the commonalty, the Tarmachan, about the size of a Red-cock, and its flesh much of the same nature; feeds, as that bird doth, on the seeds of the bullrush, and makes its protection in the chinks and hollow places of thick stones, from the insults of the eagles, which are in plenty, both the large gray and the black, about that mountain." Red-deer, ptarmigan, and eagles are now all alike extinct; but so late as 1811, in the *General View of the Agriculture of the County of Ayr*, the following passage occurs :—" Eagles formerly abounded so much about Loch Doon, in the higher parts of Carrick, as to prove formidable enemies to the helpless sheep for many miles round their haunts. They have been much reduced in their numbers by the shepherds, but they are by no means extirpated. They still hatch in the most inaccessible rocks, and occasionally carry off, in their powerful talons, a lamb to feed themselves and their young."

BENNYLÒW.   ' Kirkcowan.'

BÈOCH (*P.* Baoch, Bioch, Byochs ; *Inq. ad Cap.* 1600, Beauch). ' Inch,' ' Kirkpatrick Irongray,' ' Penninghame,' ' Tungland.' *Beithach* [bayoch], a place of birches. *Cf.* Beith in Ayrshire, and Beagh, Behagh, and Behy in Ireland. Slieve Beagh is written *Sliabh beatha* by Muircheartach.

BERE HILL. ' Kirkmaiden.' A.S. *bere,* barley (BR. SC. *bear*) + LAT. *far,* corn.

BESSIE YON. ' Glasserton.' Bessie's oven ; *cf.* Yorkshire *yoon,* an oven — A.S. *ofen, ofn* + DU. *oven* + ICEL. *ofn,* later *omn* + SWED. *ugn* + G. *ofen* + GOTH. *auhns* + ERSE *amhan* + GAEL. *amhuinn, uamhainn.* In northern dialects it is not uncommon to prefix *y* before a vowel ; thus BR. SC. *yin,* one, *yow,* ewe, *yeild,* eild, age, etc.

BETTY KNOWES.   ' Loch Rutton.'

BIÀNGENS.   ' Kirkmaiden.'

BIÀWN. ' Kirkmaiden.' *Badhun* [?] [bawn], a cattle pen (literally *bo dun,* cattle fort). Hence Bawn, a common name in Ireland. O. ERSE and GAEL. *bó,* a cow, W. *bu, buw,* also *buwch,* a cow, *biw,* cattle, C. *biuch,* B. *bio'ch* (the final *ch* is unaccounted for) + DU. *koe* + ICEL. *kýr* + SWED. and DAN. *ko* + O.H.G. *chuo, chuoa,* M.H.G. *kuo, ku,* G. *kuh* + A.S. *cú,* plur. *cý* (whence M.E. *cu, cou,* plur. *ky, kie, kye,* E. *cow,* plur. *kine,* BR. SC. *coo,* plur. *kye*) + LAT. *bos,* an ox + GK. βοῦς + SKT. *go,* a bull or cow. The common Aryan form is *gau,* an ox, from √GU, to low, to bellow ; SKT. *gu,* to sound. (*Skeat, s.v.* Cow.)

BILEÒW (a cave mouth). 'Kirkmaiden, s.c.' (*twice.*) *See under* BELLEW.

BINE HILL.   'Kirkcolm,' 'Port Patrick.'

BIRKETS HILL. 'Urr.' A.S. *beorc* or *birce wudu*, birch wood. E. *birch*, BR. SC. *birk*—A.S. *beorc, birce* (whence M.E. *birche*) + DU. *berken boom* + ICEL. and SWED. *björk* + DAN. *birk* + G. *birke* + RUSS. *bereza* + SKT. *bhúrja*, a birch. *See under* AIKET.

BISHOP BURN. 'Penninghame.' Named from the Bishop of Galloway's palace, which formerly stood at Clary.

BISHOPTON (*P.* Bishoptoun; *W. P.* MSS. Bisscoptoun). 'Twynholm.' The bishop's house.

BÌZZIARD FELL. 'Kirkcowan.' *Cf.* BAZARD LANE.

BLACKBEAST.   'Rerwick.'

BLACKCRAIG (*P.* Black-kraig Hill). 'Dalry.' *Cf.* CRAIGDHU.

BLACK GAIRY (*P.* Blakghary). 'Kells.' *Garry* or *gairy*, a common term in Galloway for a rough hill-side or stony place, — ERSE *garbh* [garriv], rough. Not in *Jamieson*.

BLACKDUBS. 'Minigaff.' "*Dub*, (1) a small pool of rain-water; (2) a gutter" (*Jamieson*)—ERSE *doub*; "*in doub*," the stream (*Broccan's Hymn*, l. 54; *Windisch*, p. 33). "*Dob*, river, stream."—*O'Reilly*. Probably from the root word *dub*, dark, which is emphasised in the present case by the prefix.

BLACKGRANE. 'Carsphairn.' "*Grain, grane*. 3. The branch of a river. 4. It also signifies the branches of a valley at the upper end, where it divides into two, as Lewishope Grains. 5. In plur. the prongs of a fork."—*Jamieson*.

BLACKGROUND. 'Old Luce.' *Cf.* TARDOW.

BLACKHEAD. 'Port Patrick, s.c.' *Cf.* CUNDEE.

BLACK ISLE, THE (a meadow in the moors). 'New Luce.' *See under* ALLANDOO and INKS.

BLACKMARK. 'Dalry.' *Mark* is a common name for lands in Galloway, and though it often means "*merk, merkland*, a denomination of land from the duty formerly paid to the sovereign or superior" (*Jamieson*), it has often, as in this case, another meaning, *i.e.* "*Markstane*, a landmark, Galloway; synon. *Marchstane*" (*Jamieson*). *See under* MARK.

BLACKMORROW WELL. 'Kirkcudbright.' Said to have received its name from an outlaw named Black Murray, on whose head a reward was set by the Crown. One of the Maclellan family found him asleep, and drove a dagger through his head, which is supposed to be the origin of the cognizance of the Maclellans.

BLACKMYRE. 'Kirkmabreck.' A place where black dye-stuff was obtained. "Notwithstanding their seeming neglect of their persons, these islanders were not without a spice of vanity, for they had invented dye-stuffs to diversify the colours of their clothes ; and their dying materials were (all of them) the produce of their own soil ; the principal these three : a kind of mud called *mireblack*, made a very deep and durable black ; a kind of stuff called *carker*, scraped off the rocks, made a very fine red ; and a kind of plant almost the same, and of the same effect, as madder."—*An Historical Essay on the Dress of the Ancient and Modern Irish*, by Joseph Walker, 4to, Dublin, 1788. "At the bottom of some deep bogs a half-liquid stuff, as black as jet, is found, which was formerly used by the peasantry all over Ireland for dyeing black. It gives frieze and other woollens an excellent dye." —*Joyce*, ii. 270. *Cf.* DOCHIES.

BLACKNOOK. 'Kirkinner.' Black corner. E. *nook*, BR. SC. *neuk* (M.E. *nok*), enters into many names in Galloway. *Lucas* (*s.v.* Newk) compares Norse *knúkjr*, a nob, peak, eminence ; but it may be taken generally as signifying a corner, equivalent to ERSE and GAEL. *cuil*.

BLÀDNOCH [*pron.* Blaidnoch], (*Cott.* MS. 1563, Blaidno, Blaidnoo ; *Pont's* MS., Bluidnoo ; *Inq. ad Cap.* 1643, Bladzenoche ; *Symson*, Blaidnoch). A river in Wigtonshire.

BLAIKET (*Inq. ad Cap.* 1548, Blaikat ; 1552, Blaket ; *P.* Blakitt). 'Wigton.' A.S. *blæc wudu*, black wood. M.E. *blak wode* or *wde*. A.S. *blac. blæc* (whence M.E. *blak*, E. *black*) + ICEL. *blakkr* (used to describe the colour of wolves) + DAN. *blæk*, ink + SWED. *bläck*, ink ; SWED. dialect *blaga*, to smear with smut. The idea seems to be smoky, smutty, arising from the root of *blow*, in the sense of a flaring fire, *cf.* O.H.G. *pláhan*, M.H.G. *blüjen*, G. *blähen*, to blow, to melt in a forge. *Cf.* AIKET.

BLAIR (*P.* Blaar, Blair ; *W. P.* MSS. Blair). 'Sorbie,' 'Stoneykirk.' "*Blàir*, a plain, a field ; a dispute, contention, a battle."— *O'Reilly.* GAEL. "*Blar*, a battle, engagement, battle-field ; ground, plain."—*Macalpine.* The word does not seem to occur in Irish names, nor is it noticed by *Lluyd, Windisch*, or *Joyce*. The primary meaning is probably that of "a plain," and then a battle from the place chosen for it. The Scottish historian Buchanan's gloss upon it is "*solum arboribus liberum*," ground clear of trees, such as, in a densely wooded country, would naturally be chosen for a battle.

BLAIRBÙIE (*W. P.* MSS., Blairbowy). 'Glasserton.' *Blár buidhe* [buie], yellow plain. This word, or Blairfin, would graphically designate a piece of cultivated land, corn, or light-coloured grass, among surrounding moor or wood. In common parlance, arable pasture is now spoken of as "white land" in the sense of pale. *Cf.* BLAIRFIN, WHITEFIELD, WHITEHILLS; also Blarbuidhe in Iona. *See under* BARBUIE.

BLAIRBÙIES (*Inq. ad Cap.* 1604, Glenure, *alias vocata* Blairboyis; *P.* Blairbuy). 'Minigaff.' *See under* BLAIRBUIE.

BLAIRDÈRRY (*P.* Blairdyrry). 'Old Luce.' *Blár doire* [dirry], plain of the oak wood. ERSE "*doire*, a grove, a wood, a place full of bushes."—*Lluyd.* It means specially an oak wood, from *dair, darach*, an oak. *See under* ARNDARROCH.

BLAIRFÌN. 'Kirkcolm.' *Blár fion* [fin], white field. *See under* BLAIRBUIE, WHITEFIELD. O. ERSE *find, fin*, W. *gwyn*, C. *guydn, guyn*, B. *gwen*. GAEL. *fionn*.

BLAIRGÒWER. 'Penninghame.' *Blár gobhar* [gowr], plain of the goats. *See under* ALGOWER. Blairgowrie in Perthshire represents the genitive singular *goibhre* [gowrie].

BLAIR HILL. 'Kirkcowan,' 'Kirkinner.' Here the name of the plain, *blár*, has been transferred to the hill. *See* GLAIK, LAG.

BLAIRÌNNIE (*Inq. ad Cap.* 1608, Blairinny; *P.* Blairynny). 'Crossmichael.' *Blàr roinne* [rinnie], plain of the point or division of land. *See under* RHINNS.

BLAIRMÀKIN [*pron.* maukin], (*Inq. ad Cap.* 1581, Blairmalkein; *P.* Blairmakyn). 'Kirkinner.'

BLAIRMÌCHAEL [*pron.* Blairmeeghl, *gutt.*]. 'Crossmichael.' *Blár Micheil* [meeghl], (St.) Michael's field.

BLAIRMÒDDIE. 'Kirkcowan.' *Blár madadh* [maddy], plain of the dogs, or perhaps of the wolves. "There are two words in common use for a dog, *cu* and *madadh* or *madradh* [madda, maddra], which enter extensively into local names. Of the two forms of the latter, *madradh* is more usual in the south and *madadh* in the rest of Ireland."—*Joyce*, i. 479. *Cf.* W. *madrin, madyn*, a fox.

BLAIRMÒRE. ' Kirkcolm.' *Blár mór*, great plain.

BLAIRNAGÒBBER. ' Kirkcowan.' *Blár na gobur*, plain of the horses or goats. The unaspirated form of genitive. *See under* ALGOWER.

BLÀIROCH. ' Penninghame.' *Blárach*, a level place, deriv. of *blar*.

BLAIRS (*P*. Blairs). ' Kirkmabreck.' *Blár*, a plain, to which E. plural has been added. *See under* BLAIR.

BLAIRSHÌNNOCH (*P*. Blairshinnock). ' Kirkgunzeou,' ' Kirkinner.' *Blár sionach* [shinnagh], plain of the foxes. *See under* AUCHENSHINNOCH and TODDLY.

BLANYVÀIRD (on the shore of Loch Ochiltree). ' Penninghame.' *Blean a' bhaird* [blainavaird], creek, curve, or bay of the rhymer. *See under* BARNBOARD and DIRVAIRD. O. ERSE *blén*, inguen, the groin; ERSE *bléan*; GAEL. *blian*, the groin; " in a secondary sense it is applied to a creek branching off either from the sea or from a lake, or formed by the mouth of a river." —*Joyce*, ii. 264. *Cf.* LINBLANE, in Old Luce, and Blean, Blane, and Blaney, in various parts of Ireland; Bleanalung (the boat-creek, *bléan a' luing*), in Lough Erne, etc.

BLAWQUHÀIRN [*pron*. Blaw-whairn]. 'Dalry.' *Blár chairn* [harn] [?], plain of the cairn. *See under* AUCHENCAIRN and BLAIR.

BLAWRÀINIE (*P*. Blairenny). ' Balmaclellan.' *Blár raineach*, ferny plain. O. ERSE *raith* (*raithnech*, ferus—*Cormac trans*., p. 143), ERSE *raithneach*, W. *rhedyn*, C. *reden*, B. *raden*, GAEL. *raineach*, fern, bracken.

BLAWRÌNNIE (*P*. Blairennies). ' Balmaclellan.' *See under* BLAIRINNIE.

BLAW WEARY. ' Balmaclellan,' ' Urr.' *Blár iarach* or *iarthagh* [eeragh], west field. *See under* BALSHERE. *Cf.* CANEERIE, CASTLE WEARY; and, in Ireland, Baurearagh, a hill in Cork, and Cloonearagh in Kerry and Roscommon.

BLINDWALLS. ' Whithorn.'

BLOODMIRE Moss. ' Kirkpatrick Durham.' Probably named from the colouring given in various places by oxide of iron in the springs.

BLOODY SLOUCH. ' Kirkcolm, s.c.' *See under* BARRACK SLOUCH.

BLOODY WIEL (a pool on the Luce, where the Hays and the Linns of Larg had a bloody encounter). ' New Luce.' BR. SC. *wiel, wele*, a whirlpool, a pool on a river where the water revolves—A.S. *wella, well, wyll* (M.E. *wel*, E. *well*)+ICEL. *vell*+

DU. *wel*, a spring+DAN. *væld* (*væll*) a spring+G. *welle*, a wave
or surge (BR. SC. *wall*, a wave—*Jamieson*). All from TEUT.
base WAL, to turn round, from √WAR, to turn round. SKT.
val, to move to and fro.—*Skeat, s.v.* Well (2).

BLOWPLAIN.   ' Balmaclellan.'

BLUE MIRE (on the Palnure). ' Minigaff.' Named from the
bluish alluvial clay banks exposed by the fall of the tide.

BLYTHEMAN'S RIG.   ' Kells.'

BO STANE, THE. ' New Luce.' *Bo*, a cow. This is the name of
a large black rock in mid-channel of the Luce, below the
Loups of Kilfeather. In 1874 a gentleman who was fishing
asked the keeper why it was so called, " Just because it's
like a black stot " (bullock), was the reply. The name,
though not given in any map, has been orally handed down
from Gaelic-speaking times, the sense having been also preserved, which does not often happen. *See under* BIAWN.

BOAK PORT. ' Kirkcolm, s.c.' *Boc*, a he-goat [?]. *See under*
AUCHNIEBUT.

BOAT DRAUGHT. ' Girthon, s.c.' A place where fishing-boats
are drawn up. *See under* TARBERT.

BODDON'S ISLE (an island in the Dee).   ' Kells.'

BODEN WALLS WELL.   . ' Glasserton.'

BÒGGRIE MOSS. ' Girthon.' Soft, boggy moss—ERSE *bogur* (a
derivative of *bog—Lluyd*), *bogurach*, *bogreach*. *See under*
BOGUE.

BÒGHOUSE (*P*. Boighouse). ' Mochrum.' House of the bog, or
soft land.

BÒGRIE (*P*. Boggryleinn). ' Kirkpatrick Irongray.' Formerly
Boggrie Lane, the boggy stream, as shown by *Pont*.

BOGUE. ' Minigaff.' *Bog*, soft; O. ERSE *bocc*. Referred to the
same root as E. *bow*, to bend.

BOGUE FELL. ' Dalry.' *See under* BOGUE. *Fell*, a hill—ICEL.
fjall, fell, a mountain+DAN. *field*+SWED. *fjüll*. *Skeat* suggests
probably originally applied to open flat down=E. *field*.

BOGUE QUAY (a landing-place in the Solway). ' New Abbey.'
See under BOGUE.

BÒMBIE (*P*. Bouiby (*misprint*), Bomby).   ' Kirkcudbright.'

BONÈRICK.   ' Kirkpatrick Irongray.'

BONSACK. . ' Urr.'

BONYLÀGOCH (*Inq. ad Cap.* 1600, Bonylagoch).   ' Kirkcowan.'

BÒRELAND (*Inq. ad Cap.* 1605, Bordland ; *P.* Boirlant, Boirland).
A frequent name all over Galloway.   Dr. John Cowell in his
Law Dictionary says, " Bordlands signifie the desmenes which
lords keep in their hands for the maintenance of their board
or table."   If this is the correct meaning, then this name is
the equivalent of a "home-farm"; but it is more probably
bere-land, that is, land on which bere or barley was grown.
The natives pronounce it *Beurland*.

BÒRGAN (*P.* Boirgan).   ' Minigaff.'

BORGAN FERRACH.   'Minigaff.'   *Farrach* [?], a rendezvous, a
meeting-place.   *Cf.* CLAYFARAS ; and, in Ireland, Farragh in
Cavan, Farra in Armagh, Farrow in Westmeath and
Leitrim, Gortnafurra in Tipperary, etc. (*Joyce*, i. 207).

BORGUE (*P.* Boirg, Borg ; *Charter of David II. (Crauf.* MS.), Borgg).
'Borgue.'   A parish in the Stewartry; +O. ERSE *borg, brog,
borce* ("brogg thromm Temra," Tara's mighty burgh; *Fél.,
Prol.* 165), ERSE *buirg, brugh, bruighean,* GAEL. *borgh,* B. *burch*+
SCAND. *borg,* a fort+ICEL. *borg*+DU. *burg*+GOTH. *baurgs,* a
town+O.H.G. *puruc* (G. *burg,* A.S. *burh, burg* (whence M.E. *burgh,
borgh,* BR. SC. *burgh,* E. *borough*), from *beorgan,* to defend,
protect+GOTH. *bairgan,* to hide, preserve, keep+LITH. *brukù,*
to press, constrain+LAT. *farcire,* to stuff+GK. φράσσειν, to
shut in—GK. √ΦΡΑΚ.

BORRON.   ' Kirkbean.'

BOUGHTY BURN.   ' Penninghame.'   The winding burn.   "*Bought,
boucht,* a curvature or bending of any kind."—*Jamieson.*
—A.S. *búgan,* to bend+DU. *buigen*+ICEL. *beyjia,* to bend
(tr.)+SWED.' *böja*+DAN. *böie,* to bend (tr. and intr.)
+GOTH. *biugan*+O.H.G. *piocan* (G. *beugen*)+LAT. *fugere,* to
turn to flight+φεύγειν, to flee+SKT. *bhuj,* to bend — √BHOGH,
to bend. (*Skeat, s.v.* Bow.)

BOÙROCK.   ' Loch Rutton.'   "*Bowrach, bowrock, bowrick,* 3. a
shepherd's hut, Galloway."—*Jamieson.*   *See under* BORGUE,
of which this seems to be another form.

BOW [*pron.* Boo], (*P.* Bow).   ' Glasserton,' 'Rerwick.'   *Both* [bo],
a hut.   "*Boo, bow,* a term sometimes used to denote a manor-
house, or the principal farm-house, or a village."—*Jamieson.*

Cf. Bough in Carlow and Monaghan. O. ERSE and ERSE *both*, GAEL. *buth*+ICEL. *buð* (whence M.E. *bothe*, E. *booth*)+SWED. and DAN. *bod*+G. *bude*, a booth,— √BHÚ, to be; *cf.* SKT. *bhavana*, a house, a place to *be* in— *bhú*, to be (*Skeat*).

BOW BURN. 'Carsphairn.' *See under* BOW.

BOWDY-HOUSE BRAE. 'New Luce.' A singular name to occur in the middle of wild moors.

BOWHILL. 'Colvend.' *Buachaill* [bōghel], a boy; a name often applied in Ireland to upright stones, as Boughil near Kenmare, and many townlands called Boughill and Boghill.—*Joyce*, ii. 435. *Buachaill*, a boy, a cow-herd—*bo*, a cow.

BRACKENIECÀLLIE. 'New Luce.' *Breacnach cailleaich* [?], spotted land of the old woman or nun. *Cf.* Bracknamuckley in Antrim, broken land of the swine-pasture; also Bracknagh, Brackenagh, and Brackney, occurring frequently as names of places in Ireland, *i.e. breacnach* (from *breac*, see under Aucha-brick), a variegated, freckled place. The alternative ERSE *breaclach* and *breacnach* has its parallel in the cognate E. *freckle* (spelt *frekell* by Sir T. More), and *freken* (used in plu. by Chaucer, *Cant. Tales*, 2171). *Cf.* BRECKENIHILL, BREAKOCH HILL, BRECKLACH HILL, BRECKNACH.

BRACO MOAT (*P.* Bracoch).   'Kirkpatrick Irongray.'

BRADEYARD.   'Colvend.'

BRÀDOCK. 'Kirkcolm, s.c.' *Braghadóg* [brahdog], a throat or gulley; dim. of *braghad*. O. ERSE *bráge*, gen. *bragat, braget*, the neck; ERSE and GAEL. *braghad*+O.W. *brouant*, W. *breuant*, the windpipe; which *Rhys* (p. 66) refers to same root as LAT. *gurges*, an abyss, *gurgulio*, the windpipe + O.H.G. *guërca*, O. NORSE, *kverkr*, the throat. *Cf.* BRADINA and BREDDOCK; and, in Ireland, Braddocks in Monaghan, Bradoge, a tributary of the Liffey, and another stream at Bundoran in Donegal.

BRAE (*P.* Brae). 'Loch Rutton.' *Brá, brí*, a hill-side, GAEL. *braigh*, a summit. It is interesting to trace this word *brae* from the SKT. √*bhur*, to move quickly; whence *bhrú*, eyebrow, PERS. *abrú*, GK. ὀφρύς, ERSE *brá*, a brow, M.H.G. *bár*, the eye-lid, A.S. *brú* (a pronunciation retained in Broad Scots when speaking of the face, but in speaking of the hill-brow *brae* is used, although *hill-broo* is not uncommon). Ignorant of the figurative origin of *brae* the Lowland Scots often speak of the *brae-face*=hill-face, that is, literally, the face of the forehead. The Dutch also show how far the word has travelled from the original root-sense, for they call the eyebrow *wenk-braauw,* wink-brow or wink-wagger ; *wenk* being from a root, WAK, WAG, to move aside.

BRAIDEN'S KNOWE.   'Carsphairn.'

BRAIDENOCH (a hill of 1000 feet). 'Carsphairn.' The next adjacent hill is called Bardennoch.

BRAID PORT. 'Girthon.' The broad landing-place. BR. SC. *braid* —A.S. *brád* (changing according to rule to M.E. *brod, brood,* E. *broad*)+DU. *breed*+ICEL. *breiÿr*+SWED. and DAN. *bred*+ GOTH. *braids*+O.H.G. *preit,* G. *breit.* Origin uncertain.

BRAID FELL, broad hill.   'Inch.'

BRANDEDLEYS. 'Urr.' A.S. brown or burnt meadows. "*Branded, brannit,* having a reddish brown colour as if singed by fire. *A branded cow* is one that is almost entirely brown."—*Jamieson.* The E. *brown* contains the sense of burning. "*Brown* may be considered as a contract form of the old past part. signifying *burnt.*"—*Skeat. See under* BRUNTLAND. A.S. *ledh, leá* (whence M.E. *ley,* E. *lea, ley, lay*)+provin. G. *loh,* a morass, bog, or forest (as A.S. *fledh,* E. *flea*+G. *floh*), (thus Waterloo = water-*lea* or meadow)—TEUT. base LAUHA—TEUT. √ LUH, to shine+LITH. *laukas*+LAT. *lucus,* a grove (thus showing a curious commentary on the proverbial *lucus a non lucendo*)+ SKT. *loka,* space, the world—SKT. *loch,* to see—SKT. *ruch,* to shine—√ RUK, to be bright. (*Skeat.*)

BRANNETRIGG. 'Kirkgunzeon.' Burnt hill. *See under* BRANDEDLEYS.

BRANNIT MOAT. 'Carsphairn.' *See under* BRANDEDLEYS.

BRANYÈA [*pron.* yae], a hill of 1125 feet. 'Girthon.' *Breánsheach* [?] [branyagh], (a) stinking (place), deriv. of *bréan* ; or else *bréan chaedh* [brān hay], stinking bog, a name which has travelled from the bog to the hill. O. ERSE *brén,* ERSE *bréan,* GAEL. *breun* [brānn], stinking, foul, is an epithet often applied to bogs or swamps. "One of the indications that led Colonel Hall to the discovery of copper mines at Glandore in Cork, was the fetid smell emitted from a fire of turf cut in a neighbouring bog, which turned out to be strongly impregnated with copper. This bog was known as the 'stinking bog' (*móin bhréun*), and the people had it that neither cat nor dog could live in the house where the turf was burnt."—*Joyce,* ii. 397 (quoting Mrs. Hall's *Ireland,* i. 142). This smell, as in Harrogate water, etc., arises from sulphur in combination with copper.　*Cf.* Brenter in Donegal, *i.e. bréan tir*, stinking ground, named from a sulphurous spring; Breandrum in several places in Ireland; Breansha, near Tipperary (*i.e. bréanseach*, a stinking place), etc.

BRATNEY WA'S.　　　　　　　　　　　　　　' Kirkinner.'

BREÀCKOCH HILL (*P.* Brakoch).　'Leswalt.'　*Breacach* [brăkogh], brindled, broken.　*See under* BRACKENICALLIE.

BRÈCKLACH HILL (865 feet).　'Minigaff.'　*Breaclach*, broken, variegated.　*Cf.* Bracklagh, a frequent name in Ireland.　*See under* BRACKENICALLIE.

BRECKENIHILL [*pron.* Brecknihill].　'Buittle.'　*See under* BRACKENI-CALLIE.

BRÈCKNACH.　'Dalry.'　*Breacnach*, broken, variegated.　*See under* BRACKENICALLIE.

BRECONSIDE (*P.* Brakansyde).　'Kirkgunzeon.'　A.S. or BR. SC. the hillside of brackens.　A.S. *bracce*, fern, pl. *braccan* (whence M.E. *braken*, BR. SC. *breckan*, E. *bracken*)+SWED. *brăken*, fern+DAN. *bregne*+ICEL. *burkni*, fern, *brok*, sedge.　*Side*—A.S. *síde*, generally means the edge or border, but also a tract, as in BR. SC. *country-side*, the district.

BRÈDDOCK (*P.* Briddachan).　'Kirkmaiden, s.c.'　*See under* BRADOCK.

BREEDIE BURN.　'New Luce.'　*Brighde* [breedie], gen. of *Brigid*, Bridget.　Dedications to St. Bridget or Bride are numerous. In this case the Gaelic prefix has been dropped.　*See under* HILL MABREEDIA (which is in the immediate vicinity).

BRÈNNAN.　'Balmaclellan.'　*Bruigheandn* [breanan], a dwelling, a mansion; dim. of *bruighedn*, itself a dim. or derivative of *bruigh*. *Cf.* Breenaun in Galway.　*See under* DRUMABRENNAN.

BRÈOCH.　'Buittle.'　*Bruigh*, a house, a dwelling. *See under* BORGUE.

BRÍGIE BRAES.　　　　　　　　　　　　　　' Kirkmaiden.'

BRÍSHIE BRIDGE.　　　　　　　　　　　　　' Penninghame.'

BRÍSHIES (*P.* Bryishyish).　　　　　　　　　' Minigaff.'

BROACH (*P.* Browach).　'Kirkmabreck.'　*Bruigh*, a house.　*See under* BORGUE.

BROADWALL.　　　　　　　　　　　　　　' Kirkmaiden.'

BROCHDOO.　'Kirkcolm.'　*Bruach dubh* [doo], black hill, or *brugh dubh*, black house.　*See under* BROUGHHILL.

BRÒCKLAN BRAES. 'Kirkmaidcn.' A.S. *broc land,* badger ground. *See under* BROCKLOCH.

BROCKLAW. 'Sorbie.' A.S. *broc hlaew,* badger hill.

BRÒCKLOCH (*P.* Brokloch). 'Carsphairn,' 'Inch,' 'Kirkcudbright,' 'Kirkpatrick Durham,' 'Minigaff,' 'Penninghame,' 'Port Patrick.' *Broclach,* a badger warren. Brocklagh is the form assumed in modern Irish topography. ERSE, GAEL., M. *broc*+W., C., and B. *broch,* from *breac,* parti-coloured, in allusion to the animal's striped face, just as *breac,* a trout, from his spots (the Irish form *brech* for *broc* also appears). From the Celtic was borrowed the A.S. *broc,* whence M.E. *brok,* BR. SC. *brock. See under* AUCHABRICK.

BRÒCKLOCH BÈNNAN. 'Carsphairn.' *Broclaich beanndn,* hill of the badger warren.

BRÒCKLOCHS. 'Minigaff.' *See under* BROCKLOCH.

BROCK'S COVE. 'Kirkmaiden, s.c.' Badger's cave, *see under* BROCKLOCH. "*Cove,* a cave."—*Jamieson.* This authority rightly derives *cove* − A.S. *cófa,* a chamber, a cave+ICEL. *kofi,* a hut, a shed+G. *koben,* a cabin, a pig-stye. It has no connection with *cave, alcove, coop,* nor *cup,* though often erroneously connected with these words. *Cove,* or more commonly *co',* is the usual name for a cave in Galloway.

BROÒKLANDS. 'Kirkpatrick Durham.' In the absence of old forms of spelling it is impossible to say if this may not be corrupted from *broclan* (*see* BROCKLAN BRAES). It is probably, however, A.S. *brooc lands,* a name commonly applied in England to low-lying, marshy ground (*cf.* ERSE *leana*). *Brook* is not of common occurence in Scotland (even in A.S. districts) −M.E. *brouke*—A.S. *bróc, brooc*+DU. *broek,* a marsh, a pool+ O.H.G. *pruoch* (G. *bruch*), a marsh, a bog.

BROOMHASS. 'Minigaff.' "*Hass of a hill,* a defile, *q.* the throat or narrow passage; used in a general sense to signify any gap or opening."—*Jamieson.* Hence this would be a pass or hollow where broom grows. BR. SC. *hass, hals, hawse*=the throat, the neck.

BROOMY KNOWE. 'Leswalt,' 'Mochrum.' BR. SC. *knowe,* a hillock, a knoll—A.S. *cnol* (whence M.E. *knol,* E. *knoll*)+DU. *knol,* a turnip (in the sense of a lump)+DAN. *knold,* a knoll+SWED. *knöll,* a knob. *Skeat* considers the word of Celtic origin, *quasi knokel,* dim. of *knok,* ERSE and GAEL. *cnoc,* W. *cnol,* a hillock. *Cf.* AUCHENGILSIIIE, KNOCKGILSIE, etc.

BROUGH [broogh, *gutt.*]. 'Kells.' *Bruach*, a brink or hill, or *brugh*, a house. *See under* BORGUE. ERSE *bruach*, lit. big-bellied; also "a border, brink, edge, bank, mound " (*O'Reilly*) —*bru*, the womb, the belly+W. and C. *bryn*, a hill, *bryncu*, a hillock, C. *bron*, a round protuberance, a breast, the slope of a hill; akin to E. *brink*. The idea is that of " roundness,"— √BHRV, to swell, boil. (*Skeat.*)

BROUGH HILL (*Inq. ad Cap.* 1625, 1647, Burgh Jerg; 1670, Brugh jarg). 'Kirkcolm.' *Brugh dearg* [dyarg], red house (*see under* BORGUE), or *bruach dearg*, red brink, border, or hill. *Cf.* Broughderg in Cavan, Fermanagh, and Tyrone, and Dergbrough in the latter county, which *Joyce* assigns to *bruach* (ii. 210).

BROUGHTON (*gutt.*) (*P.* Brogtoun; *W. P.* MSS. Brochetoun). 'Whithorn.' A.S. *burg tún*, two words of almost identical meaning. It is possible that it first received a Celtic name, ERSE *brugh*, and then in A.S. times *tún*, an enclosure, a farm-house (BR. SC. *toon*) was added; the sense being, the *tún*, or dwelling-place of *brugh*, the old house or fort.

BROUGHTON SKEOG, *i.e.* Broughton of the hawthorns (*W. P.* MSS. Brochetoun Skeoche). 'Whithorn.' *See under* AUCHEN-SKEOG.

BRUNTIS. 'Minigaff.' Burnt land.

BRÙNTLAND. 'Glasserton.' Burnt land.

BÙCHAN (*P.* Bukunstoun; MS. 1527, Buchane). 'Minigaff.' *Bothán* [bohan], a hut. *See under* BARBÙCHANY and BOW. *Cf.* Bohaun in Galway and Mayo.

BUCHAN BURN (*P.* Ess Bouchany). 'Minigaff.' Named from the farm-house standing on this burn (*see* BUCHAN). *Pont* preserves the old Celtic name *eas bothanach* [ess bohanagh], the torrent or cascade of the huts. *See under* ASS OF THE GILL, BARBUCHANY, and BOW.

BUCHT DOÙLOCH CRAIG. 'Minigaff.' The crag of the sheep-pen of the black lake (*see under* DOULOCH), or the sheep-pen at the crag of the black lake. " *Boucht, bought, bught, bucht,* a small pen usually put up in the corner of the field, into which it was customary to drive the ewes when they were to be milked."—*Jamieson.*

BUCKDÀSS OF CAIRNBÀBER. 'Minigaff.' SCAND. *bukkr dass*, the he-goat's ledge. *Dass* is used in the hill districts of Galloway to express a shelf or ledge on a cliff. " Yon sheep's clinted on the dass," said of a sheep which has fed along a grassy ledge till it cannot turn, and will either fall over or die there.

BÙCKIE HILL. ' Whithorn.' "*Buckies*, fruit of a certain kind of briar."—*Mactaggart.* The berries of the burnet rose (*rosa spinosissima*).

BÙCKIE KNOWE. ' Kirkmaiden.' *See under* BUCKIE HILL.

BUCK LOOP. ' Minigaff.' The he-goat's leap. BR. SC. *loup*—A.S. *hlýp* (+ICEL. *hlaup*, a leap+G. *lauf*, a course), from the verb — *hleápan*, to run, to leap (of which the past tense is *hleóp*)+ O. SAX. *hlópan*, to run+O. FRIES. *hlapa*+DU. *loopen*, to run (of which past tense *liep*)+ICEL. *hlaupa*+DAN. *löbe*, to run+SWED. *löpa*, to run+GOTH. *hlaupan*, to leap+O.H.G. *hlaufan* (M.H.G. *loufen*, G. *laufen*) from TEUT. base HLAUPAN, to leap.

BÙITTLE (a parish in the Stewartry), (*Inq. ad Cap.* 1572, Butill; 1605, Butehill; MS. 1527, Buthlc; *P.* Butill). *Cf.* Bootle in Lancashire.

BULGIE FORD.   ' Minigaff.'

BÙLLET. ' Kirkmaiden, s.c.' *Builg* [bullig], bellows; "a word which generally occurs on the coast, where it is applied, like *seidán*, puffing-holes, to rocks or points that break and spout up water during storms; and it is commonly anglicised Bullig, which is a name constantly met with all along the western coast from Donegal to Cork."—*Joyce*, ii. 249. O. ERSE *bolc, bolg*, a bag; ERSE *builg* or *bolg*, a sack, pair of bellows; GAEL. *bolg*, a belly, womb, or bellows; W. *bol*+A.S. *bælig, belg*, a bag+DU, *balg*, the belly+SWED. *bälg*, belly, bellows+DAN. *bälg*, shell, belly. All these words come from an early base BHALGH, to swell, common to both Teutonic and Celtic speech, to which may be referred *ball, boil* (subs.), *bowl, bilge, bulge, belly, bag, bulk, boll*, etc. (*Skeat.*)

BUNKER'S HILL.   ' Borgue.'

BURNGRAINS.   ' Kirkpatrick Irongray.'

BURNYARD. ' Borguc.' *See under* BARNYARD.

BURROW HEAD (*P.* Burrow Head). ' Whithorn, s.c.' *Borg, brugh*, a fortification. This headland, like most others on this coast, has been strongly fortified. *See under* BORGUE.

BUSS, THE (*P.* Buss). A wood or thicket. M.E. *busk, busch* (E. *bush*) —DAN. *busk* + SWED. *buske*, a bush + DU. *bosch*, a wood, forest + O.H.G. *busc*, G. *busch*. The L. LAT. *boscus*, IT. *bosco*, F. *bois* are derived from the Teutonic.

BUTTER CAIRN.   ' Penninghame.'

BUTTER HOLE. ' Buittle,' ' Dalry,' ' Kirkgunzeon,' ' Terregles.'
The bittern's hole. "*Boytour, butter,* the bittern (*Acts. Ja.* VI.)."
—*Jamieson.* M.E. *bitoure, bytoure* — F. *butor* — L. LAT. *butorius.*

BUTTERLUMP. ' Balmaghie.' *See under* BUTTER HOLE.

BÙYOCH [*pron.* Boyoch], (*P.* Buyesh). ' Whithorn.' GAEL. " *Bathach*
[bayach], a cow-house, a byre " (*Macalpine*), *i.e. bo theach* ; or
else " *bothach* [boyach], a bog, a fen, a marshy place "
(*O'Reilly*).

BYNG HILL. ' Kirkinner.' " *Bing,* a heap in general."—*Jamieson.*
Cf. BINE HILL.

CADGERHOLE (*P.* Cadgerhal). ' Carsphairn.' *Cadger,* a
hawker, a dealer. " *Cadger,* a miller's man who goes from
house to house collecting corn to grind, and returning it in
meal."—Grainge's *History of Nidderdale,* 1863.

CÀDLOCH.   ' Kirkcolm, s.c.'

CÀGGRIE. ' Inch.' *Cudhogreach* or *cathagreach* [?] [caagragh], adj.
form from ERSE *cudhóg,* GAEL. *cathag* [cawg], a jackdaw,
frequented by jackdaws. *Cf.* CAIGRIE.

CÀIGRIE. ' Urr.' *See under* CAGGRIE.

CÀIRDIE WIEL (a pool on the Cree near the village of Clauchan-
easy). ' Penninghame.' Probably the tinker's pool. BR. SC.
caird, cairdie, a tinker, a gipsy — ERSE *ceard,* a tinker — O. ERSE
cerd, a smith. Or perhaps from *cearda,* a workshop, a forge
— O. ERSE *cerda,* a forge (*O'Reilly*), to which has been added
BR. SC. *wiel* (*see under* BLOODY WIEL).

CÀIRN. *Carn,* a cairn. Many places are called simply The Cairn
without other adjunct. *See under* AUCHENCAIRN.

CAIRNAGREÈN. ' Leswalt.' *Carn na greine* [greenie], cairn of the
sun ; or perhaps more probably from a proper name like
Cairngranny, near Antrim, which *Joyce* (i. 335) refers to
Carn Greine, Grian's Cairn (a woman's name). " A whimsical
circumstance relative to these *Crom-liaghs* I cannot omit.
They are called by the ignorant natives *Grannie's beds.* This
Grannie is fabled to be the mother of Finmacoal or Fingal,
and of her, as well as of her son, they have wonderful
traditions. The source, however, of the appellation of
Grannie's bed I conceive to be a corruption of the original
Irish name of these altars. Grineus is, we know, a classical
name of Apollo. In Cambden's *Lauden* we meet with an

inscription '*Apollini Granno*,' and Grian is a common name for the sun in Irish."—*A Philosophical Survey of the South of Ireland, in a Series of Letters to John Watkinson, M.D.*, 8vo, London, 1777.

CAIRNARZÈAN [*pron.* reean].   'Inch.'

CAIRNBÀBER (*P.* Garnbabbyir Hill).   'Minigaff.'

CAIRNBRÒCK (*Inq. ad Cap.* 1600, Cairnebrek). 'Kirkcolm.' *Carn broc*, cairn of the badgers. *See under* BROCKLOCH.

CAIRNBÙIE (*Inq. ad Cap.* 1624, Cairnbuy ; *P.* Karnbuy). 'Kirkcolm.' *Carn Buidhe* [buie], yellow cairn. *See under* BARBUIE.

CAIRNBÙY. 'Mochrum.' *See under* CAIRNBUIE.

CAIRNDÀRROCH. 'Kells.' *Carn darach*, cairn of the oaks. *See under* ARNDARROCH.

CAIRNDÈRRY. 'Minigaff.' *Carn doire* [dirry], cairn of the oak wood. *See under* DERRY.

CAIRNDÒNALD. 'Kirkcolm.' *Carn Domhnuill* [Donnill], Donald's cairn.

CAIRNDÒNNAN. 'Kirkcolm.' *Carn Donnain*, Donnan's cairn. *Donnán*, a man's name, from *donn*, brown. (*O'Don. Topgr.*, p. [55].)

CAIRNDOÒN (*Inq. ad Cap.* 1600, Kerindoun ; *W. P.* MSS. Cairmdowne). 'Glasserton.' *Carn duin*, cairn of the fort. The modern farm-house occupies the site of the fort.

CAIRNDÙBBIN. 'Carsphairn.' *Carn Dubaghain*, Dubagan's or Dougan's Cairn.

CAIRN EDWARD (*P.* Karn Edward).   'Kells.'

CAIRNEY HILL, in several parishes ; hills upon which there are or have been cairns.

CAIRNEYWÀNIE (a hill of 1065 feet). 'Kirkmabreck.'

CAIRNFIELD (*P.* Kairnfields). 'Kirkinner.' There used to be cairns here, now removed, and a circle of large stones, of which only one remains. "Cairn" and "Antique Cairn" are marked on an estate map of 1777.

CAIRNFÒRE. 'Minigaff.' *Carn mhór* [vore] [?] great cairn. *Cf.* CAIRNMORE.

CAIRNGÀAN (*P.* Karngan ; *Inq. ad Cap.* 1610, Carnegayne). 'Kirkmaiden.'

CAIRNGÀRROCH (*P.* Karnygyrach and Karngyroch; *Inq. ad Cap.* 1610, Carnegirroch). 'Kirkmaiden,' 'Stoneykirk.' *Carn gcarroch* [garrogh], rough cairn. *See under* BARHARROW.

CAIRNHÀGGARD. 'Stoneykirk.' *Carn shagairt* [haggart], the priest's cairn. *Cf.* Drumhaggart in Donegal. *See under* ALTAGGART.

CAIRNHÀNDY.   'Stoneykirk.'

CAIRNHÀPPLE (*P.* Karnchaple). 'Leswalt.' *Carn chapul* [happul], cairn of the horses. *See under* BARHAPPLE.

CAIRNHÀRROW. 'Anwoth.' *Carn charroch* [harrogh], rough cairn. Aspirated form of CAIRNGARROCH, *q.v.*

CAIRNHÌNGEY.   'Stoneykirk.'

CAIRNHÒLLY.   'Kirkmabreck.'

CAIRNIE FINNART.   'Kirkmaiden.'

CAIRNIEWÀ.   'Inch.'

CAIRNIEWÈLLAN.   'Kirkmaiden.'

CAIRN KÈNNAGH. 'New Luce.' *Carn Cainneaich,* or possibly *Cinaeidh* [kinneh], Kenneth's cairn. Both occur as proper names from very early times. From Canneagh of Agha Boe, named St. Kenny (*Four Masters,* 598) is derived the name of Kilkenny.

CAIRNKÈNNY. 'Inch,' 'New Luce.' *Cf.* Cairnkenny in Tyrone. *See under* CAIRN KENNAGH.

CAIRN KÌNNA. 'Minigaff.' *Carn Cinaeidh* [kinneh], Kenneth's cairn. *See under* BENNIGUINEA.

CAIRNLÈES. 'Crossmichael.' *Carn liath* [lee], grey cairn; *cf.* Carnlea in Antrim, or *carn lios* [lis], cairn of the fort.

CAIRN MACNEELIE. 'Inch,' 'New Luce.' M'Neil's cairn. The resemblance to Karnmenelez in Cornwall (translated by *Borlase,* in his *Nœnia Cornubiæ,* the cairn-stones of the angels) is singular, though accidental.

CAIRNMÒN. 'Stoneykirk.' *Carn na-mban* [carnamān], cairn of the women. *Cf.* Carmoan in Cornwall. *See under* BARNAMON.

CAIRNMÒRE. 'Kirkmaiden,' 'Mochrum.' *Carn mór,* the great cairn.

CAIRNMÙLTIBRUGH (*Inq. ad Cap.* 1607, Carnemulktibrugh; *P.* Kairn Multibrugh). 'Inch.'

CAIRN-NA-GATH. ' New Luce.' *Carn na' gcat* [gaat], cairn of the wild cats. *Cf.* Carnagat in Antrim and Tyrone. *See under* ALWHAT.

CAIRNPÀT, CAIRNPIÒT, or PIOT FELL (*P.* Karn Patt). ' Port Patrick.' (St.) Patrick's Hill.

CAIRNRÀWS.   ' Kells.'

CAIRNSCÀRROW. ' Inch.' *Carn scaïrbhe* [1] [scairvie, scarrow], cairn of the ford. But *see under* BARSCARROW and CAIRNS-GARROCH.

CAIRNSGÀRROCH. ' Carsphairn.' *Carn g-carroch*, rough cairn, with redundant *s* as in Cairnsmore. *Cf.* CAIRNSCARROW.

CAIRNSÌM.   ' Stoneykirk.'

CAIRNSMORE of Carsphairn, of Dee, and of Fleet, three hills in the Stewartry (*P.* Karnsmoor H., Kairnsmoort Hil).

> " Cairnsmore o' Fleet and Cairnsmore o' Dee,
> And Cairnsmore o' Carsphairn, the biggest o' the three."
> *Local Rhyme.*

See under CAIRNMORE.

CAIRNTÀMMOCK. ' Girthon.' *Carn tomach*, bushy cairn — ERSE *tom*, dumetum (*Llwyd*), a thicket, GAEL. *tomach*, bushy. Or, possibly, BR. SC. the cairn hillock. " *Tammock, tommack*, a hillock, Galloway."—*Jamieson.*

CAIRNTÒOTAN.   ' Kirkcolm.'

CAIRNTÒSH (*P.* Kairntoish). ' Girthon.' *Carn tùas* [1], upper cairn, or perhaps *carn tess*, south cairn. Ò. ERSE *sùas, tùas* (adverb), above (do-úas 1, *Windisch*). O. ERSE *tess, dess* (adverb), southerly. *See under* BARCHESKIE.

CAIRNWÈIL.   ' Stoneykirk.'

CAIRNYÀRD. ' Kirkmabreck,' ' New Abbey.' *Carn ard*, high cairn. *See under* AIRD.

CÀITANS [*pron.* Catyens].   ' Whithorn.'

CÀLDONS (*Inq. ad Cap.* 1602, Caldonis ; 1616, Caldanis ; *P.* Kaldouns, Kalduns, Caldun). ' Minigaff,' ' Stoneykirk.' *Coll-dean*, the hazels (plur. of O. ERSE *collde*), E. plur. added. *See under* AUCHENHILL.

CALDOW (*P.* Kaildow ; MS. 1527, Caldow). ' Balmaclellan.' *Coill dubh* [kyll doo], dark wood. *Cf.* BLAIKET.

CALDRON, THE HOWE OF THE. 'Minigaff.' A secluded Alpine valley on the east shoulder of Cairnsmoor. "*How.* (1) Any hollow place; (2) a plain."—*Jamieson.* *How*+A.S. *holh,* a hollow, an extended form from *hol,* a hole. *Caldron* is the equivalent of GAEL. *coire,* applied to a gorge or contracted glen. *See under* BALQUHIRRIE.

CALF KNEES (a hill of 1803 feet). 'Carsphairn.' Probably another form of "ness," a headland—A.S. *næs, nes*; 1. the ground; 2. a promontory or headland+ICEL. *nes*+DAN. *næs,* SWED. *näs.* "The sense of 'promontory' is due to some confusion with *nose,* but it is not quite certain that the two words are related."—*Skeat.* But *see under* GLOON.

CALGÒW (P. Koulgaw). 'Minigaff.' *Cuil gobha* [gow], the smith's corner, or *cul gobha,* the hill-back of the smith. The change from *u* sound to *a* is very unusual. Close by is Challoch, *i.e. tealach,* the forge. *See under* ALDERGOWAN.

CALHÀRNIE. 'Penninghame.'

CÀLLAN HILL. 'Balmaghie.' *Cuillean* [?] [cullan], holly. *See* COLLIN HILL.

CALLIEDÒWN. 'Kirkmaiden, s.c.'

CALLY (*Inq. ad Cap.* 1572, Calie *and* Caliegirtoun; *P.* Kelly; Charter 1418, ze Cale; *also written* Kalecht-Girthon *and* Kalacht). 'Girthon.' "*Cala, caladh,* a port, harbour, haven, ferry."—*O'Reilly,* who says Calais has this origin. "The word *caladh,* which in other parts of Ireland denotes a ferry or a landing-place for boats, is at present used in this district (Roscommon) to signify a low, flat district, extending along a lake or river, like the word *strath* in Ulster and Scotland."—*Hy Many,* p. 74, *note.* Either meaning suits the character of this place.

CALNAVÌE or CALNIVÀE. 'Penninghame.' *Coill, cuil,* or *cul na bheith* [vey], wood, corner, or hill-back of the birches.

CAMBRET HILL. 'Kirkmabreck.' *Ceann breac* [kenn brek], brindled or dappled hill. O. ERSE *cend,* W.B. and O.C. *pen,* C. *pedn*; ERSE and GAEL. *ceann,* a head, summit or point. *Cf.* CAMBRICK.

CÀMBRICK HILL (2250 feet). 'Minigaff.' *See under* CAMBRET.

CÀMELON LANE. 'Balmaghie.' *Cam linn,* crooked pool. *Cf.* CAMLING, LINCOM. Several small streams in Ireland are called Camling and Cameline. Cameline is a river in Antrim which runs through a glen called Crumlin. The latter is a common name in Ireland; in one instance, near Dublin, the *Four Masters* (A.D. 1595) write it Cruimghlinn [Crumhlinn], *i.e. crum ghleann*, crooked glen. *Crom* and *cam* are equivalent in meaning.

CÀMER [*pron.* Cammer]. 'Minigaff.' *Cf. Pont*: "Camyir-hill, a hill separating the shriffdome of Renfrew and the country of Cuninghame, wich should be callit Quamyir-hill."—*Cuninghame*, p. 111. *Cf.* BARHAMMER.

CÀMFORD (*Charter* 1578, Camquhart; *P*. Camfurr). 'Kirkinner.' *Ceann phort* [kenfort], chief residence, head fort. On this farm there is a hill formerly fortified. All traces of the fort have disappeared under the plough, save where a fence intersects the line of the ancient enclosure, but in an estate-map of 1777 there is given a rectangular camp marked "Roman camp," whereas a fort on the hill of Drumtrodden, not far distant, is given in the same map as circular, and marked "Brittish Camp" (*sic*). This *ceann phort*, then, may have been a Roman camp. Samian ware and bronze Roman vessels were found in 1863 and 1884 on the crannogs in the adjoining Loch of Dowalton; and the Roman camp at Rispain, near Whithorn, is distant about six miles. Cean-annus (now Kells) in Meath, was anglicised Headfort, on which the Irish gloss was Kenlis (*ceann lis*).

CAMLING (a pool in Pulmaddy Burn). 'Carsphairn.' *See under* CAMELON.

CAMPBELTON (*P*. Kammiltoun, and near it Balmackamil, which is the GAEL. equivalent, *i.e. baile mic Cathmail*). 'Twynholm.' Campbell's house.

CAMP DOUGLAS (*Inq. ad Cap.*, Camdudzeall, *vocatus* the Maynes of Balmaghie). 'Balmaghie.'

CAMRIE (*Inq. ad Cap.* 1633, Camary; *P*. Kamary). 'New Luce.' Probably *camrach*, crooked, winding, in allusion to the windings of the Luce, formed from *cam* as *claonrach* from *claon*. *See under* CLANERIE.

CANABONY.   'Kirkbean.'

CANÈERIE. 'Parton.' *Ceann iarach* or *iarthagh* [eeragh], western headland. *Cf.* Canearagh in Ireland. *See under* BLAWWEARIE and CAMBRET.

CANT. 'Kirkmaiden, s.c.' O. ERSE *cend* [?], a headland. *See under* CAMBRET.

CANTIN WIEL.   'Minigaff.'

CARDONÈSS (*Inq. ad Cap.* 1556, Cardeneis; *P.* Kardeness). 'Girthon.'

CÀPENOCH (*Inq. ad Cap.* 1572, Capanach; *P.* Keapanagh). 'Kirkinner.' *Joyce* (ii. 346) gives Coppanagh, a common name in Ulster, Connaught, and Leinster, as *copanach*, full of dockens, adj. form of *copachán, copán*; but the pronunciation here points rather to *ceapanach*, from *ceapa*, a stump, full of stumps, where timber has been felled (*see under* BALLOCHA-KIP), or to *ceapach* [cappagh], a garden plot, which enters into many Irish names.

CARDÒON. 'Kirkmabreck.' *Carr duin*, rock of the fort. "The word *carr*, though not found in the dictionaries, is understood in several parts of Ireland to mean a rock, and sometimes rocky land."—*Joyce*, i. 419. *See under* AUCHENCAIRN. Perhaps *ceathramhadh* [carhow] *duin*, land-quarter of the fort.

CARDÒRCAN (*P.* Garrowdorkan (on Pooldorken B.)). 'Minigaff.' *Ceathramhadh* [carrou], the land quarter. The meaning of *-dorcan* is obscure, perhaps a man's name. *See under* CARHOWE.

CARDRÀIN (*P.* Kardrain). 'Kirkmaiden.' This and the following name are those of places very near one another. Either would bear the interpretation of *ceathramhadh cathair* or *carr draighean* [drain], the land-quarter fort or rock of the blackthorns. *See under* DRANGAN.

CARDRỲNE (*Inq. ad Cap.* 1616, Cardryne; *P.* Kardryin). 'Kirkmaiden.' *See under* CARDRAIN.

CÀRGEN (*P.* Kargan). 'Loch Rutton.' *Carraican* or *Carraigan*, a little crag, or a rocky place, dim. of *carraic*. *Cf.* Cargan, Cargin, and Crarigeen, a common name in the north of Ireland, from the latter of which "Carrigeen moss," an edible seaweed, takes its name.

CARGHIDÒUN. 'Whithorn, s.c.' *Carraig a' duin*, crag of the fort, or *cairge duin*, the crags of the fort. *Carraig*, plur. *cairge*, in Mod. Gael. invariably means a sea-cliff or rock, as distinguished from *creig, creag*, an inland rock, and this distinction seems to be an old one. O. ERSE *carric*, a stone, ERSE *carraig* + W. *carrec* + C. *karak* + B. *karrek* — √CARR. *See under* AUCHENCAIRN.

CARGHISION.   'Whithorn.'

CARHOWE. 'Twynholm.' *Ceathramhadh* [carhow], a quarter, a division of land, "a plough-land" (*O'Reilly*), a fourth part of a *baile*. About thirty townlands in Ireland are called Carhoo, and over seven hundred Carrow (*Joyce*, i. 244). In Galloway local names it is generally worn down in composition to *Car-*, *Cur-*, or *Kerrie-*. O. ERSE *cethramad* (ERSE *ceathramhadh*, GAEL. *ceathramh*) + W. *pedwaredh*, C. *padzhwera*, a fourth part, derivatives of O. ERSE *cethir*, *cetheóir*, GAEL. *ceithir*, W. *pedwar*, C. *padzhar*, *pezwere*, B. *pevar*, *peder*, M. *kiare* + A.S. *feówer* (whence M.E. *feowur*, *fower*, *feour*, *four*, BR. SC. *four* [pron. *fow-er*], E. *four*), O. FRIES. *fiower*, *fiuwer*, *fior* + ICEL. *fjórir* + DAN. *fire* + SWED. *fyra* + DU. *vier* + GOTH. *fidwor* + O.H.G. *fior*, G. *vier* + LAT. *quatuor* + GK. τέτταρες, τέσσαρες (dialect πίσορες) + RUSS. *chetvero* + SKT. *chatvar*, *chatur*, all from an original form KWATWAR (*Skeat, s.v.* Four). *Mr. Ellwood* has collected a list of numerals in different dialects and languages, which *Mr. Lucas* quotes in his *Studies in Nidderdale*. It includes several curious forms of sheep-scoring numeration still in use in various districts. The numeral *four* appears in this list under the following forms besides those given above :—Hindustani, *char* ; Gipsy, *stor* ; Knaresborough, Yorkshire (sheep-scoring), *methera* ; Nidderdale, *peddero* ; Swaledale, *mether* ; Kirkby Stephen, Westmoreland, *maed'ere* ; Teesdale, *mether* ; Coniston, *medderte;* Borrowdale, *methera*; Millom, Cumberland, *peddera*; Eskdale, Cumberland, *meddera*; Wastdale Head, Cumberland, *anudder* ; Epping, Essex, *fethera* ; Maine, U.S., *fither* ; Hebron, Connecticut, *fedhur* ; Cincinnati, *feather*. The last three are from numeration used by Red Indians, originally taught them, no doubt, by earlier settlers.

CARLÀE (*P.* Korle).   'Dalry.

CÀRLETON (*Charter* 1250, Karlaton ; *W. P.* MSS. Cairiltoun ; *P.* Kairlton, Karltoun). 'Borgue,' 'Glasserton,' 'Kirkcolm.' A name which is of frequent occurrence throughout A.S. districts. Supposing it, in this case, to be A.S., the meaning would be *ceorla tún*, the enclosure or dwelling of the husbandmen (*cf.* Dindinnie), which is, in fact, the exact form of the name in the charter of 1295, Karlaton. From A.S. *ceorl* comes M.E. *cherl*, *cheorl*, E. *churl* + A.S. *carl*, a male + DAN. and SWED. *karl*, a man + ICEL. *karl*, a male, a man + BR. SC. *carle*, a fellow + O.H.G. *charal*, G. *karl*, a man. The proper name *Charles* (*Carolus*) is another form of TEUT. *carl*, *karl*, male.

CÀRLIN BED and HOUSE. 'Kirkmaiden, s.c.' Witch's bed and house. *See under* CARLIN'S CAIRN.

CÀRLINGWARK (*P.* Carlingworck, Carlingwoorck; *Bishop Pococke's Letters,* Caerlwark). 'Balmaghie.' A.S. *ceorla weorc,* the work (*opus*) of the countrymen, or men. *See under* CARLE-TON. A.S. *weorc, worc, werc* (whence M.E. *werk,* BR. SC. *wark,* E. *work*) + DU. *werk* + ICEL. *verk* + DAN. *værk* + SWED. *verk* + O.H.G. *werch,* G. *werk* + GK. ἔοργα, I have wrought; ZEND. *vareza,* a working + PERS. *warz-hâr,* a ploughman, a labourer — TEUT. base WARK — √WARG, to work.

CARLIN'S CAIRN (a hill 2650 feet) (*P.* Karlingkairn). 'Cars-phairn.' The old woman's cairn. Said to have been erected by a miller's wife, who gavé shelter to Robert the Bruce by hiding him among some sacks of meal while the soldiers of Baliol searched the premises. After his subsequent success the king granted the lands of Polmaddie to his preserver, who, in gratitude, is said to have erected this cairn.—(*Unique Traditions, chiefly of the West and South of Scotland,* by John Gordon Barbour, 1833.) " *Carlin, carling,* an old woman, a witch."—*Jamieson. See under* CRAIGENCALLIE.

CÀRLIN STONE. 'Mochrum.' Witches' stone. A monolith which until lately had a circle of stones round it. *See under* CARLIN'S CAIRN.

CARLOCHAN. 'Crossmichael.' *Carr, ceathramhadh* [carrow], or *cathair* [caer] *lochain,* the rock, land-quarter, or fort of the lakelet.

CARMÌNNOW (*Inq. ad Cap.* 1615, Kirremonnow; *P.* Karmunnow). 'Carsphairn.' *Ceathramhadh meadhonach* [minnough], the middle land-quarter. *Cf.* Carrowmenagh in Ireland. *See under* CARHOWE.

CARNÀVEL. 'Carsphairn.' *Ceathramhadh n-abhall* [?] [carrow naval], land-quarter of the apples. ERSE *abhall,* W. *afal* + LITH. *obolýs* + O. BULG. *jablŭko* + F. *apple. Cf.* Gartnavel in Lanarkshire, *i.e. gart n' abhall* [navall], the appleyard, orchard (GAEL. *abhallghart*). *Cf.* AIRIEWHILLART.

CARNÈLTOCH. 'Kells.' *Carr n' eilte,* rock of the hind. *Cf.* Curr-na-heillte near Burrishoole, Clonelty in Limerick and Ferma-nagh (*cluain eilte*), Rahelty in Kilkenny and Tipperary (*rath eilte*). ERSE *eilidh,* a hind, gen. *eilte* — O. ERSE *elit* (*ag allaid,* a stag—*Cormac*)+ ICEL. *elgr* (whence E. *elk*), SWED. *elg,* an elk + O.H.G. *elaho,* M.H.G. *elch* + RUSS. *oléne,* a stag + DU. *eland,* an elk + LAT. *alces* + GK. ἄλκη. Perhaps *carn ealtaidhe* [eltahy], white cairn. " *Ealtaidhe,* white."—*O'Reilly.*

CARNÌNE.   'Minigaff.'

CARRICKABÒYS. 'Whithorn, s.c.' *Carraicán buidhe* [buie], yellow crag. *See under* CARGEN and BENBUIE. *Cf.* CRAIGENBOY, CRAIGENBUY, CRAIGENBUYS.

CARRICKADÒYN. 'Kirkcolm, s.c.' *See under* CARGHIDOUN.

CARRICKAFLIÒU. 'Kirkmaiden, s.c.' *Carraicán fluich*, wet crag. O. ERSE *fluich*, GAEL. *fliuiche*, wet + LAT. *fluxus* (whence, through F. *flux*, E. *flush*) + GK. φλύειν, to overflow + SKT. *pluta*, wet. But *cf.* Carrigafly near Cork, which *Joyce* (ii. 79) interprets *carraig a' phlaigh*, the crag of the plague; *plaigh* — LAT. *plaga* + GK. πληγή, a blow, a plague.

CARRICKAHÀWKIE. 'Kirkmaiden, s.c.'

CARRICKALÌG. 'Stoneykirk, s.c.' *Carraic a' lige*, crag of the flat stone. *See under* AUCHENLECK.

CARRICKAMÌCKIE. 'Kirkmaiden, s.c.'

CARRICKAMÙRLAN. 'Kirkmaiden, s.c.' (*twice*). *Carraic a' murlain*, crag of the rough top. "*Murlán*, a rough top or head."— *O'Reilly. Cf.* MURLIN STRAND and KNOCKMORLAND.

CARRICK BURN. 'New Luce.' Divides Ayrshire (Carrick) from Wigtonshire.

CARRICKCÀMRIE. 'Kirkmaiden, s.c.' *Carraic am-reidh* [amrey], rugged crag. O. ERSE *am-reid* ("*bid reid riam cach n-amreid*," "everything unsmooth shall be smooth before him," *Goid.*, p. 56), ERSE *aimhreidh* — *am*, a negative prefix, and *reidh* [ray], smooth. *Cf.* CROFTANGRY, TYDAVERYS.

CARRICKCÀRLIN. 'Kirkmaiden, s.c.'

CARRICKCÒIL. 'Kirkmaiden, s.c.'

CARRICKCÒNE. 'Kirkmaiden, s.c.' *Carraic con*, craig of the dog.

CARRICKCÒRIE. 'Kirkmaiden, s.c.' *Carraic caithre* [?] [caarie], crag of the fort, gen. of *cathair*.

CARRICKCÒW. 'Kirkcolm, s.c.' *Carraic dhubh* [oo, ow], black crag. *Cf.* CRAIGDHU.

CARRICKCÙNDIE. 'Kirkmaiden, s.c.'

CARRICKÈE. 'Kirkmaiden, s.c.' *Carraic fhiadh* [?] [ee], crag of the deer.

CARRICKFÙNDLE. 'Kirkcolm, s.c.'

CARRICKGÌLL. 'Kirkmaiden.' *Carraic geal* [?] [gal], white crag. O. ERSE *gel*.

CARRICKGLÀSSEN. 'Stoneykirk.' *Carraic glasain* [?], crag of the sea-weed. "*Glasán*, salad, a sort of edible sea-wrack."—

O'Reilly. Not, as might be supposed, from *glasin*, a streamlet, as there is no stream here.

CARRICK KÌBBERTIE. 'Kirkmaiden, s.c.' *Carraic thiprat* [iprat], crag of the well, irregular gen. of *tipra*, one of the many forms of *tobar*, a well. *See under* TIBBERT.

CÀRRICK POINT. 'Girthon, s.c.' *Carraic*, a crag. *See under* CARGHIDOUN.

CARROCH LANE. 'Dalry.' *Carroch*, rough, rocky, applied to the land through which the "lane" or stream runs, and whence it takes its name.

CARRÒUCH (*P.* Kerroch), [*pron.* Cărrūghe]. 'Girthon.' Probably *ceathramhadh* [carhow, carrow], a quarter-land. *See under* CARHOWE.

CARRÙCHAN. 'Terregles.' *Ceathramhadh ruadhán*[?] [carhoo roohan], red land-quarter. Situated on the new red sandstone, which here lies unconformably on the grey Silurian rock composing most of Galloway, and gives the land a red hue.

CARSE (*P.* Kars). 'Kirkcudbright.' Meadowland. "*Carse, kerss*, low and fertile land, generally that which is adjacent to a river. SU. G. *kaerr*, ISL. *kiar*, *kaer*, a marsh."—*Jamieson.* A word in common use in BR. SC. *Carse land*, alluvial land. It appears in place-names as a prefix with GAEL. qualitative, *e.g.* Carseglass, etc., and seems to have been early adopted into GAEL. speech as well as into BR. SC.

CARSCRÈUGH (*Charter* 1563, Carscrue, Cascrv ; *P.* Karskeroch). 'Old Luce.'

CARSDÙCHAN (*Inq. ad Cap.* 1582, Carsdowgan ; *P.* Karssduchan ; *Charter* 1513, Corsidochquhan). 'Minigaff.'

CARSE DUNCAN. 'Minigaff.' Duncan's Carse.

CARSEGLÀSS. 'Dalry.' *Carse glas*, green carse. *See under* BARGLASS and CARSE.

CARSEGÒWAN. 'New Abbey.' *Carse gobhain* [gowen], the smith's carse. *See under* ALDERGOWAN.

CARSEGÒWN. 'Kells,' 'Wigton.' *See under* CARSEGOWAN.

CARSEMÌNNOCH (*P.* Carshmeanach). 'Minigaff.' *Carse meadhonach* [minnagh], middle carse. *See under* BALMINNOCH.

CARSENÈSTOCK (*P.* Carsnestak). 'Penninghame.' *Cf.* PORT NESSOCK, which *Pont* writes Port Nustak.

CARSERÌGGAN (*P.* Casriggen).   'Penninghame.'

CARSETHÒRN.   'Kirkbean.'

CARSEVÈIGE.   'Minigaff.'

CARSEWÀLLOCH (*P.* Karskullagach). 'Kirkmabreck.' *Pont's* spelling points to a *g* or *qu* sound softened into *w.*

CARSFAD (*P.* Karsfod). 'Dalry,' 'Kells.' *Carse fada,* long or far carse. *Cf.* CARSWADA.

CARSINDÀRROCH. 'Minigaff.' *Carse an daraich,* carse of the oak tree. *See under* ARNDARROCH.

CARSKÈEL. 'Kirkmabreck.' *Carse caol* [keel], narrow carse. *Cael, caol,* narrow ; W. *cul. Cf.* DRUMKEEL, PORT KALE ; also Glenkeel in Fermanagh, Cork, and Leitrim, and many places in Ireland called Keal, Keale, and Keel.

CARSNAW. 'Minigaff.' *Carse an atha* [*aha, aa*], carse of the ford. There is here a ford on the tidal channel of the Cree. ERSE and GAEL. *áth,* gen. *atha*+W. *bais*+ICEL. *vað,* a ford, *vada,* to wade+G. *wat,* a ford+LAT. *uadum* (*vadum*)+SWED. *vada*+ O.H.G. *uatan*+A.S. *wadan* (pt. t. *wód*) to wade (whence M.E. *waden,* E. *wade,* BR. SC. *wad,* to wade)+SKT. *gádham,* to move forward, *gádha,* shallow, a place where a footing may be obtained, probably from a base GADH, an extension of √GA, to go. (See *Skeat, s.v.* Wade.) *Cf.* CRAIGNAW, LOCHNAW, KNOCKNAW ; and, in Ireland, Drumaa in Fermanagh.

CARSLÙITH (*P.* Karsluyith). 'Kirkmabreck.'

CARSNABRÒCK. 'Minigaff.' *Carse na broc,* carse of the badgers ; a meadow beside the river Minnick. *See under* BROCKLACH.

CARSPILÀIRN (a village and parish in the Stewartry). 'Carsphairn.' *Carse fearn* [farn], carse of the alders. *Cf.* Elder Holm in Dalry (the next adjacent parish), which should be Alder Holm, the BR. SC. for "elder" being *bourtree. See under* BALFERN.

CARSWÀDA. 'Loch Rutton.' *Carse fhada. See under* CARSEFAD.

CARTY. 'Penninghame.' *Cearda* [carda], a workshop. *See under* CAIRDIE WIEL.

CASH BAG. 'Kirkmaiden, s.c.' *Còs beag,* little hole or fissure. "*Còs,* a fissure."—*O'Reilly.* GAEL. "*Cos,* a crevice, a hole." —*Macalpine.*

CÀSPIN. 'Kirkcolm, s.c.' *Cf.* HESPIN, also on the sea-coast.

CASSALANDS. 'Troqueer.'

CASSENCÀRIE (*P.* Kassinkary). 'Kirkmabreck.' *Casan caora,* footpath of the sheep, or *casan caithre* [caarie], footpath of the fort, gen. of *cathair. See under* AIRYILASSAN.

CASSENGÌLSHIE. 'Wigton.' *Casan giolchach* [gilhyagh], rushy, reedy footpath. *See under* AIRIECHASSAN and AUCHENGILSHIE.

CASSENVÈY (*P.* Cassinbe ; MS. 1527, Cassinvey). 'Balmaclellan.' *Casan bheithe*, footpath of the birch tree. *See under* AIRIE-HASSAN and AUCHENVEY.

CASTLE BAN. 'Kirkcolm.' *Caiseal* [cashel] *bán*, white fort, or perhaps Bann's fort. *Cf.* Castlebane and Castlebawn in Ireland.

CASTLE CRÈAVIE. 'Rerwick.' *Caiseal craebhe* [creevy], castle of the tree, or *caiseal craebhach* [cashel creevagh], castle of the wooded place. *Craebhach*, adjective from *craebh*, a branch, a tree, a bush. "There are more than thirty townlands called Creevagh, *i.e.* branchy or bushy land (in Ireland)."—*Joyce*, i. 501. *Cf.* KNOCKCRAVIE, CORNCRAVIE ; also Moheracreevy in Leitrim (*mothar na craebhe*, fort of the tree).

CASTLE DAFFIN.   'Rerwick.'

CASTLE DOUGLAS. 'Balmaghie.' A modern name given to Carlingwark by one Douglas who built mills here.

CASTLE FEATHER. 'Whithorn.' *Caiseal Pheaduir* [feddur], Peter's castle. *Cf.* KILFEATHER.

CASTLE FERN (*P.* Castell Fairne). 'Dalry.' *Caiseal fearn*, castle of the alder trees. *See under* BALFERN.

CASTLE GOWER (MS. 1640, Cassilgour). 'Buittle.' *Caiseal gobhar*, castle of the goats.

CASTLE LÀRICK. 'Inch.' *Larach*, a dwelling-place, a site. *See under* LARROCH. Close by is Tripolarick.

CASTLEMÀDDIE (*P.* Castle maddyes ; MS. 1527, Castlemady). 'Carsphairn.' *Caiseal madadh* [madda], castle of the dogs. *See under* BLAIRMODDIE.

CASTLEMÀNOCH. 'Kelton.' *Caiseal manach*, castle of the monks. *See under* ARNMANNOCH.

CASTLE MUIR.   'Rerwick.'

CASTLE NAUGHT (*gutt.*). 'Stoneykirk, s.c.' *Caiseal nochd* [?], naked, bare, exposed castle ; O. ERSE *nocht*, ERSE *nochd* (*O'Reilly*), naked, GAEL. *nochta*+W. *noeth*, B. *nôaz*, C. *noath*+A.S. *nacod*, naked + O.F. *nakad*, *naken* + DU. *naakt* + ICEL. *naktr*, *nakinn*+DAN. *nögen*+SWED. *naken*+G. *nackt*, M.H.G. *nacket*, O.H.G. *nachot*+GOTH. *nakwatus*+RUSS. *nagoi*+LITH. *nugas*+ LAT. *nudus* (*nugdus*, *nogdus*, *nagdus*)+SKT. *nagna*, all with the meaning "naked, stripped." (See *Skeat*, *s.v.* Naked.) *Cf.* BARNEIGHT, AUCHENEIGHT.

CASTLE SHELL.   'Inch.'

CASTLE SOD.   'Twynholm.'

CASTLE WEARY. 'Old Luce.' *Caiseal iarach* [eeragh], western castle. *See under* BLAWWEARY.

CASTRÀMONT, DOUN OF (*Inq. ad Cap.* 1610, Castraman; *P.* Karstromen; *War Committee*, 1646, Carstraman). 'Girthon.'

CATEBRÀID. 'Port Patrick, s. c.' *Cat braghad* [?] [brahad], the gully (lit. the throat) of the wild-cats. *See under* ALWHAT and BRADOCK. Although the qualitative noun rarely comes first, still it seems to do so in this and the two following instances, as it does in AUCHNESS, *q.v.*

CATELIG. 'Port Patrick, s. c.' *Cat liag* [leeg], the stone of the wild-cats. *See under* CATEBRAID and AIRIELICK.

CATEVÈNNAN. 'Port Patrick, s. c.' *Cat bhennan* [vennan], the hillock of the wild-cats. *See under* BENNAN and CATEBRAID.

CATOAK or COTTACH. 'Troqueer.' Possibly from W. *coed*, a wood.

CÀUCHIE STONE. 'Kirkmaiden, s. c.' ·

CAUGH MOSS. 'Girthon.'

CAULDSIDE. 'Whithorn.' Cold side or place; probably referring to the soil. It is a wonder that the Ordnance Surveyors have not Anglicised this name, as they have Brigg-end into Bridge-end, Alt Water into Old Water, etc. Old Northumbrian *cald =* A.S. *ceald* + ICEL. *kaldr* + DU. *koud* + GOTH. *kalds* + G. *kalt* + LAT. *gelidus.*

CAULKERBUSH. 'Colvend.'

CAUSEWAYEND [*pron.* Causènd], (*P.* Causayend). 'Balmaghie,' 'Penninghame.' End of the causeway. *See under* AIRIE-HASSAN.

CÀVAN. 'Kells.' *Cabhán* [cavvan], "a hollow plain, a field."— *O'Reilly.* Like other names for hollows this is often transferred to the hill beside the hollow. Thus O'Donnell, in his *Life of St. Columba*, translates it *collis. Cf.* Cavan, which occurs about twenty times in Ireland. *See also* KEVANDS, COLVEND, KEVAN BRAES, etc.

CÀVENS (*P.* Kovenns). 'Kirkbean.' *See under* CAVAN.

CAVE ÒCHTREE. 'Leswalt.' *Uchtraidh* [Ughtrie], Uchtred's cave; the GAEL. construction, with the qualitative last.

CAWN LANE. 'Glasserton.'

CAWVIS HILL. 'Wigton.' Calves' hill. BR. SC. *cauf*, a calf, pl. *cawvies.*

H

CHÀLLOCH (*P.* Chellach). *Teallach* [tyallagh], "a hearth" (*O'Reilly*).
   GAEL. "*Teallach*, a smith's fire-place or forge, a hearth or
   fireplace. Occurs without adjunct as a place-name about a
   dozen times in Wigtonshire, and once at least in the
   Stewartry. In Galloway it may be assumed to mean 'a
   forge,' though not used in that sense in Ireland, where
   teallach means 'a tribe, a family.'"—*O'Reilly.* *T,* followed
   by a diphthong, is weakened nearly to E. *ch.* A similar change
   of sound may be observed in *nation, action,* etc. *See under*
   AUCHENGIBBERT. Mr. Skene writes :—"There is a great
   hill in Wester Ross called the Challoch, as the word is there
   pronounced, and the popular meaning in the district is the
   Furnace Hill, which the people as frequently call it."

CHALLOCHBLÈWN (*P.* Chellachblawis ; *W. P.* MSS. Challochbhel-
   lin). 'Glasserton.'

CHALLOCHGLASS [*pron.* Chillàss], (*P.* Shellachglass). 'Mochrum.'
   Tealach glas, green forge (hill). The hill seems to have
   derived its name Challoch from the forge, and subsequently
   to have received the qualitative suffix which applies to the
   hill and not to the forge. Had the old spelling not survived
   the change in pronunciation, the etymology of Challochglass,
   as now pronounced, might have been sought in vain.

CHALLOCHMÙNN (*P.* Challachmun). 'Old Luce.' *Tulach* [tyallagh],
   Munna [?]. Munna's hill. *Cf.* Kilmun in Argyllshire,
   Munna's (or Fintan's) church, Taghmon in Wexford (*teach
   Munna*), Munna's house. *See under* KNOCKIEFOUNTAIN.

CHANG (*Inq. ad Cap.* 1636, Schaing ; *P.* Chang). 'Mochrum.'
   Teanga [tyanga], a tongue or strip of land. For change of *t*
   to *ch, cf.* CHALLOCH and CHIPPERFINIAN. O. ERSE *tenge,*
   ERSE and GAEL. *teanga* + GOTH. *tuggo* (=*tungo*) + O.H.G.
   zunga, G. *zunge* + DAN. *tunge* + ICEL. and SWED. *tunga* + DU.
   tong + A.S. *tunge* (whence M.E. *tunge, tonge,* E. *tongue*) + O. LAT.
   dingua, LAT. *lingua,* FR. *langue.* *Cf.,* however, ICEL. *tangi,* a
   spit or projection of land, which has a different origin from
   ERSE *teanga,* being allied to E. *tangi* and *tongs.* (See *Skeat* on
   these words.) The form as well as the sense of these words
   run together. Thus in the *Prompt. Parv.* we read, " *Tongge* of
   a bee, *Aculeus ; Tongge* of a knife, *Pirasmus.*"

CHAPEL FINIAN. 'Mochrum.' *See* CHIPPERFINIAN.

CHAPELÈRNE. 'Crossmichael.' Perhaps a dedication to St. Ernan,
   one of St. Columcille's twelve companions in his mission to
   Alban. *Cf.* Killearn in Stirlingshire, and Killearn or Kiler-

nadale, formerly a parish in Jura. On the other hand, the name may be A.S., signifying the *ærn*, place or dwelling of the chapel.

CHAPELHERON. 'Whithorn.' *See* CHIPPERHERON.

CHAPELRÒSSAN. 'Kirkmaiden, s. c.' *Caipeal rosain*, chapel of the promontory. GAEL. *caipeal* (Reeves's *Adamnan*, 426) – L. LAT. *capella* (whence O.F. *chapelle*, E. *chapel*). The word took its origin from the shrine wherein was preserved the *cappa* or cope of St. Martin (*Skeat, s.v.* Chapel). It is one of the words introduced into Erse speech with Christianity. That this is an old word, and not merely E. *chapel* prefixed to Rossan, the name of the promontory, seems to be shown by the name of the adjacent hill, Knocktaggart, the priest's hill. *Rosán*, dim. of *ros, see under* ROSS. *Cf.* Ardrossan in Ayrshire, "so named," says *Pont*, "in respecte it is situated on a suelling knope of a rock runing frome a toung of land advancing from ye maine land in ye sea, and almost environed vith ye same, for Ross in ye ancient Brittich tounge signifies a Biland or peninsula."—*Cuninghame*, p. 56.

CHÀPMAN. 'Kirkinner.' *See under* CHAPMANLEYS.

CHAPMANLEYS. 'Troqueer.' The merchant's fields. A.S. *ceáp-man* (*cf.* ICEL. *kaupmaðr*, G. *kaufmann*, a merchant), whence M.E. and E. *chapman* (of which E. *chap*, a fellow, is a familiar abbreviation)—A.S. *ceáp*, price, sale, bargain, business (*Bosworth*), whence M.E. *chep, cheap, cheep* (subst.), barter, price, becoming in modern E. an adjective, *cheap*+DU. *koop*, a purchase+ICEL. *kaup*, a bargain+SWED. *köp*, price, purchase+DAN. *kiöb*, purchase+GOTH. *kaupon*, to traffic+O.H.G. *coufón*, G. *kaufen, kauf*, to buy, a purchase. "*B. Curtius* (i. 174) affirms that all these words, however widely spread in Teutonic tongues, must be borrowed from Latin. Indeed we find O.H.G. *choufo*, a huckster, which is merely LAT. *caupo*. The further related words are *capa*, a barmaid, *caupona*, an inn; GK. κάπηλος, a pedlar; RUSS. *kupite*, to buy." (*Skeat, s.v.* Cheap). A.S. *leáh, leá*, a field, a place. *See under* BRANDEDLEYS.

CHÀPMANTON (*P.* Chapmantoun). 'Crossmichael.' The merchant's house. *See under* CHAPMANLEYS and BALDOON.

CHERRY CRAIG.   'Dalry.'

CHILCÀRROCH (*P.* Chalkarroch).   'Mochrum.'

CHÌNCOUGH WELL. 'Glasserton.' Whooping-cough well. A spring in the rocks just above high-water mark at Kirkmaiden in Glasserton (*see under* KIRKMAIDEN), the water of which is said to be a remedy for whooping-cough. BR. SC. *kink-cough* or *kink-hoast.* "*To kink,* to labour for breath in a severe fit of coughing."—*Jamieson.* "*Kink* is a nasalised form of a root *kik,* to choke" (*Skeat*)+DU. *kinkhoest,* O. DU. *kiechhoest*+SWED. *kikhosta,* whooping-cough, *kikna,* to gasp, to become choked+DAN. *kighoste,* whooping-cough+G. *keichen,* to pant+E. *chincough.* *Choke* is another form of the root KIK, which is imitative.

CHIPPERDÌNGAN WELL. 'Kirkmaiden.' *Tiobar Dingain,* Dingan's or Ninian's well. *See under* TIBBERT. The form "Dingan," as well as "Ninan," occurs in Geoffrey Gaimar's *Estorie des Engles,* written about the middle of the twelfth century, line 967 :—

> "Ninan aveit ainz baptizé
> Les altres Pictes del regné :
> Ce sunt les Westmaringiens
> Ki donc esteient Pictiens.
> A Witernen gist Saint Dinan
> Long tens vint devant Columban."

The change of *t* to *ch* and *k* in this word *tiobar* is a common one. *See under* CHALLOCH and KIBBERTIE KITE WELL.

CHIPPERFÌNIAN (*P.* Chappel finian). 'Mochrum.' *Tiobar Finnain,* (St.) Finnan's well. There is a ruined chapel here. St. Finnan was elected Bishop of Lindisfarne in A.D. 652.

CHIPPERHÈRON or CHAPELHÈRON (*Inq. ad Cap.* 1600, Tibertquharaine ; *W. P.* MSS. Schippirquharraine). 'Whithorn.' *Tiobar Chiarain* [heeran], St. Kieran's or Ciaran's well. There are several individuals called *Ciarán* in the Irish hagiology and hierarchy. The most celebrated of these, founder of Clonmacnoise, died A.D. 548 ; but miracles were imputed to him as late as 1018. See *Four Masters* under that year : "*Scrín Ciardin do orgain do Domhnall mac Taidhg, agus a marbhadh fein a cceand seachtmhaine tria fiortaibh Dé agus Ciardin,*" *i.e.* "The shrine of Ciaran was plundered by Domhnall, son of Tadhg, and he himself was killed at the end of a week, through the miracles of God and Ciaran." The following places, among others, are also dedicated to St. Ciaran (whose name is rendered in Latin *Queranus* or *Kyranus,* and in Cornish *Piran*)—Kilkerran in Kintyre, Kilkerran and Dalquharran in Ayrshire, Kilcheran or Kilkeran in Islay, and St. Kieran's well in Glenbervie. *Ciarán* (from *ciar,* black) means the dark man.

CHIPPERKÝLE. 'Kirkpatrick Durham.' *Tiobar.*

CHIPPERMÒRE (*P.* Chippertmoir). 'Mochrum.' *Tiobar mór*, the great well. Probably the land got the name Tipper or Chipper from Chipperfinian (which is on this farm), and *mór* was added subsequently as a distinctive name of part of the land.

CLÀCHAN. *Clachan,* stones. A word of very frequent occurrence and of varying meaning. Generally it means a hamlet, from the stone foundations of circular huts or wigwams in prehistoric times, or, later, from the *stones* of which walls were built ; but it also is used to designate a church or churchyard. Pagan places of worship (*see under* CLACHANARRIE) consisting of monoliths, either solitary or in groups or circles, were adopted by Christian missionaries as sites for churches and cells, hence *clachan*, the stones, became synonymous for the church or churchyard. O. ERSE and ERSE *cloch*, GAEL. *clach.* The name is common in Ireland as Cloghan, Cloghane, and Cloghaun.

CLACHANAMÙCK. 'Kirkinner.' *Clachan na muc,* the swine's stones.

CLACHANÀRRIE. 'Mochrum.' *Clachan aoraidh* [aray], stones of worship. In Perthshire, on Findowie Hill, Strathbraan, there is a circle of stones called *Clachan Aoradh,* or the worshipping stones (*Proc. Soc. Ant. Scot.* 1884-5, p. 42).

CLACHANÈASY. 'Penninghame.' *Clachan Iosa* [?] [eesa], the hamlet of Jesus. A hamlet near St. Ninian's chapel of the Cruives. *See under* ALLANEASY.

CLACHANHÈAD. 'New Abbey.' Head of the clachan or hamlet.

CLACHANLÀUKES.   'Whithorn.'

CLACHANMÒRE. 'Stoneykirk.' *Clachan mór,* the great stones, or big village. There is no village here now.

CLACHANPLÙCK. 'Inch.' Lauriston, in Girthon parish, formerly bore this name also.

CLACHRÀWER. 'Dalry.' *Cf.* STRANRAER.

CLÀCHRUM (*P.* Clachrum). 'Kells,' 'Penninghame.' *Clacherin,* a stony place, deriv. of *clach.* *Cf.* CLAUCHTREM, and, in Ireland, Cloghereen near Killarney.

CLACK HILL. 'Balmaghie.' *Clach,* a stone. *Cf.* TOOMCLACK HILL.

CLÀUCHRIE (*Inq. ad Cap.* 1599, Clauchreid ; *P.* Clachory, Clachary, and Clachred). 'Kirkinner,' 'Minigaff,' 'Wigton.' *Clach-*

arach or *cloichreach*, a stony place.   *See under* CLACHRUM.
Cf. Cloghera in Clare and Kerry.

CLÀUCHTREM.   'Carsphairn.'   *See under* CLACHRUM.

CLÀWBELLY (*P.* Clabelly).   'Kirkgunzeon.'   *Clach baile* [claw bally], stone town, enclosure, or house.   *Cf.* Cloghbally and Cloghvalley, frequent names of Irish townlands.

CLADDIOCHDÒW.   'Kirkcolm, s. c.'   *Claddach dubh* [doo], black beach. *Claddach* is still in use in the speech of the country folk in its original sense of a stony or shingly beach.   "*Cladach*, a flat, stony shore."—*O'Don.*, Appendix to *O'Reilly*.   *Cf.* CLADY HOUSE, and, in Ireland, Clady in Tyrone, Antrim, and Armagh ; Clydagh, Cloydach, Clodagh, Cleedach, Clodragh, Cleady, Clodiagh, Clyda, all forms of the same word ; also Claddagh, a river running into Loch Erne, and Claddagh, part of the town of Galway.   Clady in Tyrone is written Claideach by the *Four Masters*.   "*Clidyoch, Clydyoch*, the gravel bed of a river, Dumfr."—*Jamieson*.

CLADY HOUSE.   'Inch.'   The beach house.   A house on the shore of Loch Ryan.   *See under* CLADDIOCHDOW.

CLAFÀRAS.   'Penninghame.'   *Clach farraich* [?], the stone of meeting.   *See under* BORGAN FERRACH.

CLAINGE (*P.* Kloyintz).   'Kirkmabreck.'   *See under* CLAUNCH. *Pont* writes it very nearly according to the old pronunciation.

CLAIRBRAND (*Inq. ad Cap.* 1628, Clairbrand ; *P.* Clarckbraind). 'Crossmichael.'

CLAMDALLY.   'Rerwick.'   *Claon dealg*, the slope of the thorny thicket.   *Claon* (adj.), sloping ; *see under* CLENE.   For the change of *n* to *m* in this word see *Pont's* spelling of Clannoch, Klemmeock.   *Dealg* (O. ERSE *delg*) occurs in Irish names, as Moneydollog in Antrim (*muine dealg*), Kildellig in Queen's County.   Delliga in Cork is given by the *Four Masters* (A.D. 1580) as *Deilge*, the plur. of *dealg*.   *Cf.* DALLY, DAILLY, DRUMDALLY.

CLAMDISH.   'Parton.'   *Claon dess*, southern slope.   O. ERSE *dess*, the right hand, or south.

CLÀNERIE (*P.* Cloynary).   'Kirkmabreck.'   *Claonrach*, sloping. *Cf.* CLENARIE, CLENDRIE, forms of the same word.   Cleenrah in Longford and Cleenrath in Cork are referred (*Joyce*, ii. 422) to *claen rath* [cleen raw], sloping fort.   "*Is aire is claen an lis*," this is why the fort slopes (*Cormac*).   *See under* CLAMDALLY.

CLANGHIE POINT [*pron.* Clanzie]. 'Kirkmaiden, s. c.' *Claona*, the slopes. *Cf.* Cleeny, near Killarney.

CLANNOCH (*P.* Klemmeock). 'Minigaff.' *Claonach*, sloping. *Cf.* CLENNOCH, and, in Ireland, Clenagh and Cleenagh in Donegal, Fermanagh, and Clare.

CLANTIBÙIES (*Inq. ad Cap.* 1582, Clontagboy.) 'Kirkinner.' *Cluainte buidhe* [cloonty buie], yellow meadows. Plur. of *cluain* (*see under* CLONE), E. plur. added. *Cf.* Cloontabonniv, Cloontakillow, Cloonboy, Clonboy, etc., in Ireland. *See under* BENBUIE and CLONE.

CLÀNYARD (*P.* Cloynard, Kloynard; *Inq. ad Cap.* 1610, Cloinzeard). 'Kirkmaiden.' *Cluain ard*, high meadow, or *claonárd*, "an inclining steep" (*O'Reilly*). *Cf.* Clonyard. In Ireland the name occurs several times as Clonard, Cloonard. *See under* AIRD, CLAMDALLY, and CLONE.

CLARE HILL. 'Kirkcowan.' *Clár*, a level place, a plain (lit. a table or board), a name transferred from the level ground to the hill. "The county of Clare was so called from a village of the same name; and the tradition of the people is that it was called Clare from a board formerly placed across the river Fergus to serve as a bridge."—*Joyce*, i. 428. This village, however, is called *Clár-mór* by the *Four Masters*, which looks rather as if it took its name from flat land. Clarehill in Derry and Clarkill in Armagh, Down, and Tipperary are corruptions of *clár choill* [hill], level wood.

CLÀRY (*P.* Clary), anciently the Bishop of Galloway's palace. 'Penninghame.' *Clerech*, a clerk or priest (*clericus*). *See under* BARNYCLEARY.

CLÀRY PARK (a field on the farm of Prestrie, *i.e.* Priest-ery). 'Whithorn.' *See under* CLARY.

CLASH. 'Borgue,' 'Kirkmaiden,' 'Leswalt.' *Clais* [clash], a trench, ditch, or pit; a cleft in a hill. The name of many townlands in Ireland. "*Clash, claisch*, a cavity of considerable extent in the acclivity of a hill."—*Jamieson*.

CLASHBRÒCK. 'Carsphairn.' *Clais* [clash] *broc*, the badger's pit or den. *Cf.* Clashnamrock [*clais-nambroc*] near Lismore. *See under* BROCKLACH and CLASH.

CLASHDÀN.   'Minigaff.'

CLASHDÒOKIE.   'Minigaff.'

CLASH HILL. 'Kirkmaiden.' *See under* CLASH.

CLASHMAHÈW. 'Inch.' *Cf.* Kilmahew in Argyllshire.

CLASHMÙRRAY. 'Kirkcolm.' *Clais Muireadhaich* [clash Murragh], Murray's or Murphy's trench or grave. *See under* BAL-MURRIE.

CLASHNÀRROCH.   'Leswalt.'

CLASHNEÀCH, NICK OF. 'Minigaff.' *Clais n-ech*, the trench or cleft of the horses. *Clais* and *Nick* here express the same idea, *i.e.* a cleft in the hill. *See under* AUCHNESS.

CLASHWHÀNNON WELL.   'Kirkmaiden.'

CLASH WOOD. 'Kirkmabreck.' *See under* CLASH.

CLATTERINSHÀWS (*P.* Clattranshawes). 'Kells.' The echoing 'shaws' or woods. A.S. *clatrung*, anything that makes a clatter-ing, a drum, a rattle, *cleadur*, a rattle. *See under* SHAW BRAE.

CLÀUCHAN. 'Girthon.' *See under* CLACHAN.

CLÀUCHANDÒLLY. 'Borgue.' *Clachan dealg* [dallig], stones or houses of the thorns. *Cf.* AUCHENDOLLY, CLAMDALLY.

CLÀUCHAN WELL (beside the ruins of Kirkchrist). 'Old Luce.' Clauchan here bears the meaning of a church, *i.e. clachan*, the stones; the memorial or pagan worshipping stones (*see under* CLACHANARRIE), on the site of which the Christian churches were often erected.

CLAUCHLÒUDOUN.   'Kirkmabreck.'

CLAUNCH (*Inq. ad Cap.* 1631, Clonsche; *P.* Cloyinsh; *W. P.* MSS. Clonche). 'Sorbie.' *Cladh innse* [claw inshe], bank or ditch of the river-meadow. *Cf.* CLAINGE, also Clawinch, an island in Loch Ree, Ireland, where *innis* bears the alternative mean-ing of "island."

CLAYCRÒFT. 'Buittle,' 'Minigaff.' The croft or small farm of clay land. *Croft* — A.S. *croft*, a field + DU. *kroft*, a hillock, O. DU. *krochte, crocht*, a field on the downs, high, dry land + GAEL. *croit*, a hillock, a croft, whence the guttural (which is pre-served in *cruach*, a hill) has disappeared. *Skeat* suggests that *croft* may have come from ERSE *cruachd* before the disappearance of the guttural. Not akin to *crypt*—as some philologers have suggested—from being *shut in*, for crofts are not fenced like farms, at least in their primitive condition, but cattle, etc., are herded off them. Before the adoption of draining, the *croit, cruach*, hillock, being naturally drained, was the only part of the land that would bear a crop.

CLAYCRÒP. 'Kirkinner.' *See under* CLAYCROFT.

CLAYGRÀNE. 'Carsphairn.' *Cladh greane* [claw graney], the mound or ditch of the gravel, or possibly in the sense of a grave, *cladh greine*, Grian's grave (*see under* CAIRN-NA-GREEN). *Grean*, gravel + B. *grouan* + C. *grow*, gravel + W. *gro* + SKT. *grávan*, a stone, a rock. Not, as suggested by some, connected with LAT. *granum*, which is from √GAR, to grind.

CLAYGÙGAN. 'New Luce.' Cladh *Geoghagain* or *Eochagain* [?], Geachan's grave.

CLAYHILTS. 'Balmaclellan.'

CLAYMÒDDIE (*P.* Clymady; *W. P.* MSS. Glenmaddie). 'Glasserton.' *Cladh madadh* [claw maddie], the mound of the dogs; but the name as it appears in the Whithorn Priory rental points to *gleann madadh*, the dog's glen. *Cf.* Glennamaddy in Galway.

CLAYSHÀNT (formerly a parish), (*P.* Klachshant). 'Stoneykirk.' *C ach séant* [shant], holy stone — LAT. *sanctus*, O. ERSE *sanct*.

> "Ni bu *Sanct* Brigit suanach."
> *Broccan's Hymn*, line 21.

and

> "Ateoch érlam *Sanct* Brigte
> Co *sanctaib* Cille dara."—*Ibid.*, line 95.

CLAYSHÈEN. 'Inch.' *Cladh sidheain* [claw shean], mound of the fairies' house (*cf.* FAIRY KNOWE); or perhaps from *sian* [sheen], foxglove (called also in E. fairy-finger, fairy-thimble).

CLAYS OF CHANG (the site of an ancient village). 'Minigaff.' *Clays* [*pron.* Clies], is not an uncommon name for a deserted site, where the foundations of houses remain as grassy mounds. From *cladh* [claw, cly], a mound, with E. plural added. *See under* CHANG.

CLAYS OF CULNÒAG (the site of an ancient village). 'Sorbie.' *See under* CULNOAG.

CLAYWHÀRNIES. 'Inch.'

CLAYWHÌPPART. 'Whithorn.' *Cladh* [claw] or *clach thiprat* [ippart], mound or stone of the well. *See under* TIBBERT.

CLÈNARIE (*P.* Cloynary). 'Glasserton.' *See under* CLANERIE.

CLÈNDRIE (*P.* Kloynary and Clonary). 'Inch,' 'Kirkbean,' 'Old Luce,' 'Kirkcolm.' *See under* CLANERIE.

CLENE. 'Girthon.' *Claon* [clane] or *claen* [cleen] (adj.), sloping. Used as a substantive in place-names. *See under* CLAMDALLY, CLAMDISH. *Cf.* Cleen in Fermanagh, Leitrim, and Roscommon.

CLÈNNOCH (*Inq. ad Cap.* 1642, Clannoch). 'Carsphairn,' 'Inch.' *Claenach,* sloping. *See under* CLANNOCH.

CLERKSBURN. 'Glasserton.' The clerk's or priest's burn; close to Kirkmaiden. *Cf.* ALTAGGART, CLARY.

CLEUGH [*gutt.*] (*P.* Kleugh). 'Kirkmaiden, s. c.' "*Cleuch, cleugh.* 1. A precipice, a rugged ascent. 2. A straight hollow between precipitous banks, or a hollow descent on the side of a hill." —*Jamieson.* From A.S. *clough,* "a cleft of a rock, or down the side of a hill" (*Bosworth*).

CLEUGHBRAE. 'Terregles.' The brow of the cleugh. *See under* BRAE and CLEUGH.

CLEUGH HEAD (from estate map of Cuil). 'Kirkmabreck.' The head of the cleugh. *See under* CLEUGH.

CLEUGH OF THE EGLIN. 'Girthon.' *See* EGLIN LANE.

CLIES OF CHANG, etc. 'Mochrum,' 'Sorbie.' *See under* CLAYS OF CHANG, etc.

CLINKING HAVEN. 'Twynholm.' "*Clinking Co's,* caverns which make a tinkling noise when stones are thrown into them."— *Mactaggart.*

CLINT MAELUN. 'Kells.' "*Clint,* a hard or flinty rock."— *Jamieson.* *Cf.* Clint, the name of a place in Yorkshire. "DAN. and SWED. *klint,* the brow of a hill, promontory."— *Lucas.* Maelun possibly = *maolain; maolán,* a beacon (*O'Reilly*); but *Maelan* and *Maeleoin* are names of several personages mentioned by the *Four Masters. Cf.* Letter Maelain in Clare, written *Leitir Maoilín* by the *Four Masters.* " *Maelan* was, I believe, a leguminous plant, and not a cereal one, as is shown by the *maelan milce* being applied to the tuberous bitter vetch, *Orobus tuberosus,* the tuberous roots of which were formerly much prized for making a kind of drink by the Highlanders, and used in times of scarcity as food. The *Orobus niger,* or black bitter vetch, which is said by some to have supported the Britons when driven into the forests and fastnesses by the Emperor Severus, was also called *Maelan.*" —*Sullivan's Intr. to O'Curry,* ccclxiii.

CLINTS OF DRUMORE. 'Minigaff.' "*Clints*, limited to the shelves at the side of a river."—*Jamieson.* This limitation is not observed in Galloway, and certainly does not apply in this case, for these Clints are far from a river. "*Clints*, little awkward-lying rocks."—*Mactaggart.* Neither is this a suitable definition, for these Clints are bold precipitous cliffs on high ground. *Cf.* Clent Hills in Staffordshire. *See under* CLINT and DRUMORE.

CLINTS OF THE BUSS. 'Minigaff.' *See under* BUSS.

CLINTS OF THE SPOUT [*pron.* spŏŏt]. 'Minigaff.' "*Spout*, a boggy spring in ground."—*Jamieson.* But it also means a waterfall. *Spout* (M.E. *spouten* — SWED. *sputa*, the sound of which is well preserved in BR. SC. *spŏŏt*) has lost the *r*, and was originally from the same root as *sprout*, just as *speak* stands for *spreak* (*Skeat*).

CLOAK HILL. 'Carsphairn.' *Cloch*, a stone [?]. *See under* CLACHAN.

CLOCHCLÙAIN. 'Kirkcolm.' *Clach cluain* [cloon], stone of the meadow. *See under* CLACHAN and CLONE.

CLONE (*P.* Cloyin). 'Buittle,' 'Kells,' 'Mochrum.' *Cluain* [cloon], a meadow. Clone in Mochrum appears in *Inq. ad Cap.* 1600 as Clontrunnaight, *i.e. cluan traona* [trana], or the longer form *tradhnach* [trannagh], meadow of the corncrakes. *Cf.* Cloonatreane in Fermanagh, with the same meaning, Lugatryna in Wicklow, etc. "*Cluan*, a lawn, a retired or sequestered place." —*O'Reilly. Cluan* or *cluain* enters into many names both in Ireland and Scotland.

CLONE FELL (*Inq. ad Cap.* 1604, Clone; *P.* Klon). 'Kells.' The hill above the *cluain*, or great meadow at the head of Loch Ken. *See under* CLONE.

CLÒNKINS. 'Kirkpatrick Durham.' *Cluain caoin* [cloonkeen], fine or beautiful meadow. Cloonkin and Clonkin is a common name in Ireland, and Clonkeen in Galway is given in *Hy Many, Cluain-cain-Cairill*, Cairill's fair field.

CLONSHANK. 'Buittle.'

CLONYARD (*Inq. ad Cap.* 1628, Clonzeard). 'Buittle,' 'Carsphairn.' *See under* CLANYARD. *Cf.* Clonard in several places in Ireland ; but Clonard in Meath is *Cluain Eraird*, Erard's meadow.

CLOSING. 'Minigaff.'

CLOSS HILL. 'New Luce.' "*Close.* 3. An area beside a farm-house in which cattle are fed, and where straw, etc., are deposited. 4. An enclosure, a place fenced in."—*Jamieson.* It is pronounced *closs* in BR. SC.

CLOVEN CRAIG. 'Old Luce.' *Cf.* CRAIGBIRNOCH.

CLOWNSTANE.   'Kirkcudbright.'

CLOY POINT. 'Kells.' *Cladh* [claw, cly], a mound. *See under* CLY.

CLUDEN WATER.   'Troqueer.'

CLUGGIE LINN.   'Minigaff.'

CLÙGSTON (*Inq. ad Cap.* 1600, Clugistoun). 'Kirkcowan.'

CLÙNIE HILL. 'Terregles.' *Cluain* [cloon], a meadow. *See under* CLONE.

CLÙTAG (*Inq. ad Cap.* 1681, Clontage ; *P.* Cloutaig). 'Kirkinner.'

CLY. 'Penninghame.' *Cladh* [claw, cly], a mound, ditch, or grave. O. ERSE *clad* + W. *clawdd, cloddian.* "An artificial mound, dyke, or rampart of any kind, . . . pronounced *cly* or *clee* in the south half of Ireland, and *clee* or *claw* in the north. The word is also applied to the raised fences, so universal in Ireland, separating field from field."—*Joyce*, ii. 219. It occurs in the sense of a grave in *Compert Conculaind*, 2, *L.U.* (*Windisch*, 425).

COCKLÈATH (*pron.* Cocklay). 'Buittle.' O. NORSE, *hlatha*, a barn.

COCKLICK (*Charter* 1532, Cockleiks ; *Charter* 1634, Cocklex). 'Urr.'

COCKPLÀY (a hill of 950 feet).   'Dalry.'

COCKRÒSSEN.   'Tungland.'

CÒCKTRIES HILL.   'Urr.'

CÒGARTH (*P.* Kogart ; *Retour* 1616, Cowgairth). 'Parton.' A.S. *cú geard* [cow garth], cow-pen.

CÒGERSHAW. 'Kirkpatrick Irongray.' The "shaw" or wood of Cogarth.

COLDSIDE. 'Sorbie.' *Cf.* CAULDSIDE.

CÒLFIN. 'Port Patrick.' *Cuil fionn* [finn], white nook or corner. *Cf.* Coolfin and Coolfune in Ireland, the latter representing the pronunciation of *fionn* in the south. *Joyce*, ii. 272.

CÒLLEGE GLEN and HILL (1175 feet). 'Dalry.'

CÒLLIN (*P.* Colynn). 'Rerwick.' *Cuileann,* holly. *See under*
ALWHILLAN and KNOCKWHILLAN. *Cf.* Cullane, Cullaun,
Collon, and Cullan in various parts of Ireland.

CÒLLIN HILL. 'Buittle.' Close by is Knockwhillan. *See under*
COLLIN.

COLLIN ISLAND (in the Dee). 'Dalry.' *See under* COLLIN. A
little further down the stream is Holly Island.

CÒLLOCHAN. 'Terregles.' *Cam lochan,* crooked lakelet. *See under*
CAMELON.

COLVEND (a parish in the Stewartry), (*P.* Covenn, Cawenn ; *Inq.
ad Cap.* 1560, Colven ; 1610, Culwen). *Cabhán* [cavan], a
hollow. *See under* CAVAN.

COMPSTONE (*P.* Kumstoun, Cumstou). 'Twynholm.'

CÒNCHIETOWN (*Inq. ad Cap.* 1603, Conquhiton ; 1605, Conquech-
toun). 'Borgue.' Conkie's house. M'Conchie is a common
surname in Galloway. The *Four Masters* record the death of
Conchadh [Conchie, *gutt.*], son of *Cuanach,* in A.D. 732, and of
Dermot Mac Conchagadh, a priest, in A.D. 1488.

CONGÈITH. 'Kirkgunzeon.'

CONHUITH. 'Terregles.'

CONNIVEN. 'Kirkgunzeon.'

COO LOCHANS. 'Minigaff.'

CÒORAN LANE (part of the head waters of the Dee), (*P.* Sawchs of
Kowring). 'Minigaff.'

COPIN KNOWE. 'Minigaff.' The hill of bargaining. "To cowp, coup,
cope. 1. To exchange, to barter. 2. To expose to sale. 3. To
buy and sell, to traffic ; commonly used in this sense, but only
of an inferior kind of trade."—*Jamieson.* E. *to cope,* to vie
with, originally meant to chaffer. It was introduced into
England, says *Skeat,* by Dutch and Flemish traders – DU.
koopen, to buy. For the connection with E. *cheap, chapman,
chaffer, see under* CHAPMANLEYS.

CÒRAN OF PORTMARK. 'Carsphairn.' *Corán,* dim. of *cor,* a round
hill (*O'Don. Suppl. to O'Reilly*) + *corr,* a snout, bill, beak
(*O'Reilly*). *Cf.* Corann in Connaught, where, in A.M. 4532,
the *Four Masters* record a great battle to have taken place.

CORANSCLÙIE (*P.* Kornsleu H.). 'Carsphairn.' *Cor an sleibhe* [slewie], hill of the moor. *See under* SLACARNACHAN.

CORBÈLLY (*P.* Carbelly, Corbyilly). 'Kirkbean.'

CÒRBIETON (*Inq. ad Cap.* 1604, Corbertoun; *P.* Corbettoun). 'Buittle.' Corbet's house. David I. granted the lands of Barschain in this parish to Robert Corbet (*M'Kerlie*).

COREHILL. 'Kirkmaiden,' 'Stoneykirk' (*twice*). *Cathair* [caer], a fort, or perhaps *cor*, a round hill.

COREHOLM. 'Kirkmaiden.'

CÒRKET. 'Kirkmaiden, s. c.' *Corcur*, red ; a lichen called in BR. SC. *staneraw*, used for dyeing red. *See under* BARNCORKRIE.

CORNÀRROCH. 'Minigaff.' *Cordn charroch* [harrogh], rough hill. *Cf.* CORNHARROW, ROUGH GIBB. *See under* CORAN.

CORNCRÀVIE. 'Stoneykirk.' *Cordn craebhach* [cravagh], wooded hill. *See under* CASTLE CREAVIE and CORAN.

CORNERS GALE. 'Minigaff.'

CORNHÀRROW. 'Dalry.' *See under* CORNARROCH.

CORNHÙLLOCH (*Inq. ad Cap.* 1582, Corhallachill *vel* Corrach hill; 1636, Carhallow; *P.* Karhalloch, Kerihalloch). 'Mochrum.' *Cor na chullach* or *cordn chullach* [hullagh], hill of the boars. O. ERSE *cullach, caullach,* a boar ; ERSE "*Cullach, callach,* a boar, a yearling calf" (*O'Reilly*).

CORNLÈE (a hill 1175 feet). 'Kirkpatrick Irongray.' *Coran liath* [lee], grey hill. *See under* CORAN and BARLAE.

CÒRRA. 'Buittle.' *Currach,* "a marsh, a bog, a fen ; a course, a level plain."—*O'Reilly.* *Cf.* the Curragh of Kildare, Curraghmore, and many other places called Curragh, Curra, and Curry in Ireland.

CÒRRA HILL. 'Balmaghie,' 'Rerwick.' *See under* CORRA.

CÒRRA POOL (on the Dee). 'Kirkcudbright.' *Coradh* [corrah], a weir. *Cf.* Corrofin in Clare, written *Coradh Finne,* Finna's weir (*Four Masters,* 1573), and Corofin in Galway, *Coradh finne,* white weir (*Four Masters,* 1451).

CORRAFÈCKLOCH. 'Minigaff.'

CÒRSBY (*P.* Korsbuy). 'Penninghame.' *Cf.* Corsbie or Crosbie in Ayrshire.

CORSE O' SLAKES. 'Kirkmabreck.' The crossing of the passes. "*Slak, slake,* an opening in the higher part of a hill or mountain, where it becomes less steep and forms a sort of pass."—*Jamieson.* " In Galloway there are no roads so wild as the one which leads over the celebrated pass of the above name between Cairnsmoor and Cairnhattie. It is a perfect Alpine pass, and was a haunt of Billy Marshall and his gang in days of yore."—*Mactaggart.*

CORSEHILL (the place of this name in Dalry is on *Kirk*land). 'Dalry,' 'Kirkpatrick Durham.' The cross hill, the place whereon probably stood a memorial cross.

CÒRSELAND. 'Kirkpatrick Durham.'

CORSEMÀLZIE (*P.* Corsmaille). 'Minigaff.' Cross Malzie, *i.e.* a ford over the Malzie.

CORSEMÀRTIN. 'Balmaghie.' *Crois Martainn,* (St.) Martin's cross. *See under* BALNACROSS. Dedicated, no doubt, like Crois Mhartain, the great cross opposite the west front of Iona Cathedral, to St. Martin, Bishop of Tours, who died A.D. 397, and to whom Ninian dedicated Candida Casa, and Fergus, Lord of Galloway, subsequently dedicated the Priory Church there in 1143.

CÒRSEWALL. 'Kirkcolm.' The cross well, well of the cross. There is here a well dedicated to St. Columba. "*Corse, cors.* 1. The cross or rood. 2. A crucifix. 3. Market-place, from the cross being formerly erected there."—*Jamieson.*

CORSERÌNE. 'Kells.'

CORSEWOOD. 'Balmaghie.'

CORSEYARD. 'Balmaghie,' 'Borgue.'

CÒRSOCK (*Inq. ad Cap.* 1607, Corsak; MS. 1527, Karsok; *P.* Corsock). 'New Abbey,' 'Parton.'

CORVÌSEL (*P.* Kerivishel) [*pron.* Corveesel]. 'Penninghame.' *Coire iseal* [kirrie eeshal], low pool (caldron). There is a swirling pool here in the Cree, into the foot of which high tides flow; the lowest pool in the river, *i.e.* the one next the sea. *Cf.* Agheeshal in Monaghan (*ath iseal,* low ford), Athassel, with the same meaning, on the Suir in Tipperary, Gorteeshall in Tipperary; Meeshall, Myshall, Mishells (*magh íseal*, low field), and Dunishel (*dún, íseal*). ERSE *íseal*, GAEL. *íosal* — O. ERSE *íssel* + W. *isel*, low, inferior. *Cf.* DRUMMIE-HISLIE.

CÒRWALL.   'Mochrum.'

CÒRWAR (*P.* Korwar ; *W. P.* MSS., Corver). 'Penninghame,' 'Sorbie.'

COTTACH. 'Troqueer.' *See* CATOAK.

CÒUNAN [*pron.* Coonan]. 'Glasserton, s. c.' *Cuaindn,* a landing-place, a haven. "It 'll be bad weather, for I hear Counan roaring;" said when the surf breaks on Glasserton shore in calm weather.

CÒWAN HILL. 'Kirkinner.' *Cabhan,* a hollow. *See under* CAVAN.

COWANS. 'Kirkmaiden.' *Cabhan,* a hollow ; E. plural added. *See under* CAVAN.

CÒWEND. 'Port Patrick.' *Cabhan,* a hollow. *See under* CAVAN.

COWLOOT.   'Parton.'

CRABBEN POINT.   'Kirkcolm, s. c.'

CRÀCHAN. 'Kirkcowan.' *Cruachán,* a hill ; dim. of *cruach,* a stack. *Cf.* Croaghan, Croaghaun, Croghan, and Crohan in Ireland. *See under* CROACH.

CRAE (*P.* Krae). 'Balmaghie.' *Craebh* [crave], a tree.

CRÀICHIE (*P.* Krachy). 'Parton.' *Cruachach,* hilly, deriv. of *cruach. See under* CROACH. *Cf.* CROACHIE, which also *Pont* spells Krachy.

CRAICHMÒRE (*P.* Kroochmoir). 'Leswalt.' *Cruach mór,* great stack or hill. *Cf.* CROCHMORE. *See under* CROACH.

CRAIG. In many places. *Creag,* a rock. or inland cliff. W. *craig* (whence M.E. *crag, cragge*). "The original form is clearly *car,* a rock ; whence, with suffixed *t,* the Irish *ceart,* a pebble, and E. *chert,* also with suffixed *n* the GAEL. *carn.*"—*Skeat.* A contracted form of *carraic. See under* CARRICK.

CRAIGÀDAM.   'Kirkpatrick Durham.'

CRAIGALCARIE. 'Balmaclellan.' *Creag an caora* (carey), rock of the sheep.

CRAIGÀMMIN. 'Inch.'

CRAIGANALLY. 'Crossmichael.' 'Mochrum.' *Creagán ailich* [elligh], crag of the stone fort. *Aileach*, deriv. of *ail*, a stone (*ail-theach*, stone house, according to *Michael O'Clery*), enters into many Irish names, such as Greenan-Ely, the ancient palace of the northern kings in Derry, always referred to as *Aileach* by the old writers; Caherelly in Limerick, Cahernally in Galway, Ardelly, Ellagh, and Elagh, etc. The stones of which these forts were made have generally been removed for dyke-building. The name might also signify *creagán eilidh* [elly], crag of the hinds (*cf.* CARNELTOCH, CRAIGNELDER), but the former meaning is perhaps the more probable. *Cf.* CRAIGENELLIE.

CRAIG ANTHONY. 'Port Patrick.'

CRAIGANTỲRE. 'Stoneykirk, s. c.' *Creagán t-iar* [tear], west craig. *See under* BALTIER.

CRAIGÀRIE (*P.* Kraigary). ' 'Kirkcowan.' *Creag airidh* [airey], crag of the shieling, or *creag aedhaire* [airey], shepherd's crag.

CRAIGBÈLL. 'Kirkcolm.'

CRAIGBÈNNOCH. 'Minigaff.' *Creag beannaich*, crag of the hilly ground; an adjectival form of *beann* often used as a substantive, *e.g.* Bannaghbane and Bannaghroe in Monaghan, the white and red hilly ground.

CRAIGBÈRNOCH (*P.* Kraigbyrronach). 'New Luce.' *Creag béarnach*, cloven crag. *Cf.* CLOVEN CRAIG; also Caherbarnagh in Cork, Clare, and Kerry, Rathbarna in Roscommon. "*Béarnach*, gapped, full of gaps."—*O'Reilly.* *See under* BARNEYWATER.

CRAIGBÌLL (*Inq. ad Cap.* 1604, Craigbull). 'Terregles.'

CRAIGBÌTTERN. 'New Abbey.'

CRAIGBÒNNY. 'Balmaclellan.' *Creag banbh* [bonniv], crag of the young pigs. *See under* AUCHNABONY.

CRAIGBRÀCK. 'Girthon.' *Creag breac*, spotted, variegated crag.

CRAIGBRÈX. 'New Abbey.' *See under* CRAIGBRACK.

CRAIGBRÒCK. 'Inch.' *Creag broc*, badgers' crag. *See under* BROCKLACH.

CRAIGBUIE. 'Mochrum.' *Creag buidhe* [buie], yellow crag.

CRAIGBÙRDIE. 'Kirkmaiden.'

I

CRAIGCÀFFIE (*Charter K. Rob. Bruce*, Kellechaffe; *Inq. ad Cap.* 1600, Nether Craigie, *alias* Craigcaffie; *P.* Karkophy). 'Inch.'

CRAIGCHÈSSIE. 'Carsphairn.' *See under* BARCHESSIE.

CRAIGCRÒCKET. 'Carsphairn.' *Creag crochaid*, crag of the hanging. *See under* AUCHENROCHER.

CRAIGCRÒON. 'Penninghame.' The syllable *cron* or *crun* is difficult to identify, as it represents several different words. In this case it may represent either *creag crón*, brown crag, *creag crúan* [croon], red crag (*O'Reilly*), or *creag cruain* [croon], crag of the copper (*O'Reilly* and *Windisch*). Copper has in recent times been mined for, though with indifferent success, in the immediate neighbourhood of Craigcroon.

CRAIGCRÙN. 'Inch.' *See under* CRAIGCROON.

CRAIGDÀRROCH. 'Kirkinner.' *Creag daraich*, oak-tree crag; perhaps *creag dearg*, red crag; the two words assume the same form in composition. *See under* ARNDARROCH.

CRAIGDÈWS (*P.* Kraigdewhous). 'Minigaff.' *See under* CRAIGDHU.

CRAIGDHU or CRAIGDOW (*P.* Kraigdow, Kreigdow; *W. P.* MSS., Craigdow). 'Glasserton,' 'Kirkcowan.' *Creag dubh* [doo], black crag. *Cf.* CARRICKCOW, CRAIGDEWS, CRAIGDUFF, CRAIGENDOUS, and, in Ireland, Cregduff.

CRAIGDÌSTANT.   'Minigaff.'

CRAIGDÙFF. 'New Abbey.' *See under* CRAIGDHU.

CRAIGÈACH (*P.* Kraigailch). 'Minigaff.' *Creag eich* [egh], gen. of *each*, crag of the horse. *Cf.* Carriganegh in Antrim. *See under* AUCHNESS.

CRAIGEÀFF. 'Inch.' Probably the same as Craigeach.

CRAIGÈAZLE. 'Inch.' *Creag íseal* [eeshal], low crag. *See under* CORVISEL.

CRAIGÈLLAN. 'Urr.' *Creag alluin* [?], crag of the hind. Or perhaps *creag álluinn*, beautiful crag, which is the meaning *Joyce* gives to Carrigallen in Leitrim. *Alluin*, a hind, a fawn (*O'Reilly*), akin to *eilidh*. *See under* CARNELTOCH.

CRAIGENBÀRROCH. 'Kirkmaiden.' *Cf.* BARNBARROCH.

CRAIGENBÀY. 'Kells.' *Creagán beith* [bey], crag of the birches.

CRAIGENBÈN.   'Inch.'

CRAIGENBÒY. 'Kirkmabreck.' *Creagán buidhe* [buie, buy], yellow crag. *Cf.* CARRICKABOYS, CRAIGENBUY, CRAIGENBUYS; and, in Ireland, Craigenboy.

CRAIGENBÙY (*Inq. ad Cap.* 1604, Craiginbay). 'Inch.' *See under* CRAIGENBOY.

CRAIGENBÙYS. 'Penninghame.' *See under* CRAIGENBOY.

CRAIGENCÀILLIE (*P.* Kraiginkailly Hill). Minigaff.' *Creagán cailleaich*, crag of the old woman. Said to have been named from the woman who gave shelter to Robert the Bruce the night before the battle of Raploch Moss. *See under* CARLIN'S CAIRN.

CRAIGENCÀRSE. 'Dalry.'

CRAIGENCÒLON. 'Carsphairn.'

CRAÌGENCÒR (*P.* Kragincor). 'Dalry,' 'New Luce.'

CRAIGENCRÒSH. 'New Luce,' 'Stoneykirk.' *Creagán crois* [crosh], crag of the cross, or of the gallows. *See under* BALNACROSS. *Cf.* Carrickmacross in Ireland.

CRAIGENCRÒSS. 'Port Patrick.' *See under* CRAIGENCROSH.

CRAIGENCRÒY. 'Stoneykirk.'

CRAIGENDÒUS [*pron.* dooze]. 'Minigaff.' *Creagán dubh* [doo], black crags; E. plural added. *Cf.* CRAIGDEWS.

CRAIGENÈLLIE. 'Balmaghie.' *See under* CRAIGANALLY.

CRAIGENGÀLE. 'Inch,' 'Kirkmaiden.' *Creagán geal* [gal], white crag.

CRAIGENGÀSHEL (*P.* Kragingasheel H.). 'Minigaff.' *Creag an g-caiseail* [gashel], crag of the castle. *See under* AUCHENGASHELL.

CRAIGENGÈARY. 'Carsphairn.' *Creagán g-caora* [gairey], crag of the sheep.

CRAIGENGÈRROCH. 'Kirkcolm.'

CRAIGENGÌLLAN (*P.* Kragingullan H.). 'Carsphairn,' 'Kirkpatrick Durham.' *Creag an g-cuileainn* [guillan], crag of the holly. Or perhaps *creagán Guillin*, Guillin's crag. "*Guillin*, alias *Cualan*, from whom so many of our mountains are named, was the tutelar deity of blacksmiths, and called *Cuilean-gabha*, vulgarly *Gabhlun-go*."—*O'Reilly, s. v.* Giollaguillin.

CRAIGENGÒWER.   'Balmaclellan,' 'Glasserton,' 'New Abbey.' *Creagán gobhar* [gower], crag of the goats.   *Cf.* Carrignagower and Carricknagore in Ireland.

CRAIGENHÒLLY.   'Old Luce.'

CRAIGENJÌG.   'Minigaff.'

CRAIGENKÈELIE.   'Minigaff.'

CRAIGENLÈE (*P.* Kraigenluy).   'Port Patrick.'   *Creagán liath* [lee], grey crag.

CRAIGENLÈES.   'Inch.'   *See under* CRAIGENLEE.

CRAIGENLÌE.   'New Luce.'   *See under* CRAIGENLEE.

CRAIGENLÌGGIE.   'New Luce.'   *Creagán ligce* [leeggie], crag of the flat stone or tomb.   *See under* AIRIELICK.

CRAIGENRÌNE (a shoulder of Cairnsmore).   'Carsphairn.'

CRAIGENRÒY.   'Minigaff.'   *Creagán ruadh* [roo], ruddy crag.

CRAIGENS.   'Inch,' 'Kirkcudbright,' 'Minigaff.'   *Creagán*, the crags ; E. plural superadded.

CRAIGENSÀLLIARD.   'Minigaff.'

CRAIGENSKÙLK.   'Minigaff.'   *Creag an scoloic*, the crag of the "scoloc," or small farmer.   "*Scológ*, a petty farmer."—*O'Reilly.* The original meaning of scholar or clerk has been lost — ERSE *scol* — LAT. *schola.*   "The Scolocs seem to have been the lowest order of the ecclesiastical community, and to have been clerics who were undergoing a course of training and instruction to fit them for performing the service of the church. Their Pictish name was *Scolofthes*, as we learn from Reginald of Durham, who mentions the clerics of the church (of Kirkcudbright), 'the Scolofthes, as they are called in the Pictish speech,' and gives 'Scholasticus, a scholar,' as its Latin equivalent. We find them under the name of *Scolocs* in three of the churches belonging to St. Andrews. . . . In 1387 the church lands of Ellon are called the Scolog lands, and were hereditary in the families of the Scologs who possessed them. . . . In an inquest regarding the lands of the Kirkton of Arbuthnot, in the Mearns, held in the year 1206, we find the ecclesiastical territory held by certain tenants called parsons, who had sub-tenants under them, having houses of their own and cattle which they pastured on the common ; and the tenants of these lands are termed by several of the witnesses Scolocs, and are also termed the bishop's men. . . . The name of Scoloc is also found in connection with one of the Columban monasteries in Ireland; for in one of the charters preserved in the Book of Kells, which must have been granted between the years 1128 and 1138, we find that among the functionaries of the monastery, after the Coärb of Columcille, or the abbot, the *Sacart* or priest, the *Ferleiginn* or lecturer, the *Aircennech* or Erenach of the house of guests, and the *Fosaircennech* or vice-Erenach, appears the *Toisech na Scoloc*, or Chief of the Scologs."—Skene, *Celt. Scot.* ii. 446.

"There is an unfortunate class of men known under the name of Scallags. The Scallag, whether male or female, is a poor being, who, for mere subsistence, becomes a feudal slave to another, whether a sub-tenant, a tacksman, or a laird. The Scallag builds his own hut with sods and boughs of trees. Five days in the week he works for his master; the sixth is allowed to himself for the cultivation of some scrap of land on the edge of some moss or moor, on which he raises a little kale or coleworts, barley, and potatoes."—Buchanan's *Travels in the Western Hebrides from* 1782 *to* 1790. So that what originally meant "a scholar," has come to mean a cottar or squatter.

CRAIGENTÈASY.   *Cf.* BARCHESSIE.   'Minigaff.'

CRAIGENVÈOCH.   'Old Luce.'   *Creagán bhfiaich* or *bhfithich* [veeagh], crag of the raven.   *See under* BENNAVEOCH and KNOCKNAVAR. Macdonald of Glengarry displays as his crest a raven perching on a crag, with the motto, "*Creagán an fithich*," *i.e.* "Rock of the raven."

CRAIGENVÒLLEY.   'Balmaclellan.'   *Creag an bhaile* [valley], crag of the house.   *Cf.* SHANVOLLEY.   *See under* BAILIE HILL.

CRAIGENWÀLLIE.   'Carsphairn.'   *Cf.* CRAIGENVOLLEY.

CRAIGFÀD.   'Carsphairn.'   *Creag fada*, long, or far crag.   *Cf.* Carraig-fada in Iona; Craigfad and Carrigfadda in Ireland.

CRAIGFÌNNIE.   'New Abbey.'   *Creag mhuine* [?] [vinny], crag of the thicket.   *Cf.* CRAIGWHINNIE, and, in Ireland, Leaffony in Sligo (*liath mhuine*, grey thicket).

CRAIGFÒLLY.   'New Luce.'

CRAIG GILBERT (*P.* Kraigilbert).   'Kells.'

CRAIGGÒRK.   'New Luce.'   *Creag orc* [?] [ork], crag of the pigs. "*Orc . i . muc*" (*O'Davoran*, p. 109)=*torc*, *thorc*, a pig+W. *porch*, *twrch*+LAT. *porcus* (whence F. *porc*, E. *pork*)+LITH. *parszus*, a pig+A.S. *fearh* (whence E. to *farrow*).

CRAIGGÙBBLE. 'Inch.' *Creag gcapuil*, crag of the horse. *See under* BARHAPPLE.

CRAIGHÀLLOCK. 'Mochrum.' *Creag challoch* [?] [hallogh], crag of the boar. *See under* CORNHULLOCH.

CRAIGHÀNDLE 'Minigaff.' *Creag Fhingaill* [?] [hingal], the Norseman's Crag. *See under* CARRICKFUNDLE, in *Addenda*.

CRAIGHÀR. 'Buittle.' *Creag ghar* [?] [har], near crag.

CRAIGHÀRDY. 'Kirkcolm.' *Creag chearda* [harda], crag of the workshop. *See under* CAIRDIE WIEL.

CRAIG HELEN. 'Penninghame.'

CRAIGHÈRRON. 'Buittle,' 'Girthon.' *Creag chaerthinn* [?] [heerinn], crag of the rowan-tree. "*Cairthainn*, a mountain ash."—*Joyce*, i. 513.

CRAIG HET. 'New Luce' (*twice*). *Creag chuit* [hit], crag of the wild-cat, cat's craig.

CRAIGHÌT. 'Carsphairn.' *See under* CRAIG HET.

CRÀIGHLAW (*Inq. ad Cap.* 1633, Crauchlaw M'Kie, *alias* Drumbuie; *P.* Craichlaw). 'Kirkcowan.'

CRAIGHÒRE. 'Kirkcowan.'

CRAIGHÒRN. 'Carsphairn.'

CRÀIGIE (*P.* Kraigoch). 'Penninghame.' *Creagach*, craggy, a rocky place.

CRAIGIECÀLLEN. 'Kirkcowan.'

CRAIGIECÒOL. 'New Luce.'

CRAIGIEDALZELL. 'Tungland.'

CRAIGIEGÒWER. 'New Luce.' *See under* CRAIGENGOWER.

CRAIGIE LINN. 'Dalry.' *See under* CRAIGIE and CRAIG LINN.

CRAIGIEWHÌNNIE. 'Kirkcowan.'

CRAIGINCÒRE. 'Leswalt.' *See under* CRAIGENCOR.

CRAIGINNÈE. 'Stoneykirk.' *Creag an fhiaidh* [ee], crag of the deer. *Cf.* DRUMANEE, LAROCHANEA ; and, in Ireland, Drumanee in Derry, Knockanee in Limerick and Westmeath, Clonea in Waterford, meaning the ridge, the hill, and the meadow of the deer. "The word *fiadh* [fee] originally meant any wild animal, but its meaning has been gradually narrowed, and in Irish writings it is almost universally applied to a deer."—*Joyce*, i. 476.

CRAIGKNÙCKLE. 'Inch.' *Cf.* CRAIGNEUKALD.

CRAIGLÀRIE (*P.* Kraiglary). 'Mochrum.' *Creag laira,* the mare's crag; a hill, part of which is called Craignagapple, which means the same thing. *See under* AUCHENLARIE.

CRAIGLÀUKIE. 'Kirkmaiden.' *Cf.* CLACHANLAUKES and KNOCK-MILAUK.

CRAIGLEARIE. 'Glasserton.' *See under* CRAIGLARIE.

CRAIGLÈBBOCK. 'Kirkbean.'

CRAIGLÈE (*P.* Kraigly hil). 'Minigaff.' *Creag liath* [lee], grey crag. *Cf.* CRAIGENLEE, etc., also, in Ireland, Craglea, Carrick-leagh, Carriglea, etc.

CRAIGLEMÌNE [*pron.* Craiglmine] (*W. P.* MSS. Craigilmayne). 'Glasserton.'

CRAIGLETEMON. 'Mochrum.'
CRAIGLEWHÀN. 'Kirkpatrick Durham.'
CRAIGLEY. 'Urr.'
CRAIGLINGAT. 'Carsphairn.'

CRAIGLÌNN (on the Ken). 'Dalry.' *Creag* and *linn,* a pool, both being adopted into BR. SC. are here used, the former qualifying the latter, *i.e.* the linn or pool of the crag.

CRAIGLÒCHAN. 'Inch.' *Creag lochain,* crag of the tarn or lakelet.

CRAIGLÒFT. 'Kirkpatrick Irongray.'
CRAIGLÒOM. 'Minigaff.'

CRAIGLÒSK. 'Balmaclellan.' *Creag loisg* [lusk], burnt crag. *Cf.* Ballylusk in Leinster. "*Loisg, loisgthe,* burnt" (*O'Reilly*). +W. *llosg,* a burn, C. and B. *losc*+ICEL. *log,* a flame (whence M.E. *lo3he,* BR. SC. *low*), akin to LAT. *lux, lumen, luna,* etc. — √RUK, to shine.

CRAIGLÒUR HAWSE [*pron.* Craigloor]. 'Dalry.' *Creag lobhair* [loor], crag of the cripple or sick man. *Cf.* Craiglure in Ayrshire. *See under* BARLURE. "*Hawse.* 1. The neck. 2. The throat. 3. Any narrow passage. 4. It is used to denote a defile; a narrow passage between hills."—*Jamieson.*

CRAIGLÒWRIE. 'Girthon.' *Creag labhairadh* [lowra], speaking crag (probably from an echo). *Cf.* Cloghlowrish in Water-ford, and Clolourish in Wexford.

CRAIGMABRÀNCHIE. 'Penninghame.' *Creag ma Branchu* [?], Branchu's crag. The *Four Masters* relate the death of Branchu, son of Bran, at a great battle in Ulster in 728. For the use of the prefix *ma,* expressing affection or venera-tion, *see under* HILL MABREEDIA.

CRAIGMAHÀRB.   'Inch.'

CRAIGMÀTH.   'Urr.'

CRAIG MÌCHAEL [*pron.* meehull] (*P.* Kraigmichel).   'Kells.'
  Creag Michaeil, Michael's crag.

CRAIGMÌNE.   'Dalry.'   *Cf.* CRAIGLEMINE and CRAIGMINN.

CRAIGMÌNN.   'Minigaff.'   *Creag meadhon* [meun], middle crag.

CRAIGMITCHELL.   'Carsphairn.'   *See under* CRAIG MICHAEL.

CRAIGMÒDDIE (*P.* Kraigmaddie).   'Kirkcowan.'   *Creag madadh*
  [maddy], the dog's or wolf's crag.   *See under* BLAIRMODDIE.
  Cf. Carricknamaddry, Carrignamaddy, and Craignamaddy, in
  Ireland.

CRAIGMÒRE.   'Girthon,' 'Glasserton,' 'Loch Rutton,' 'Parton.'
  Creag mór, great crag.   Occurs both as Craigmore and Creg-
  more in Ireland.

CRAIGMÙLE.   'Kirkmabreck.'   *Creag maol* [meul], bald crag.
  See under MEAUL.

CRAIGMÙLLEN.   'Rerwick.'   *Creag muileain* [meullan], crag of
  the mill.

CRAIGMÙLLOCH.   'Dalry.'   *Creag mullaich*, crag of the summit.
  See under MULLACH.

CRAIGMÙRCHIE.   'Minigaff.'   *Creag Murchaidh* [Murchie], Murchadh's crag.   Murchadh is an ancient Erse name (modern-
  ised Morrough), the first of that name mentioned by the
  Four Masters being the son of Diarmaid, Lord of Leinster,
  A.D. 713.

CRAIGNACRÀDDOCH.   'Minigaff.'   *Creag na craideach* [?], crag of
  the scald crows (*O'Reilly*).

CRAIGNAGÀPPLE.   'Mochrum.'   *Creag na gcapul* [gappul], crag
  of the horses.   Part of this hill is called Craiglarie, which is
  synonymous.   *Cf.* CRAIGGUBBLE.

CRAIGNAHÈRRIE.   'Kirkmaiden, s. c.'

CRAIGNÀIR.   'Balmaclellan,' 'Whithorn.'   *Creag an air*, crag of
  the slaughter.

CRAIGNÀLLY.   'Kirkcolm.'   *See under* CRAIGENALLY.

CRAIGNÀLTIE.   'Inch.'   *Creag na eilte* [?] [elty], crag of the hind.
  See under CARNELTOCH.

CRAIGNÀNE.   'Carsphairn.'   *Creag n-en* [nane], crag of the birds.
  See under BARNEAN.

CRAIGNAQUÀRROCH [*qu* hard] (*P.* Korynahowarach).   'Port Patrick.'

CRAIGNÀRBIE. 'Kirkcowan.' *Creag an earbuil* [?], crag of the point. *See under* DARNARBEL.

CRAIGNÀRGET (*P.* Kraiginargit). 'Minigaff' (*twice*), 'Old Luce,' 'Penninghame.' *Creag an airgid*, crag of the silver. *Cf.* SILVER CRAIG. In Minigaff the name occurs twice among the lead mines, where the ore is rich in silver. O. ERSE *argat*, ERSE *airgiod*, W. *arian*, C. *argan*, B. *arghant* + LAT. *argentum* + GK. ἄργυρος, connected with ἀργός, white + SKT. *rajata*, white, silver (from *ráj*, to shine), and *arjuna*, white— √ARG, to shine.

CRAIGNÀW (*P.* Kraigna). 'Minigaff.' *Creag an atha* [?] [aha, awe], crag of the ford, or of the kiln (*O'Reilly*). *See under* CARSENAW.

CRAIGNAWÀCHEL. 'Kirkcolm.' *Creag na bhuachail* [?] [vooghal], crag of the boys or herd-boys. *See under* BOWHILL.

CRAIGNÈLDER. 'Minigaff.' *Creag na eilte* [?], the hind's crag. *See under* CARNELTOCH.

CRAIGNÈLDRICKEN.   'Minigaff.'

CRAIGNÈLL (*P.* Kraignall H.).   'Minigaff.'

CRAIGNÈSKET, an island in Fleet Bay (*P.* Kraigneskan). 'Girthon.' *Creag fheusgan* [essgan], rock of the mussels (*cf.* Mussel Clauchan in Colvend). Both in this name and in Stranfasket (*q. v.*) the final *t* is written *n* by Pont. "*Fasgan, feusgán*, the shell-fish called the muscle" (*O'Reilly*).

CRAIGNÈUK. 'New Abbey.' *Creag niuic* [nook], crag of the nook or corner ; ERSE *niuc*, whence E. *nook*, BR. SC. *neuk*.

CRAIGNÈUKALD. 'Minigaff.' *Cf.* CRAIGKNUCKLE.

CRAIGNÌE.   'New Luce.'

CRAIGNIEBÀY. 'New Luce.' *Creag na beith* [bey], crag of the birches. *Cf.* CRAIGENBAY.

CRAIGNIEGÒWRIE. 'New Luce.' *Creag na goibhre* [gowrie], crag of the she-goat : gen. sing. of *gobhar*. *Cf.* CRAIGENGOWER.

CRAIGNIEVÀLLEY. 'New Luce.' *Creagán a' bhaile* [vallie], crag of the house, or *creagán a' bheallaich* [vallagh], crag of the pass or roadway. *See under* BAILIE, BALLOCH, and SHINVALLEY.

CRAIGNÌNE (*P.* Kraignym).   ' Kirkmabreck,' ' Minigaff.'

CRÀIGOCH (*P.* Kraigoes). 'Kirkcolm.' *See under* CRAIGIE.

CRAIGÒNERY. 'Penninghame.' *Creag fhainre* [?] [anry], uneven, sloping crag. *See under* CROFTANGRY.

CRAIG-ON-RÌCKETS.   ' New Luce.'

CRAIGÒWER. 'Inch,' ' Kells.' *Creag odhar* [owr], grey crag, or *creag gobhar* [gowr], goat's crag.

CRAIGRÀPLOCH. 'Rerwick.' There is a large fort here. The village at the foot of the rock on which Stirling Castle stands is called the Raploch. *Cf.* RAPLOCH MOSS.

CRAIGRÀRIE.   ' Kirkmaiden, s.c.'

CRAIGRÌNE, a hill of 1075 feet. ' Kells.'

CRAIGRÒAN.   ' Rerwick.'

CRAIGRÒCKALL.   ' Kirkbean.'

CRAIGRÒNALD. 'Girthon.' *Creag Raonuill* or *Raghnaill*, Ronald's crag.

CRAIGRÒUNAL (*P.* Kraig Randell). 'Minigaff.' *See under* CRAIG-RONALD.

CRAIGRÒW [*pron.* roo]. 'Rerwick, s.c.' *Creag rudha* [roo], crag of the point. *See under* ROW.

CRAIGSHÌNGING.   ' Girthon.'

CRAIGSHÌNNIE (*P.* Kraigsindy). 'Kells.' *Creag sionach* [shin-nagh], crag of the foxes. *Pont* shows the *d* of the older form *sindach.* *See under* AUCHENSHINNOCH.

CRAIGSHÙNDIE (*P.* Kraigsunday hil). 'Borgue.' *Creag sindach* [shindy], crag of the foxes. *Sindach,* an old form of *sinnach, sionnach* (*Windisch, s.v.*).

CRAIGSKÌMMING.   ' Sorbie.'

CRAIGSLÀVE. 'Port Patrick.' *Creag sleamh* [?] [slav], crag of the elm-trees. *See under* CRAIGSLOUAN.

CRAIGSLÒUAN. 'New Luce.' *Creag sleamhan* [?] [slavan, slawan], crag of the elm-trees. *Cf.* Carrickslavan in Leitrim. "*Leamhan* (is) used in the south, and *sleamhan* in the north." —*Joyce*, i. 507. *See under* BARLUELL.

CRAIG SPIER.   ' Inch.'

CRAIGSTRÙEL. 'Kirkcolm.' *Creag sruthair* [sruhar], crag of the stream. The final *r* is frequently and systematically changed into *l*, and *t* as frequently inserted after *s*. Struell, near Downpatrick, is written Tirestruther in a charter *circa* 1178 (*Joyce*, i. 458). Sroolane and Srooleen are names of streams in the south of Ireland. *Cf.* STROOL BAY. "The original root (of stream) √SRU, to flow ; *cf.* SKT. *sru*, to flow, GK. ῥέειν (put for σρέ-ειν), to flow, IRISH *sroth*, a stream, LITH. *srowe*, a stream. The *t* seems to have been inserted for greater ease of pronunciation, not only in Teutonic, but in Slavonic ; *cf.* RUSS. *struia*, a stream. The putting of *sr* for *str* occurs contrariwise in IRISH *sráid*, a street, from LAT. *strata.*"—*Skeat, s.v.* Stream.

CRAIGTÀPPOCK. 'New Abbey.'

CRAIGTÀRSON. 'Carsphairn.' *Creag tarsuinn*, thwart crag. *See under* BALTERSON.

CRAIGTÈRRA. 'Buittle.' *Creag t-searrach* [terragh], crag of the foals. *Cf.* Aghaterry and Clonterry in Queen's County. *See under* BARSHERRY.

CRAIGTÈRSAN. 'Minigaff.' *See under* CRAIGTARSON.

CRAIGVÈY (*P.* Kraginbae). 'Kells.' *Creag bheith* [vey], crag of the birches. *See under* CRAIGENBAY, CRAIGNIEBAY.

CRAIGWELL. 'Urr.'

CRAIGWHÀR. 'Carsphairn.' *See under* CRAIGHAR.

CRAIGWHÌLL. 'Dalry.' *Creag chuill* [hwill], crag of the hazel. *See under* BARWHILL.

CRAIGWHÌNNIE. 'Girthon,' 'Kirkmaiden, s. c.' *See under* CRAIGFINNIE.

CRAIGWÒUGHIE. 'Stoneykirk.'

CRAIGY THORN. 'Dalry.' *See under* CRAIGIE.

CRAIKNESS. 'Kirkcudbright.' M.E. *crag ness*, the "ness" or point of the crag.

CRÀILLOCH (*P.* Krellach). 'Mochrum,' 'Port Patrick.' *Crithlach* [creelagh], a shaking bog, from *crith*, to shake, with suffix *-lach*. *Cf.* Creelogh in Galway, Creelagh in Queen's County, and Crylough in Wexford.

CRÀMMAG [*pron.* Crummogh]. 'Kirkmaiden, s.c.' *Crumóg*, a sloping place ; deriv. of *crom* or *crum*. " Cromane and Cromoge, two diminutives, signify anything bending or sloping, and give names to many places (in Ireland) : whether they are applied to glens, hills, fields, etc., must be determined by the character of the particular spot in each case."—*Joyce*, ii. 422. In this case it is the name of a sea-cliff with an old fort on it.

CRAMONERY.   'Minigaff.'

CRANCRÈE. 'Inch.' *Crann crìche* [?] [cree], tree of the boundary. *Crann*, a tree + W. *pren*, B. *prenn*. *See under* CREECH.

CRAN MOSS. 'Kirkmaiden.' *Crann* [?], a tree. *Cf.* Cran and Crann in Armagh, Cavan, and Fermanagh.

CRÀNNOCH ISLE (on the Dee). 'Girthon.' *Crannach*, wooded ; *cf.* many places in Ireland called Crannagh ; or " *Crannog*, a boat " (*O'Reilly*), the boat island. From *crann*, a tree. *Crannog* was also applied to artificial islands or lake-dwellings made of timber, and appears in BR. SC. as *cranok*. *Regist. Secreti Concilii*, A.D. 1608. *See under* CRANCREE.

CRAWAR.   'Kirkmaiden, s. c.'

CRAWHÈNGAN.   'Balmaghie.'

CRAW STANE. 'Inch.' The crow stone. The BR. SC. here preserves the spelling, and probably the exact pronunciation of the A.S. *craw stán*. " *Crow* is allied to *crake, croak*, and even to *crane* — √GAR, to cry out."—*Skeat*. A.S. *stán* has become E. *stone*, just as A.S. *bán* (BR. SC. *bane*) has become *bone* + DU. *steen* + ICEL. *steinn* + DAN. and SWED. *sten* + G. *stein* + GOTH. *stains*, all − TEUT. base STAINA, a stone. The base is STI, appearing in GK. στία, a stone, a pebble (*Skeat*).

CREARY HILL. 'Loch Rutton.' *Criathrach* [crearach], " wasteland " (*O'Reilly*). " *Trí bailé an Criathraigh*, the three townlands of Criathrach."—*Hy Fiachrach*, p. 203. " In Carra," says the editor of the *Hy Fiachrach*, " the term *criathrach* is applied to a flat piece of land intermixed with arable, bogs, sedgy quagmires, and brushwood."

CREE, the river dividing Wigtonshire from the Stewartry. (*Charter*, 1363, Aqua de Creth). This river formed Ptolemy's *Iena Æstuarium*. The old spelling indicates a lost guttural or aspirated dental. *Crích* [?] [cree], a boundary.

CREECH (*gutt.*) (*W. P.* MSS. Creiche). 'Sorbie.' *Críoch*, a boundary, a territory (*O'Reilly*), a field (*O'Don. Suppl.*); O. ERSE *crích*. *Cf.* Creagh, the name of many townlands in Ireland, also Cree and Creea in Cavan and King's County.

CREÈCHAN (*gutt.*) (*Inq. ad Cap.* 1610, Creicher). 'Kirkmaiden.' *Cruachan* [?], a hillock. *See under* CRACHAN. Or *criochán*, the boundary. *Cf.* Creaghaun in Galway.

CREÈTOWN (*P.* Ferrytown). 'Kirkmabreck.' Town on the Cree River.

CREMÒN. 'Kirkcolm,' 'Stoneykirk, s. c.'

CREOGHS (*Inq. ad Cap.* 1611, Meikle Creochis). 'Balmaghie.' *Cruach*, a stack or hill. *See under* CROACH.

CRÈRROCH. 'Balmaclellan.'

CREWHOLE. 'Minigaff.' *Craebh choill* [?] [crew hill], branchy wood. *Cf.* Crewhill in Kildare (*Joyce*, i. 501).

CRÌFFEL (a hill of 1850 feet). (*Map in Bodleian Library*, circ. 1330, Mons Crefel; *P.* Crafel). 'Kirkbean.'

CRÒACH (*gutt.*) 'Inch.' *Cruach*, a stack, a hill. W. *crug*, C. *cruc* +A.S. *croft*. *See under* CLAYCROFT. Croagh or Crogh is a common name in Ireland.

CROACH HILL (*gutt.*) 'Kelton.' *See under* CROACH.

CROÀCHIE (*P.* Krachy). 'Kells.' *Cruachach*, hilly. *Cf.* CRAICHIE.

CRÒCHAN. 'Borgue.' *Cruachán*, dim. of *cruach*, a hill. *Cf.* CRACHAN and CREECHAN.

CROCHMÒRE. 'Kirkpatrick Irongray,' 'Urr.' *See under* CRAICHMORE.

CROCKENCÀLLY, 'Kirkbean.' *Crocán cailleaich*, hillock of the nun. This was church land of old, and Ladyland is close by. *Cnoc* and *Cnocán* are often altered to *croc* and *crocán*, both in Ireland and Scotland.

CROCKETFORD (*P.* Crocofurd). 'Kirkpatrick Durham.'

CROFTÀNGRY. 'Wigtown.' *Croft fhainre* [anry], sloping croft. The popular derivation is *Croft an righ* [?] [ree], the king's croft; but the accent would in that case fall on the last syllable, and the *n* of the article is generally dropped in Irish names containing this word, such Monaree (*moine a' righ*, the king's bog), Dunaree, etc. "Sloping croft" exactly expresses the character of the ground, which is steep.

CROFTRÒY. 'Kirkmabreck.' *Croft ruadh* [roo], red croft. *See under* BENROACH and CLAYCROFT.

CROFT CÀPENOCH. 'Kirkmabreck.' *See under* CAPENOCH and CLAYCROFT.

CRÒGO.   'Balmaclellan.'

CRONIE.   'Urr.'

CROOK (*Inq. ad Cap.* 1620, Cruik). 'Kirkinner.' A.S. *cruce,* a cross.

CROOK, FELL OF. 'Mochrum.' Probably *cruach,* a hill. *See under* CROACH.

CROOKS HILL. 'Dalry.' Probably *cruach,* a hill. *See under* CROACH.

CROOKS (POW). 'Terregles.' *See under* CROOK. "*Pow,* a slow-moving rivulet in flat lands " (*Jamieson*) — A.S. *pol,* a pool, just as BR. SC. *fu'* — A.S. *full,* and *ha'* — A.S. *heal, hal,* a hall.

CRÒSHERIE (*Inq. ad Cap.* 1596, Crosvrie ; 1598, Crosherie, M'Kie ; *P.* Kroshari and Croishare). 'Kirkcowan.' *Crosra, croissaire* [croshary], cross-roads, deriv. of *crois.* *Cf.* Crossera and Crussera, two townlands in Waterford.

CROSSMÌCHAEL [*pron.* meeghil] (*Inq. ad Cap.* 1607, Crocemichael ; *Charter* 3 Rob. II., Corsmychell ; *P.* Korsmichel). A parish in the Stewartry. *Cros Michil* [meeghil], St. Michael's cross.

CRÒTTEAGH HILL. 'Kirkcowan.' *Croiteach* [cruttyagh], lumpy, humpy, from "*croit,* a hump on the back ; a small eminence " (*O'Reilly*). *Cf.* Crotta and Crutta in Kerry, Tipperary, and Cork, from the plural *crotta.* W. *crwt,* a round, dumpy fellow, *crwth,* fem. *croth* + GK. κυρτός, curved, humped. *See under* CLAYCROFT.

CROWS [*pron.* Crowze]. 'Kirkinner.' *Crúadhas* [crooas], hard land, deriv. of *cruadh.* *Cf.* Croase in Wexford. O. ERSE *crúaid,* probably cognate with ICEL. *hardr* + SWED. *hård* + DAN. *haard* + DU. *hard* + A.S. *heard* (whence E. *hard*) + GOTH. *hardus* + G. *hart* + GK. κρατός, strong, κρατερός, καρτερός, valiant, all from a base KART — √KAR, to make. *Skeat* says there is a little doubt about the connection with GK. κρατύς ; he does not mention the O. ERSE *crúaid,* which seems a link in the connection.

CROW'S NEST.   'Old Luce.'

CROW WHIT'S WELL.   'Balmaghie.'

CROYS. 'Kirkpatrick Durham.' *See under* CROWS.

CRÙGGLETON (*P.* Cruggeltoun ; *Inq. ad Cap.* 1620, Crugiltoun-Cavenis ; *W.P.* MSS. Crugiltonn). 'Sorbie.'

CRUISE. 'Old Luce.' *See under* CROWS. *Cf.* CROYS.

CRUISY. 'Penninghame.'

CRÙMMIE. 'Kells.' *Cromadh* or *crumadh* [crumma], the side of a hill (*O'Reilly*), from *crom*, crooked, sloping. *Cf.* CRAMMAG.

CRUMQUHÌL. 'Tungland.' *Crom choill* [hwill], crooked, *i.e.* sloping wood. *Cf.* Cromkill in Ireland. *Crom*, W. *crwm*, fem. *crom*, curved, bent.

CRÙNGIE. 'Penninghame.'

CRUNLAE FELL. 'Kirkcowan.'

CÙBBOX. 'Balmaclellan.'

CUBBY FAULDS. 'Minigaff.'

CUCÀLLA. 'Minigaff.'

CUFF. 'Kirkmaiden, s. c.'

CUIL (*P.* Kool, Keul ; *Inq. ad Cap.* 1604, Cuill). 'Buittle,' 'Kirkmabreck.' *Cúil*, a corner, a nook. *Cf.* Coole, a barony in Fermanagh, name from a point or corner of land running into Lough Erne. Coleraine is translated by *Colgan Cuil-rathinn, secessus filicis,* or the corner of the ferns. It is difficult, however, to distinguish between this word in composition and *cúl*, a back.

CUIL HILL. 'Anwoth,' 'Colvend.' *See under* CUIL.

CULBÀE (*P.* Coulbee). 'Kirkinner.' *Cúil* or *cúl beith* [bey], corner or hill-back of the birches. *Cf.* Coolavehy in Limerick (*cuil an bheithe*).

CULBÈE. 'Kirkcolm.' *See under* CULBAE.

CULBRÀTTEN. 'Penninghame.' *Cúil* or *cill Breatain* [?], Bretan's corner or church. *Cf.* Kilbritton in Cork, which the *Four Masters* (1430) write Cill-Britain. Or *cuil Bretain*, the Briton's or Welshman's corner, as Dumbarton, formerly Dunbretan, was the fort of the Britons. *Cf.* DRUMBREDDAN.

CULCÀIGRIE (*P.* Koulghagary). 'Twynholm.' *Cuil coigriche*, stranger's corner. *See under* DRUMCAGERIE.

CULCÀLDIE. 'Inch.' *Cúil* or *cúl calldtin*, corner or hill-back of the hazel. *See under* CALDONS.

CULCHÌNTIE. 'Kirkcolm.'

CULCRÀE or CULCRÈE. 'Tungland.' *Cuil craebhe* [crew], corner of the tree.

CULCRÈUCHIE (*gutt.*) (*P.* Coulcreochy). 'Penninghame.' *Cúl croiche*, hill-back of the gallows. The old name of Penninghame House. Close by is Galla Hill, *q. v.*; the gallows being probably an appanage of Castle Stewart in Glenraazie. *Croich*, a gallows, W. *crog-bren*, a gallows, *i.e.* a hanging-tree + LAT. *crux*.

CULCRÒNCHIE (*P.* Kilwhronchy). 'Kirkmabreck.'

CULDÈRRY (*P.* Couldury). 'Sorbie.' *Cúl doire* [dirry], hill-back of the oak wood. *Cf.* Coolderry in Ireland.

CULDÒCH (*P.* Kouldowoch). 'Twynholm.' The back of the weir, a hybrid word, ERSE *cúl*, the back, and BR. SC. *doach* or *doagh* (*gutt.*), a weir or cruive. *See under* DOACH.

CULDRÀIN (*P.* Couldrein). 'Kirkgunzeon.' *Cúil draighean* [drain], corner of the blackthorns. *See under* DRANGAN.

CULFÀD (*Inq. ad Cap.* 1640, Culfad). 'Kirkinner,' 'Kirkpatrick Durham.' *Cúil* or *cul fada*, long or far corner, or back.

CULGÀRIE (*P.* Coulghary). 'Glasserton,' 'Kirkinner.' *Cúil* or *cúl g . caera* [gairey], corner or hill-back of the sheep. *Cf.* Calgary in Argyllshire.

CULGHÌE (*P.* Koulgaw). 'Minigaff.' *Cúil gaeth* [gee], corner of the winds, windy corner.

CULGRÀNGE. 'Inch.'

CULGRÒAT (*Inq. ad Cap.* 1543, Cullingrott; 1675, Cullingrott; *P.* Coulgrawit). 'Stoneykirk.'

CULGRÙFF (*P.* Coulgruiff). 'Crossmichael.' *Cúil creamha* [?] [gravva], corner of the wild garlic. *Cf.* Clooncraff in Roscommon (recorded in the *Irish Annals* as *Cluain-creamha*), Inishcraff in Loch Corrib, which is written in the same Annals *Inis-creamha*. The eclipse of *c* by *g* in this word may be noted in Drumgramph in Fermanagh. *Joyce* (ii. 349) says, "It appears probable that the correct form of this word is *cneamh* [knav], and that this has been corrupted to *creamh* like *cnoc* to *croc*."

CULHÒRN (*P.* Coulhorn; *Charter* 1647, Culquhorne). 'Inch.' *Cúil eórna* [orna], corner of the barley. *Cf.* Coolnahorna in Wexford and Waterford; also Craignahorn in Derry, Taonahorna in Antrim, Mulnahorn in Fermanagh and Tyrone, Glennyhorn (*Cluain na eórna*) in Monaghan, Cappaghnahoran in Queen's County.

CULKÀE (*Inq. ad Cap.* 1620, Culcay; *W. P.* MSS. Culcay; *P.* Coulka). 'Sorbie.' *Cùil* or *cúl caedhe* [kaey], corner or back of the quagmire. *Cf.* Coolquoy in Dublin, another form of the same name.

CULKIÈST (*P.* Coulkist). 'Kirkgunzeon.' *Cf.* DALKEST.

CULLACH (*P.* Coulclach). 'Penninghame.' *Cùil* or *cùl clach* [?], stony corner or hill-back.

CULLÀCHIE (HEIGH and LAIGH), (two fields in Glasnick). 'Penninghame.' *Cúl achadh*, back field.

CULLÈARY RIG (*P.* Koulkery). 'Kells.' *Coill* [kil], *cúil* or *cúl iarach* [eeragh], western wood, corner, or hill-back. Pont's rendering is probably a misprint. *See under* BLAW WEARY.

CULLENDÈUGH (MS. 1527, Culindaich). 'New Abbey.' *See under* CULLENOCH. Perhaps the *d* is intrusive here; if it is regarded as organic, then the meaning would be *cuileann dabhoch* [davogh, daagh], the farm or land of the hollies. "*Dabhoch,* a farm that keeps sixty cows."—*O'Reilly.*

CÙLLENDOCH (*P.* Cullendach; *Inq. ad Cap.* 1608, Culleindoch). 'Girthon,' 'Kirkmabreck.'

CULLENOCH (*War Committee,* 1646, Cullenoch, *callit* Clauchane-pluck). 'Balmaghie.' *Cuileannach,* a place of hollies; from *cuileann. Cf.* Cullenagh, a frequent name in Ireland. *See under* ALWHILLAN.

CULLINAW. 'Buittle.' *Cúl an atha* [?] [aha], back of the ford.

CÙLLOCH (*P.* Culloch). 'Urr.'

CULLÙRPATTIE FELL (*P.* Coulurpetty; *Inq. ad Cap.* 1668, Killurpatie). 'Inch.'

CULMÀIN (*P.* Coulmeinn). 'Urr.'

CULMÀLZIE (*P.* Coullmalzie). 'Kirkinner.' *Cúl* or *cúil Malzie,* the back, or the corner or angle of the Malzie burn. *See under* CORSEMALZIE and MALZIE. *Cf.* Kilmalie, a parish in Argyll-shire, written also Kilmailze and Kilmalzie.

CULMÀRK (*P.* Gulmark, Gulmarck). 'Dalry.' A hybrid name; *cúl,* the back, and A.S. *mearc,* a boundary (E. and BR. SC. *march*), the back march. *See under* MARK.

CULMÌCK (*Inq. ad Cap.* 1543, Culmuk; 1691, Kilmick; *P.* Culmuck). *Cúil muic* [mick], the pig's corner. *Cf.* Coolna-muck in Ireland.

K

CULMÒRE (*P.* Culmoir). 'Stoneykirk.' *Coill mór*, the big wood. *Cf.* Kilmore in Cork (written by the Annalists *coill mohr*); Kylemore in Connemara, etc., also Cuilmore. *See under* KILLIEMORE.

CULNÀUGHTRIE (*P.* Colnachtyr). 'Rerwick.' *Uachdarach*, upper (*see under* AUCHNOTTEROCH); prefix uncertain.

CULNÒAG (*Inq. ad Cap.* 1620, Culnog; *W. P.* MSS. Culnoik; *P.* Culnowack). 'Sorbie.' Resembles Cullenoge in Wexford, which *Joyce* derives from *culeainóg*, a place of hollies; but the accent would, in that case, probably be as in CULLENOCH.

CULQUHÀ [*pron.* Culhwa] (*Inq. ad Cap.* 1601, Culquha; *P.* Koulwha). 'Twynholm.' *See under* CULKAE.

CULQUHÀSEN [*pron.* Culhwàsen] (*P.* Coulwhoisen).　'Old Luce.'

CULQUHÌRK [*pron.* Culhwirk] (*Barnbarroch Papers*, 1583, Cowlquhork). 'Wigton.' *Cùil choirce* [hurkie], corner of the oats. *Cf.* Coolacork in Wicklow, Gortachurk in Cavan. *See under* AWHIRK.

CULREÒCH [*pron.* Culroigh] (*P.* Culreoch). 'Inch.' *Cùil riabhach* [reeagh], grey corner. *Cf.* Coolreagh in Ireland.

CULRÒY. 'Old Luce.' *Cùil ruadh* [rooa, roy], red corner. *Cf.* Coolroe in Ireland.

CULSCÀDDEN (*P.* Coulskadden). 'Sorbie.' *Cùil sgadan*, corner of the herrings. On the shore of Wigton Bay; named, probably, from being a landing-place for fishing-boats. *Cf.* Coolscadden in Dublin County, a place where herring were sold. *See also* LOCHANSCADDAN. O. ERSE *scatán*. The word seems akin to names of other fish, as ICEL. *skata*, a skate + LAT. *squatus* + ERSE and GAEL. *sgat*, a skate + A.S. *sceadda*, a shad.

CULSHÀBBEN.　　　　　　　　　　　　　　　　'Mochrum.'

CULSHÀN (*Inq. ad Cap.* 1604, Culscheinchane; 1607, Culzeane [?]). 'Kirkpatrick Durham.'

CULSHÀRG. 'Minigaff.' *Cùil dearg* [dyarg], red corner. *Dearg* is frequently softened into *jarg*, whence the transition is easy to *sharg*.

CULTAM HILL.　　　　　　　　　　　　　　　'Crossmichael.'

CULTIEMORE. 'Minigaff.' *Coillte mór*, big woods. *Cf.* Kiltybegs, in Longford and Monaghan, in the opposite sense, *i.e.* little woods.

CULTS (*W. P.* MSS. Cultis). 'Inch,' 'Sorbie.' *Coillte* [kilty, culty], woods; plur. of *coill*.

CULVÈNNAN (*P.* Coulvennan). 'Crossmichael,' 'Kirkcowan.' *Cul bhennain* [vennan], back of the hill. The place of this name in Crossmichael was named by the Gordons after their lands in Kirkcowan.

CUMLÒDEN. 'Minigaff.'

CÙMNOCK KNOWES. 'Carsphairn.' *Cam cnoc,* crooked or sloping hill. *Cf.* KNOCKCAM.

CUNDÈE (three hills, Near, Mid, and Far). 'Penninghame.' *Ceann dubh* [ken doo or dew], black head. *Cf.* KINDEE.

CÙNNOCH. 'Whithorn, s. c.' *Cuinneóg,* "a churn, a pail" (*O'Reilly*), *i.e.* where the waves are churned. *Cf.* RUMMLEKIRN. GAEL. *cuinneag,* W. *cynnog,* a pail or pitcher.

CUPAR'S CAIRN (a hill 2000 feet). 'Minigaff.' Said to be named from Coupar, Bishop of Galloway, who, with Archbishop Maxwell, was the principal reviser of the prayer-book submitted to King James in 1616.

CURATE'S NEUK. 'Kirkcolm.' BR. SC. *neuk,* a nook or corner (of land), M.E. *nok.* From ERSE *niuc,* a nook.

CÙRCHIEHILL [*pron.* kurchie, as in *church*]. 'Minigaff.'

CURDEN. 'Balmaghie.'

CURGHÌE [*pron.* Curgee, *g* hard] (*Inq. ad Cap.* 1610, Corghie; *P.* Karghy). 'Kirkmaiden.' *Cor* or *cathair* [caer] *gaeth* [gee, gwee], hill or fort of the wind. *Cf.* (with the latter meaning) Cahernageeha and Dungeeha in Ireland (*cathair na gaeithe, dun-gaeithe,* windy fort), and from the plural (as in the present instance) *gaeth* or *gaoth,* Tonderghie, Drumagee, Mullingee, in Longford, *i.e. muileann gaeith,* wind-mill. O. ERSE *gáeth, góeth,* gen. *gáithe,* ERSE *gaeth, gaoth* + W. *gwynt,* C. *guenz,* LAT. *uentus,* cognate with TEUT. base WENDA or WENTHA, wind, whence GOTH. *winds, winths* + O.H.G. *wint,* G. *wind* + DAN. and SWED. *wind* + ICEL. *vindr* + DU. *wind* + A.S. *wind* (whence M.E. *wind, wynd,* E. *wind*). The LAT. *uentus* (says *Skeat*) was originally a pres. participle, meaning "blowing," from √AW or WA, to blow, from the latter of which is the SKT. *vá,* to blow. The ERSE *gáeth,* has either lost the *n,* or has travelled by a different road from the root WA, which it has nearly approached in pronunciation again. *Cf.* CURLEYWEE.

CURLEYGÒWER (a hill). 'Minigaff.' *Cor na gabhar* [?], the goat's peak.

CURLEYWÈE (a hill of 2405 feet). 'Minigaff.' *Cor na gaeth* [?] [gee], peak of the winds, by usual change of *g* to *w*. *See under* CURGHIE, WINDY HILL, WINDY STANDARD, etc.

CURLÙCKIE (a shoulder of Cairnsmore of Dee). 'Kells.'

CURNÈLLOCH. 'Kells.' *Corr n-eilidh* [?] [elleh], peak of the hinds (*see under* CARNELTOCH); or perhaps *cathair* [caher], or *corr n-ailich*, as Caherelly in Limerick, written in Irish *cathair ailigh*. "A union of two synonymous terms, the *caher* of the stone fort. So also in Cahernally in Galway, which is called *Cathair-na-hailighi* in an ancient document quoted by Hardiman."—*Joyce*, i. 293. *See under* CRAIGANALLY.

CURRAFÌN [*pron.* Corriefeen]. 'New Luce.' *Coire fionn* [fin], white pool (caldron), a salmon pool on the Luce. *Coire* is applied to both deep, swirling pools in a river, and also to contracted, pot-like dells. O. ERSE *core*+W. *callor*, also (by change of *c* to *p*) *pair*+C. *caudarn*+O.F. *caldaru*+LAT. *caldarium* (—*caldus, calidus*, hot) whence M.E. *caldron, caudron*, E. *caldron*. *Cf*. SKT. *crá*, to boil. *Cf*. CURRYDOW.

CURRIE RIG. 'Carsphairn.' *Coire* [currie], a caldron, a glen, and A.S. *hric, hrycg*, or BR. SC. *rig*, a ridge.

CURRIESTANES (*P.* Creustoun). 'Troqueer.'

CÙRROCHTRIE (*P.* Korrachty). 'Kirkmaiden.' This farm is situated next to Garrochtrie; their juxta-position and the similarity of the names suggest that the two last syllables in each may represent respectively *uachdar* [ougher], upper, and *íochdar* [eighder], lower. This would agree with the relative position of the farms, and if this be a correct supposition, then Currochtrie would represent *ceathramhaidh* [carhoo] *íochdarach*, the lower land-quarter, and Garrochtrie *ceathramhaidh uachdarach*, the upper land-quarter. *Cf*. Curryeighter and Curryoughter in Ireland, from *currach*, a marsh or moor, Moyeightrach (*mach íochdar*, lower plain) near Killarney, and Moyletra (*mael íochdar*, lower hill) in Derry. But into these Galloway names it is hard to say whether *Ochtraidh* [Ochtrie] does not enter. The lands have long been held by the Macdouall family, in which Ochtraidh or Uthred is of very ancient and frequent occurrence. *Cf*. KIRROUCHTRIE and GARROCHTRIE.

CURRYDÒW (*P.* Corydow), a glen on Garpel Burn. *Coire dubh* [currie doo], the black caldron (pool or glen). *See under* CURRAFIN.

CUSHIEMÀY. 'Buittle.' *Cos a' maighe* [?] [cush a' maye], foot of the field. *Cf*. Cushaling in Tyrone (*cos a' linne*, foot of the pool); Cushendun and Cushendall in Antrim (the foot of the river Dun and of the river Dall), Coshquin in Londonderry, Coshlea in Limerick, etc., etc. (*Joyce,* i. 527). O. ERSE *coss,* ERSE *cos,* GAEL. *cas*+LAT. *pes*+GK. $\pi o\hat{v}\varsigma$+GOTH. *fotus*+G. *fuss* +SWED. *fot*+DAN. *fod*+ICEL. *fótr*+DU. *voet*+A.S. *fót,* pl. *fét* (whence M.E. *fot, foot,* BR. SC. *fut, fit,* E. *foot*)+SKT. *pad, pád*— √PAD, to go. *Magh, see under* MAY.

CUTCLÒY [*pron.* Cuckloy] (*Inq. ad Cap.* 1585, Cutcloy; *P.* Cotcloy; *W. P.* MSS. Cottcloye). ' Whithorn.'

CUTREÒCH [*pron.* Cuttroghe] (*P.* Cettreoch; *W. P.* MSS. Coitrioche). ' Whithorn.'

CUTTYMÒRE BURN. 'Minigaff.' *Ceide mór* [?], great hill. *See under* KITTYSHALLOCH.

DAFFIN.   ' Kirkmabreck.'

DAILEYBRÀCKEN.   ' Inch.'

DÀILLY. ' Urr.' *Dealghe,* the thorns. *See under* CLAMDALLY. *Cf.* Dailly in Ayrshire.

DALÀNE *or* DELÈEN (a pool in the Minnick).   ' Minigaff.'

DALÀRRAN.   ' Balmaclellan.'

DALBÈATTIE (*Inq. ad Cap.* 1599, Dalbatie; 1604, Dalbaittie; *P.* Dalbety). ' Urr.'

DALBÒNNITON.   ' Carsphairn.'

DALHÀMMEN.   ' Kirkcowan.'

DALKÈST (*P.* Dalchist).   ' Kirkcolm.'

DALLÀSH (*P.* Dallash). ' Minigaff.' *Cf.* Dallas, a parish in Moray, which *Shaw* translates *dal uis,* watered plain.

DÀLLY. ' Kirkcolm.' *Dealghe,* the thorns. *See under* CLAMDALLY and DAILLY.

DALMÀLIN BURN.   ' Girthon.'

DALMÀNNOCH (*Inq. ad Cap.* 1668, Croftmannoch *prope burgum de* Innermessan). ' Inch.' *Dál manach,* the field or land-portion of the monks. *Dál* has two significations, the principal and (in Celtic) original being " a portion, a share ;" the other, probably borrowed from the Scandinavian, being " a dale, a low place between hills." " *Dál* i. *rand* (a portion), inde dicitur Dal Riata."—*Corm.* p. 47. The E. *deal* is cognate in origin and sense, its primary meaning being a share, a division, hence, a quantity; and, further, a thin board of timber, from the slicing or dividing of the tree (*Skeat*).   *Cf.* E. *share* (A.S. *land scearu*, a portion or share of land), from the idea of shearing or cutting.   ERSE *dál*, a portion + DU. *deel*, a share + A.S. *dél*, a share (whence M.E. *deel, del*, E. *deal*) + DAN. *deel*, a portion + SWED. *del*, a part, a share + ICEL. *deild, deilð*, a dole, a share + GOTH. *dails*, a part + O.H.G. *teil*, G. *theils*.   In the other and, probably, later sense of a dale between hills, "the original sense was 'cleft' or 'separation'" (*Skeat*), and from the same base as 'deal' come E. *dale — dell —* A.S. *del* (plur. *dalu*), a valley + ICEL. *dalr*, a dale + DAN. *dal* + SWED. *dal* + DU. *dal* + O. FRIER. *del* + O. SAX. *dal* + GOTH. *dul* + G. *thal*. As a prefix *dal* in place-names is not always to be distinguished from *dur*, *i.e. dobhar*, water, owing to the interchange of *l* and *r*.   *See under* DARGALGAL.

DALMÒNEY.   'Urr.'   *Dál muine* [minnie], field of the thicket, or *dál mónadh* [munnie], of the moor or peat.   *Móin*, gen. *mónadh*, a mountain, an extensive common; a bog, moss, turf, peat. W. *mawn*, peat, *mynydd, mwnt*, a mountain, GAEL. *monadh*, a moor + B. and C. *monedh* + A.S. *munt* + LAT. *mons*, gen. *mont-is* — √MAN, to project; *cf.* LAT. *e-min-ere*, to project.

DALNÀDER.   'Minigaff.'

DALNÀW (*P.* Dalna).   'Minigaff.'   *Dál an atha* [aha, awe], field of the ford.

DALNIGÀP, DOLNIGAP, or DARNIGAP (*Inq. ad Cap.* 1633, Dalnagap).   'New Luce.'

DALQUHÀIRN (*P.* Dalwharn, Dalahorn, Dalwhairns).   'Carsphairn,' 'Kirkpatrick Irongray.'   *Dál chairn*, field of the cairn. *See under* AUCHENCAIRN.

DALREAGLE [*pron.* Darrègal].   'Kirkinner.'   *Deargail* [?], a red place, red land.   *Cf.* Dargle in Wicklow, Darrigil in Mayo, Darrigal in Waterford.   Deriv. of *dearg* (*Joyce*, ii. 39).

DALRÝ (a town and parish in the Stewartry).   'Dalry.'   The same name occurs in Ayrshire.

DALSCÀIRTH (*P.* Dalskairth).   'Troqueer.'   *Dál sceirach* [?], rocky field.   *See under* BARSCARROW.

DALSHÀNGAN (*P.* Dalchangan).   'Carsphairn,' 'Minigaff,' 'New Luce.'   *Dál seangan*, field of the ants. *See under* BARNSHANGAN.

DALSHÌNNIE (*Inq. ad Cap.* 1604, Dalschynnie). 'Terregles.' *Dál sionach* [shinnagh], the field of the foxes. *Sionagh* was a common name of men in Celtic times, just as Fox in England and Ireland, and Todd in Scotland, are now. Thus O'Carthar-naigh, Lord of Teffia, took the name of Sinnach; and from the O'Caharneys are descended Fox of Foxville in Meath, and Fox of Foxhall in Longford. Dalshinnie, therefore, may be the portion of a man called Shinnach (*O'Don. Top. Poem,* ix. (35)). *Cf.* AUCHENSHINNOCH, BLAIRSHINNOCH, etc. *See* page 33, *note.*

DALTÀLLOCHAN (*P.* Lein of Daltallachan). 'Carsphairn.'

DALTÀMIE. 'Minigaff.'

DALTORAE. 'Minigaff.' *Dál tòruidhe* [?] [tory], the hunter's field. *Cf.* Ballytory in Wexford, Ratory in Tyrone. *Tòruidhe*, from *tóir*, pursuit, *tór*, a pursuer, came to mean an outlaw or *tory*; thus becoming a term of reproach, as it is still among the lower orders in Scotland and North Ireland. As such it was applied to a political party by their opponents, and the Tories in return dubbed their foes the Whigs, a term of contempt having its origin in the sour milk or whey (whig), which was an ordinary article of diet among the " hill folk."

DALVÀIRD. 'Minigaff.' *Dál bhaird* [vaird], the rhymer's field. *Cf.* Dalnavaird in Forfar and Kincardine, and Dalnavert in Inverness-shire. *Cf. also* DERVAIRD. *See under* BARNBOARD.

DALVÀDIE [*pron.* Dalvaddy]. 'Kirkmaiden.' *Dál mhadaidh* [vaddie], the dog's field. *See under* BLAIRMODDIE.

DALWHÀT. 'Balmaclellan.' *Dál chat* [haat], the wild cat's field. *See under* ALWHAT.

DÀMLOCH STRAND. 'Kirkcowan.'

DAMNAGLÀUR. 'Kirkmaiden.'

DAMNAHÒLLY. 'Kirkmaiden.'

DÀNEVALE. 'Crossmichael.'

DÀNNERS. *See* FOUNTAIN DANNERS.

DÀRACHANS. 'Minigaff.' *Darachean*, the oaks, E. plur. added.

DARGÀLGAL. 'Penninghame.' *Dobhar gall Gaidheal* [?] [dour gall gael], the water of the stranger Gaels. *See under* GALLOWAY. The prefix is evident, but the remainder is purely speculative, suggested by the proximity of the place to the Deil's Dyke, the ancient rampart separating Gallgaidhel, or Galloway, from the kingdom of Strathclyde.   O. ERSE *dobur* (i . *uisce,* unde dicitur *dobar-chú* i . *dobran—Corm.* p. 15), ERSE *dúr* (*O'Reilly*) + W. *dwfr, dwr,* B. *dour,* C. *dour, douar, dower,* water. *Cf.* "Drow, an indefinable quantity of water."—*Mactaggart.* This word occurs as the prefix *dar, der, dir, dur,* and some-times *dal,* principally in the moorland and uncultivated districts of Galloway.

DARGÀLL LANE.   'Minigaff.'   *Dobhar* [dour] *gall* [?], water of the foreigners or standing stones.   *See under* DERGALL.

DARGÒALS (*P.* Dyrgaals ; *Inq. ad Cap.* 1668, Dirgoills).   'New Luce.'

DARHÒMINY.   'Minigaff.'

DARLÒSKINE (*Inq. ad Cap.* 1633, Dirloskane).   'Kirkcowan.' *Dobhar* [dour] *loscain* or *losgan,* water of the frogs.   *Cf.* LIN-LOSKIN.   The old northern English equivalent to these names appears in Dumfriesshire as Paddockhole.

DARNAGÌE [*pron.* gee, *hard*].   'New Luce.'   *Dobhar na gáeth* [gee], water of the winds.

DARNÀRBEL.   'Minigaff.'   *Dobhar an earbil* [dour-an-arbil], water of the point, *i.e.* a tail or extremity of land.   "Often applied to the extremity of any natural feature, such as a long, low hill, or to any long strip of land."   *Cf.* DRUMMINARBEL ; also in Ireland, Urbal, the name of several townlands in North Ireland, Urbalkirk in Monaghan, Urbalshinny in Donegal (*i.e.* fox's brush), and Warbleshinny in Derry, etc. etc.   "*Ear-bull,* a tail, *i.e. iar ball,* hindward member."—*O'Reilly.*

DARNÀW BURN.   'Minigaff.'   *Dobhar* [dour] *an atha* [aha, awe], water of the ford.   *Cf.* DALNAW.

DARNCRÈE.   'Girthon.'   *Dobhar* [dour] *na criche* [creehie], water of the boundary, or perhaps *dobhar na' craebh* [crave, creev], water of the trees, wooded stream.   *Cf.* CREE, POLCREE, etc.

DARNGÀRROCH (*Inq. ad Cap.* 1604, Darnegarroch ; *P.* Darnghey-rach).   'Kirkpatrick Durham.'

DARNIMÒW (*P.* Dyrnamow).   'New Luce.'   *Dobhar na mbo* [dur-namoe], water of the cows.   *Cf.* Annamoe in Wicklow (*ath-na-mbo,* the cows' ford), Carrigeennamoe in Cork (*carruigan-na mbo,* the cows' crag).

DARNSHÀW (a tributary of the Water of Deugh).   'Carsphairn.'

DARÒW BURN.   'Girthon.'   *Dobhar dhubh* [?] [oo], black water.

DÀRROCH. · 'Stoneykirk.' *Darach*, a place of oaks. *Cf.* Darragh in Limerick, and Derragh in Cork, Longford, Mayo, Down, and Clare. Adjective from *dair* (O. ERSE *daur*), an oak.

DARROW (a hill of 1500 feet) (*P.* Darry). 'Kells.' Probably from *darach* or *doire*, an oak wood. *See under* DERRY.

DARSÀLLOCH (*P.* Darsalloch). 'Kells.' *Dobhar saileach*, water of the willows. *See under* BARNSALLIE.

DARSNÀG. 'Mochrum.'

DARWOOD. 'Kells.' Seems to be a compound from *dair*, an oak, with E. *wood* added.

DAVENHOLM. 'New Luce.'

DEE, a river in the Stewartry (*Ptolemy*, Deva). Probably from the base *dub, dubh*, black, the dark water; the aspirated labial being shown in the Latin form Deva.

DEER'S DEN. 'Carsphairn,' 'Dalry,' 'Minigaff.' " *Den*, a hollow, a dingle " (*Jamieson*).—A.S. *denu, dene, den*, a valley, a plain ; M.E. *dene*. This word commonly occurs in English names, *e.g.* Tenterden, Hazeldean, etc.

DELHÀBIECH (*P.* Dalchappock ; *Inq. ad Cap.* 1600, Dalcopokc). 'Inch.'

DENDÒW or DISDÒW. 'Girthon.'

DENDÒWNIES. 'New Luce.'

DENNIEMÙLK. 'Minigaff.'

DENNOT. 'Leswalt.' *See* LONG DENNOT.

DERGÀLL. 'Kirkmabreck.' The existence here of megalithic circles suggest the origin *dobhar gall*, water of the standing stones, but this is pure conjecture (*see under* DERGALGAL). *Gall*, literally a foreigner, is also a name for a standing stone ; given, if we are to believe *Cormac*, because they were first erected in Ireland by the Galli, or primitive inhabitants of France. This, however, is, to say the least, improbable ; and if *gall*, a standing stone, is the same word as *gall*, a foreigner, it was probably applied figuratively. *See under* BOWHILL. *Gall*, a Gaul, *Gallicus*. " This word was first applied by the Irish Annalists to the Danes or Scandinavians from their first arrival in the eighth century to the twelfth, when it was transferred to the English."—*O'Don. Suppl.* *Gall*, foreign + O.H.G. *walah* + A.S. *wealh* (E. *walnut* = A.S. *wealh knut*, foreign

nut), from " Teutonic type WALHA, a stranger, a name given
by Teutonic tribes to their Celtic and Roman neighbours "
(*Skeat*).   *Cf.* A.S. *Wealhas*, the Welsh, whence E. *Wales.*

DERHÀGIE.   ' Old Luce.'

DERLÒCHLIN. ' Old Luce.' *Dobhar* [dour] *Lochlinn* [?], Lauchlan's
    stream. *See under* BARLAUCHLINE.

DERLÒNGAN.   ' Old Luce.'

DERNACÌSSOCK [*c* soft]. ' Kirkcowan.' *Dobhar na' siosg* [?] [shisk],
    water of the sedges or reeds. " *Siosg*, a sedge, reed grass,
    sheer grass ; carex."—*O'Reilly.*   GAEL. *scasg* + LOW G. *segge*
    + A.S. *secg* (whence M. E. *segge*, DR. SC. *seg*, E. *sedge*). " The
    lit. sense is ' cutter,' *i.e.* sword-grass, from the sharp edge or
    sword-like appearance ; *cf.* LAT. *gladiolus*, a small sword,
    sword-lily, flag. From the Teut. base SAG, to cut = √SAK,
    to cut."—*Skeat.* LAT. *sec-are*, etc. *Cf.* DRUMACISSOCK ; and
    in Ireland, Cornashesk in Tyrone and Cavan, Cornashesko,
    in Fermanagh, Glenshesk in Antrim, Glenshisk in Waterford,
    etc. *See under* SEG HILL and STARRY HEUGH.

DERNAFRÀNIE.   ' Old Luce.'

DERNAFÙEL.   ' Old Luce.'

DERNAGLÀUR. ' Old Luce.' *Cf.* DAMNAGLAUR.

DERNÀIN (*P.* Derneen). ' Old Luce.' *Dobhar* [dour] *n-en* [?]
    [ane], water of the birds. *See under* BARNEAN.

DERNEMÙLLIE.   ' New Luce.'

DERNIEMÒRE (*P.* Lein of Dyrgonmoir).   ' Old Luce.'

DERRISCÒAL.   ' New Luce.'

DERRY (*P.* Dyrry). ' Kirkcowan,' ' Mochrum,' ' Penninghame.'
    Doire [dirrie], a wood, especially an oak wood. Londonderry
    was anciently *Doire Calgaich*, rendered by Adamnan *Roboretum
    Calgachi*, Calgach's oakwood, it then got the name of *Doire-
    Columcille*, from the monastery which St. Columba founded
    there in 546, and, finally, when James I. gave a charter
    thereof to a company of London merchants it was called
    Londonderry.

DERRYGÒWAN (*Inq. ad Cap.* 1680, Darregoun).   ' Balmaghie.'
    Doire gobhain [gowan], the smith's wood. *See under* ALDER-
    GOWAN.

DERRYS, THE. 'Penninghame.' *Doire*, an oak wood (*see under* DERRY), E. plur. added. This is often done to express the Gaelic plural, but in this case it has probably happened in some such way as this: a house or farm gets the name of Derry, then another house is built, or the farm is subdivided, when the group would be called collectively the Derrys, with perhaps, further definition as High Derry, Low Derry, etc. There is, however, prevalent an indiscriminate use of the plural in country speech: thus the Earl of Stair is commonly spoken of as Lord Stairs.

DERVÀIRD (*Inq. ad Cap.* 1633, Dirvairdis; 1668, Dirwardie; *P.* Dwrboird). 'Old Luce.' *Dobhar bhaird* [dour vaird], the water of the rhyme. *Cf.* DALVAIRD. *See under* BARNBOARD. *Pont* gives the unaspirated form.

DERWHÌLLAN. 'Old Luce.' *Dobhar chuillain* [dour hillan], water of the hollies.

DERWÌNDLE. 'New Luce.' *Cf.* DRUMFUNDLE. *See under* CARRICKFUNDLE in Addenda.

DEUGH, WATER OF (*Inq. ad Cap.* 1550, Ottroduscan (*i.e.* Water o' Duskan)). 'Carsphairn.' *Dubh uisce* [doo iskie], black water. The old spelling retains the *s*. *Cf.* Dusk Water in Ayrshire.

DIAMOND LAGGAN. 'Parton.' *See under* LAGGAN.

DIAN, EAST. 'Kirkcowan.' *Daingean*, a stronghold. " In the north of Ireland the *ng* in the middle of this word is pronounced as a soft guttural, which, as it is very faint and quite incapable of being represented by English letters, is suppressed in modern spelling, thereby changing *daingean* to *dian*, or some such form."—*Joyce*, i. 307. *Cf.* Dian and Dyan in Tyrone and Monaghan.

DÌBBIN CRAIG and LANE.   'Dalry.'

DIDDLE'S HILL.   'Inch.'

DILDAWN (*Inq. ad Cap.* 1604, Daldawen; MS. 1527, Daldawane). 'Kelton.'

DILENOCH.   'Kirkmaiden, s. c.'

DINCHÌNPON. 'Buittle.' *Dún tiompain*, fort of the hillock: by the common change of *ti* to *ch* (*see under* CHALLOCH). " *Tiompan*, a hillock (Antrim)."—*O'Don. Suppl. to O'Reilly.* *Cf.* DUNJUMPIN; and in Ireland, Timpan in Antrim, Timpaun in Roscommon, Reanadimpaun in Waterford (*reidh na dtiom-*

pan, to which *Joyce* gives the meaning of the mountain-flat of the standing stones), Tempanroe in Tyrone, Craigatempin in Antrim, etc. *Tiompán* also means a harp or drum, hence Dunchimpon may mean the fort of the harps, from some long-forgotten incident.

DINDÌNNIE (*P.* Doundunny). 'Leswalt.' *Dún duine* [dinny], fort of the men, the folk's fort. ERSE *duine*, a man, a person + W. *dyn* + C. *dên*, B. *den.*

DINDÙFF (*Inq. ad Cap.* 1616, Dunduff; *P.* Dunduff). 'Kirkcolm.' *Dún dubh* [duv], black fort.

DIN HILL. 'Twynholm.' *Dún*, a fort.

DÌNNANS (*W. P.* MSS. Dunnance; *P.* Dounen). 'Whithorn.' *Dúnan*, a fort, dim. of *dún*, E. plural added. *Cf.* Doonans in Antrim; Dooneens and Downings the names of many townlands in Ireland.

DÌNNINS (a hill of 1050 feet). 'Carsphairn.' *See under* DINNANS.

DINVÌN (*P.* Duntin (*misprint*); *Inq. ad Cap.* Dunevin). 'Port Patrick.' *Dún fionn* [fin], white fort.

DERCLÀUCH. 'Carsphairn.' *Dobhar* [dour] *clach*, water of the stones.

DÌRLETON. 'Kirkinner.'

DIRNÈARK [*pron.* Durnyark] (*P.* Dyrnairp; *Inq. ad Cap.* 1698, Darnyerk). 'Kirkcowan.'

DIRNÒW [*pron.* Durnoo] (*P.* Dyrnagrow). 'Kirkcowan.'

DIRSKÈLPIN *or* DIRSKÈLVIN (*Barnbarroch* 1563, Dyrreskylben, *Inq. ad Cap.* 1668, Dirsculvyne; *P.* Dyrskilby). 'Old Luce.'

DIRVÀCHLIE (*P.* Dyrvachlie; *Inq. ad Cap.* 1698, Darvachlan). 'Kirkcowan.'

DIRVANÀNIE (*P.* Dwrrymannany, Dyrrymannany). 'Kirkcowan.' The prefix here seems to be, not *dobhar* but *doire*. *See under* DERRY.

DISDÒW (*Charter*, 1664, Duirsdow). 'Girthon.'

DIVOT, THE (a salmon pool in the Dee). 'Kirkcudbright.' *See under* DIVOT HILL.

DÌVOT HILL. 'Dalry.' The hill of the sods. "*Divot, divet, diffat*: a thin, flat, oblong turf, used for covering cottages, and also for fuel."—*Jamieson.* *Cf.* Knockascree, Nogniescree.

DOACH, MEIKLE, and PRIORY DOACH (on the Dee near Tungland Abbey). 'Kirkcudbright.' " *Doach, doagh*, a weir or cruive." —*Jamieson*. *Cf.* CULDOCH.

DOACH STEPS (across Pulharrow Burn). 'Kells.' *See under* DOACH.

DOAMS. 'Tungland.'

DÒCHIES. 'Kirkcolm.' *Dubh ais* [?], black hill. *Cf.* Divis in Down County, Divish in Mayo, Dooish in Donegal (*Joyce*, ii. 270). *Cf.*, however, Duffus, a parish in Moray, which *Shaw* interprets *dubh uisg*, black water.

DODD HILL. 'Carsphairn' (*thrice*), 'Dalry.' Dodd appears locally as a hill name. Meaning uncertain. Perhaps related to " *Doddy, doddit.* 1. Without horns. 2. Bald, without hair."—*Jamieson*. In this sense it would=*mael*, bald, so common as a hill name. *See under* MEAUL, MULL.

DODD OF TROQUHÀIN [*pron.* Trohwane], (a hill of 1139 feet). 'Balmaclellan.'

DOGSTONE HILL. 'Kirkcolm.'

DOGTAIL CROFT. 'Mochrum.'

DOGTÙMMOCK (a hill of 1631 feet). 'Colvend.' *See under* DODD, of which this is probably a corruption. " *Tummock.* A tuft, or small spot of elevated ground."—*Jamieson*.

DOLT. 'Kirkmaiden, s. c.' *Dubh alt* [?] [doo alt], black height or glen.

DOMINS. 'Girthon.'

DONALDBÙIE. 'Kells.' *Dúnach* or *dúnadh buidhe* [buie], yellow fort. *Cf.* Doonachboy in Clare. *Dúnach*, a derivation of *dún* (*Joyce*, ii. 5), or *dúnadh* (*O'Reilly*), is liable to confusion with *domhnach*, a church.

DÒNNAN HILL. 'Stoneykirk.' *Dúnan*, a fort. *Cf.* DINNANS, DOONEND, DOUNAN; and, in Ireland, Dooneen, Downing, and Downeen.

DOON, DOON CASTLE, HILL, etc., of frequent occurrence throughout the district. *Dún*, a fort. Doon and Down are equally common names in Ireland and Scotland. O. ERSE *dún*+W. *din*, a hill-fort or fortified hill+A.S. *dún*, a hill (whence M.E. *dun, doun*, E. *down*, a hill), cognate with A.S. *tún* (M.E. *toun*, E. *town*). The original idea is " a fence "+DU. *tuin*, a fence+

ICEL. *tún*, an enclosure, a homestead + G. *zaun*, O.H.G. *zún*, a hedge. The Celtic *dún* "is conspicuous in many old place-names, such as *Augusto-dunum, Camelo-dunum,* etc." (*Skeat*), just as the Teutonic *tún* in such names as Brighton, Hampton, Brigton, etc.

DOONAMÙCK. 'Minigaff.' *Dún na muc,* fort of the swine. *Cf.* DUNMUCK.

DOONEND (*P.* Dounens). 'Colvend.' *Dúnan,* a fort. *See under* DONNAN.

DORNELL LOCH (*Inq. ad Cap.* 1576, Dornall; *P.* Dornell). 'Balmaghie.' *Dobhar* [dour], water. *Cf.* LOCH DORNAL.

DOUGARIES. 'New Luce.'

DOULOCH (*Inq. ad Cap.* 1624, Dewlache; *P.* Dowloch). 'Kirkcolm.' *Dubh loch,* black lake. *Cf.* DOWLOCH, DOWLOCHS and DUBLOCH; also frequently in Ireland, Doolough.

DOÙNAN. 'Stoneykirk.' *See under* DONNAN. *Cf.* Doonan and Doonane in many counties in Ireland.

DÒURIE (*P.* Dowry). 'Mochrum.' *Durach, i.e. dobharach,* watery, plashy, deriv. of *dobhar, dur,* water. *Cf.* Doory, in Antrim, Kerry, King's County, and Longford; Doora in Clare and Dooragh in Tyrone.

DOVEWELL. 'Loch Rutton.' *Cf.* DOWELL.

DÒWALTON [*pron.* Dooalton] (*Inq. ad Cap.* 1620, Dowellstoun; *W. P.* MSS. Dowaltoun). 'Sorbie.' Doual's homestead. Tradition connects this place with the M'Doualls, lords of Galloway.

DOW CRAIG. 'Twynholm.' It is uncertain whether this is ERSE *dubh creag,* black crag (*see under* CRAIGDOW), or BR. SC. *doo craig,* crag of the pigeons.

DOWELL. 'Troqueer.' *Cf.* DOVEWELL.

DÒWIES [*pron.* Dooies]. 'Glasserton.' *Dubh uisc* [dooh isk], black water. A stream here runs dark through peaty ground, being, in the rest of its course, clear, on a hard bed. This name becomes "Dusk," in Dalry, Ayrshire, and is thus annotated by *Pont,* "Dow-visck, flu.: black watter, for so it is."— *Cunninghame,* p. 124.

DÒWLOCH (*P.* Douloch). 'Minigaff.' *See under* DOULOCH.

DÒWLOCHS. 'Minigaff.' *See under* DOULOCH.

DRÀNGAN. ' Kirkcolm.' *Draigheanan* [drannan], blackthorns.'
O. ERSE *droigen* (*Cormac*), ERSE *draighean*, GAEL. *draigh*, a
thorn-tree + W. *drain*, thorns, *drain duon*, blackthorns, C. *drain*
+ DU. *doorn*, a thorn + ICEL. þorn + DAN. *tiörn* + SWED. *törne* +
G. *dorn* + GOTH. *thaurnus*, a thorn (+ RUSS. *tërne*, blackthorns
+ POLISH *tarn*, a thorn) + A.S. *þorn* (whence M.E. *þorn*, E.
thorn) ; from the base THAR = √TAR, to bore or pierce (*Skeat*).
This word enters into many name of places in Scotland and
Ireland. *Cf.* CARDRAIN, DRANGOWER, DRANIEMANNER, DRAN-
NANDOW, DRONNAN, DRONNANS, DRUNGAN, etc.; and, in
Ireland, Dreenan, Drinane, Dreenaun, Drinan, Dreen, Drain,
Drains, Dreenagh, Drinagh, Driny, and Drinachan, besides
composite names.

DRANGÒWER (*P.* Drongangour). ' New Luce.' *Draigheanan gobhar*,
blackthorn thicket of the goats. *See under* ALGOWER and
DRANGAN.

DRANIEMÀNNER. ' Minigaff.

DRANNANDÒW (*Inq. ad Cap.* 1572, Drongandow ; *P.* Drongandow)
' Minigaff.' *Draigheanan dubh* [drannan doo], dark black
thorns. *Cf.* W. *drain duon* (*see under* DRANGAN). Perhaps,
however, *dronnán dubh*, black ridge (*see under* DRONNAN).

DRIGMÒRN (a hill of 2000 feet) (*P.* Dyrrickmoirn ; MS. 1666,
Drumockmoirne). ' Minigaff.' *Cf.* GREYMORN.

DROCHFÒRE. ' Parton.'

DROCH HEAD (an insulated rock in the sea). ' Kirkcolm, s. c.'
Drochaid, a bridge. *Cf.* the DEVIL'S BRIDGE, a similar rock
on Whithorn coast. *See under* BARDROCHWOOD.

DRÒNAN HILL. ' Penninghame.' *See under* DRANGAN and
DRONNAN.

DRÒNNAN, THE. ' Minigaff.' *Dronnán*, a back, a ridge, akin to
druim ; or else *draigheanan* [dranan], blackthorns (*see under*
DRANGAN). The two words assume the same form in composition.

DRÒNNANS (*Inq. ad Cap.* 1620, Dronganis). ' Kirkinner.' *Dronnán*, a ridge, or *draigheanan*, blackthorns. *See under* DRANGAN
and DRONNAN.

DROUGHANDRÙIE. ' Minigaff.' *Drochaidh an druidhe* [?] [drog-
handreehy], the druid's or magician's bridge. There is a
stream here.

DROUGHDÒOL (*P.* Drochduil). ' Old Luce.'

DRÙCHTAG (*Inq. ad Cap.* 1582, Dreuchdag; *P.* Dreugtak). 'Mochrum.'

DRUM (*P.* Druym). 'Loch Rutton,' 'New Abbey.' *Druim*, a ridge, *lit.* a back, corresponding exactly in meaning and application to BR. SC. *rig* — A.S. *hrycg*, a back, and to the W. *cefn*. *Druimm, druim*, a back, a ridge + W. *trum* + LAT. *dorsum* + GK. δειράς, a mountain-ridge, δειρή, δερή, a neck, a ridge. Of extremely frequent occurrence in Scotland and Ireland, both separately and as a prefix.

DRUMABRÈNNAN (*Inq. ad Cap.* 1638, Drumalbreinan). 'Kirkcowan.' *Druim Ui Braenain* [?], O'Brennan's ridge. The O'Brennans or Brennans of Ireland are descended from one named after Brendan of Birr, the patron saint of Kerry.

DRUMACÀRDIE. 'Old Luce.' *Druim a' cearda* [cairda], ridge of the forge or workshop. *Cf.* CAIRDIE WIEL, CARTY; and, in Ireland, Farranacardy in Sligo, Tullynagarda in Down.

DRUMACÀRIE (*P.* Druymnachory). 'Kirkcowan.' Names ending in *carie* are very common and may have various origins. *Pont* preserves the *n* of the plur. article, and his writing would accord with *druim-na-caera*, ridge of the sheep (*see under* CULGARIE); but the name might as probably come from *druim na cairthe* [carha], ridge of the pillar stones, which *Joyce* assigns as the derivation of Drumnacarra in Louth.

DRUMACÌSSOCK. 'Inch.' *Druim na' siosg* [shissug], ridge of the sedges, sedgy hill. *See under* DERNACISSOCK.

DRUMACLÒWN. 'Kirkcowan.' *Druim na cluain* [cloon, clone], ridge of the meadows. *See under* CLONE.

DRUMACRÀE.   'Whithorn.'

DRUMADRỲLAND. 'Inch.' *Druim na dreólan* [?], ridge of the wrens. *Cf.* Gorteenadrolane in Cork, Curradrolan in Tyrone, Mulladrillen in Louth, which *Joyce* (ii. 296) refers to *dréolán*, . a wren.

DRUMAGÈE. 'Kirkcowan.' *Druim na gaeth* [gee], windy ridge. *Cf.* Drumnageo in Antrim. *Cf. also* WINDY HILL. *See under* CURGHIE. Of course, like BALMAGHIE, the name may signify M'Ghie's ridge.

DRUMAGÈRDY. 'Inch.' *Druim a' g-cearda*, hill of the forge. *Cf.* Tullynagardy in Down. *See under* DRUMACARDY.

DRUMAGÌBBEN.   'Old Luce.'

DRUMAGÌLLOCH. ' Glasserton.' *Druim a' g-coilleaich* [gillach], hill of the cock (? grouse or blackcock). *Cf.*, in Ireland, Cornagillach in Leitrim, Longford, and Monaghan, Coumnagillach in Tipperary, Knocknagulliaghin in Wicklow and Down, and Glannagilliagh in Kerry. +W. *ceiliog*, B. *quillocq*, C. *kuileog*.

DRUMAHÀMMIE. ' Old Luce.'

DRUMAHÈRN. ' New Luce.' *Druim a' chuirn* [?] [hirn], ridge of the cairn. *Cf.* DRUMAWHERN.

DRUMAHÒWEN. ' Leswalt.'

DRUMAKÌBBEN. ' Kirkcowan.'

DRUMALIG. ' Stoneykirk.' Perhaps like Dromaleague in Cork, which is *druim dha liag* [drum-a-leeg], ridge of the two stones; or like Dromanallig in Cork, from *druim an ailigh*, ridge of the stone fort. *See under* AIRIELIG and CRAIGA-NALLY.

DRUMÀLLOCH (*P.* Drummaloch ; *Inq. ad Cap.* 1624, Drummalocht). ' Kirkcowan.' *Druim shalach* [?] [hallagh], miry ridge. *Cf.* Drumhallagh in Ireland. *See under* BARSALLOCH.

DRUMALÒNE. ' Dalry.' *Druim na luan* [?] [lone], ridge of the lambs. *Cf.* Maloon and Malone (*magh luan*), and Gortmaloon in Ireland.

DRUMAMOSS. ' Kirkcudbright.'

DRUMANÀRY. ' Port Patrick.' *Druim an airidh* [airy], the ridge of the shieling ; or *druim an aedhaire* [airy], the shepherd's ridge. *Cf.* CRAIGARIE, and (in the latter sense) Drumaneary in Donegal, and Drumary in Fermanagh and Monaghan.

DRUMANÈE. ' Kirkcowan.' *Druim an fhiaidh* [ee], the ridge of the deer. *Cf.* Drumanee in Derry. *See under* CRAIGINEE.

DRUMÀNOGHAN. ' Wigtown.' *Druim manachan*, ridge of the monks, dim. of *manach*. *Cf.* Drummany and Drumavanagh in Cavan (the latter = *druim a' mhanaigh*).

DRUMANTRÀE. ' Stoneykirk.' *Druim an traigh*, ridge of the shore. This is a long low ridge, a raised beach, running for half a mile along the shore at Ardwell. *Cf.* KILLANTRAE ; also Fintray in Stirlingshire, Ballantrae in Ayrshire ; and, in Ireland, Baltray, Ballynatray, Monatray, Ventry (*fionn traigh*), Fintra, and Fintragh.

DRUMASKÌMMING.   ' Penninghame.'

DRUMÀSLIG. 'Port Patrick.' *Druim isle* [issly], low ridge. *See under* CORVISEL; *cf.* DRUMMAHISLIE, DRUMWHISLEY.

DRUMASTÙBBIN.   ' Kirkcowan.'

DRUMATIER. 'Penninghame.' *Druim a' t-saeir* [?] [teer], ridge of the wright or carpenter; *s* eclipsed by *t* (*see under* BALTIER *and* BARTAGGART). *Cf.* Ballinteer, near Dublin, and again in Londonderry (*baile an t-saeir*). "*Ar thal in t-sœir do gabail,*" "because he took the wright's adze."—*Félire*, p. ci. 31. O. ERSE *sáer*, ERSE *saor*, gen. *saoire* (*O'Reilly*) + W. *saer*, C. *sair*.

DRUMATWÒODIE.   ' Kirkcowan.'

DRUMATỲE. 'Glasserton.' *Druim a' tighe*, ridge of the house. The name of a singular ridge of rock on the summit of Carleton Fell, formed like the steeply-pitched roof of a house. It also goes by the name of the " Pratie Pit," from its resemblance to a pit or ridge of stored potatoes. *Cf.* Drumatihugh in Ireland, *i.e.* the ridge of Hugh's house. O. ERSE *tech*, ERSE *teach*, also *tigh* + W. *ty*, a house, *tsi*, to thatch, B. *ty*, C. *tshyi*, a house + DU. *dak*, thatch (whence E. *deck*) + ICEL. þak + DAN. *tag* + SWED. *tak* + G. *dach*, thatch + A.S. þæc (whence M.E. þak, BR. SC. *thack*, E. *thatch*), all from TEUT. base THAKA, a thatch, from TEUT. base THAK, to cover, which, having lost initial *s*, stands for STHAG = √STAG, to cover: *cf.* GK. τέγος = στέγος, a roof. From the same root comes SKT. *sthag*, to cover + GK. στέγειν + LAT. *tegere* (for *stegere*) + LITH. *stëgti* + FR. *toit* + M.E. *tigel*, E. *tile* (− LAT. *tegula*).

DRUMAWÀ. 'Kirkcowan,' 'New Luce' (*twice*).

DRUMÀWAN. 'Kirkcowan.' *Druim Shamhuin* [?] [hawan]. "The first of November was called *Samhuin* (savin or sowan), which is commonly explained *samh-fhuin*, *i.e.* the end of summer, and, like *Bealltaine*, it was a day devoted by the pagan Irish to religious and festive ceremonials."—*Joyce*, i. 202. The word occurs in many Irish names, *e.g.* Knocksouna in Limerick (called by the *Four Masters* Samhuin, and in the Book of Lismore *Cnoc-Samhna*), Mullasawney in Donegal, Drumsamney, Drumsawna, etc., in all of which the *s* is retained; but in Drumhaven or Drumhaman in Monaghan, in Carrickhawna in Sligo, and (nearest of all to the name under consideration) Drumhawan in Monaghan, the *s* is lost by aspiration.

DRUMAWÀNTY. 'Penninghame.' This name resembles Dingina-
. vanty in Cavan, translated *Daingean-a-Mhantaigh* (*Joyce*,
i. 307), Mantagh's stronghold.

DRUMAWHÈRN. 'Leswalt.' *See under* DRUMAHERN.

DRUMBÀE. 'Balmaclellan.' *Druim beith* [bey], ridge of the
birches. *See under* ALLANBAY.

DRUMBÀIN. 'Kirkcowan.' *Druim bán*, white ridge. A hill
covered with light-coloured grass in a moorland would
naturally get this name, while one covered with heather
would be called Drumdon or Drumdow. *Cf.* Drumbane and
Drumbawn in Ireland.

DRUMBÀWN. 'Stoneykirk.' *See under* DRUMBAIN. Possibly
druim badhuin (bawn), ridge of the cattle-pen. *See under*
BIAWN.

DRUMBÈCK. 'Balmaghie.' *Druim becc*, little ridge. O. ERSE
becc, little, ERSE *beag*. *See under* DRUMBEG.

DRUMBÈG. 'Glasserton,' 'Kirkcowan.' *Druim beag* [beg], little
ridge. *Cf.* Drombeg and Drumbeg in Ireland. O. ERSE *bec*,
becc ; ERSE *beag* + W. *bach, bychan*, small, and *by*, a diminutive
prefix ; C. *bîan, bihan*, B. *bíhan*.

DRUMBLÀIR (*Inq. ad Cap.* 1598, Dirreblair ; *P.* Drumblair).
'Mochrum.' *Druim blára*, ridge of the plain or of the battle.
See under BLAIR. The charter of 1598 gives a form from
doire blára, oakwood of the plain or of the battle.

DRUMBÒW. 'Twynholm.' *Druim bo*, ridge of the cows. *See
under* BIAWN. *Cf.* Drumbo in Down, written by the *Four
Masters* (A.D. 1003), *druim-bo*, and Drumbo in Donegal
(A.D. 1490), the same. *Adamnan* (*Vit. Col.*, ii. 13) writes
of the monastery which is called in Latin *Campulus bovis*, but
in the Irish Achadboe.

DRUMBÒY. 'Stoneykirk.' *See under* DRUMBUIE.

DRUMBRÈACH [*pron.* breeagh] (*Estate Map* 1777, Drumgreach
(? misprint)). *Druim bréagh* [?], ridge of the wolves. *Cf.*,
in Ireland, Caherbreagh, near Tralee.

DRUMBRÈDDAN. 'Old Luce,' 'Stoneykirk.' *Druim Breadtain*
[Breddan], Bretan's ridge, or the Welshman's ridge. *See
under* CULBRATTEN.

DRUMBRÒCHANIE. 'Minigaff.' *Druim breachnaich* [braghnagh], ridge of the broken, variegated land. *See under* BRACKENI-CALLIE.

DRUMBÙIE. 'Kirkcolm,' 'Kirkcowan.' *Druim buidhe* [buie], yellow ridge. *Cf.* DRUMBOY; also Drumbuy in Beith parish, Ayrshire, which *Pont* explains " Druym-buy, the zellow backe."—*Cuninghame*, p. 125.

DRUMBÙRN. 'Colveud.'

DRUMCÀGERIE. 'Kirkcowan.' *Druim coigeriche*, ridge of the strangers. *Cf.* STRANGER'S KNOWE. *Coigeriche*, a stranger, whence the surname MacCon-Cogry, MacCogry, which was changed to L'Estrange in consequence of legislation of Edward IV., by which the use of Irish surnames within the Pale was prohibited (*O'Don., Top. Poems*, Intr. 26).

DRUMCÀNNOCH. 'Minigaff.' *Druim ceannaich* [?] [cennogh], ridge of the purchase, of the bargaining. *Ceannaich* also means "strife" (*Shaw*). *Cf.* DRUMTRODDAN, STRIFE RIG, etc.

DRUMCÀPENOCH. 'Glasserton.' *Druim ccapanach* [?], ridge of the stumps; deriv. of *ceapán*, a stump. *See under* CAPE-NOCH.

DRUMCÀRRICK. 'Old Luce.' *Druim carric*, ridge of the crag.

DRUMCÀUCHLIE. 'Penninghame.'

DRUMCHÀLLOCH. 'Kirkcowan.' *Druim tealaich* [tyallach], ridge of the forge. *See under* CHALLOCH.

DRUMCHÈATE. 'Urr.'

DRUMCHÈSNIE. 'Minigaff.' *Cf.* BARCHESNIE.

DRUMCLÈIGH. 'Minigaff.' *Druim cliabh* [?] [cleeve], ridge of the baskets. *Cf.* Drumcliff, near Sligo, which is always written in Irish MSS. *Druim-chliabh* (*Four Masters*, A.D. 871, 1011, 1239, etc.); also Drumcliff in Clare and Donegal, Drumcleave in Tipperary, and Lisdrumcleve in Monaghan. *Cf.* DRUMCLEUGH.

DRUMCLÈUGH. 'Girthon.' *Cf.* DRUMCLEIGH.

DRUMCLÒY. 'Balmaclellan.' *Druim cloiche*, ridge of the stone, or *druim cladha* [cly, claw], ridge of the mound or grave.

DRUMCLÝOR. 'Kirkpatrick Durham.'

DRUMCÒLTRAN (*P.* Drumcauran). 'Kirkgunzeon.' *Druim Cultrain,* the ridge of Cultran. In the 12th and 13th centuries this land belonged to the Abbey of Holm Cultran in Cumberland. The old tower, now a farmhouse, bears over the doorway the following inscription :—

CELA . SECRETA . LOQVERE
PAVCA . VERAX . ESTO.
AVARO . CAVE . MEMENTO
MORI . MISERICORS . ESTO.

DRUMCÒW. 'Colvend.'

DRUMCRÀICHIE. 'Balmaclellan.'

DRUMCRÒY. 'Kirkcudbright.' *Druim cruadh* [croo], hard ridge.

DRUMCÙIL. 'Minigaff.' *Druim cúl,* back ridge.

DRUMDÀLLY. 'Stoneykirk.' *Druim dealg* [dallig], ridge of the thorns. *See under* CLAMDALLY.

DRUMDÀRRACHY. 'New Luce.' *See under* DRUMDARROCH.

DRUMDÀRROCH. 'Mochrum.' *Druim darach,* ridge of the oaks. *See under* DARROCH.

DRUMDÈLLY. 'Dalry.' *See under* DRUMDALLY.

DRUMDÈNNEL. 'Penninghame.' *Druim d-tenneail* [?] [dennal], ridge of the bonfire. *Cf.* KNOCKTINKLE, KNOCKTINNEL. *Tenneal (Joyce),* a bonfire, deriv. of O. ERSE *ten,* fire ; ERSE *leine,* W. *tan,* B. and C. *tân.*

DRUMDÒAN. 'Old Luce.' *See under* DRUMDON.

DRUMDÒCH (*Inq. ad Cap.* 1623, Drumdooche). 'Inch.' *Druim dubh* [doov, doo], dark ridge. *Cf.* Dromduff and Drumduff in Ireland.

DRUMDÒN. 'Glasserton.' *Druim donn,* brown ridge.

DRUMDÒNNIES. 'Mochrum.'

DRUMDÒW. 'Glasserton,' 'Kirkcolm,' 'Kirkcowan,' 'Mochrum.' *See under* DRUMDOCH.

DRUMDÒWN. 'New Luce' (*thrice*), 'Old Luce,' 'Penninghame.' *See under* DRUMDON.

DRUMDRÒCHAT. 'Minigaff.' *Druim droicheaid,* the ridge of the bridge, bridge-hill (near the bridge over the Penkiln). *Cf.* Drumnadrochat on the Highland railway, Drumadried in Antrim, Drumadrehid in Clare. *See under* BARDROCHWOOD.

DRUMFÀD (*P.* Drumfad). 'Minigaff,' 'Terregles.' *Druim fada,* long, or far ridge. This form and Drumfada occur frequently in Ireland. *See under* DRUMMODDIE.

DRUMFÀRNACHAN. 'Kirkcolm.' *Druim fearnachán,* alder ridge. *Cf.* Mullafernaghan in Down, Carrowfarnaghan in Cavan. *See under* BALFERN.

DRUMFEÀTHERIN. 'Penninghame.'

DRUMFÈRN. 'Kirkgunzeon,' 'Minigaff.' *Druim fearn,* ridge of the alders. *See under* BALFERN. *Cf.* DRUMFARNACHAN and DRUMFERNIE.

DRUMFÈRNIE. 'Parton.' *Druim fearna,* ridge of the alder-tree. *See under* BALFERN.

DRUMFLÈICH. 'New Luce.' *Druim fliuch,* wet ridge. *Cf.* Drumflugh in Ireland. *See under* CARRICKAFLIOU.

DRUMFLÒWER [*pron.* Drumflure]. 'Penninghame.' *Druim lobhair* [?] [louwer], the leper's, sick, or infirm man's ridge. *Cf.* Dromalour in Cork, and Drumalure in Cavan. Knocka-lower, in Sligo, is called in English Flowerhill, a similar change to that which it is suggested has taken place in Drumflower. *See under* BARLURE.

DRUMFÒRK. 'Dalry.'

DRUMFRÌEL (*Inq. ad Cap.* 1616, Drumfrid (*misprint*)). 'Inch.'

DRUMFÙNDLE. 'Inch.' *Druim Finngael* [?], the Norseman's ridge. *Cf.* CARRICKFUNDLE (in Addenda) and DERWHINDLE.

DRUMGÀLDER. 'Old Luce.'

DRUMGLÀSS (*P.* Drümglash). 'Balmaghie,' 'Minigaff.' *Druim glas,* green ridge.

DRUMGÌLL. 'New Abbey.' *Druim goill* [?], the foreigner's ridge. *See under* INCHIGUILE.

DRUMGÒRTH (*P.* Barnagoirt). 'Kirkcowan.' *Druim guirt* [?], ridge of the enclosure or garden. O. ERSE *gort, gart,* a garden or cultivated field (*gloss* hortus, Zeuss MSS. prædium, *Colgan*), more common in Irish names than in Scotch + W. *gardd* + ICEL. *garðr* (whence BR. SC. *garth*) + DAN. *gaard* + SW. *gard* + O.H.G. *garto,* G. *garten* + RUSS. *gorod',* a town + LAT. *hortus* + GK. χόρτος, an enclosure + A.S. *geard,* an enclosure, a court (whence M.E. *yerd,* E. *yard*). (The M.E. *gardin,* E. *garden,* O.F. *gardin,* F. *jardin* come from the genitive of O.H.G. *garto,* a garden.) From Teut. base GARDA = Aryan GHARTA, "a place surrounded" — √GHAR, to seize, hence to surround ; *cf.* SKT. *hri,* to seize, *harna,* the hand, GK. χείρ, the hand (*Skeat*).

DRUMGÒWAN. 'Penninghame.' *Druim gobhan* [gowan], the smith's hill ; or *druim gamhan* [gowan], the calves' hill (*cf.* CAWVIS HILL). It is impossible to distinguish between *gobhan*, gen. sing. of *gobha*, and *gamhan*, gen. plur, of *gamhan*, a calf, O. ERSE *gamuin* (*Cormac*). Clonygowan in King's County is written by the *Four Masters* (A.D. 1576) *Cluain-na-ngamhan*, meadow of the calves. *Cf.* Drumgoon, also in Ireland.

DRUMGRÌLLIE. 'Kells.' *Druim greallach* [?], dirty ridge, ridge of the clay. ERSE *greallach*, clay, *adj.* dirty + ERSE *criadh*, clay, earth + W. *pridd*, earth, *priddgalch*, calcareous earth, fuller's clay ; C. and B. *prî*, clay.

DRUMHANEY.   'Old Luce.'

DRUMHÀSTIE.   'Borgue.'

DRUMHÌGH.   'New Abbey.'

DRUMHÙMPHREY (*P.* Drumhunchra).   'Kirkpatrick Durham.'

DRUMIEMÀY. 'Kirkcowan.' *Druim a' magha*, ridge of the plain. *See under* MAY.

DRUMJÀRGON (*Inq. ad Cap.* 1584, Drumgorgan ; *P.* Druymjargan). 'Kirkinner,' 'Penninghame.' *Druim deargán* [dyargan], red ridge. (For use of terminal *án* see under CARRICKGLASSEN.) *Cf.* Drumderg in Ireland. Or, possibly, *druim Deargain*, the ridge of Deargan, or the red man. *Cf.* Drumyarkin in Fermanagh, *i.e.* Yarkin's or O'Harkin's ridge. O'Harkin = O'Dheargan.

DRUMJÈNNING.   'Kirkcowan.'

DRUMJÌN.   'Glasserton.'

DRUMJÒHN (*P.* Drumjowan, Drumjoan). 'Carsphairn,' 'Kirk-gunzeon,' 'Minigaff.'

DRUMKÀRE. 'New Luce.' *Druim caer* [?] [kaer], ridge of the berries. *Cf.* Dromkeare in Kerry, Knockcoolkeare in Limerick, etc. etc. (*Joyce* ii. 323).

DRUMKÈEL. 'Balmaclellan,' 'Parton.' *Druim caol* [keel], narrow ridge. *See under* CARSKEEL.

DRUMLÀD. 'Rerwick.' Close to Drumlass and Old Man, show-ing that the names have been corrupted to suit a spurious meaning.

DRUMLÀNE. 'Wigtown.' *Druim leathan* [lahan, laan], broad ridge. *See under* AUCHLEAND.

DRUMLÀSS. 'Rerwick.' *Druim leasa* [lassa], ridge of the fort, irregular genitive of *less*, which is the old form of *lios*, " a house, habitation; a palace, court; a fortified place; enclosures or stalls for cattle " (*O'Reilly*). The regular genitive of *less* is *liss*, but *Joyce* mentions an irregular genitive *leasa* [lassa], to which he refers Gortalassa, Knockalassa, Ballinlass, Ballinlassa, and Ballinlassy; while Drumlish, Moylish, and others, are from the form *liss*. *Cf.* Drumlease in Leitrim, which is mentioned in an early MS. (*Zeuss, Gram. Celt.* 269) as "*Druimmlias, i.e. jugum tuguriorum,*" the ridge of the huts, *lias* being another form of *lios*.

DRUMLAWÀNTIE. 'Minigaff.' *Cf.* DRUMAWANTIE.

DRUMLAWHÌNNIE. 'Minigaff.' *Druim na mhuine* [vinnie], ridge of the thicket or of the mountain.

DRUMLÈICHT. 'Kirkcolm.' *Druim leacht*, ridge of the graves. *See under* LAIGHT.

DRUMLÈY. 'Kirkcowan.' *Druim liath* [lea]; grey ridge. *Cf.* Drumlea, Drumleagh, in Ireland.

DRUMLIEBÙIE.   'Kirkcowan.'

DRUMLÒCHLINN. 'Mochrum.' *Druim Lochlinn*, Lauchlan's ridge. *See under* BARLAUCHLINE.

DRUMLÒCKHART. 'New Luce.' *Druim luachair* [?], ridge of the rushes. *Cf.* BARLOCKHART, GLENLOCHAR; also Drumlougher, Drumloughra, Letterlougher, Gortlogher, and Lougher in various parts of Ireland.

DRUMLÒSKIE. 'Penninghame.' *Druim loisgthe* [luskie], burnt ridge. *See under* CRAIGLOSK.

DRUMMACÒNNEL. 'Kirkcowan.' *Druim mic Connuil*, ridge of the son of Connel, M'Connel's ridge.

DRUMMÀNISTER (*P.* Drummannister). 'Balmaclellan.' *Druim mainisdir*, ridge of the monastery. *See under* AUCHMANISTER.

DRUMMÀNOCH. 'Buittle.' *Druim manach*, ridge of the monks. *See under* ARNMANNOCH. *Cf.* DRUMANOGHAN.

DRUMMÀRGIE. 'Kells.' *Druim airgidh* [?] [argie], ridge of the silver. *See under* CRAIGNARGET.

DRUMMÀRGUS. 'Minigaff.' *See under* DRUMMARGIE.

DRUMMÀRTIN. 'Balmaclellan.' *Druim Martinn*, Martin's ridge.

DRUMMÀSTON (*W. P.* MSS. Drummastoun). 'Whithorn.'

DRUMMATRÀNE. 'Kirkcowan.' *Druim a' traona* [trana], ridge of the corncrake. *See under* CLONE.

DRUMMIEHÈRON. 'Colvend.' *See under* DRUMAHERN.

DRUMMIEHÌSLIE. 'New Luce.' *Druimín isle* [isslie], lower ridge. *See under* CORVISEL. *Cf.* DRUMWHISLEY.

DRUMMIEMÌCKIE. 'Kirkcowan.'

DRUMMIENÈLLAN. 'New Luce.'

DRUMMIENÈZER. 'New Luce.'

DRUMMIERÀUD. 'New Luce.' *Druim a' rathaid* [?] [raud], ridge of the road. *Cf.* KNOCKAROD; and, in Ireland, Drumaroad, Ballinroad, Lisnarode, etc. O. ERSE *rót* (*Cormac*), ERSE *ród*, GAEL. *rathad* + B. *rut.* Cognate with E. *road* (which is from A.S. *rád*, a journey, from *rád*, past tense of *ridan*, to ride), but not derived from it, as it occurs in the oldest Irish MSS.

DRUMMIESÙE. 'Old Luce.' *Druim a' suidhe* [?] [suie], ridge of the seat.

DRUMMÌLLAN (Pow) (*P*. Drummillem). *Druim muileain* [mullen], ridge of the mill. *See under* BARMULLIN. *Cf.* DRUMMOLLAN, DRUMMULLAN, DRUMMULLIN, and DRUMMILLAN. "*Pow*, a slow-moving rivulet in flat lands" (*Jamieson*) — A.S. *pol*, a pool, like *ba'* for *ball*, *ha'* for *hall*, etc.

DRUMMINÀRBEL. 'Kirkcowan.' *Druim an earbuil* [arbil], ridge of the point or extremity. *See under* DARNARBEL.

DRUMMÌNNOCH. 'Inch.' *Druim meadhonach* [minnogh], middle ridge. *See under* BALMINNOCH. *Cf.* Drummenagh in Armagh, Tyrone, and Fermanagh.

DRUMMÒDDIE (*Inq. ad Cap.* 1643, Drummadie; *P*. Drummady, Drummaddy; *W. P.* MSS. Drummaddie). *Druim fhada* [adda], long or far ridge. *Cf.* Dromada and Dromadda in various parts of Ireland; also Banada, which the *Four Masters* (A.D. 1265) write Beannada and (A.D. 1439) *Beann-fhoda*; and Creewood which is given in a charter of King John as *Craebh-fhoda.* It may, however, be *druim madadh* [madda], the dog's ridge. *See under* CLAYMODDIE.

DRUMMÒLLAN. 'Whithorn.' *See under* DRUMMILLAN.

DRUMMÒNACHAN. 'Glasserton.' *See under* DRUMANOGHAN.

DRÙMMOND HILL. 'Whithorn.' *Dromainn*, deriv. of *druim*, with the same meaning, a ridge. *Cf.* Dromin, Drummin, and Drumans in Ireland ; and in Ulster about twenty townlands are called Drummond.

DRUMMÒNEY. 'Kirkcowan,' 'New Luce.' *Druim mónadh* [money], ridge of the moor, or of the peat. *See under* DALMONEY.

DRUMMÒNIE. 'Kirkcowan.' *See under* DRUMMONEY and DAL-MONEY.

DRUMMÒRAL. 'Whithorn.'

DRUMMÒRE (*P.* Druimmoir). 'Kirkmaiden.' *Druim mór*, great ridge. *Cf.* DRUMORE, and, in Ireland, Dromore.

DRUMMÙCKLOCH (*Inq. ad Cap.* 1602, Drummukloch). 'Inch.' *Druim muclaich*, ridge of the swine pasture. "*Muclach*, a herd of swine" (*O'Reilly*), deriv. of *muc*.

DRUMMÙDDIOCH. 'Dalry.' *Druim m-bodach* [muddagh], ridge of the clowns or countrymen. *Cf.* Ballynamuddagh, now called Clownstown, and Rathnamuddagh, both in West Meath. ERSE and GAEL. *bodach*, a churl, a rustic, an old man + A.S. *bodig*, body (M.E. *bodi*, E. *body*, that which confines the soul, a person) + O.H.G. *potach* + SKT. *bandha*, the body, bondage — √BHADH, to bind. The ERSE *bodach* has come to be used in a familiar or somewhat contemptuous sense, just as BR. SC. *body* or "*buddie*."

DRUMMÙLLAN. 'Twynholm.' *See under* DRUMMILLAN.

DRUMMÙLLIN. 'Kirkcolm,' 'Leswalt,' 'Stoneykirk,' 'Whithorn.' *See under* DRUMMILLAN.

DRUMMÙRRIE. 'Kirkcowan.' *Druim Muireadhaich* [murragh], Murphy's or Murray's ridge. *Cf.* Drummurrie in Ireland. *See under* BALMURRIE.

DRUMNÀIL. 'Kirkgunzeon.' *Cf.* DRUMNEIL.

DRUMNAMÌNSHOCH. 'Minigaff.' *Druim nam fhuinnseog* [unshog], ridge of the ash-trees. The initial letter of *fuinnseóg* is often obliterated by aspiration, especially in the northern part of Ireland ; and corresponding to Funshion, Funshin, Funshinagh, and Funchoge in the south and west, we find Unshinagh,

Inshinagh, Unchog, and Hinchoge in the north, also Drumna-nunshin.   *Cf.* INSHANKS and KNOCKNINSHOCK.   ERSE *fuinnse, fuinnseán, fuinnseóg* + W. *on, y̅n,* B. *onn.*

DRUMNÀRBUCK.   'New Luce.'

DRUMNÀW. 'Urr.' *Druim an atha* [aa, awe], ridge of the ford. *See under* CARSNAW.

DRUMNÈIL. 'Minigaff.' *Druim Niaill* (Neel), Niel's ridge. *See under* AUCHNEAL.

DRUMNÈRLIE.   'Old Luce.

DRUMNÈSCAT (*Inq. ad Cap.* 1582, Drumniscart; *P.* Druimneskart) 'Mochrum.' *Druimín dheisceart* [?] [drumminescart], south ridge. *Cf.* Drumhuskert in Mayo, *i.e. druim thuaisceart,* northern ridge; formed in the same way by aspiration and silence of the initial consonant.

DRUMNÈSS (*P.* Drumness). 'Carsphairn.' *Druim an easa* [essa], ridge of the cascade. There is a waterfall here on Pulmaddy. *See under* ASS OF THE GILL. *Cf.* Dunass on the Shannon, Caherass in Limerick, Owenass, Pollanass, and Poulanassy, elsewhere in Ireland.

DRUMORAWHÈRN. 'Inch.' *Druim mór a' chuirn* [hirn], great ridge of the cairn.

DRUMÒRE (*P.* Drummoir ('Kirkmabreck')). 'Kirkcowan,' 'Kirk-mabreck.' *See under* DRUMMORE.

DRUMÒURS. 'New Luce.' *Druim odhar* [owr], grey ridge.

DRUMÒWRE. 'Minigaff.' *See under* DRUMOURS.

DRUMPÀIL (*P.* Drumpail). 'Old Luce.' *Druim pell* [?], ridge of the horses. O. ERSE *pell,* GAEL. *peall.*

DRUMPÀRK. 'Kirkpatrick Irongray.' *Druim pairc* [park], ridge of the fields. ERSE and GAEL. *pairc*+W. *park, parwg,* B. *park* +O.F. *parc.* The Celtic forms are probably borrowed from the Teutonic. E. *park*—A.S. *pearroc* (M.E. *parrok,* now spelt *paddock*)+DU. *perk*+SWED. and DAN. *park*+G. *pferch,* an en-closure+IT. *parco*+SP. *parque.*

DRUMQUHÀN [*pron.* Drumwhan).   'Penninghame.'

DRUMRAE (*Inq. ad Cap.* 1620, Drumroy; *W. P.* MSS. Drumra). 'Glasserton.' *Druim reidh* [?] [ray], smooth ridge, or *druim ratha* [raa], ridge of the rath or fort. *Cf.,* in the latter sense, Drumragh in Tyrone, spelt Drumrathe in the *Inquisitions.*

DRUMRÀKE.   'Kirkmabreck.'

DRUMRÀNNIE. 'New Luce.' *Druim raithne* [rahnie], ridge of the ferns. *See under* BLAWRANNIE. *Cf.* DRUMRENNIE; and, in Ireland, Dromrahnee, Drumrainy, and Drumrane.

DRUMRÀSH (*P.* Druymcaash (*misprint*)). 'Parton.' *Druim ras*, ridge of the bushes. *Cf.* RASHNACH. Probably akin to *ros*. *See under* ROSS.

DRUMRÈARIE.   'Kells.'

DRUMRÈNNIE. 'Balmaclellan.' *See under* DRUMRANNIE.

DRUMRÒBBIN.   ' 'Twynholm.'

DRUMRÙCK (*Inq. ad Cap.* 1625, Drumruckalie; *P.* Drumruck). 'Girthon.'

DRUMSCÀLLAN. 'Mochrum.' *Druim sgeallain* [?] [sgallan], ridge of the wild mustard.

DRUMSHÀLLOCH. 'Kirkcowan,' 'Penninghame' (the two places are within a mile of each other). *Druim sealg* [?] [shallug], the ridge of the chase, of the hunting. *Cf.* Drumnashaloge in Tyrone, Drumashellig in Queen's County, Derrynashallog in Monaghan, and Ballynashallog in Londonderry. It is quite possible, however, that this may be a softened form of Drumchalloch (*q. v.*), or even a corruption of *seíleach*, willows, or of *salach*, dirty (*see under* BARSALLOCH).

DRUMSHÀNGAN. 'Girthon.' *Druim seangan* [shangan], ridge of the ants. *See under* BARNASHANGAN

DRUMSHÙNE.   'Parton.'

DRUMSKÈLLY. 'Crossmichael.' *Druim sceilig*, ridge of the rocks. *See under* BALSCALLOCH.

DRUMSKEÒG [*pron.* skioghe] (*P.* Drumskioch). 'Mochrum.' *Druim sceithiog* [skeyog], ridge of the hawthorns. *Cf.* Drumskea, in Ireland. *See under* AUCHENSKEOG.

DRUMSLÈET.   'Troqueer.'

DRUMSOUL. 'Old Luce.' *Druim sabhuil* [sowl], ridge of the barn or granary.

DRUMSTÌNCHALL (*P.* Drumstinchar).   'Colvend.'

DRUMSTÌNCHAR.   'Crossmichael.'

DRUMTÒWL. 'Glasserton.' GAEL. *druim tuaitheal* [tooall], north ridge (literally, left-handed). Perhaps *Tuathail*, Tuathal's or Doual's ridge.

DRUMTÙTOR. 'Dalry.' *Druim t-súdaire* [toodery], ridge of the tanner. *Cf.* LAGTUTOR.

DRUMTRÒDDAN (*P.* Drumtrodden). 'Mochrum.' *Druim trodain,* ridge of the quarrel. Three large standing stones here perhaps commemorate the event which is perpetuated in the name. There was also a circular fort, marked in estate survey of 1777, which has now disappeared. *Cf.* Ballytroddan and Carricktroddan in Armagh.

DRUMVÈRGES. 'New Luce.'

DRUMVÒGIL. 'New Luce.'

DRUMWÀLL. 'Girthon.' *Druim gall* [?], ridge of the foreigners, the strangers, or of the standing stones.

DRUMWÀLT. 'Mochrum.'

DRUMWÀVE. 'Kirkcowan.'

DRUMWHÀR. 'Minigaff.' *Druim ghearr* [har], short ridge, or *druim ghar,* near ridge. *Cf.* Drumgar in Ireland.

DRUMWHÀT. 'Mochrum.' *Druim chat,* hill of the wild-cats. *See under* ALWHAT.

DRUMWHÌLL. 'Kirkmaiden.' *Druim chuill* [hill], ridge of the hazel. *See under* BARWHIL. *Cf.* Drumaquill in Ireland.

DRUMWHÌLLAN. 'Kirkcowan.' *Druim chuilinn* [hillin], ridge of the holly. *See under* ALWHILLAN. *Cf.* Drumacullin, Drumacullion, Drumcullen, and Drumcullion in Ireland, which are the unaspirated forms.

DRUMWHÌLLANS. 'Kirkmabreck.' *See under* DRUMWHILLAN.

DRUMWHÌN. 'Urr.' *Druim choin* [?] [hin] ridge of the dog. ERSE *cu,* gen. *coin,* W. *ci*+TEUT. type HUN-DA (whence G., DAN., SWED. *hund,* DU. *hond,* A.S. *hund,* E. *hound*), related to LAT. *canis,* GK. κυών, gen. κυνός. SKT. *çuan*— √KWAN, a dog.

DRUMWHÌNNIE. 'Colvend,' 'Kirkgunzeon.' *Druim mhuine* [?], [vinny], ridge of the moor or thicket.

DRUMWHÌRN. 'Mochrum.' *Druim chuirn* [hirn], ridge of the cairn. *See under* DRUMAHERN.

DRUMWHÌRNS. 'Penninghame.' *See under* DRUMWHIRN.

DRUMWHÌRRAN. 'Kirkcowan.'

DRUMWHÌSLEY. 'Leswalt.' *Druim isle* [issly], lower ridge. *See under* DRUMMIEHISLIE.

DRUMWHÒDYA. 'Mochrum.'

DRUNGANS. 'New Abbey,' 'Rerwick,' 'Troqueer.' *See under* DRANGAN.

DRURY LANE.   'Whithorn.'

DRÝBURGH.   'Crossmichael.'

DÙBLOCH. 'Mochrum,' 'New Luce.' *See under* DOULOCH.

DUB OF HASS (*P.* Haiss). 'Buittle.' The "dub," or pool of the "*hals*" or "*hawse*," a narrow glen. *See under* HAUSE BURN.

DUCÀRROCH.   'Stoneykirk.'

DUCHDUBS BURN. 'Inch.' A compound of ERSE *dubh* [dooh], black, and TEUTONIC *dub*, a pool. This name appears near Saltcoats, in Ayrshire, as Dudups.

DÙCHRA (*Inq. ad Cap.* 1543, Dowchrary; *P.* Dochray). 'Stoney-kirk.' *Dubh reidh* [dooh ray], black meadow. *Cf.* Dockra, Duchray, and Docraw in Ayrshire.

DÙCHRAE (*P.* Dowchra). 'Balmaghie.' *See under* DUCHRA.

DÙGLAND (a hill of 2000 feet). 'Carsphairn.'

DULLÀRG (*P.* Dullarg). 'Parton,' 'Tungland.' *Dubh learg*, black hill-side. *See under* LARG.

DULSLÒUGH.   .   'Kirkcolm, s.c.'

DUMBÈY or DUNBÀE (*Inq. ad Cap.* 1691, Dumbeg). 'Inch.' *Dún beith* [bey], fort of the birches.

DUMBIE POINT.   'Sorbie, s.c.'

DUNAGÀRROCH. 'Kirkmaiden.' *Dundn carrach* or *garbh* [garve, garriv], rough fort.

DUNAHÀSKEL.   'Kirkmaiden.'

DÙNAN. 'Kirkmaiden.' *See under* DONNAN.

DUNANDÒW. 'Kirkmaiden.' *Dúnan dubh* [doo], black fort.

DUNANRÈA. 'Stoneykirk.' *Dún an righ* [?] [ree], the king's fort. *Cf.* Dunaree in Cavan (transl. Kingscourt), and Dinn Righ on the river Barrow. (*Four Masters*, A.M. 3267, 4658); also Doonaree in Connaught, written *Dún na riogh* in the *Book of Lecan.*

DUNBÀR.   'Kirkbean.'

DUNBÈG. 'Kirkcolm.' *Dún beag*, little fort.

DUNDÈUGH (*P.* Dungeuch; *Pitcairn,* 1515, Dungeuche; *Charters*— 1630, Dingewche; 1666, Dungeuche; 1674, Dundeuch; 1700, Dindouch; 1702, Dunduff). 'Carsphairn.' The original form of the name seems to have been Dungeuch.

DUNDRÈAM. 'Kirkcolm, s.c.'

DUNDRÈNNAN (*P.* Doundrainan). 'Rerwick.' *Dún draigheanan* [?] [drannan], fort of the blackthorns. *See under* DRANGAN.

DUNÈSKET. 'Balmaghie.' *Dún dheisceart* [escart], south fort. *See under* DRUMNESCAT.

DUNFÈRMYN. 'Mochrum.' The old name given in *Pont's* atlas to the vitrified fort now called the Doon of May.

DUNGÀMEN. 'Kirkmaiden.'

DUNGÀRRY. 'Rerwick.' *Dún garbh* [garriv], rough fort. *Cf.* DUNAGARROCH.

DÙNGEON GLEN, THE. 'New Luce.' *Dúnagan* [?], rocky; deriv. of *dún.* *Cf.* Port Dunagain and Eileandunagan, in Iona.

DÙNGEON (a hill). 'Kells.

DÙNGEON (a small loch). 'Dalry.'

DUNGÙILE (a fortified hill of 1453 feet). 'Kelton.' *Dún goill* (gen. of *gall*), fort of the foreigner. *Cf.* INCHIGUILE; and, in Ireland, Dungall and Donegal, *i.e. dún na' gall*, fort of the foreigners, the latter of which is frequently mentioned by the *Four Masters* as *Dún-na-nGall.*

DUNHÀRBERRY. 'Girthon.' *Dún Chairbre* [harbrie], Cairbre's fort. Cairbre is an exceedingly common proper name in the *Annals of the Four Masters* from A.D. 10 onwards. Under the year 1538 they mention *dún Ccairbre* (now Doongarbry) in Leitrim; and the barony of Carbury, in Sligo, takes its name from Cairbre, son of Niall of the Nine Hostages, chief of this territory in St. Patrick's time.

DUN HILL. 'Carsphairn.' *See under* DOONHILL. But Dunhill in Waterford is called in *Grace's Annals* Donnoil (*i.e. dún aille*, the fort of the cliff).

DUNICHÌNNIE. 'Kirkmaiden.'

DUNIKÈLLIE. 'Kirkmaiden.'

DUNJÀRG. 'Crossmichael.' *Dún dearg* [dyarg], red fort.

DUNJÒP (*P.* Dounjopp). 'Tungland.'

DUNJÙMPIN. 'Colvend.' *See under* DINCHIMPON.

DUNKÌTTERICK. 'Minigaff.'

DUNMÀN (*P.* Doun Man). 'Kirkmaiden.' *Dún m-beann* [?] [man], fort of the hillocks, gables, or peaks. *Cf.* Dunnaman in Down and Limerick, Dunnavenny in Londonderry (from the genit. sing. *bheanna*), and Dunmanway in Cork (*dún m-beann bhuidhe*, fort of the yellow hills or peaks), given by the *Four Masters* (A.D. 1506) as *Dun-na-m-beann*.

DUNMÒRE. 'Carsphairn.' *Dún mór*, the great fort. *Cf.* Dunmore in Ireland.

DUNMÙCK. 'Kirkmaiden.' *Dún muc*, fort of the swine.

DUNMÙIR. 'Kelton.' *See under* DUNMORE.

DUNMÙRCHIE. 'Kirkcolm.' *Dún Murchaidh* [murghy, *gutt.*], Murchadh's fort. *See under* CRAIGMURCHIE.

DÙNNERUM. 'Inch.'

DÙNNANCE MOAT. 'Balmaghie.' *See under* DINNANS.

DUNNANÈE. 'Minigaff.' *Dún an fhiaidh* [ee], fort or hill of the deer. *See under* CRAIGINEE.

DÙNNANS CRAIG. 'Dalry.' *See under* DINNANS.

DUNNÒTTRIE. 'Minigaff.' *Dún uachterach*, upper fort. *Cf.* Moyotra in Monaghan.

DUNÒOL (a hill of 1777 feet). 'Carsphairn.'

DUNÒRROCH or DUNÒRA. 'Kirkmaiden.' *Dún odhartha* [owra], grey fort; a derivative of *odhar*, or perhahs *dún fhomhorach* [awragh], fort of the pirates.

DUNÒWER. 'Balmaclellan.' *Dún odhar* [ower], grey fort; or perhaps the same as Donore, in Meath, which the *Four Masters* (A.D. 1310), write *dún uabhair* [ower], the fort of pride, and Castleore in Sligo, which they write *caislén an uabhair*. To Donoure, Doonoor, Doonour, Doonore, and Dunover, are assigned the same meaning by *Joyce* (ii. 473).

DUNRÒD (*P.* Dunrod). 'Kirkcudbright.' *Dún rathaid* [raad], the fort of the road, or from the older form *ród*, the fort of the roads. *See under* DRUMMIERAUD. *Cf.*, with the same meaning, Lisnarode in Queen's County.

DUNSKÈY (*P.* Dunskay). 'Port Patrick.' "Scæodunum appellatur vulgo Dunskey, id est Arx Alata."—*Maclellan*. If this be the correct meaning, then the original name would be *dún sciathach*, the winged fort, from *sciath*, a wing, a shield, a buckler (*O'Reilly*). Donaskeagh in Tipperary is written (*Four Masters*, A.D. 1043), *Dún na sciath*, the fort of the shields.

DUNSKÌRLOCH. 'Kirkcolm, s.c.' *Dun sceirlach* [?], rocky fort; deriv. of *sceir*, a sharp sea-rock (*O'Reilly*).

DUNSÒUR. 'Kirkcolm.'

DUN'S WA'S. 'Kirkcudbright.'

DUNTING GLEN. 'Stoneykirk.'

DUNVÈOCH. 'Kells.' *Dún fithich* [feeugh], the raven's fort. *See under* BENNAVEOCH.

DUNWICK. . 'Kirkcolm.'

DÙPAL. 'Kirkmaiden.' *Dubh* [doo] *pol*, black pool or water.

DURHAM HILL. 'Kirkpatrick Durham.'

DUTCHMANSTÈRN. 'Kirkmaiden, s.c.'

DYESTER'S BRAE. 'Stoneykirk.' The dyer's brae; *dyester*, a woman who dyes. E. *dye*—A.S. *deágan*, to dye, *deág*, *deah*, colour: further origin unknown (*Skeat*). The suffix *ster* (A.S. *-es-tre*), is well explained by *Skeat*, *s.v.* Spinster. Originally it was restricted to the female sex, but was gradually extended to the other.

DYESTER'S RIG. 'Balmaclellan.' *See under* DYESTER'S BRAE.

DYRHÝMPEN. 'Mochrum.' *See under* LOCH HEMPTON.

DYRNAMÀY. 'Mochrum.' *Dobhar* [dour] *na magha*, water of the plain. This name, now disused, is that given by *Pont* to Drumwalt Loch. The farm of May, on the south-western shore of the lake, retains the last syllable of the old name.

DYRSNÀG. 'Mochrum.'

EAGLE CAIRN. 'Kirkmaiden.' *Cf.* BENYELLARY.

EÀRLSTON (*P.* Erlstoun). 'Dalry.' The Earl's homestead. Said to have been built by James, Earl of Bothwell, as a hunting-box, whence the name.

EDGARTON (*P.* Egerton, Eggertoun). 'Balmaghie.' Edgar's homestead.

EDINGHAM. 'Urr.'

EGGERNÈSS (*P.* Eggerness; *Charter of Roland, Lord of Galloway, circa* 1185 (*Crauf.* MS.), Egernesse). 'Terregles, s.c.'

M

Èglin Lane. 'Minigaff.' *Cf.* Eglin Hole in Nidderdale, Yorkshire, which *Lucas* (p. 101) derives from a man's name, a suggestion strengthened by the occurrence of the name Eglinton in Ayrshire.

Èilah Hill. 'New Luce.' *Aileach* [ellagh], a stone house or fort, from *ail*, a stone. "*Aileach* or *ailtheagh, i.e.* a name for a habitation, which (name) was given from stones."—*O'Clery's Glossary.* *Cf.* Elagh in Tyrone, and Ellagh in Mayo and Galway. *See under* Craigenallie.

Èlder Holm. 'Kells.' The river-meadow of the alders, not "elders," which in BR. SC. would be "bourtrees." M.E. *aldyr*, previously *aller* (the *d* being redundant), BR. SC. and north E. dialect, *eller*—A.S. *alr* + DU. *els* + ICEL. *elrir, elri, ölr* + SWED. *al* + DAN. *elle, el* + O.H.G. *elira, erila, erla*, G. *eller, else* + LAT. *alnus* + LITH. *elkszris* + RUSS. *olecha* — √AL, to grow, whence E. *elm*. The E. *elder* (M.E. *eller*) is probably the same word applied to a different tree.

Èldrig or Èlrig (*P.* Elrick, Elrich ; *Charter*, A.D. 1413 (*Crauf. MS.*), Ellerig). 'Kirkcowan,' 'Kirkmaiden,' 'Mochrum,' 'New Luce,' 'Penninghame,' 'Stoneykirk.' A name of very general occurrence all over Scotland. *Cf.* Olrick in Caithness.

Eldrig Ree, The. 'New Luce.' "*Ree*, a sheep-ree, a permanent sheepfold, surrounded with a wall of stone and peat."—*Jamieson.*

Ellergòwer Rock. 'Minigaff.' *Ail na' gobhar* [gower], goat's cliff. *See under* Algower.

Èmer's Isle. 'Kirkcolm, s.c.'

Ènoch [*pron.* Ennogh] (*Inq. ad Cap.* 1600, Enoche ; *P.* Enoch). 'Glasserton,' 'Stoneykirk,' 'Whithorn.' *Aenach* [ennagh], a fair. *Cf.* Enagh, the name of many places in Ireland. Liable to be confused with *eanach* [annagh], a bog.

Ènrick (*P.* Ainrik, Ainryick). 'Girthon,' 'Tungland.'

Ernàmbrie (*Inq. ad Cap.* 1628, Irnealmerie; *P.* Ardnamrie). 'Crossmichael.' The prefix *Ern-*, occurring six times in this parish, seems to be a local contraction of *ard*, a height, followed by the article ; it is possibly, however, A.S. *œrn*, a house (*see under* Whithorn), which may have found its way into Celtic speech as a loan word.

ERNÀNITY (*P.* Ardnannaty). 'Crossmichael.' *Ard na annuid,* hill of the church. *See under* ANNAT HILL.

ERNCRÒGO.   'Crossmichael.'

ERNÈSPIE. 'Crossmichael.' *Ard an espoic* [espick], the bishop's hill. O. ERSE *epscop* (*Cormac*, p. 19), *easpog, easbog* + W. *esgob,* B. *escob,* C. *ispak, escop* — LAT. *episcopus,* a bishop — GK. ἐπίσκοπος, an overseer. The gen. *espoic* occurs in the *Leabor Breac,* " *Do laim Tassaig espoic,*" "To the hand of Bishop Tassach." *Cf.* GILLESPIE and QUINTINESPIE ; also, in Ireland, Tullinespick in Down, Monaspick in Wicklow, Killaspy in Kilkenny.

ERNFÌLLAN. 'Crossmichael.' *Ard an Fillain,* Fillan's hill. The name of St. Fillan, abbot of Pittenweem, is perpetuated in many parts of Scotland. "This hermit saint had a miraculous left hand of glory, which shed from the fingers a splendour that lighted his task of translating the Holy Scriptures. Robert the Bruce possessed this luminous arm, and had it carried in a silver shrine at the head of his army. Before the battle of Bannockburn, the chaplain, fearing lest it should fall into English hands, placed the marvel-working relic in a place of safety ; but whilst Robert knelt before the empty casket, the door suddenly opened and shut, for the saint himself had replaced the arm as a sign of coming victory. In gratitude King Robert built St. Fillan's Priory at Killin, on Loch Tay."—*Mackenzie Walcott,* p. 327. *See under* KIL-FILLAN.

ERNMÌNZIE (*P.* Ardmynnies).   'Crossmichael.'

ÈRSBAL'S CAVES.   'Stoneykirk, s.c.'

ÈRSOCK (*W. P.* MSS., Erssik, Irsak, Irsyk ; *Charter* 1513, Irsalk). 'Glasserton.'

ÈRVIE (*Inq. ad Cap.* 1600, Urie).   'Kirkcolm.'

ESCHÒNCHAN [*pron.* Skyoncan] (*P.* Eshsheskewachan). 'Minigaff.' The prefix is *eas,* a waterfall. Buchan Burn (*q. v.*), which is near this place, is spelt by *Pont* Essbuchany.

EWE HILL (1900 feet).   'Carsphairn.'

EYES.   'Inch.'

EYES OF CRAIGBIRNOCH.   'New Luce.'

EYES, RIG OF THE.   'New Luce.'

F̀AGAN.   'Minigaff.'

FÀGRA.   'Rerwick.'

FAÌRGIRTH (*P.* Fairgirth). 'Kirkcowan.' Fair garth, fair cultivated field or garden. *See under* DRUMGORTH.

FAIRY KNOWES.   'Inch.'

FALBÀE. 'Kirkmabreck.' *Pholl beith* [bey], pool of the birches.
The aspirated form of *poll* is commonly met with as the prefix *Fal, Phal,* or *Phil.* *See under* POLBAE.

FALCLINTÀLLACH.   'Mochrum.'

FALCÙMNOR.   'Mochrum.'

FALGÙNZEON [*pron.* gunnion]. 'Kirkgunzeon.' *Pholl Guinnin,*
St. Winnin's pool. *See under* KIRKGUNZEON.

FALHÀR. 'Whithorn.' *Pholl ghearr* [?] [har], short pool.

FALKEÒWN BURN.   'Kirkmaiden.'

FALKIPPER. 'Mochrum.' *Phol tiobair,* pool of the well. *See
under* TIBBERT.

FALLBÀE. 'Parton.' *See under* FALBAE *and* POLBAE.

FALLBÒGUE. 'Borgue.' *Pholl bog,* soft, boggy pool or stream.
See under BOGUE.

FALLINCHÈRRIE CRAIG. 'Kells.' The prefix is probably *faill,* a
cliff, an alternative form of *aill.* *See under* ALCHERRY, which
appears to bear the same meaning as FALLINCHERRIE.

FALL OF FOURS (a field on Dunskey). 'Port Patrick.' BR. SC.
fauld, an enclosure.

FALLRÈOCH. 'Balmaclellan.' *Pholl riabhach* [reeagh], grey pool.
Cf. LOCHANOUR.

FALNÀW BURN. 'Kirkmabreck.' *Pholl an atha* [awe], pool or
water of the ford.

FALNEAR.   'Mochrum.'

FALRÈADY.   'Penninghame.'

FALSHEÙCHAN. 'Kirkinner.' *See under* SHEUCHAN.

FALWHÌRN. 'Kirkcowan.' *Pholl chuirn* [hwirn], pool or water of
the cairn. *Cf.* PILWHIRN.

FALWHÌSTLE. 'Kirkinner.' *Pholl iseal* [?], low pool. *See under*
CORVISEL.

FALYOUSE. 'Mochrum.'

FANG OF THE MERRICK. 'Minigaff.' The "fang" or claw; metaph. for the spur of a hill.

FANNYGÀPPLE (a field on Stewarton farm). 'Kirkinner.' *Faiche na geapul*, the field of the horses. O. ERSE *faidche*, a green (*Cormac*), whence BR. SC. "*Fey*, croft or infield land, Galloway."—*Jamieson.* The Cinel-Fathaidh were the people whose descendants, after the tenth century, took the name of O'Fathaidh, now written O'Fahy and Fay, and still further disguised, in obedience either to fashion or to the laws compelling the native Irish to assume English names, in the name *Green*, from the resemblance between the pronunciation of *Fathaidh* and *faithche*, a green.

FARMÀLLOCHY. 'Mochrum.'

FARRACHBÀE. 'Minigaff.' *Farrach beith* [?] [bey], trysting-place of the birches. *See under* BORGAN FERRACH.

FARY ROCK. 'Kirkmaiden, s.c.'

FAULDBÀNE. 'Mochrum.' *Pholl bán* [?], white water; or perhaps a hybrid name, *fauld bán*, the white enclosure.

FAULD BURN. 'Mochrum.' The burn of the "fauld" or enclosure.

FAULDCÀRNAHAN. 'New Luce.' Carnochan's "fauld" or enclosure. Carnochan is still a common surname in Galloway, Cairnech, Cearnach, and Cearnachan, occur frequently in the *Annals of the Four Masters*, the former being a celebrated saint and contemporary of St. Patrick. The name arises from two sources, viz. *cearnach*, victorious, from *cearn*, victory, and *carnach*, a heathen priest (*O'Reilly*), *i.e.* one who officiates at the *carn*, or cairn. The suffix *an* is the usual addition to adjectives used as names of men (*Top. Poems* [55]).

FAULDCLÀNCHIE. 'New Luce.' A hybrid word, *i.e. fauld*, an enclosure, and *cladh innse* [claw inshie], the mound or fence of the meadow-land. The place seems first to have been called Clanchie (*see under* CLAUNCH), and then called the "fauld" of Clanchie.

FAULDÌNCHIE. 'New Luce.' Prob. a hybrid word, *i.e. fauld*, an enclosure, *innse* [inshie], of the meadow-land. *Cf.* FAULD-CLANCHIE.

FAULDRÀRE, or FULRARE BURN. 'Kirkmabreck.'

FAULDRÒT or FILRÒTE WELL. 'Mochrum.'

FAULDSLÀVE. 'Inch.'

FELL, in many places, sometimes alone, at others in conjunction with English or Gaelic names, frequently pleonastic. M.E. *fel—*ICEL. *fjall, fell*, a mountain + DAN. *field* + SWED, *fjäll.* " Probably originally applied to an open flat down, and the same word as E. *field.*"—*Skeat.* The prevalence of this word in Galloway hill-names is doubtless owing to the subjection of the province to the Norsemen in the ninth and tenth centuries.

FELLNÀW. 'Tungland.' *See under* FALNAW.

FELL OF CROOK. 'Mochrum.' *Cruach*, a hill, or *croch*, gallows.

FELL OF LAGHEAD. 'Girthon.' Hill of the head of the hollow. This name, like ASS OF THE GILL, is polyglot. ICEL. *fjall*, ERSE *lag*, E. *head*.

FELLSÀVERY. 'Inch.'

FELLYÈNNAN. 'Mochrum.' *Pholl*, water. There used to be a lakelet here, formerly a swamp.

FÈRNTOWN HILL. 'Port Patrick.'

FEYMÒRE. 'Leswalt.' *Faiche mór*, great green field. *See under* FANNYGAPPLE. *Cf.* Foymore in Armagh. But Feemore, in Ireland, is *fidh mór*, great wood.

FILBÀNE HILL. 'Old Luce.' *See under* FAULDBANE.

FÍNEN HILL. 'Kirkcolm.' See *Pont's* rendering of Fingland.

FÌNENESS (three syllables) (*Inq. ad Cap.* 1576, Fynnenes; 1611, Fynnaneis; *P.* Finneness). 'Balmaghie.'

FÌNGLAND (*P.* Fingen). 'Dalry.'

FÌNLOCK. 'Stoneykirk, s.c.'

FÌNNART. *See* CAIRNIE FINNART.

FÌNTLOCH (*Inq. ad Cap.* 1617, Fyntallachie; *P.* Fintilloch). 'Kells.' *Fionn tulach*, white hill. Part of this farm is called Whitehill. *Cf.* FYNTULLACH.

FLÈCKEDLAND. 'Penninghame.' Broken, variegated land; E. equivalent of ERSE *breac*. *See under* AUCHABRICK, KNOCKBRAKE, etc. *Cf.* the three names next following, also FRECKIT HILL.

FLÈCKIT HILL. 'Kirkpatrick Durham.' *See under* FLECKEDLAND.

FLÈCKIT KNOWE. 'Minigaff.' *See under* FLECKEDLAND.

FLÈCKIT RIG. 'Parton.' *See under* FLECKEDLAND.

Fleet (*P.* Fleet) (a river). 'Girthon,' etc. ICEL. *fljót*, a stream
+ DU. *vliet*, a brook + A.S. *fleót*, a bay or channel, *fleotan*, to
fleet, glide bye. The regular name for a creek among the
marshes of Kent is " fleet."

Fleugh Larg (*P.* Flularg). 'Penninghame.' *Fluich learg*, wet
land. *See under* Carrickafliou and Larg. *Cf.* Flush Hill.

Float (*Inq. ad Cap.* 1616, Floit ; *P.* Flot). 'Stoneykirk.'
Probably " flat " by the regular change of *a* to *o* (as in *ác* to
oak). The farm of Flat, in Largs parish, Ayrshire, is called
Flote by *Pont* (*Cuninghame*, p. 136).

Flush Hill. 'Kirkcolm.' Wet hill. *See under* Fleugh Larg.

Folk Burn. 'Kells.'

Foulflùsh. 'Whithorn, s.c.' *Faill fluich*, wet cliff. *See under*
Carrickafliou and Fallincherry.

Foulford. 'Inch. Foul or dirty road. " *Ford*, way " (*Jamieson*) ;
" E. *ford*, M.E. *ford, forth*, a passage, esp. through a river " (*Skeat*)
— A.S. *ford* + G. *furt, furth* + A.S. *faran*, to go + DU. *varen* +
ICEL. and SWED. *fara* + DAN. *fare* + O.H.G. *faran*, C. *fahren* +
GOTH. *faran*, to go + GK. πορεύομαι, I go, travel, πόρος, a way
through, περάω, I pass through + LAT. *experior*, I pass through,
experientia + SKT. *pri*, to bring over — √PAR, to cross, pass
over or through.

Fountain Danners. 'New Luce.'

Foremànnoch (*P.* Faumenach ; *Charter* 1799, Forminogh, Fomin-
ogh). 'Parton.' *Faiche meadhonach* [menagh], middle field.
See under Balminnoch and Fannygapple.

Fòrket Glen. 'Kirkgunzeon.' Forked, divided glen. *Cf.*
Glenhowl.

Fox Hunt. 'Glasserton.'

Fox Rattle. 'Stoneykirk, s.c.' *Rattle*, a heap of boulders and
debris at the foot of a cliff. M.E. *rattlen* — A.S. *hrætele*,
hrætelwyrt, rattlewort, *i.e.* the plant that rattles + DU. *ratelen*, to
rattle + G. *rassel*, a rattle + GK. κροταλίζειν, to rattle — KRAT,
to knock (imitative, as in *rat-tat-tat*). In the sense of a heap
of stones, from the noise made by stones falling from a cliff.

Foxes' Rattle. 'Kirkmaiden, s.c.' *See under* Fox Rattle and
Inchshannoch.

Fox Yird. ‘Carsphairn.’ Fox earth. br. sc. “*Yird, yerd,* earth.” —*Jamieson.* The technical expression for a fox’s hole in E. is an “earth.” br. sc. *yird* — icel. *jörd* + dan. and swed. *jord* + goth. *airtha* + G. *erde* + a.s. *eorðe* (whence m.e. *eorþe, erþe, erthe,* E. *earth*).

Fràngo Hill. ‘Kirkcolm.’ *Franco,* a Frenchman. *See under* Auchenfranco.

Frànkie Hill. ‘Minigaff.’ *See under* Frango Hill.

Frecket Hill. ‘Stoneykirk.’ *See under* Fleckit Hill.

Freuch (*Inq. ad Cap.* 1666, Gallindalloch, *nunc vocata* Frewch). ‘Stoneykirk.’ *Fráech,* heather. There are several places in Ireland called Freagh and Freugh. o. erse *frdech* + w. *grug,* B. *bruc.*

Friar’s Yard (close to New Abbey). ‘New Abbey.’ The friar’s garden. “*Yard, yaird,* a garden, properly of pot-herbs. . ‘ The bonny *yard* of ancient Eden’; *Ferguson.*”—*Jamieson.* m.e. *yerd* — a.s. *geard. See under* Drumgorth.

Fuffock (a lakelet).   ‘Minigaff.’

Fùffock Hill (*P.* Fuffock ; ms. 1527, Fuchik) (1050 feet). ‘Twynholm.’

Fùffock, Kiln of the.   ‘Kirkmaiden, s.c.’

Fulràre. ‘Kirkmabreck.’ *See* Fauldrare.

Fumart Liggat. ‘Dalry.’ Polecat’s gate. “*Fowmarte,* a polecat.” —*Jamieson.* m.e. *fulmart, folmart, fulmard.* From m.e. *ful* — a.s. *fúl,* foul, stinking, and o.f. *marte, martre,* a martin ; thus a.s. *fúl mear* , stinking, foul martin = *foul martin.* But *Lucas* (*Studies in Nidderdale,* p. 130) devotes a chapter to show that *foumart,* a polecat, is a distinct word from *fomud,* Yorksh. for the Pine Marten (which has no smell), and which he derives from o. norse *fóa,* a fox, and *mördr,* a martin = the fox-martin, as we speak of the martin-cat. *See under* Liggat-cheek.

Fùnlan.   ‘Mochrum.’

Furbar.   ‘Kelton.’

Fùrmiston Craig and Lane.   ‘Carsphairn.’

Fyntùllach (*P.* Fintilloch). ‘Penninghame.’ *See under* Fint-loch.

Gabarruning. 'Kirkmaiden, s.c.' *Gab, gob,* a mouth, beak, snout (*O'Reilly*). Applied to the point of a hill or cliff. BR. SC. "*gab, gob,* the mouth" (*Jamieson*), W. *gob,* a heap, a mound.

Gab Hill. 'Kirkmaiden.' *Gab, gob,* a snout.

Gabsnòut. 'New Luce.' Appears to be a pleonastic compound of *gab* and *snout. See under* Gabarruning.

Gahàrn (a hill of 2000 feet). 'Minigàff.'

Gaìgrie. 'Buìttle.' *See under* Caggrie.

Gaìral. 'Kirkmaiden, s.c.' *Gar aill* [?], near cliff. There are several islands off the coast of Ireland called Garinish, *i.e.* near island.

Gaìrland Burn (*P.* Ghairland). *Gar linn,* the near pool, or *gearr lin,* short pool (the former most likely). *Cf.* Garline in Inverness-shire. ·

Gàirloch (*P.* Loch of Gherloch). 'Kells.' *Gar loch,* near loch, or *gearr loch,* short loch.

Gàiry. A name commonly applied to an elevated place, a hillside (not to be confounded with "garry")—A.S. *gára,* a projecting point of land—A.S. *gár,* a spear. Or perhaps it comes from ICEL. *geiri,* a triangular piece of land, from *geirr,* a spear; BR. SC. "*gair,* a slip of tender, fertile grass in a barren situation"—*Jamieson.* This is the same as E. "*gore,* a triangular piece let into a garment, a triangular slip of land" (*Skeat*), from the pointed shape.

Gàla Lane (*P.* Gallua Lein). 'Carsphairn.'

Gàldenoch (*Inq. ad Cap.* 1543, Galdynnoch). 'Leswalt,' 'Old Luce,' 'Stoneykirk.' *Gallnach,* a place of foreigners, stranger's dwelling. *See under* Dergall.

Gale Island. 'Minigaff.'

Gàlla Hill. 'Penninghame.' The gallows hill (*see under* Culcreuchie)—*galga, gealga,* a cross, a gibbet, whence M.E. *galwe,* by usual change of *g* to *w* + ICEL. *gálgi* + DAN. and SWED. *galge,* a gibbet + DU. *galg* + GOTH. *galga,* a cross + G. *galgen.* Root unknown (*Skeat*).

Gallant Buoys. 'Borgue, s.c.'

Gallie Craig. 'Kirkmaiden, s.c.'

GALL KNOWE.   'Rerwick.'
GALL MOSS OF DIRNEÀUK.   'Kirkcowan.'

GÀLLOWAY, the province comprising the shire of Wigtown´ and
the Stewartry of Kirkcudbright. "During the latter years
of Kenneth's reign (A.D. 844-860) a people appear in close
association with the Norwegian pirates, and joining in their
plundering expeditions, who are termed Gallgaidhel. This
name is formed by the combination of the two words 'Gall,'
a stranger, a foreigner, and 'Gaidhel,' the national name of
the Gaelic race. It was certainly first applied to the people
of Galloway, and the proper name of this province, Galwethia,
is formed from Galwyddel [pronounced *Gallwythel*], the Welsh
equivalent of Gallgaidhel. It seems to have been applied to
them as a Gaelic race under the rule of 'Galls,' or foreigners;
Galloway being for centuries a province of the Anglic kingdom of Northumbria, and the term 'Gall' having been
applied to the Saxons before it was almost exclusively appropriated to the Norwegian and Danish pirates."—Skene, *Celt.
Scot.* i. 311. For the survival of the ERSE form of the name
see under DRUMGALGAL.

GALLOWAY ISLES. 'Minigaff.' The meadows beside the stream
called *Gallua Lein* in *Pont's* map (*see* GALA LANE). "Isle" is
here used in the sense of a meadow beside a stream, just as
innis (BR. SC. *inch*, ink) and *eilan* are sometimes used in ERSE.
See under MILLISLE.

GALLOWHÀE. 'Kirkinner.' The gallows height—A.S. *galga hehŏe*,
the *g* becoming *w* in M.E. according to rule. *See under*
GALLA HILL.

GALLOLECK. 'Colvend.' The gallows stone, a hybrid word,
from M.E. *galwe*, a gallows, and ERSE *leac*, a stone. "*Leck*,
any stone that stands a strong fire, as greenstone, trap, etc."
—*Jamieson.*

GALLRÌNNIES. 'Balmaclellan.' *Cf.* GILLROANIE.

GALTNEY or GALTWAY (formerly a parish, variously written Gata,
Gultneyis, etc.). 'Kirkcudbright.'

GÀNNOCH. 'Minigaff.' *Gaineach, gainmheach,* sandy, a sandy
place; adj. from *gaine* or *gaineamh*, sand. *O'Reilly* also gives
gainneach, a place where reeds grow. *Cf.* GENOCH, GLEN-
GAINOCH, GLENGUNNOCH; also, in Ireland, Gannoughs,
Gannow and Gannaveen in Galway, Gannaway in Down
(called Gannach in the *Inquisitions*), Gannavagh (*gainmheach*)
in Leitrim, Ganniv in Cork, and Gannew in Donegal.

GÀRCHEW (*Inq. ad Cap.* 1580, Garskeogh, *alias* Garskere *vel* Garkere; 1664, Garneskeoch, *alias vocata* Garkerie, *also* Garcherow; *P.* Garchery). 'Penninghame.' *Gar ceathramhaidh* [carrou], near land-quarter. The alternative name seems to have been *gar sceithiog* [skyōg], the near hawthorn-tree. *See under* CARHOWE.

GÀRCHRIE. 'Leswalt.' *See under* GARCHEW.

GARCRÒGO (*P.* Garnechraggow, Garcraggow). 'Balmaclellan.'

GÀRGRIE (*P.* Gargry). 'Kirkcowan,' 'Mochrum.' *See under* GARCHEW.

GÀRHEUGH (*Inq. ad Cap.* 1582, Garkerrow; *P.* Garcherow). 'Mochrum.' *See under* GARCHEW.

GARÌNNER STRAND (a stream). 'Kells.' *Gar inbher* [inver], the near junction (of two streams).

GARLAFFIN (a hill of 1050 feet). 'Dalry.'

GARLÀIKEN. 'Minigaff.' *Gar leacain* [lackan], the near hill-side. *See under* LAKIN.

GARLICK. 'Minigaff.' *Gar leac*, the near stone.

GARLIEHÀWISE. 'Kirkcolm.'

GÀRLIES (*P.* Ghairlyis, Gairleyis). 'Minigaff.' *Gar lios* [liss], the near fort. The ruins of a mediæval castle stand here.

GARLOFF (*P.* Loch of Gherloch). 'New Abbey.' *Gar* or *gearr loch*, near or short lake.

GARMARTIN (*P.* Gormairtinn). 'Kirkpatrick Durham.'

GÀRMILL. 'Penninghame.' *Gar meall*, near hill. O. ERSE *mell*, ERSE " *meall*, a globe, a ball; a lump, a mass, a heap; a hill, hillock, eminence " (*O'Reilly*). Perhaps akin to LAT. *moles* (E. *mole*, a pier). In composition sometimes difficult to distinguish from *maol*, bare; in fact, as a mountain name, the two words seem to have run together in Welsh, for *moel*, adj., means towering, piled up, and also bald, bare (*Pughe*).

GARNAVLAHAN. 'Stoneykirk, s.c.'

GARNIEMÌRE. 'Girthon.'

GARNSHÒG. 'Mochrum.' *Gcarn seobhag* [garn shyōg], cairn of the hawks. *Cf.* Carrickshock in Kilkenny. O. ERSE *sebac*, ERSE *seabhac*, GAEL. *seobhag* + W. *hebog* + O.H.G. *hapuk*, G. *habicht* + A.S. *heafoc* (whence M.E. *hauk, hauek*, E. *hawk*) + DU. *havic* + ICEL. *haukr* + SWED. *hök*, from Teutonic base HAB, to seize = LAT. *capere*.

GARNSKEÒG. 'Mochrum.' *Carn sceithiog* [skeyog], cairn of the hawthorns.

GÀRPEL BURN (*P.* Garvepool B.). 'Balmaclellan.' *Garbh* [garve] *poll*, rough water.

GÀRRACHER (*P.* Garchur). 'Kirkcowan,' 'Kirkmabreck.' *See under* GARCHEW.

GARRAHÀSPIN. 'Stoneykirk, s.c.' *Cf.* CASPIN, HESPIN.

GÀRRAMIE. 'Kells.'

GÀRRARIE (*Inq. ad Cap.* 1582, Garrore; *P.* Garery; *W. P.* MSS. Gararye). 'Glasserton,' 'Kells.'

GÀRRARIE FORD. 'Minigaff.' Robert the Bruce is said to have crossed the Minnick here.

GÀRRIE. 'Stoneykirk.' A word used in Galloway to express a rough, stony space of ground, a moraine—*garbh* [garve, garriv], rough. "A garry o' stanes" is a common expression.

GARRIEFÀD. 'Kirkmabreck.' *Gáradh* or *gárrdha fada* [garra faada], long garden. This name, Garrienae, and Garrieslae appear in the estate-map of Cuil along with such names as Peggie Murray's garden, J. Adam's garden, M'Kie's garden, etc. *Gárrdha* or *gáradh* is not to be distinguished in composition, except by local circumstances, from *garbh, carroch,* and *garradh.* It is akin to *gort. See under* DRUMGORT.

GARRIENÀE. 'Kirkmabreck.'

GÀRRIES. 'Port Patrick,' 'Stoneykirk.' *See under* GARRIE.

GARRIESLÀE. 'Kirkmabreck.'

GARRIEWHÌNS. 'Carsphairn.'

GÀRROCH (*P.* Garrach) 'Crossmichael,' 'Twynholm.' *G-carrach,* a rough, stony place.

GÀRROCH BURN. 'Kells.' *See under* GARROCH.

GÀRROCHTRIE (*P.* Garachty). 'Kirkmaiden.' *Ceathramhaidh* [carrou] *uachdarach,* the upper land-quarter. *See under* CURROCHTRIE.

GARRYÀIRD (*P.* Garrowairg, Garyaird). 'Dalry.' *Garbh* [garve, garriv] *ard* ; rough height. *Cf.* Garryard in Ireland.

GARRYHÀRRY. 'Stoneykirk, s.c.'

GÀRRY HILL. 'Balmaclellan.' *See under* GARRIE.

GARRYHÒRN (*P.* Garyhorrn).   'Carsphairn,' 'Crossmichael.'

GARSÀLLOCH.   'Kirkcolm.'   *Gar seileach,* the near willow-tree. Garrysallagh in Cavan and elsewhere is interpreted *garadh seileach,* willow garden, or *garadh salach,* dirty garden. *See under* BARNSALLIE.

GARSTÙBBIN (*P.* Garstubb).   'Dalry.'

GÀRTHLAND (*P.* Garthland; *Charter,* A.D. 1295 (*Crauf.* MS.), Garochloyne; *Charter,* A.D. 1413 (*Crauf.* MS.) Garrichloyne; *Charter,* A.D. 1426 (*Crauf.* MS.), Garflane. 'Stoneykirk.'

GARTHLEÀRY (*Inq. ad Cap.* 1656, Garthlerie).   'Inch.'   *Gort láira,* paddock of the mare.   *Cf.* Gartnalaragh in Munster.

GARVÈLLAN (an island in Fleet Bay) (*P.* Garvellan).   'Girthon.' *Garbh* [garve] *eilean,* rough island.   *Cf.* Garvillaun in Ireland.

GARVÌLLAN.   'Kirkcolm.'   *See under* GARVELLAN.

GARVÌLLAND LOCH (*P.* Garvellan).   'New Luce.'   *See under* GARVELLAN.

GARWÀCHIE (*P.* Garvacchy).   'Penninghame.'   *Garbh achadh* [garv-aha], rough field.

GARWALL.   'Minigaff.'

GASS (*P.* Gaiss).   'Old Luce.'

GATE, (*P.* Gaits).   'Kells.'   "*Gate,* a way."—*Jamieson.*   M.E. *gate, yate* (the latter form is preserved in BR. SC. *yett,* a gate)—A.S. *geat* + DU. *gat,* a hole, opening, gap, mouth + ICEL. *gat,* an opening (*see under* TAYLOR'S GAT), *gata,* a way, path, street + SWED. *gata,* a street, lane + DAN. *gade,* a street + GOTH. *gatwo,* a street + G. *gasse,* a street.   From the same root as A.S. *gitan,* to get, to arrive at, to reach, so that *gate* = a way to *get* at anything, a passage (*Skeat*).

GATE CREASE.   'Port Patrick, s.c.'

GÀTEGILL BURN (*Inq. ad Cap.* 1560, Gaitgill M'Ilvernok, Gaitgill M'Illinsche; 1602, Gaitgill M'Nische; 1603, Gaitgill Mundwell). 'Girthon.' ICEL. *gat gil,* the ravine of the gap. *See under* GATE.

GÀTEHOUSE. 'Girthon.' BR. SC. the house on the " gate " or road. *See under* GATE.

GÀVELS MOOR.   'Balmaclellan.'

GAVINGILL. 'Kirkbean.' Prob. the *gill* or ravine of Cavens, as it is close to the place of that name. *See under* CAVENS.

GAWINTOMS.   'Minigaff.'

GED STRAND. 'Balmaclellan.' BR. SC. the pike stream.

GELSTON (*Inq. ad Cap.* 1605, Glesto *rel* Glestoun *v.* Gelstoun ; *P.* Ghalstoun ; *Rag. Roll*, 1296, Gevelestone; *Robertson's Index*, 1300, Gauyliston, Guiliston ; *Pitcairn*, 1509, Gileston). 'Kelton.'

GÈNOCH (*P.* Ganoch). 'Kirkcolm,' 'Old Luce.' *See under* GAINOCH.

GIB, ROUGH. 'Kirkcowan,' 'Wigtown.' BR. SC. *gib*, a snout, a name for a hill. "The beak or hooked lip of a male salmon." —*Jamieson.* —ERSE *gob*, a snout. *See under* GAB HILL.

GIBANÀRG (a sea rock). 'Port Patrick, s.c.' *Gob an uirc* [?], the swine's snout; genit. of *orc.* *See under* CRAIGGORK and GABARRUNING.

GÌBBON. 'Rerwick.' *Gobín*, little snout. *Cf.* Gubbeen in Cork.

GILHÒW. 'Glasserton.' ICEL. *gil*, a ravine, *haug*, a hillock, a tumulus, a grave. The ravine of the hillock or grave. It is at the head of Physgill glen.

GILLÀRTHUR. 'New Abbey.' The *gill* or stream which runs out of Loch Arthur.

GILLÈSPIE (*Inq. ad Cap.* 1668, Gillespeck ; *P.* Killespick). 'Old Luce.' *Cill espoic* [espick], the bishop's cell or chapel. *See under* ERNESPIE. *Cf.* Killaspy in Kilkenny, which used to be written Killaspucke, and has dropped the final consonant in the same way as Gillespie. The surname Gillespie, common in Scotland, has a different origin, viz., *giolla espoic*, the bishop's servant.

GILLFOOT. 'Kirkbean.' The foot of the "*gil*" or ravine.

GILLRÒANIE.   'Kirkcudbright.'

GILLS LOCH. 'Kells.' *Loch gile* [gilly, *hard*], loch of the brightness. *See under* LOCH GILL.

GÌLSHIE FEYS (*P.* Achingilshy). 'Kirkinner.' A hybrid word, *guilchach*, rushy, and BR. SC. *feys*, meadows. *See under* AUCHENGILSHIE and FEYMORE.

GIRGÙNNOCHY. 'Stoneykirk.' *Cf.* Gargunnock in Stirlingshire.

GIRNIEL.   'Sorbie.'

GIRSTENWOOD (*P.* Girsten Parck).   'Rerwick.'

GIRTHON (a parish in the Stewartry) (*P.* Girtoun).

GIRVELLAN (a peninsula). 'Rerwick.' *See under* GARVELLAN.

GLADSMOOR.   'Kirkcolm.'

GLAIK (*Inq. ad Cap.* 1616, Glayk; *P.* Glaik). 'Leswalt.' *Glac,* a narrow glen (*O'Reilly*); literally, the palm of the hand. Applied, like most names of hollows, to the neighbouring hill.

GLAISTERS (*P.* Glaisters). 'Kirkpatrick Durham.' *Glas tír,* green land. E. plur. added. Glaisterlands, near Rowallan in Ayrshire, shows the English pleonastic addition of *lands.* *Tír* + W. *tir*; allied to LAT. *terra* = older form *tersa* + GK. ταρσός (Attic ταρρός) a stand or frame for drying things upon, any broad, flat surface, akin to *torrere,* to parch—√TARS, to be dry; and through this root connected with E. *thirst, torrid* (*Skeat*).

GLASNICK (*P.* Glasnick; *Inq. ad Cap.* 1604, Glasnycht, *vulgariter nuncupatus* Garglasnycht). 'Penninghame.'

GLASSERTON (*P.* Glastoun) [*locally ·pron.* Glais'ton]. A parish. *See under* WHITHORN.

GLASSOCH (*P.* Glassoch). 'Penninghame.' *Glaiseachd* [glassaghd], verdure, a grassy place. *Cf.* Glassoch in Fenwick parish, Ayrshire, which *Pont* describes thus: "Glasschach, a grassey plot" (*Cuninghame,* p. 186).

GLASTER, RIG OF THE. 'New Luce.' *See under* GLAISTERS.

GLEDE BOG. 'Carsphairn.' Perhaps from BR. SC. *gleid, glede,* a fire (*Jamieson*) —A.S. *gled.*

GLEDMEIN.   'Mochrum.'

GLEIKMALLOCH. 'Minigaff.' *See under* GLAIK.

GLENAMOUR (*P.* Glenaymer). 'Minigaff.' *Gleann amuir,* glen of the trough. *See under* BALLOCHANARMOUR. *Gleann* + W. *glyn*: derivation uncertain.

GLENARM (*Charter,* 1665, Glenearn). 'Urr.' There is a well-known place of this name in Antrim.

GLENCAIRD. 'Minigaff.' *Gleann ceard* [kaird], glen of the tinkers or workers in metal. O. ERSE *cerd,* ERSE and GAEL. *ceard,* whence BR. SC. *caird,* a gipsy, a travelling tinker, a sturdy beggar (*Jamieson*).

GLENCHÀMBER (*P.* Gleyschambrach). ' New Luce.' *Gleann seamar* [shammar], glen of the clover. *Pont* uses the adjectival form *seamrach* [shamragh], abounding in clover, which appears in several of the Irish writers in the form *scoith-seamrach*, flowery with clover. "*Seamar, seamróg*, trefoil, white clover, white honeysuckle " (*O'Reilly*), is used with the usual looseness of botanical names in early times, but seems to mean "clover," which is probably the "shamrokes" mentioned by Spenser as being devoured by the people in time of famine. It would be at least as edible as woodsorrel. *Cf.* GLENSHIMEROCK ; also Aghnashammer in Fermanagh, Mohernashammer in Roscommon, Knocknashammer in Cavan and Sligo (the latter of which places is also called Clover Hill), Coolnashamrogue in. Cork and Limerick, etc. The form Glenchamber arises from an attempt to Anglicise the Scottish word *chammer*, *chalmer*, into *chamber*. Instances of this process may be seen in Gleniron, Old Water.

GLENCRÈE. ' Penninghame.' The glen of the river Cree.

GLENCÙRROCH. ' Kirkcolm, s.c.' *Gleann corraich* [?], glen of the boat, boat glen (it is a glen opening upon the shore), or *gleann curraich*, glen of the bog or moor (*see under* CORRA). *Corrach*, a boat + W. *corwyg*, a carcase, a trunk (whence *cwrwgl*, a coracle).

GLENDÀRROCH. ' Kirkcowan.' *Gleann darach*, glen of the oaks. *Cf.* Glendarragh in Ireland.

GLENÈMBE.   ' Kirkinner.'

GLENFÈY. ' Kirkmaiden.' *Gleann faiche*, glen of the green field. *See under* FANNYGAPPLE.

GLENGÀINOCH (*P.* Glengeynett). ' Girthon.' *Gleann gaineach*, sandy glen. *See under* GANNOCH. *Cf.* Glenganagh in Down.

GLENGÀP (*P.* Glenghaip). ' Twynholm.' Probably shortened from GLENGAPPOCH, *q.v.*

GLENGÀPPOCH (*Inq. ad Cap.* 1607, Glengoppock ; *P.* Glengappock). ' Crossmichael.' *Gleann copógach* [?], glen of the dock-leaves. *Cf.* Glencoppogagh in Tyrone, and many other names in Ireland ending in *goppoge* and *gappoge*.

GLENGÀRREN (*P.* Glengheiren). ' Minigaff. *Gleann garain*, glen of the thicket. "*Garán*, thicket, underwood ; *Garran*, a grove or wood " (*O'Reilly*) ; or *gleann gearrain*, glen of the horse.

GLENGÌTTER.   ' Leswalt.'

GLENGRÙBOCH.   'Minigaff.'

GLENGÙNNOCH.   'Parton.'   *See under* GLENGAINOCH.

GLENGÝRE (*P.* Glenghyir).   'Kirkcolm.'

GLENHÀPPLE (*Inq. ad Cap.* 1645, Glenchappell ; *P.* Glenchappel).
    'Inch,' ' Penninghame.'   *Gleann chapul* [happle], the glen of
    the horses.   *See under* BARHAPPLE.

GLENHÀRVIE.   'New Abbey.'   *Gleann gharbh* [harv], rough glen.
    Cf. Glengarrif in Ireland.

GLENHÌE.   'Stoneykirk.'

GLENHÌNNIE.   'Old Luce.'

GLENHÒISE (*P.* Klonwhoisk).   'Minigaff.'   *Cf.* BARHOISE.

GLENHÒWL or GLENHOUL (*Barnbarroch*, 1563, Glenhovyll ; *P.*
    Glenhowill ; *Inq. ad Cap.* 1668, Glenhovill).   'Carsphairn,'
    'Kirkcowan,' ' Penninghame.'   *Gleann ghabail* [houl], glen of
    the fork (junction of streams).   *See under* ADDERHALL and
    FORKET GLEN.   *Cf.* Glengavlin on the Shannon, which the
    Four Masters (A.D. 1390) write *gleann gaibhle.*   The word also
    occurs in Ireland as Gole, Goul, Gowel, and dimin. Golan,
    Goulaun, Gowlan, etc.   *See* GOWLAN GLEN.   From *gabhal*
    probably comes BR. SC. "*Gowl*, a hollow between hills. Perthsh.
    The *goul* o' a stook, the opening between the sides of a shock
    of corn. Aberd."—*Jamieson.*

GLENÌRON (*P.* Klonairn).   'Old Luce.'   *Gleann* or *cluain iairn,*
    glen or meadow of the iron, or *cluain airne,* meadow of the
    sloes.   This name is an instance of spelling being modified to
    interpret a name supposed to be BR. SC.   Thus *airn* is BR. SC.
    for *iron ; Pont* shows that the name was so pronounced in
    his day ; modern writers, looking upon Broad Scotch as
    corrupt English, have attempted to make the word intelligible
    by putting it in its present form.   The sense remains the
    same, which in such cases rarely happens ; *e.g.* OLD WATER,
    GLENCHAMBER, etc.   Old Gaulish *isarn* (*Rhys,* p. 26)+ERSE
    iarn, iarand+W. *haiarn,* B. *houarn*+ICEL. *járn* (contr. from
    older *isarn*)+DU. *ijzer*+A.S. *iren* (older *ísen*), O.H.G. *isarn,* G.
    eisen+GOTH. *eisarn.*

GLENÌRON SÈVERAL.   'Old Luce.'   Separate Gleniron.   *See under*
    SEVERAL.

GLENJÒRIE (*P.* Gleniowarie).   'Kirkcowan,' ' Old Luce.'

GLENKÈNS (*Inq. ad Cap.* 1550, Glenken).   A district in the
    Stewartry consisting of the parishes of Balmaclellan, Dalry,
    Kells, and Carsphairn, through which runs the river Ken.

N

GLENKÌLN (*P.* Glenkill).   ' Kirkpatrick Irongray.'

GLENKÌTTEN (*P.* Glenkitten).   ' New Luce.'

GLENLÀGGAN (formerly Kilcrouchie). ' Parton.' *Gleann lagain,*
glen of the hollow. *See under* LAGGAN.

GLENLÀGGIE. ' Port Patrick.' *See under* GLENLAGGAN.

GLENLÀIR. ' Parton.' *Gleann láir* [?], glen of the mares.

GLENLÈE. ' Kirkmaiden.' *Gleann liath* [lee], grey glen.

GLENLÈY (*P.* Glenly). ' Kirkgunzeon.' *See under* GLENLEE.

GLENLÌNG (*P.* Glenling).   ' Mochrum.'

GLENLÒCHAR. ' Balmaghie.' *Gleann lúachair,* glen of the rushes.
See under DRUMLOCKHART.

GLENLÙCE. ' Old Luce.' The glen of the Water of Luce. The
village of this name was formerly called Ballinglauch. *See
under* LUCE.

GLENLÙCKLOCH (*Inq. ad Cap.* 1663, Glenluchak; *Charter* 1719,
Glenlochoch; *P.* Glenluichak). ' Penninghame.'

GLENLÙFFAN.   ' Colvend.'

GLENMÀLLOCH, THE TORS OF. ' Minigaff.' *Cf.* GLEIKMALLOCH.
See under TORRS.

GLENNÀPP. ' Rerwick.' *Cf.* Glenapp in Ayrshire, which is probably Glen Alpinn, where Alpin (son of Eochaidh), king of
Scottish Dalriada, was slain, A.D. 750 (*Skene, Celt. Scot.* i. 291).

GLENÒGIE (*P.* Klonvogie).   ' Penninghame.'

GLENÒRCHIE.   ' Mochrum.'

GLENÒWRIE (*Inq. ad Cap.* 1604, Glenure, *alias vocata* Blairboyis).
' Minigaff.' *Gleann iubhar* [?] [yure], glen of the yews or of
the juniper. *See under* PALNURE.

GLENQUÌCKEN (*P.* Glenquikkin).   ' Kirkmabreck.'

GLENRÀZIE [*pron.* raazie] (*P.* Klonrassy).   ' Penninghame.'

GLENRIE.   ' Kells.'

GLENRÒAN.   ' Crossmichael.'

GLENRÙTHER (*Inq. ad Cap.* 1600, Clonryddin; *P.* Kloniridder).
' Penninghame.'

GLENSÈLLIE. ' Old Luce.' *Gleann seileach,* glen of the willows.
See under BARSALLOCH.

GLENSHÀLLOCH. ' Minigaff.' *Gleann scalg* [?] [shallug], glen of
the hunting. *See under* DRUMSHALLOCH.

GLENSHÌMEROCK (*P.* Glenshymbrock). 'Dalry.' *Gleann seamarach* [shammeragh], glen of the clover. *See under* GLENCHAMBER.

GLENSÒNE. 'New Abbey.'

GLENSTÒCKADALE (*Inq. ad Cap.* 1616, Glenstakadaill; *P.* Glenstokkadell). 'Leswalt.'

GLENSTÒCKING. 'Colvend.' *Gleann stuacìn* [?], glen of the little stack or hill. *See under* STOCKING HILL.

GLENSWÌNTONS (*P.* Glensuyntouns).

GLENTÌRROW or GLENTARA. 'Inch.' *Cf.* CRAIGTERRA; also Moytirra in Mayo.

GLENTRÌPLOCH (*P.* Glentrybloc; *Inq. ad Cap.* 1675, Glentriploch). 'Mochrum.'

GLENTRÒOL (contains Loch Trool and Trool Burn) (*P.* Truiyll, Truyil). 'Minigaff.' *See under* TROOL.

GLENTRUIL. 'Borgue.' *See under* GLENTROOL.

GLENVÈRNOCH (*P.* Glenbarrana, Glenbarranach). 'Penninghame.' *Gleann bhearnach* [varnagh], gapped glen. *Pont* preserves the original unaspirated form. *See under* CRAIGBERNOCH.

GLENWHÌLLY. 'New Luce.' *Gleann choille* [hwilly], glen of the wood.

GLENWÌLLIE. 'Port Patrick.' *See under* GLENWHILLY.

GLENYÈRROCK (*Inq. ad Cap.* 1615, Glenzairock). 'Rerwick.' *Gleann dhearg* [yerrug], red glen. *See under* BARYERROCK.

GLOON BURN and RIG OF GLOON. 'Minigaff.' *Gluing* [gloong], a shoulder, or *glùn* [gloon], the knee. *Cf.* Gloonpatrick (*Glùn Phadruig* in the *Book of Lecan*) in Roscommon, named from a stone said to bear the impression of St. Patrick's knee. In the present case it means a projecting shoulder or " knee " of the hill. *Cf.* CALF KNEES.

GOAT CRAIG (in many places). *Cf.* CRAIGENGOWER.

GOAT STRAND. 'Carsphairn.' The goat stream.

GOBAWHÌLKIN. 'Kirkmaiden, s.c.' *Gob*, a snout. *See under* GABARRUNING.

GOLDIELÈA (formerly Drungans). 'Troqueer.' Goldie's *lea* or field, a modern name given by Major Goldie, who owned it in 1799.

GOOL HILL. 'Penninghame.' *Gabhal* [?] [goul], a fork. *Cf.* Gole, Gowel, Goul, in various parts of Ireland. *See under* ADDERHALL and GLENHOWL.

GÒRDONSTON (*P.* Gordonstain). 'Dalry.' Gordon's *tún*, or homestead.

GÒRMAL HILL. 'Girthon.' *Gorm aill* [?], blue cliff. *Cf.* Gorminish (*gorm innis*) in Lough Melvin, Gormagh in King's County (*gorm achadh*). If this derivation happen to be correct, it is the only instance occurring in Galloway of this word *gorm*, which is frequently used in other Celtic countries.

GÒRRACHER. 'Kirkcowan.' *Gar* or *gearr achadh* [aha], near or short field.

GÒRTIE HILL. 'Kirkcowan.' *Gar tigh*, near house. *See under* DRUMATYE.

GOUK HILL. 'Whithorn.' BR. SC. Cuckoo's Hill. *Gouk* is connected with the same imitative sound as LAT. *cuculus*, M.E. *cukkow, coccou*, O.F. and F. *coucou*, GK. κόκκυξ, SKT. *kokila*, all meaning a *cuckoo*.

GOUK THORN. 'Balmaclellan.' *See under* GOUK HILL.

GÒUNIE. 'Kirkmaiden, s.c.' *Gamhnach* [gownah], a heifer.

GÒURLEY. 'Kells.'

GOW HILL. 'Colvend.' Hill of the gulls [?]. "*Gow*, the old generic name for the gull."—*Jamieson.*

GÒWLAN GLEN. 'Penninghame.' *Gabhailan* [goulan], a little fork (of a stream), dim. of *gabhal* (*see under* ADDERHALL, GLENHOWL, GOOL HILL, etc.). *Cf.* Gowlan, Gowlane, and Gowlaun, in several parts of Ireland.

GRACE HILL. 'Old Luce.'

GRÀDDOCK (*P.* Gradock). 'Minigaff.' Probably connected with *·greadán*, the parching of corn in an open fire; *greadadh* [graddah], a scorching, whence BR. SC. "*Graddan*, grain burnt out of the ear."—*Jamieson.*

GRAINY FORD. 'Balmaghie.' *Greanach* [grannagh], gravelly. *Cf.* GRANNEY FORD; and, in Ireland, Greanagh, a stream in Limerick; Granagh, Grannagh, Granny, and Granig in other counties. *Grean* [grăn], gravel, liable, as *Joyce* says, to confusion in compound words with *grán*, grain, and *grian*, the sun + W. *graian*, B. *grouan*, C. *grou*, probably akin to O.F.

grave (of which O.F. *gravelle* is a dimin., whence M.E. *grauel*, E. *gravel*). *Cf.* SKT. *grávan*, a stone, rock.

GRANGE (in many places, such as Grange of Bladenoch, Grange of Cree, of Urr, etc.). A farmhouse. M.E. *grange, graunge* — O.F. *graunge*. *Cf.* SPAN. *granja*, a grange — LOW LAT. *granea*, a barn — LAT. *granum*, corn.

GRÀNNAN. 'Kirkmaiden.' *Grianan* [greenan], lit. a sunny spot, from *grian*, the sun. It is glossed by Irish writers *solarium, terra solaris.* The usual meaning is the residence of a chief or important personage. Grenan, Greenan, Greenane, and Greenaune, are the names of about forty-five townlands all over Ireland. In another form, *Grianóg*, it gives name to three places in Ireland called Greenoge, and also to Greenock in Scotland. *Cf.* BARGRENNAN, GRENNAN. For a full account of the word *grianan* see " The Battle of Magh Rath," p. 7, *note.*

GRANNEY FORD (on the Cree). 'Penninghame.' *See under* GRAINY FORD.

GRÀPLIN. 'Borgue.'

GRAVE SLUNK. 'Leswalt, s.c.' *See under* BANDOLIER SLUNK.

GREENDASS. 'Kells.' Green ledge. *See under* BUCKDASS.

GREEN ELDRIGS. 'Old Luce.' *See under* ELDRIG.

GREENFAULD. 'Kirkmabreck.' Green fold or enclosure.

GREENGÀIR HILL. 'Dalry.' Green strip. "*Gair*, a slip of tender, fertile grass in a barren situation."—*Jamieson. See under* GAIRY.

GREENLANE. 'Kelton.'

GRÈENLAW (*P.* Greenlaw). 'Crossmichael.' Green eminence. BR. SC. *law* — A.S. *hlœw, hlaw,* "tractus terræ paulatim ascendens" (*Bosworth*).

GREENMERSE. 'Troqueer.' "*Merse.* 1. A fertile spot of ground between hills, a hollow. 2. Alluvial land on the side of a river."—*Jamieson.* M.E. *mersche*, a marsh — A.S. *mearsc*, which is a contraction of *mer-isc* — *mere*, a mere, pool, lake.

GREENTOP. 'New Luce.' English equivalent of Barglass ; *q.v.*

GREENTOP OF DÙCHRAE (a hill of 900 feet). 'Dalry.'

GREENYARD. 'Twynholm.' Green garden. *See under* FRIAR'S YARD.

GREGGANS. 'New Abbey.' Probably *graigán*, a little village, dim. of *graig*, to which *Joyce* assigns the origin of Gragane and Graigeen in Limerick, Gragan in Clare, and Grageen in Wexford.

GREGGARY.   'Port Patrick, s.c.'

GRÈGORY. 'Kirkgunzeon.' *Cf.* GREGGARY.

GRÈNCHIE.   'Kells.'

GRÈNNAN (*Inq. ad Cap.* 1550, Grenane; 1643, Mongreinan; *P.* Grenen, Grinen, Granen; *W. P.* MSS. Grenane). 'Dalry,' 'Glasserton,' 'Kirkmaiden,' 'Minigaff,' 'Old Luce.' *See under* GRANNAN.

GRÈTNA. 'Old Luce.' Probably borrowed from the celebrated place of that name.

GREY HILL (in several parishes).

GREYMÒRN. 'Troqueer.' *Cf.* DRIGMORN.

GRÌBDIE.   'Kirkcudbright.'

GRÒBDALE (*Inq. ad Cap.* 1548, Grobdaill; 1611, Groibdaill; *P.* Grobdeill). 'Girthon.'

GROOSY GLEN. 'Stoneykirk.' *Gleann greusach* [?], glen of the cobblers. *See under* BALGRACIE.

GÙFFOGLAND (M.S. 1527, Guffokland).   'Buittle.'

GUILHILL. 'Penninghame.' *See* KILLHILL.

GULLY HILL. 'Balmaghie.' "*Gully*, a channel worn by water." —*Skeat.* A shortened form of *gullet*, a throat — F. *goulet*, dimin. of O.F. *gule*, *goule* (F. *gueule*) — LAT. *gula* — √GAR, to devour. *Cf.* SKT. *gri*, to devour, *gal*, to eat.

GÙNION HILL. 'Mochrum.' *Cf.* BALLOCHAGUNION.

H ACKETLEATHS [*pron.* -laze] (*P.* Haketlaiths; M.S. 1527, Halkokleis; *Synod of Galloway* MS. 1664, Hacketlies). 'Buittle.' *See under* COCKLEATH.

HACKLE ROCK.   'Stoneykirk, s.c.'

HAG. 'Parton.' *Hag* is a term used for copsewood; the year's hag is the part annually cut; but it also means "Moss ground formerly broken up" (*Jamieson*).

HAGGAMALÀG, HOWE HILL OF.   'Whithorn.'

HA HILL. ' Wigtown.'   Hall hill.

HAIRY HÒRRACH.   ' Port Patrick, s.c.'

HALFERNE.   ' Crossmichael.'

HALFMARK. ' Carsphairn.'   *See under* MARK.

HALFMIRE.   ' Dalry.'

HALLMIRE (*P.* Halmyir).   ' Urr.'

HALMYRE (*Inq. ad Cap.* 1604, Nether Kelton *alias* Halmure).
    ' Kelton.'   *Cf.* HALFMIRE.

HANGMAN HILL. ' Kirkbean.'   *See under* ACHENROCHER.

HARDTHORN (*P.* Harthorn).   ' Terregles.'

HARKING HILL.   ' Borgue.'

HART BURN.   ' Kirkcudbright.'

HASS. ' Buittle.'   *See under* HAUSE BURN.

HAUGH WILLIAM. ' Port Patrick, s.c.'   " *Haugh,* low-lying flat
    ground, properly on the border of a river, and such as is
    sometimes overflowed."—*Jamieson.*

HAUSE BURN. ' Kells,' ' Kirkgunzeon.'   " *Hals, hause.* 1. The
    neck. 2. The throat. 3. Any narrow passage. 4. A defile,
    a narrow passage between hills."—*Jamieson.* —A.S. *hals,* the
    neck.   Used in the same metaphoric sense as ERSE *braghad*
    (*see under* BRADOCK), *sluig* (*see under* SLOCHANAWN), and F.
    gully (*see under* GULLY HILL).

HAWKHILL. ' Kirkinner.'   *Cf.* Hawkhill or Halkshill in the
    parish of Largs, Ayrshire.   The name has nothing to do with
    " a hawk " (although the proximity of Whauphill suggests an
    ornithological origin), but is the same word as appears as
    Halkhead or Halket in Dalry parish, Ayrshire.

HELENA ISLAND. ' Old Luce.'   Said to have been named in
    commemoration of Napoleon's imprisonment ; but the name
    is suspiciously like *eilean-na.*   Perhaps an old name was
    adapted to a modern historical event.

HENMUIR.   ' Rerwick.'

HÈNSOL. ' Balmaghie.'   A modern name given in recent years
    by the proprietor, in compliment, it is said, to a friend called
    Hensol.   The old name was Duchra.

HERRIES SLAUGHTER. 'Kirkcudbright.' *Pitcairn (Crim. Trials,* vol. i. part i. p. 242) records the remission in 1528 of "Andro Hereis, bruþer to Williame Lord Hereis (and others) for þe tressonabill raising of fyre within þe realme, birnyng of þe peile of Knokschenoch (Knockshinnie, in this parish); slauchter of umq^le Patrik Hereis, etc." This may be the tragedy which gives name to this place.

HESPIE'S LINN (on the Penkiln).   'Minigaff.'

HÈSPIN. 'Whithorn, s.c.' *Cf.* CASPIN.

HESTAN ISLAND (*P.* Heston Yle).   'Rerwick.'

HEUGHYARD.   'Kells.'

HILLMABRÈEDIA. 'New Luce.' *Chill mo Brighde* [Brèedia], chapel of St. Brigid or Bride. *Cf.* BREEDIE BURN and KIRKBRIDE; also, in Ireland, Kilbreedie and Doonabreedia. Dedications to St. Brigid are very frequent. "The syllables *mo* and *do* or *da* were often prefixed to the names of Irish saints as terms of endearment or reverence; thus Conna became Mochonna and Dachonna. The diminutives *án, ín,* and *óg* were also often postfixed; as we find Ernan, Ernog, Baiethin, Baethan, etc. Sometimes the names were greatly changed by these additions; thus Aedh is the same name as Maedhog (*Mo-Aedhog,* my little Aedh), though when pronounced they are quite unlike, *Aedh* being pronounced Ai (to rhyme with *day*), and *Maedhog,* Mogue."—*Joyce,* i. 148 *note.*

HILLSBOROUGH.   'Sorbie.'

HILLYORE.   'Mochrum.'

HIND CRAIG (part of Benbrack, just as Craignelder is part of Cairnsmore). 'Kells.' *See* CRAIGNELDER.

HIRLIE (the name of a field). 'Sorbie.' The common cry to cows, in use to this day. Few, perhaps, of *Maclaggart's* verses are worth repetition, but the following from his *Galloway Encyclopædia* are musical and full of rural feeling:—

I.

"O yonder's my Nannie gatherin' the kye,
   Whar the e'ening sun is beaming,
Awa' on the hazly brae, doun by
   Whar the yellow nits are leaming.
And aye she cries 'Hurly Hawkie!
String awa', my crummies, to the milking loan,
   Hurly, hurly hawkie.'

2.

" How sweetly her voice dinnles through my heart,
    I'll wyle roun' and her foregather,
Tak a kiss or twa and then gae part,
    For fear o' her crusty father.
And aye she cries ' Hurly hawkie !
String, string awa hame to the milking loan,
    Hurly, hurly hawkie.'

3.

" Now all in a flutter she lies in my arms
    On the hinny smelling bank o' clover ;
Wha would be sae base as steal her charms ?
    It shall na be me her lover.
I'll let her cry ' Hurly, hawkie !'
And wize the kye hame to the milking loan,
    Hurly, hurly hawkie. "

HÒDDOM. ' Parton.' *Cf.* HODDAM in Dumfriesshire.

HOG HILL. ' Carsphairn.' *Cf.* DRUMMUCKLACH, etc.

HOGUS POINT. ' Kirkbean.'

HOLE CROFT. ' Kirkmabreck.' " *Holl, howe* ; hollow, deep."— *Jamieson.*

HOLE GINKINS. ' Port Patrick.'

HOLEHOUSE. ' Rerwick.'

HOLLAND ISLE (in the Dee). ' Balmaghie.' " *Holland,* of or pertaining to the holly."—*Jamieson.* —A.S. *holen, holegn,* holly. *See under* ALWHILLAN.

HOLLEN BUSH. ' Sorbie.' Holly bush. *See under* ALWHILLAN.

HOLLY ISLAND (in the Dee). ' Girthon.' *Cf.* HOLLAND ISLE.

HONEY PIG. ' Old Luce.'

HOODIE CAIRN. ' Kirkcowan.' The carrion or *hooded* crow's cairn. " *Huddy craw,* a carrion crow."—*Jamieson.*

HOOIES, THE. ' Stoneykirk, s.c.'

HOPE HILL. ' Kells.' " *Hop, hope.* A sloping hollow between two hills, or the hollow that is formed between the two ridges on one hill."—*Jamieson.*

HORNEY. ' Stoneykirk, s.c.' (*twice*).

HORNHEAD. 'Penninghame.'

HORSE ISLES. 'Buittle,' 'Glasserton.' Horse pasture. *Isle, inch, inks* are used like the Erse equivalents *eilean* or *oilean* and *innis*, in the alternative meanings of island or pasture beside a river. *See under* AUCHNESS.

HORSE MOAT. 'Carsphairn.'

HOUSTARD. 'Colvend.'

HOWE HILL OF HAGGAMALÀG. 'Whithorn.'

HOWE HOLE OF SHADDOCK. 'Whithorn, s.c.' "*How*, hollow."— *Jamieson.* — A.S. *holh*, a hollow.

HOWELL. 'Kirkcudbright.'

HOWE OF THE CALDRON, THE. 'Minigaff.' "*How*, any hollow place."—*Jamieson.* — A.S. *holh*, a hollow, spelt also *holg, healoc* (whence E. *hollow*), an extended form of *hol*, a hole. *Caldron* is used figuratively as ERSE *coire*, a caldron.

HOWE POT. 'Minigaff.' *See under* HOWE OF THE CALDRON.

HÙMPHREY. 'Mochrum.' *Cf.* DRUMHUPHREY.

HUNGRY STONE. 'Kirkmabreck.'

HUNT HA' (*P.* Hunthall). 'Carsphairn.' *Cf.* DRUMSHALLOCH.

HURKLEDOWN HILL. 'Parton.'

I LAN-NA-GÙY. 'Kirkcolm, s.c.' *Oiléan na gaoith* [gwee], island of the winds. *See under* BARNAGEE.

INCH (a parish in the shire). *Inis*, an island. Named from the natural island in the White Loch of Inch (called by *Pont* Loch of the Inch), near which the old parish church stood. In Loch Inchcrindle (now called the Black Loch of Inch), which is connected by a canal with the White Loch, there is a large crannog, *inis Crindail. Pont* calls this L. Ylen Krindil. *Inis*, gen. *inse* + W. *ynys*, B. *enes*, C. *ennis*, apparently akin to LAT. *insula* (whence, through the French, E. *isle*). Assumes the form of *inch* in BR. SC., in the sense of island or of holm, *i.e.* pasture near water; and *inks*, or *links*, pasture liable to be overflowed, or, at least, near the sea, a river, or lake. In Ireland this word appears in place-names as Ennis, Inis, Inish, and Inch. The primary meaning is an island, but it is applied like *oilén, eilean*, to pasture or meadow-land near water.

INCH (an island in Kirkcudbright Bay). 'Kirkcudbright.' *Inis*, an island.

INCH (*P.* Yinch; *W. P.* MSS. Inche). 'Sorbie.' *Inis*, holm or pasture beside water.

INCHBÀNE. 'Kirkcolm.' *Inis bán*, white holm or pasture.

INCHBRÈAD. 'Inch.'

INCHIGÙILE. 'Sorbie.' *Inis a' Goil*, the stranger's holm or pasture. *Cf.* Inchagoill in Lough Corrib, which the Irish writers render *Inis-an-Goil-chraibhthigh*, the isle of the devout foreigner, namely, Lugnat, pilot of St. Patrick, who established himself as a hermit there. The Hebrides were called by the Chroniclers *Innsi-Gall*, the isles of the foreigners, when they became occupied by the Norsemen, who named them the Sudreyar, or southern isles, a name still preserved in the Bishopric of *Sodor* and Man.

INCHMÀLLOCH. 'Kirkcowan,' 'Kirkinner.' Probably the same as Inchmulloch.

INCHMÌNNOCH. 'New Luce.' *Inis meadhonach* [minnogh], middle holm.

INCHMÙLLOCH (*P.* Inch Mullach). 'Kirkmaiden,' 'Leswalt,' 'Old Luce.' *Inis mullaich*, holm of the height.

INCHNAGÒUR. 'Kirkmaiden, s.c.' *Inis na' gobhar* [gour], island of the goats. Close by is Slochnagour. *See under* ALGOWER.

INCHSHÀNNOCH. 'Kirkmaiden, s.c.' *Inis sionach* [shinnagh], island of the foxes. It is an isolated rock, opposite to which, on the mainland, is a cliff called Foxes' Rattle. *See under* AUCHENSHINNOCH.

INCHSLÌTHERY. 'Kirkmaiden, s.c.'

ÌNGLESTON (*Inq. ad Cap.* 1605, Inglistoun; *P.* Englishtoun). 'Twynholm.' The *tún*, homestead of Inglis or of the Englishman.

INK Moss. 'Kirkcowan.'

INKS, in several places along the banks of tidal estuaries. *Inis*, pasture beside water. *See under* INCH.

INNERMÈSSAN (*Inq. ad Cap.* 1668, Innermessan; *P.* Innermessen). 'Inch.' *Inbher* [inver] *Messain* [?], mouth of the Messan Burn. The stream to which *Pont* gives the name of Messan Burn does not bear it now, but takes the names of the various farms through which it flows. Innermessan has been tentatively identified with Ptolemy's Rerigonium, a town of the Novantes, on Rerigonius Sinus (Loch Ryan). *Cf.* KNOCK-MASSAN in the next parish.

INNERWÈLL (*P.* Innerwell).   'Sorbie.'

ÌNSHANKS (*P.* Inschacs, Inchacks ; *Inq. ad Cap.* 1610, Inschanke). 'Kirkcowan, 'Kirkmaiden.' *Uinnse, uínnseóg* or *uinnseann* [inshie, inshug, or inshin], the ash-tree. *Uinnseann* is the word in the north of Ireland which appears as *fuinnseann* in the south. *See under* DRUMNAMINSHOG. *Cf.* Unshog in Armagh, and Hinchoge in Dublin.

ÌNSHAW HILL.   'Whithorn.'   *Uinnse, uinnseóg* [inshie, inshug], an ash-tree. *See under* INSHANKS.

ÌRELANDTOWN (*P.* Yrlandstoun).   'Twynholm.'

IRONCRÀIGIE. 'Balmaclellan.' *Ard na creage*, height of the crag. *Cf.* Ardencraig in Bute. *See under* ERNAMBRIE.

IRONGÀLLOWS.   'Carsphairn.'

IRONGRAY (*P.* Arngra).   Kirkpatrick (formerly Kilpatrick) Irongray (a parish in the Stewartry).   *Ard an gréaich* [graigh], height of the moor.   "*Gréach*, a mountain flat, a level moory place, much the same as *reidh*. It is common as an element in townland designations in the counties of Cavan, Leitrim, Roscommon, Monaghan, and Fermanagh. Greagh, the usual Anglicised form, is the name of several places, Greaghawillin in Monaghan, the mountain flat of the mill ; Greaghnagleragh in Fermanagh, of the clergy ; Greaghnagee in Cavan, of the wind."—*Joyce*, ii. 393. *Cf.* AUCHENGRAY and KNOCKGRAY.

IRONHÀSH.   'Colvend.'

IRONLÒSH. 'Balmaclellan.' *Ard na loise* [?], hill of the fire (*O'Reilly*).

IRONMACÀNNIE.   'Balmaclellan.'

IRONMÀNNOCH. 'Parton.' *Ard na' manach*, hill of the monks.

IRON SLUNK. 'Stoneykirk, s.c.' The "slunk" or gully of the iron.

ISLAND BUOY. 'Stoneykirk, s.c.' *Oiléan buidhe* [buie], yellow island.

ISLAYFÌTZ.   'Port Patrick, s.c.'

Isle-na-Gàrroch.   'Port Patrick, s.c.'

Isle-na-Gòwer (on the Bladenoch).   'Kirkcowan.' *Oilèan na' gobhar* [gour], the pasture of the goats. *Cf.* Inchnagour.

Isle of Lanna.   'Stoneykirk, s.c.'

Isle of Pins (in the Fleet R.).   'Girthon.'

Isle Rig (a hill of 800 feet). 'Dalry.' *Aill* [?], a cliff (*see under* Algower); or *isle*, pasture (*see under* Inch).

J

Jardinton.   'Kirkpatrick Irongray.'

Jàrkness (a hill).   'Minigaff.'

Jean's Wa's. 'Balmaclellan.' A place on the Garpel where traces of buildings remain. According to the popular belief Miss Jean Gordon, of the family of Shirmers, having been jilted by her lover, retired to this place, and died of a broken heart.

Jedburgh Knees (a hill of 2021 feet). 'Carsphairn.' *Cf.* Calf Knees.

Jenoch.   'Anwoth.'

Jerry Peak's Craig.   'Minigaff.'

Jerusalem Park. 'Old Luce.' A field close to Kirkchrist.

Jib. 'Kirkmaiden.' *Gob*, a snout. *Cf.* Gibb.

Jocklig (*Inq. ad Cap.* 1604, Jakleig).   'Colvend.'

Jòrdieland.   'Kirkcudbright.'

Juniper Face. 'Leswalt, s.c.' The wild juniper, though well-nigh extinct in Galloway, still survives in a few places on the sea cliffs, and inland on the moors of Penninghame.

K

Kainton.   'Girthon.'

Kells (a parish in the Stewartry) (*P.* Kells). There are several places of this name in Ireland, the principal, in Meath, deriving from *ceann lis*, chief fort; the others, says *Joyce* (ii. 235), "are all probably the Anglicised plural of *cill*, namely *cealla* [kella], signifying churches." It is more probable that this parish takes its name from *coill*, wood.

Kells Burn.   'Colvend.'

Kelton (a parish in the Stewartry) (*P.* Keltoun).

KÈMPLETON.   ' Twynholm.'

KÈNDLUM.   ' Rerwick.   *Cf.* KENLUM.

KÈNDOWN.   ' Girthon.'   *Ceann don*, brown head or hill.   *See under* CAMBRET.

KÈNICK WOOD (*Inq. ad Cap.* 1548, Canknok; 1607, Kammuik, *v.* Kandnik; 1611, Candnik; *P.* Keandnick).   ' Balmaghie.'   *Cam cnoc* [?], crooked or sloping hill.   *Cf.* CUMNOCK.

KÈNLUM HILL (1001 feet).   ' Anwoth.'   *Cf.* KENDLUM.

KÈNMORE (*Inq. ad Cap.* 1598, Kenmoir; *P.* Keandmoir).   ' Kirkcowan.'   *Ceann mór*, big head.   *See under* CAMBRET.

KÈNMUIR.   ' Kirkmaiden,' ' Stoneykirk.'   *See under* KENMORE.

KÈNMURE (*P.* Kenmoir).   ' Balmaclellan.'   A place on the river Ken,—the moor of the Ken.

KÈNNAN.   ' Balmaghie.'   *Ceanndn*, dim. of *ceann*, a head.

KÈNNANS HILL.   ' Tungland.'   *See under* KENNAN.

KÈNTIE BURN and HILL.   ' Minigaff.'

KEN, WATER OF.   ' Carsphairn,' etc.   The stream that gives the name to the GLENKENS and to KENMUIR.

KEÒCH LANE (a stream).   ' Carsphairn.'

KÈRBERS.   ' Kelton.'

KERMÀNACHAN.   ' Kirkcolm.'   *Ceathramhaidh* [carrou], *manachan*, quarter-land of the monks.   Referred to in *Inq. ad Cap.* 1590, as " Monkis Croft, pertaining to the Abbey of Glenluce."

KET, THE (a stream).   ' Whithorn.'

KÈVAN BRAES.   ' Whithorn.'   *Cabhán* [cavan], a hollow.   *See under* CAVAN.

KÈVANDS (*W. P.* MSS., Crugiltoun Kevennis; *Inq. ad Cap.* 1695, Cavenscroft).   ' Sorbie.'   *Cabhán*, a hollow.

KÈVAN HOWE.   ' Whithorn.'   *Cabhán*, a hollow, and BR. SC. *howe*, hollow (pleonastic).

KÌBBERTIE KITE WELL.   ' Kirkmaiden.'   *Tiobar tigh Cait*, the well of Kate's house.   Catherine's croft is the name of the adjacent land, the remains of an early dedication to St. Catherine.   The change from *tiobar* to *chipper* and *kibber* is a common one.   *See under* TIBBERT.

Kìdsdale (*W. P.* mss. Kiddisdaill).   'Glasserton.'

Kilbrèen.   'Stoneykirk.'

Kilbùie. 'Kirkmaiden.' It is impossible to distinguish, except by local circumstances, between *cill*, a cell or chapel, and *coill*, a wood. *Cuil*, a corner, and *cul*, a back, posterior part, also get corrupted into the same sound. This is probably *coill buidhe*, yellow wood, like Kilboy in Ireland.

Kilcòrmack or Kirkcormack (*Inq. ad Cap.* 1605, Kirkcormok). 'Kelton.' *Cill Cormaic*, Cormac's cell or chapel. *Skene* mentions this place as the only known dedication in Scotland to St. Cormac-na-Liathain ; but the old name of the parish of North Knapdale was Killmochormac. For an account of Cormac's life see *Reeves's Adamnan*, ii. 42 *and* iii. 17, *pp.* 166 *and* 219, and *Celt. Scot.* ii. 131. O. ERSE *cell* (kell), ERSE *cill* (kill), literally, a cell, hence an oratory, a church — LAT. *cella* + GK. καλία, a hut + SKT. *khala*, a threshing-floor ; *çâlâ*, a stable, a house — √KAL, to hide (whence LAT. *celare*, E. *conceal*).

Kilcròuchie (now called Glenlaggan) (*P.* Coulcreachie). 'Parton.' *Cuil croiche*, the gallows corner.

Kildàrroch (*P.* Kildarrac). 'Kirkinner.' *Coill darach*, oak wood. *See under* Auchendarroch.

Kildònan (*P.* Kildonnan). 'Stoneykirk.' *Cil Donain*, St. Donnan's church. St. Donnan was an Irish disciple of St. Columba, and was put to death, with fifty companions, in the island of Egg by a band of pirates in 617. Places called Kildonan and Kildonnan, perpetuating his memory, exist in Egg, in Sutherland, in South Uist, in Ross-shire, Skye, Argyllshire, Arran, and Ayrshire (*Reeves's Adamnan*, p. 309).

Kìldroch Burn.   'Kirkmaiden.'

Kildròchat (*Inq. ad Cap.* 1543, Killedroquhat ; *P.* Kernadrochat). 'Stoneykirk.' *Coill, cul, cuil,* or *cill droichid,* the wood, back, corner, or church of the bridge. *Cf.* (in the latter sense) Kildrought in Kildare. *See under* Bardrochwood.

Kilfàd. 'Kirkinner.' *Cuil fada,* long corner.

Kilfàiry (near the ruins of Kilgallioch).   'Kirkcowan.'

KILFÈATHER (*P*. Kildhelir (*misprint*)). 'New Luce.' *Cill Phetir* or *Pheadair* (St.) Peter's church. Though there are here no ecclesiastical ruins that can be traced, yet the names immediately adjacent, Altibrair, Knockiebriar, Altaggart, bear evidence of religious occupation. *Cf.* Kilpeter in South Uist, sometimes written Kilphedre. *See under* CASTLE FEATHER.

KILFÈRN. 'Twynholm.' *Coill fearn* [kill farn], alder wood. *See under* BALFERN.

KILFÌLLAN (*P*. Kilphillen, Kilphillan ('Sorbie')). 'Old Luce,' 'Sorbie.' *Cill Faolain*, Fillan's church. St. Faolan of Cluain-Maoscna in West Meath, known in Scotland as St. Fillan, left his crozier, now called the Quegrith, in the hands of one of the pilgrims who accompanied him in his wanderings. It is now in the Museum of Scottish Antiquaries. St. Fillan was called '*an lobar*,' the leper. *See under* BARLURE and ERNFILLAN.

KILGÀLLIOCH (*P*. Kilgaillach ; *Inq. ad Cap.* 1600, Cullingalloch ; 1698, Killgalloch). 'Kirkcowan.' *Cill gallach* [?], the church of the standing stones, adjective formed from *gall*, a standing stone (*see under* DERGALL), like *carrach*, rocky, from *carr*, a stone (*Joyce*, i. 344). *Cf.* Cangullia in Kerry (*ceann gaille*), and several places in Ireland called Gallagh. Kilgallioch is close to Laggangarn, where there are some very remarkable standing stones (*see under* LAGGANGARN). There are some interesting remains here. Close by the site of the old church, which has been pulled to pieces for dyke-building, there are three holy wells (Wells of the Rees), each under a separate dome of rough stones.

KILHÈRN. 'New Luce.' *Cul chuirn* [?] [hirn], hill-back of the cairn. Remains of a large cairn exist here, enclosing eight cists made of immense stones. It is called, locally, the Caves of Kilhern. *Cf.* KILQUHIRN and KILWHIRN ; also, in Ireland, Kilcarn, which is from the genit. plur. *carn*.

KILHÌLT (*Barnbarroch*, 1568, Kenhelt ; *P*. Kinhilt). 'Port Patrick.' *Ceann eilte* [?], the hill of the hind. *Cf.* Annahilt in Down, Cloonelt in Roscommon. *See under* CARNELTOCH.

KILLÀDAM. 'Kirkcowan.'

KILLANTRÀE (*Inq. ad Cap.* 1582, Kerantra ; 1600, Kerintraye ; *P*. Killentrae). 'Mochrum.' *Ceathramhaidh* [carrou] *cill* or *cathair* [caer] *an traigh*, land-quarter, church, or fort of the shore. *See under* DRUMANTRAE.

KILLANTRÌNGAN (*P.* Kilantrinzean). 'Port Patrick.' *Cill sheant* [hant] *Ringain*, church of St. Ringan, another form of Ninian. *See under* CHIPPERDINGAN and CLAYSHANT.

KILLÀSER (*Barnbarroch*, 1562, Kyllasser; *P.* Killaister). 'Stoney-kirk.'

KILLÀUCHIE. 'Penninghame.' *Cúil* or *cul achaidh* [aghie], corner or back of the field. But *cf. Cill achaidh*, or the church of the field, in the *Martyrology of Donegal*.

KILLBRÒCKS. 'Inch.' *Coill broc*, wood of the badgers.

KILLÈAL (*Inq. ad Cap.* 1604, Kilzeild ; *P.* Coulleill). 'Penning-hame.'

KILLERAN. 'Girthon.'

KILLÈRN (*Inq. ad Cap.* 1575, Killerne ; 1611, Killarne ; *P.* Kill-orin). 'Anwoth.' Doubtful whether this is a dedication to St. Kieran (*see under* CHIPPERHERON) or, as *Pont's* rendering suggests, to *Odhran* [Oran], a co-temporary of Columba at Hy, whose name is lent to Killoran in Colonsay.

KILLHILL, THE, or GUILHILL. 'Penninghame.' The hill of the *kill* or kiln, for drying grain. The BR. SC. *kill* preserves one of the M.E. forms given in the *Promptorium Parvulorum* (1440), "*kylne, kyll*, for malt dryynge." —A.S. *cyln*. The *n* is integral, as the word is borrowed from LAT. *culina*, a kitchen.

KILLIBRÀKES. 'Mochrum.' *Coillidh bréc* [killy brake], dappled, variegated woodland. *Coillidh*, woodland, a deriv. of *coill*. *See under* AUCHABRICK and BARNHILLIE.

KILLIEGÒWAN (*Inq. ad Cap.* 1604, Killigoune; *P.* Killigawin). 'Anwoth.' *Coillidh gobhan* [killy gown], the blacksmith's wood.

KILLIEMACÙDDICAN. 'Kirkcolm.' *Cille mo Cudachain* [?], church of St. Cuthbert. Apparently a diminutive of the name of the famous saint. *See under* KIRKCUDBRIGHT.

KILLIEMÒRE (*P.* Kaillymort). 'Penninghame.' *Coillidh* [killy] *mór*, great wood. *Cf.* CULMORE.

KILLIMÌNGAN. 'Kirkgunzeon.'

KÌLLINESS (*P.* Kellyness). 'Kirkmaiden, s.c.'

KILLÒCHIE. 'Balmaclellan.' *Cf.* KILLAUCHIE.

KILLÙMPHA (*Inq. ad Cap.* 1661, Kilumpha-Agnew ; *P.* Killumpha). 'Kirkmaiden.'

KILLYBÒY. 'Kirkinner.' *Coillidh buidhe* [killy buie], yellow woodland. *Cf.* KILBUIE.

KILLYLÒUR. 'Kirkpatrick Irongray.' Perhaps *cill an lobhair* [lour], St. Fillan the Leper's church. *See under* BARLURE and KILFILLAN.

KILLYMÙCK or KILLINIMÙCK (*Inq. ad Cap.* 1633, Kelenemuck). 'Penninghame.' *Coillidh* [killy] *na muc*, wood of the swine. *See under* CLACHANAMUCK.

KILLYWHÀN. 'Kirkgunzeon.'

KILMACFÀDZEAN (*P.* Kilmakphadzen). 'New Luce.' *Cill mic Phaidín*, the cell or church of the son of *Paidín*, or little Patrick; Macfadzean's church. *See under* BARFADDEN.

KILMÀLLOCH. 'New Luce.'

KILMÒRIE (*Inq. ad Cap.* 1668, Kilmirring). 'Kirkcolm.' *Cill Muire*, (St.) Mary's church. There are about fifty townlands in Ireland called Kilmurry and Kilmorey. w. *Meir, Mair,* Mary.

KILNÀIR. 'Kells.'

KILNBÙT. 'Kells.' *Cúil na boc* [?], corner of the he-goats. *See under* AUCHNIEBUT.

KILQUHÌRN [*pron.* Kilhwern]. 'Wigtown.' *Cill, cúil,* or *coill chuirn* [hirn], the church, corner, or wood of the cairn. *See under* KILHERN.

KILQUHÒCODALE (*Inq. ad Cap.* 1670, Killquhowdaill; *P.* Kailchockadale). 'Kirkcowan.'

KILSTÀY. 'Kirkmaiden.'

KILSTÙRE (*P.* Kilstyre; *Inq. ad Cap.* 1620, Kilsture; *W. P.* MSS. Calstuir). 'Sorbie.'

KILTÈRSAN (*P.* Kiltersan). 'Kirkcowan.' *Coill tarsuinn*, the wood athwart. But *cf.* Kiltarsna, written *cill tarsna* (the church of the crossing), in the *Martyrology of Donegal*. *See under* BALTERSAN.

KILWHÀNIDY (*P.* Kilwhonnaty; *War Committee*, 1640, Kilquhennady). 'Kirkpatrick Durham.'

KILWHÌRN. 'Kirkmabreck.' *See under* KILHERN.

KINCÀRRACK. 'Kirkbean.' *Ceann* [ken] *carroch*, rocky hill, or *ceann carric*, head of the crag.

KINDÈE. 'Kirkmaiden, s.c.' *Ceann dubh* [doo, duv], black head. *Dubh* often becomes *dee* in composition. On the opposite coast of Antrim is Kenbane (*ceann bán*), the white headland. *Cf.* Kinduff in Ireland.

KÌNDRAM (*P.* Keandramm). 'Kirkmaiden, s.c.' *Ceann droma*, head of the ridge; genitive of *druim*.

KINGANTON. 'Borgue.'

KING'S LAGGAN. 'Anwoth.'

KING'S WELL (within the old fortifications at the Mull of Galloway, and near two other wells called KIPPERNED and KIBBERTIE KITE WELL). 'Kirkmaiden.'

KINHÀRVIE (*P.* Kinharvy). 'New Abbey.' *Ceann gharbh* [harve], rough head. *Cf.* Kingarve, Kingarrow, and Kingarriff in Ireland. O. ERSE *garb*, rough, ERSE and GAEL. *garbh*.

KIPP (*P.* Kipp). 'Colvend.' "*Kip.* 1. A sharp pointed hill. 2. Those parts of a mountain which resemble round knobs, jutting out by the side of the cattle path."—*Jamieson.* Probably from ERSE *ceap* [cap], gen. *cip*, a tree-stock, stump, or block. *O'Reilly* also gives to *ceap* the meaning of "a piece of ground."

KIPPERNÈD. 'Kirkcolm.' *Tiobar*, a well. *See under* CHIPPER-HERON.

KÌPPFORD. 'Colvend.' The road or ford of Kipp. *Cf.* Knockakip in Clare, which the *Four Masters* (A.D. 1573) write *Bel-an-chip*, the (ford) mouth of the *cip* or tree-trunk.

KIRBRÈEN or KIRKBREEN (*P.* Keribroyn). 'Kirkinner.' *Ceathramhaidh bruigheain* [?] [carrou breen], land-quarter of the dwelling-house. *See under* CURROCHTREE and BORGUE.

KIRCÀLLA. 'Penninghame.' The only evidence of ecclesiastical occupation here is that a hill close by is called BARNEYCLEARY, *q. v.*

KIRCLÀCHIE. 'Inch.' *Ceathramhaidh* [carrou] *cloiche* [?], land-quarter of the stone. *See under* CARHOWE.

KIRCLÒY. 'Mochrum.' *See under* KIRCLACHIE.

KIRKÀNDERS or KIRKANDREWS (formerly a parish) (*IV. P.* MSS. Kirkandirrs; *Rag. Roll.* Eglise de Kircandres). 'Borgue.' *Circ Aindrea*, church of (St.) Andrew. BR. SC. *kirk* = M.E. *chirch, chireche, kirk, kirke* — A.S. *cyrice, circ* + DU. *kerk* + DAN. *kirke* + SWED. *kyrka* + ICEL. *kirkja* + O.H.G. *chiricha*, G. *kirche* — GK. κυριακόν, a church — κύριος, the Lord. Occupying, as it frequently does, the first part of a name, it is easy to see that it has been substituted for the ERSE *cill*, or made interchangeable as A.S. speech spread among the Celtic population.

In names of directly A.S. or BR. SC. origin *circ* is placed last, such as Stoneykirk (Steenie's or St. Stephen's kirk). In Ireland, whither A.S. speech did not penetrate, *circ* does not appear in the topography. *See under* KIRKLEBRIDE.

KIRKBÈAN (a parish in the Stewartry) (*P.* Kirbyinn). *Circ Beain,* Bean's church ; Bishop of Mortlach about A.D. 1012. Near Mortlach is Balvanie, written in Irish *Bal-bheni mor,* the dwelling of Bean the Great. *Kal. Scot. Saints,* p. 277.

KIRKBRÌDE (*P.* Kirkbryid ; *Charter by Uchtred, Lord of Galloway,* 1170, Ecclesia Sanctae Brigide de Blacket). 'Kirkgunzeon,' 'Kirkmabreck,' 'Kirkmaiden.' *Circ Brighde,* (St.) Brigid's church. The 'Mary of Ireland,' who died in 523, was extensively honoured in Scotland.

KIRKCÀRSEL (*Barnbarroch,* 1562, Kyrcarsall, Kyr-castell). 'Rerwick.'

KIRKCLÀUGH (*Inq. ad Cap.* 1605, Kirreclaugh ; *P.* Kareclauch ; *War Committee,* 1640, Kirriclauche). 'Anwoth,' 'Buittle.' *Ceathramhaidh clach,* land-quarter of the stones, as Carrownagloch in Connaught, which is written *Ceathramhaidh-na-gcloch* in the Book of Lecan. *Cf.* KIRCLACHIE.

KIRKCHRÌST (*P.* Kirkcrist, Kirkchrist). ' Kirkcudbright,' ' Old Luce,' ' Penninghame.' *Circ Crioisd,* Christ's kirk.

KIRKCÒLM [*pron.* Kirkcùm] (*Act. Ed. I.,* A.D. 1296, Kyrkum). *Circ Coluim,* (St.) Columba's church. Dr. Reeves enumerates fifty-six of this celebrated saint's dedications and foundations in Scotland.

KIRKCÒNNEL (*P.* Karkonnell, Kirkonnell). 'Tungland.' *Circ Connaill,* church of (St.) Connall. *Cf.* Tirconnel in Ireland, called *Terra Connallea* in a MS. life of St. Modvenna. A semi-vowel has been dropped ; the name was formerly Convall, as is shown in another life of St. Modvenna, where Tirconnell is called *populus Convalleorum* = W. *Cynwal,* O. W. *Congual,* and, on an inscribed stone in Cornwall, CVNOVALI (*Rhys,* p. 86). "There are seven saints of this name in the Irish lists. It is impossible to identify any of them with him who gives his name to Kirkconnell."—*Kal. Scot. Saints,* p. 311.

KIRKCÒRMACK. ' Kelton.' *See under* KILCORMACK.

KIRKCÒWAN (a parish in the shire) (*Synod of Galloway* MS. 1664, Kirkuan). *Circ Comhghain* [cowan], Comgan's church. He was the brother of St. Caentigerna (the recluse of Inch

Cailleach on Loch Lomond), and uncle of St. Fillan. He fled from Ireland to Ross-shire, where there is a dedication to him, Kilchoan, as well as numerous others in Scotland. *Kal. Scot. Saints*, p. 310. *Simpson* remarks the name is pronounced (as at the present day) Kircuan. *Cf.* LINCUAN.

KIRKCÙDBRIGHT [*pron.* Kirkçoobry] (*Rag. Roll*, Kircuthbright; *Maclellan*, Fanum Cudberti; *P.* Kircubright). 'Kirkcudbright.' A.S. *circ Cuðbert*, Cuthbert's kirk. "On one occasion Cudberct went to the land of the 'Niduari Picts,' or Picts of Galloway, who were then under the dominion of the Angles. He is described as quitting his monastery (Melrose) on some affairs that required his presence, and embarking on board a vessel for the land of the Picts who are called *Niduari*, accompanied by two of the brethren, one of whom reported the incident. They arrived there the day after Christmas, expecting a speedy return, for the sea was smooth and the wind favourable; but they had no sooner reached the land than a tempest arose, by which they were detained for several days exposed to hunger and cold; but they were, by the prayers of the saint, supplied with food under a cliff where he was wont to pray during the watches of the night; and on the fourth day the tempest ceased, and they were brought by a prosperous breeze to their own country. The traces of this visit have been left in the name Kirkcudbright."—*Skene* (quoting *Bede's Vit. S. Cud.*), *Celtic Scotland*, ii. 208.

KÌRKDALE [*pron.* Curdle, formerly a parish] (*P.* Kirkdall; *W. P.* MSS. Kirkdaill). 'Kirkmabreck.' AS. *circ dœl*, church portion, *i.e.* glebe.

KIRKÈNNAN (*Inq. ad Cap.* 1611, Kirkcunane, Kirkinane *P.* Kerekennan). 'Buittle,' 'Minigaff.' *Kirk Adhamhnain* [?] [eunan], (St.) Adamnan's church. Although there is no authority for adding these places to the list of Scottish dedications to this Saint given by *Dr. Reeves* (*Adamnan*, lxv.), yet the similarity of the name to those of other places sacred to his memory certainly suggest it, especially the old spelling, Kirkcunane. *Cf.* Killeunan in Argyllshire, Killonan in Limerick, etc. Perhaps *circ Fhinnain* [innan], a dedication to St. Inan or Finnan. *See under* KIRKGUNZEON.

KIRKEÒCH (*P.* Kirkock). 'Twynholm.'

KIRKGÙNZEON [*pron.* Kirkgunnion] (a parish in the Stewartry) (*P.* Kirkguinnan, Carguinnan; *Charters of* 12*th century*

Kirkwinnyn and Kirkwynnin). *Circ Finnain*, St. Winnin's church.   On the church bell, cast in 1640, Kirkwinong. Kilwinning and Southennan in Ayrshire are dedicated to the same Saint, whom Dr. Skene identifies with the Welsh Saint Vynnyn or Ffinnan, *i.e.* St. Finnan of Clonard, educated by St. Patrick, and patron of Lumphanan in Aberdeenshire, the name of which is a corruption 'of the Welsh *Llanffinan.*

KIRKHÒBBLE (*P.* Kerychapell ; *Inq. ad Cap.* 1645, Keirchappell). 'Penninghame.'   *Ceathramhaidh chaipeail* [carrou happle], the quarter-land of the chapel. The next farm is GLENHAPPLE, *q.v.   See also under* BARHAPPLE.

KIRKÌNNA.   'Parton.'

KIRKÌNNER (*Inq. ad Cap.* 1584, Kirkinver ; *P.* Kirkynnuir). 'Kirkinner.'   *Kirk Cennera*, St. Kennera's Church.   St. Kennera, virgin and martyr, was one of the maidens who accompanied St. Ursula to Rome.   Her story is told at length in the *Breviarium Aberdonense*, vol. i. fol. cxxxiii. *et seq.*   She lived with her parents, Aurelius and Florencia, " *in Orchada minore ad urbem dictam Orchadam.*"   On returning from Rome, when St. Ursula and the other virgins were massacred at Cologna, the king of the Rhine " *ob ejus eliganciam miram motus* " (moved by her wonderful beauty) threw his cloak over her and took her to the Rhenish town where he dwelt.   There she lived a life of piety, " *ibat de virtute in virtutem,*" and became so honoured by the king that he gave into her charge the keys of his realm, and preferred her above all his household.   Not unnaturally the queen became jealous, and tried to make him believe evil of Kennera.   " *Sed quia vincit opus verbum,*" the king would not believe the slander, so the queen resolved upon the removal of the maiden.   The king having gone hunting, she caused Kennera to be strangled with a towel (*manitergium*) and buried in the stable.   On the king's return he asked at once where was Kennera.   The queen replied that while he had been absent the parents of the maiden had come and taken her away.   Meanwhile the king's horse, having been led round to the stable where Kennera was buried, neither by blows nor coaxing could he be induced to enter.   He was therefore taken to another stable which he entered at once.   The king went to bed, but was aroused by his groom, who, having had occasion to enter the stable where Kennera lay, was terrified at seeing burning candles in the form of a cross.   Accompanied by his household the king entered the stable, where the candles still were burning. On his approach they disappeared; but on search being made the newly-disturbed floor led to the discovery of the body of Kennera with the napkin round her neck. She was canonised, and the 27th October set apart as her day. *Scta. Keñera vgo. et mr. patrona de Kirkyner in Galvvedia.* *Chalmers* says the old name of Kirkinner was CARNESMOEL, and quotes, among others, a charter of Edward II. in 1319, giving presentation to Carnesmeol in the diocese of Candida Casa.

KIRKLAND, in many places, = church land, glebe.

KIRKLANE. 'Kelton.' The stream of the church.

KIRKLÀUCHLANE (*Inq. ad Cap.* 1596, Kerelauchleine; *P.* Keirlachline). 'Stoneykirk.' *Cathair* [caher] *Lochlinn,* Lauchlan's fort. *See under* BARLAUCHLINE. O. ERSE *cathir* + W. and C. *caer,* B. *karia.*

KIRKLEBRIDE (*P.* Kirkilbryde). 'Kirkpatrick Durham.' *Kirk cill Brighde,* (St.) Brigid's church. We have here the BR. SC. *kirk* prefixed to the ERSE *cill Brighde.* *See under* KIRKANDERS and KIRKBRIDE.

KIRKLÈISH.   ' Kirkmaiden.'

KIRKLOCH.   ' Minigaff.'

KIRKMABRÈCK. A parish in the Stewartry. *Circ mo Brice,* church of St. Bricius or Brecan. (For the use of the pronoun *mo, see under* HILLMABREEDIA.) Of Bricius (*episcopus et confessor*) it is narrated in the *Aberdeen Breviary* that in his youth he bore great enmity to St. Martin. Once, when a certain sick person was seeking St. Martin, Bricius mocked him, saying: "If you are looking for that madman, there he is, staring at the sky as usual, like a lunatic." When he afterwards denied having said this, Martin said: "I have obtained this from God, that you shall be bishop after me; but know this, that in your bishopric you shall encounter much tribulation." Bricius, hearing this, derided him, and continued in enmity to him; but the blessed Martin was ever praying for him, saying: "If Christ bore with Judas, why shall I not bear with Bricius?" For the rest of his acts see the *Aberdeen Breviary,* vol. i. fol. clix. Another saint, whose name may be commemorated in KIRKMABRECK, is *Brioc* or *Brieuc,* a disciple of Germanus of Auxerre, and the patron saint of Rothesay. *Bryak Fair* is mentioned at the 16th Nov. in the Aberdeen Almanack 1665, and DUNROD, in the Stewartry, was dedicated to St. Mary and St. Brioc. *Kal. Scot. Saints,* p. 291.

KIRKMABRÌCK (*P.* Kirkmabrick). 'Stoneykirk.' *See under* KIRK-
MABRECK.

KIRKMADRÌNE [*pron.* Kirkmadreen] (*P.* K. Madrym). 'Sorbie.'
'Stoneykirk.' Both of these were formerly parishes. *Dr.
Stuart* held that they were Gaulish dedications to Mathurinus
of Sens, but *Bishop Forbes* holds with more probability that
Medran, mentioned in the *Martyrology of Donegal,* is herein
commemorated.

KIRKMÀGILL (*Inq. ad Cap.* 1616, Carmagyll; *P.* Kyrmagil).
'Stoneykirk.' *Cathair* [caer] *mic Giolla* [?], M'Gill's fort.
There are ruins here, behind the dwelling-house on Bal-
greggan Mains, but nothing to indicate a church.

KIRKMÀIDEN (*P.* Kirkmadin, Kirkmaiden o' the sea). 'Glasserton,' 'Kirkmaiden.' A parish in the shire. Formerly there
were two parishes of this name in Wigtownshire, one of
which is now conjoined to Glasserton, the other being the
southernmost parish in Scotland. The name is derived,
according to the *Aberdeen Breviary,* from a dedication to St.
Medana, who is described as an Irish maiden who took upon
herself a vow of perpetual chastity, and being solicited by a
certain *miles nobilis,* who would not take "no" for an answer,
sailed for Scotland with two handmaidens. Landing in the
Rhinns of Galloway (*partes Galvidie superiores que ryndis
dicuntur*), she led a life of poverty. But the knight followed
her, and drove her to take refuge with her two companions
on an insulated rock in the sea. This rock, in answer to
her prayers, became a boat, in which she was carried a
distance of 30 miles, *ad terram que farnes dicitur* (Kirkmaiden
in Glasserton), where the relics of the holy virgin (Medana)
now repose. Again the knight followed her to her retreat,
and arrived at the house where she and her two maids were
sleeping. A cock crew and awoke her, when she took refuge
in a high tree. "What do you see in me," said she, "to
excite your passion?" "Your face and eyes," he replied :
whereupon she tore out her eyes and flung them at his feet.
He, moved to penitence, departed ; she descended from the
tree, and, being in want of water to wash her bleeding face,
a fountain miraculously sprang from the root of the tree.
The rest of her life she spent in sanctity and poverty under
St. Ninian. There is a holy well at Kirkmaiden in Glasserton still repaired to by the country-people as a cure or pre-
ventive of whooping-cough, hence called the Chincough Well.

In Kirkmaiden parish, near the Mull of Galloway, is the cave and exterior chapel of St. Medan, locally pronounced Midden.

KIRKMÌRRAN (*Inq. ad Cap.* 1605, Kirkmirrein; 1615, Kirkmyrring). 'Kelton.' *Circ Meadhrain* [merran], church of (St.) Meadhran or Merinus, of the order of Clugny, buried at Paisley.

KIRKMÙIR. 'Kirkmabreck.'

KIRKPATRICK-DURHAM (a parish in the Stewartry) (*Inq. ad Cap.* 1607, Kirkpatrick Dirrame). 'Kirkpatrick Durham.' *Kirk Pádric*, church of (St.) Patrick. Formerly called *Cella Patricii*, or Kilpatrick-on-the-moor.

KIRKPATRICK-IRONGRAY (*P.* Arngra). 'Kirkpatrick Irongray.' *See* IRONGRAY.

KIRMÌNNOCH (*P.* Kerymeanoch). 'Kirkcolm.' *Ceathramhaidh meadhonach* [carrou mennagh], middle land-quarter. *See under* BALMINNOCH and CARHOWE.

KIRMÌNNOCH (*P.* Kerimanach; *Inq. ad Cap.* 1620, Kerimannoch; 1643, Kerriemanoche). 'Inch,' 'Kirkinner.' *Ceathramhaidh* [carrou] *manach*, the monk's land-quarter. *See under* CARHOWE, KERMANACHAN, and KIRVENNIE. *Cf.* Carrowanmeanagh in Roscommon.

KIRNÀUCHTRY. 'Stoneykirk.' *Carn uachdarach*, upper cairn. *See under* AUCHNOTTRIE.

KIRÒUCHTRIE (*Inq. ad Cap.* 1570, Kerrochrie, Kerreochrie, Kerdochrie; 1572, Kirreuchrie). 'Minigaff.' *Cathair* [caer] *Ochtraidh* [oughtra], Uchtred's fort.

KIRREÒCH [*pron.* Kirry-oghe] (*Inq. ad Cap.* 1572, Correith). 'Carsphairn.'

KIRRIEDÀRROCH. 'Minigaff.' *Coire darach*, corrie or glen of the oaks. *See under* CURRAFIN.

KIRRIEMÒRE (*P.* Kerymoir). 'Minigaff.' *Coire mór*, great corrie.

KIRRIERÒACH [*pron.* -roghe] (*P.* Kererioch, Kereryoch). 'Minigaff.' *Coire ruadh* [rooh], red corrie, or, as *Pont's* spelling seems to indicate, *coire riabhach* [reeagh], grey corrie.

KIRRÒNE (*P.* Kyrronh). 'Minigaff,' 'Mochrum.'

KIRRONRÀE. 'Kirkcolm.' *Ceathramhaidh an reidha* [carrou an ray], land-quarter of the flat field. A name truly expressing the ground, which is a wide flat on the shores of Loch Ryan. *See under* CARHOWE and REPHAD.

KIRSHÍNNOCH. ' Minigaff.' *Carr, cathair* [caer], or *coire* [kirrie] *sionach* [shinnagh], rock, fort, or corrie of the foxes. *See under* AUCHENSHINNOCH.

KIRVÈNNIE (*P.* Kerenwanach). 'Wigtown.' *Ceathramhaidh* [carrou] or *cathair* [caer] *mhanach* [vannagh], land-quarter or dwelling of the monks. *Cf.* Drumavanagh in Cavan. *See under* KIRMINNOCH.

KIRWAR. ' Mochrum.' *Ceathramhaidh ghar* [carrou har], near land-quarter.

KIRWÀUGH (*P.* Kirriwauchop, Kerywacher ; *Charter* 1513, Kerowoltok). ' Kirkinner.' *Ceathramhaidh* [carrou] *mhagha* [wagha] [?], land-quarter of the plain or level ground. *Pont* shows an alternative form from *machair*, a synonym of *magh*. *See under* MAY and MACHAR.

KÍSSOCK (*P.* Kissoktoun).   ' New Abbey.'

KÍTTRICK. ' Minigaff.' *See* DUNKÍTTERICK.

KITTYSHÀLLOCH. ' Minigaff.' *Ceide* or *ceadach sealg* [?] [kiddie shallug], hill of the hunting. " *Ceide*, a hillock, a compact kind of hill, smooth and plain at the top" (*O'Brien*). *Cf.* Keadydrinagh in Sligo, written *Ceideach droighneach* (*Four Masters*, 1526).

KNÀRIE (*Inq. ad Cap.* 1605, Knarie).   ' Kirkpatrick Durham.'

KNOCK (*W. P.* MSS., Knok of Kirkmadin). ' Glasserton.' An exceedingly common name, usually as a prefix, but frequently, as in this case, standing alone. *Cnoc*, a hill (the initial hard *c* is pronounced in Erse and Gaelic). Probably akin to A.S. *cnol* (as if *cnocel*, a dim. of *cnoc*), W. *cnol*, a knoll + DU. *knol*, a turnip (from its roundness ; and it is to be remarked that *O'Reilly* gives " navew " or turnip as one of the meanings of *cnoc*).

KNOCKADÒON. ' Balmaclellan.' *Cnoc a' duin*, hill of the fortress. *Cf.* KNOCKDOON, KNOCKDOWN, and KNOCKDUN.

KNOCKAHÀY. ' Old Luce.' *Cnoc na aithe* [?] [aiha], hill of the kiln. *See under* AUCHENHAY.

KNOCKALÀNNIE.   ' Kirkcowan.'

KNOCKÀLDIE.   ' Leswalt,' ' Penninghame.'

KNOCKÀLLAN. ' Stoneykirk.' *Cnoc aluin*, beautiful hill, *cnoc alluin*, hill of the hinds, or *cnoc Alain*, Alan's hill. *See under* CRAIGELLAN.

KNOCKÀLPIN. 'Stoneykirk.' *Cnoc Alpinn*, Alpin's Hill. *See under* LEIGHT ALPIN.

KNOCKAMAD.   'Penninghame.'

KNOCKAMÀIRLY.   'Stoneykirk.'

KNOCKAMÒORY.   'Port Patrick.'

KNOCKÀMOS.   'Kirkpatrick Durham.'

KNOCKÀN (*P.* Knokkan). 'Kirkinner.' *Cnocán*, little hill. The farm on which this is situated is called Little Hills. The stress, unlike the ordinary pronunciation of Erse in Galloway, but like that of Ireland, is in the last syllable. *Cf.* KNOCKANS; also Knockane, Knockaune, Knockeen, and Knickeen, the names of about seventy townlands in Ireland.

KNOCKANÀROCK. 'Stoneykirk.' *Cnocán dharaich* [arragh], hill of oak; or *dhearg* [arrig], red hill.

KNOCKANDÀRICK. 'Tungland.' *Cnoc an daraich*, hill of the oak, or *cnocán dearg*, red hill. *Cf.* KNOCKINDARROCH.

KNOCK AND MAIZE (*P.* Maze).   'Leswalt.'

KNOCKANÈARY. 'Minigaff.' *Cnocán iarach* [eeragh], western hill. *See under* BLAW WEARY.

KNOCKANÈED.   'Stoneykirk.'

KNOCKANHÀRRY. 'Whithorn.' *Cnocán charragh* [?] [harragh], rough little hill. *Cf.* KNOCKENHARRY; also Knockauncarragh in Ireland.

KNOCKANÌCKEN. 'Kirkcowan.' *Cnoc an cnuicin* [?] [nikkin], hill of the hillock.

KNOCKANRÀE. 'Kirkmaiden.' *Cnocán réidh* [ray], smooth hill, *cnoc an réidhe* [ray], hill of the green pasture, or perhaps, like Knockanree in Wicklow, *cnoc an fhraeich* [ree], hill of the heather.

KNÒCKANS. 'Minigaff.' *Cnocán*, the hillock; E. plur. added.

KNOCKANTÒMACHIE. 'Kirkmaiden.' *Cnocán tomach* [?], bushy hill.

KNOCKÀRDY. 'New Luce.' *Cnoc cearda* [carda], hill of the workshop or forge. *See under* CAIRDIE WIEL.

KNOCKARÒD. 'Kirkcolm,' 'Leswalt,' 'Port Patrick,' 'Stoneykirk.' *Cnoc a' rathaid* [?] [raud], hill of the road. *See under* DRUMMIERAUD.

KNOCKASCRÈE.   'Port Patrick.'

KNOCKATÒOL.   'Inch,' 'Port Patrick.'   *Cnocán tuatheal* [tooal], northern hill.   *See under* DRUMTOWL.

KNOCKATOÙAL.   'Kirkcowan.'   *See under* DRUMTOWL.

KNOCKAWÌNE   'Minigaff.'

KNOCKBRÀKE.   'Kirkcowan' (*twice*), 'Old · Luce,' 'Mochrum.'   *Cnoc bréc,* brindled, variegated hill.   *See under* AUCHABRICK and FLECKIT HILL..   *Cf.* Knockbrack in Ireland.

KNOCKBRÀX.   'Kirkinner.'   *See under* KNOCKBRAKE.

KNOCKBRÈAK.   'Kirkcowan.'   *See under* KNOCKBRAKE.

KNOCKBRÈMEN.   'Stoneykirk.'

KNOCKBREX.   'Penninghame.'   *See under* KNOCKBRAKE.

KNOCKBÙIE.   'Carsphairn.'   *Cnoc buidhe* [buie], yellow hill.   *See under* BENBUIE.   *Cf.* Knockboy in Ireland.

KNOCKCÀIRNACHAN.   'Stoneykirk.'   *Cnoc Cearnachain,* Carnachan's hill.   *See under* FAULDCAIRNACHAN.

KNOCKCÀIRNS.   'Port Patrick.'   *Cnoc cairn,* hill of the cairn.   *See under* AUCHENCAIRN.

KNOCKCÀNNON.   'Balmaghie.'   *Cnoc ceann fhionn* [canhon], speckled, variegated hill.   The literal meaning of *ceann fhionn* (*fh* silent) is white-headed; but is commonly applied to a cow with a white star on the forehead, and, generally, to anything freckled.   Thus KNOCKCANNON is the equivalent of KNOCKBRAKE.   *Cf.* Foilcannon, Clooncannon, Carrigcannon, Drumcannon, Lettercannon, etc., in Ireland.

KNOCKCÀPPY.   'Kirkmaiden.'

KNOCKCÀRNEL.   'Parton.'

KNOCKCLÀYGIE.   'Minigaff.'   *Cnoc claigeain,* hill of the skull, or of the arable field.   *See under* BARNYCLAGY.

KNOCKCLÙNE.   'Kells.'   *Cnoc cluain* [cloon], hill of the meadow.   *See under* CLONE.

KNOCKCÒARS.   'Kirkmaiden.'

KNOCKCÒCHER.   'Kirkcowan.'

KNOCKCÒM.   'Minigaff.'   *Cnoc cam,* crooked hill.   *Cf.* CUMNOCK.

KNOCKCÒRE.   'Stoneykirk.'

KNOCKCRÀVEN.   'New Luce.'   *See under* KNOCKCRAVIE.

KNOCKCRÀVIE.   'Kirkcowan,' 'Stoneykirk.'   *Cnoc craebhach* [creevagh], wooded hill, or *craebhe,* hill of the tree.   *See under* CASTLE CREAVIE.

KNOCKCRÈAVIE. 'Balmaclellan.' *See under* KNOCKCRAVIE.

KNOCKCROE. 'Mochrum.' *Cnoc crodh* [croe], hill of the cattle, or *cnoc ruadh* [rooh], red hill.

KNOCKCRÒSH. 'Balmaclellan.' *Cnoc crois* [crosh], hill of the cross or gallows, or *cnoc roiss*, hill of the wood or promontory (*see under* ROSS), or *cnoc ros*, hill of the roses. *Cf.* KNOCKROSH.

KNOCKCRÙNGE. 'Old Luce.'

KNOCKCÙDDY. 'Minigaff.'

KNOCKCÙLLIE (*Inq. ad Cap.* 1633, *Pecia terrarum de* Stranrawer, *vocata* Knockinkelzie). 'Leswalt.' *Cnoc coille*, hill of the wood. *Cf.* KNOCKHILLY and KNOCKWHILLY.

KNOCKCÙNNOCH. 'Carsphairn.' *Cnoc conaidh* [connah], hill of the firewood (*Joyce*, ii. 351); *Cf.* Killyconny in Westmeath, written *Coill an chonaidh* (*Four Masters*, 1445), Kilconny in Cavan; Druminacunna in Tipperary; Clooncunna, Clooncunny, and Cloonconny, in various parts of Ireland. ERSE *conadh*, W. *cynnud*, B. *cenneuden*. Perhaps cognate with E. *kindle*, which is akin to *candle* — LAT. *candere* (*accendere*) — √SKAND, to shine.

KNOCKCÙRRY. 'Parton.' *Cnoc coire*, hill of the caldron, or kettle-like glen. *See under* CURRAFIN.

KNOCKDÀILY. 'Balmaghie.' *Cnoc dealg* [?] [dallig], hill of the thorns. *See under* CLAMDALLY.

KNOCKDÀNIEL. 'Balmaclellan.'

KNOCKDÀVIE. 'Kells.' *Cnoc t-samhaidh* [?] [tavie], hill of the field-sorrel. *Cf.* Knockatavy in Louth. *Samhadh*, sorrel, pronounced *saua* or *sow* in the south, and *sauva* in the north of Ireland, generally loses the initial *s* in composition by eclipsing *t*. It appears in many Irish names (*Joyce*, ii. 341).

KNOCKDÀWN. 'Girthon.' *Cnoc don*, brown hill.

KNOCKDÒLLOCHAN. 'Dalry.' *Cnoc da lochan* [?], hill of the two lakelets.

KNOCKDÒLLY. 'Parton.' *See under* KNOCKDAILY.

KNOCKDON. 'Mochrum.' *See under* KNOCKDAWN.

KNOCKDÒON. 'Kirkmabreck.' *Cnoc duin*, hill of the fort. *See under* KNOCKADOON.

KNOCKDÒWN. 'Stoneykirk.' Probably *cnoc duin*, hill of the fort; but an attempt to Anglicise what was supposed to be BR. SC.

doon, has turned it into E. *down.* The same name occurs, however, in Kerry and Limerick, and is referred by *Joyce* to *cnoc don*, brown hill.

KNOCKDRÒNNAN. 'Parton.' *Cnoc draighnean* [drannan], hill of the blackthorns. *See under* DRANGAN.

KNOCKDÙN. 'Minigaff.' *See under* KNOCKDOON.

KNOCKÈANS. 'Kirkmabreck.' *Cnocín*, little hill. *Cf.* KNOCKANS.

KNOCKEEN. 'Kirkcolm,' 'Kirkmaiden.' *Cnocín*, little hill (*see under* KNOCKAN), or perhaps *cnoc caein* [keen], pretty hill, corresponding to Bonny Knowes, which is not far from Knockeen in Kirkcolm. *Cf.* Drumkeen and Dromkeen, the names of fifteen townlands in Ireland (*Joyce*, ii. 64). O. ERSE *cdin* (bonus. Z^2. 30)+W. *cain*, beautiful, *can*, bright, white ; B. *can*, C. *can* ; ⁇ akin to LAT. *candĕre*, to shine—LAT. *candĕre*, to kindle, which appears in *ac-cendere, in-cendere*+SKT. *chand*, to shine— √SKAND, to shine.

KNOCKÈFFERRICK (*P.* Knokafarik). 'Kirkinner.' Perhaps named from Afreca, daughter of Fergus, Lord of Galloway, who, after peace had been contrived between the Norsemen and the people of Galloway in the twelfth century, married Olave, the Norwegian king.—*Celt. Scot.* iii. p. 34.

KNOCKÈLDRIG. 'Kirkmaiden.' *See under* ELDRIG.

KNOCKENCÙLE. 'Kirkmaiden.' *Cnoc an cúil* [⁇], hill of the angle or corner. Probably a syllable has been lost, the original meaning having been the hill of the corner of something; as Knockcoolkeare in Limerick, the hill of the corner of the berries.

KNOCKENCÙRR (*P.* Knokinkurr).   'Kirkinner.'

KNOCKENDOCH. 'New Abbey.' *Cnocán dubh* [dooh], black hill.

KNOCKENDÙRRICH. 'Twynholm.' *See under* KNOCKANDARICK.

KNOCKENHÀRRY. 'Kirkcolm.' *See under* KNOCKANHARRY.

KNOCKENHÒUR. 'Colvend.' *Cnocán odhar* [owr], grey hill. *Cf.* Knockoura in Cork and Galway, from the derivative *odhartha* [owra], greyish.

KNOCKENSÈE. 'Kells.' *Cnoc an suidhe* [see], hill of the seat. O. ERSE *sude, suide*, ERSE *suidhe*, a seat, often occurring in Irish place-names, generally as a prefix; *suidhim*, I sit+DAN. *sidde* +DU. *zitten*+GOTH. *sitan*+ICEL. *sitja*+O.H.G. *sizzan*, G. *sitzen* +A.S. *sittan* (whence M.E. *sitten*, E. *sit*), all from TEUT. base

SAT, akin to √SAD, to sit, whence SKT. *sad*, GK. ἕξομαι, LAT. *sedere*, LITH. *sĕdĕti*, RUSS. *sidiete.* The E. *see*, the seat of a bishop, M.E. *se*, is from O.F. *se, sed.*

KNOCKENTARRY. 'Mochrum.' *Cnoc an tarbhe* [tarvie], the bull's hill. ERSE *tarbh*, W. *tarw*+LAT. *taurus*+GK. ταῦρος+A.S. *steor*, a young ox, whence E. *steer.* The word signifies full-grown or strong— √STU, to be strong, a form of STA, to stand (*Skeat*).

KNOCKÈRNAN. 'Kirkcowan.' *Cnoc Ernain*, Ernan's hill. Ernan was one of the twelve followers of St. Columba from Ireland to Scotland, and to him Killernan in Ross-shire is dedicated.

KNOCKÈRRICK. 'Stoneykirk.' *Cnoc dhearg* [herrig], red hill.

KNOCKÈWEN. 'Girthon.' *Cnoc Iain*, John's or Ewen's hill. *See under* BAREWING.

KNOCKFÀD. 'Kirkpatrick Durham,' 'Minigaff.' *Cnoc fada*, long, or far hill. A common name in Ireland.

KNOCK FELL. 'Old Luce.' Pleonastic addition of ICEL. *fjall* to ERSE *cnoc.*

KNOCKFÌSHER. 'Crossmichael.'

KNOCKGÀRRIE. 'Balmaclellan.' *Cnoc garbh* [garriv], rough hill. *Cf.* KNOCKANHARRIE.

KNOCKGÌLL. 'Crossmichael.' *Cnoc goill* [?], stranger's hill. *See under* INCHIGUILE. *Cf.* KNOCKGYLE.

KNOCKGÌLSIE. 'Kirkcolm.' *Cnoc guilchach*, rushy hill. *See under* AUCHENGILSHIE. *Cf.* KNOCKGULSHA, CASSENGILSIE, TARWILKIE; and, in Ireland, Knocknagilky.

KNOCKGLÀSS (*P.* Knokglash, Knockglass). 'Inch,' 'New Luce,' 'Old Luce,' 'Port Patrick.' *Cnoc glas*, green hill.

KNOCKGÒUR. 'Leswalt.' *Cnoc gobhar* [gower], hill of the goats. *See under* ALGOWER. *Cf.* Knocknagore and Knocknagower in Ireland.

KNOCKGRÀY (*P.* Knokgrey). 'Carsphairn,' 'Kirkmabreck.' *Cnoc grèaich* [graigh], hill of the elevated flat. *See under* IRONGRAY.

KNOCKGÙLSHA. 'Glasserton.' *See under* KNOCKGILSIE.

KNOCKGŶLE. 'Girthon.' *Cnoc goill*, hill of the foreigner. *Cf.* KNOCKGILL. *See under* INCHIGUILE. *Cf.* Knocknagaul in Limerick.

KNOCKHÀMMY. 'Kirkcolm.'

KNOCKHÀRNACHAN. 'Stoneykirk.' It is impossible to say what consonant is lost here by aspiration. The word may either be *cnoc Chearnachain*, Carnachan's hill (*see under* FAULDCAR-NAHAN) or *cnoc fhearnachan* (*fh* mute) hill of the alders. *See under* DRUMFARNACHAN.

KNOCKHÀRNOT. 'Leswalt.' *Cnoc ornacht* [?], hill of the barley. *Cf.* Barleymount in Kerry, formerly *Cnoc-ornacht* (*O'Don. Suppl. to O'Reilly*).

KNOCKHÀSTIE.   'Dalry.'

KNOCKHÈNRIES. 'Kirkcowan.' *Cnoc fhainre* [hàinry], sloping hill, deriv. of *fán*, a slope. *Cf.* Donaghenry, a parish in Tyrone. *See under* CROFTANGRY.

KNOCKHÌLLY (*Inq. ad Cap.* 1656, Knockinhillie). 'Leswalt.' *See under* KNOCKWHILLIE.

KNOCKHÒRNAN.   'Port Patrick.'

KNOCKIEBÀE (*P.* Knokbe). 'New Luce.' *Cnoc na beith* [bey], hill of the birch trees. *Cf.* Knockbeha in Ireland.

KNOCKIEBRÌAR. 'New Luce.' *Cnoc a' brathair*, hill of the brother (friar). *See under* ALTIBRAIR, which is close by.

KNOCKIECÒRE.   'Old Luce.'

KNOCKIEDÌM. 'Old Luce.' *Cnoc a' dtuim* [dim], hill of the village, dwelling, or grave. Genit. of O. ERSE *túaimm*, "a village, homestead ; a dyke, fence ; a grave, tomb" (*O'Reilly*).

KNOCKIEFÒUNTAIN. 'New Luce.' *Cnoc a' Fintain* [?], Fintan's hill. *Cf.* Kilfountain (Fintan's church) in Kerry, which is the Munster pronunciation of Fintan. There are several indi-viduals of this name mentioned in the old MSS. Of these, St. Finten, Munna, or Mundus was the most celebrated. He was a contemporary of St. Columba, and Adamnan thus writes of him in his life of that saint : "Sanctus Fintenus per universas Scotorum ecclesias valde noscibilis habitus est" (*Reeves's Adam-nan*, p. 22). According to the *Breviary of Aberdeen*, he was buried in Cowall, at the place now called Kilmun (Munna's church) ; but the same honour is claimed for Taghmon (*teach Munna*) in Wexford.

KNOCKIEHOURIE. 'New Luce.' *Cnoc na huidhre* [?], [hourie], hill of the dun cow (*see under* BARNHOURIE) ; or *cnocán odhartha* [owrie], grey hill.

KNOCKIENÀUSK.   'Stoneykirk, s.c.'

KNOCKIENÀWEN. 'New Luce.' *Cnoc an abhann* [?] [owen], hill of the stream (one form of the gen. sing. of *abhainn*). O. ERSE *abann* + W. *afon*, C. *awan* + LAT. *amnis* + SKT. *avani*. Or perhaps *cnocin dhonn* [onn], brown hill.

KNOCKIERÒY. 'Minigaff.' *Cnocán ruadh* [rooh], red hillock. *Cf.* Knockroe, in Ireland.

KNOCKIETÀNTER. 'Minigaff.'

KNOCKIETÌE. 'Old Luce.' *Cnoc na tighe*, hill of the house. *See under* DRUMATYE.

KNOCKIETÌNNIE. 'Kirkcowan.' *Cnoc a' teine* [tinny], hill of the fire or beacon. *Cf.* Duntinny in Donegal, Kiltinny in Antrim. W. *tān*, a fire, pl. *tānau*.

KNOCKIETÒL. 'Leswalt.' *See under* KNOCKATOOL.

KNOCKIETÒRE. 'Old Luce.'

KNOCKIETÒWL. 'Old Luce.' *See under* KNOCKATOOL.

KNOCKINÀAM. 'Port Patrick.'

KNOCKINCÀR. 'Kirkcowan.' *Cf.* KNOCKENCUR.

KNOCKINDÀRROCH. 'Balmaclellan.' *See under* KNOCKANDARICK.

KNOCKINDÈRRY. 'Old Luce.' *Cnoc an doire* [dirry], hill of the (oak) wood, or *cnocán dearg*, red hill. *Cf.* Knockaderry in Ireland. *See under* DERRY.

KNOCKJÈTTY. 'Rerwick.'

KNOCKJÌG. 'Kirkpatrick Irongray.'

KNOCKLÀNNIE. 'Kirkcudbright.' *Cf.* KNOCKALANNIE.

KNOCKLÈACH. 'Kirkpatrick Durham.' *Cnoc liag*, hill of the flat stones or tombs. *See under* AUCHLEACH.

KNÒCKLÈARN [*pron.* -lairn]. (*P.* Knoklarrin). 'Balmaclellan.'

KNOCKLERÒY. 'Tungland.' *Cnoclach ruadh* [rooh], red hilly place.

KNÒCKLOCH (*Inq. ad Cap.* 1616, Knocklie). 'Balmaclellan.' *Cnocklach*, a hilly place.

KNOCKLÝOCH. 'Kirkmaiden.'

KNOCKMÀLACHAN. 'Stoneykirk.'

KNOCKMÀN. 'Dalry,' 'Minigaff.' *Cnoc mban* [?] [man], hill of the women, genit. plur. of *bean*. *Cf.* Cornaman in Cavan and Leitrim. *See under* BARNAMON.

KNOCKMÀRLOCH. 'Kirkmaiden.' *Cf.* KNOCKAMAIRLY.

KNOCKMÀSSON. 'Leswalt.' *Cf.* INNERMESSAN in the next parish.

KNOCKMILÀUK. 'Whithorn.' *Cnoc Moluaig* [?], Moluag's hill. Moluag, the patron saint of Argyll, and founder of Lismore in Scotland, was originally called *Lughaidh*, contracted into *Lua*, familiarised *Luag*, in honorific form *Moluag*. He died in 592 (*Reeves's Adamnan*, p. 371, *note*). His name appears as *Molouach, Moloak, M'hulluoch, Malogue, Emagola*, and *Muluag*. He founded many religious houses in Scotland, and his name frequeutly occurs, especially in the west; thus we find Kilmoluag in Tiree, in Mull, in Skye; Kilmolowok in Raasay; Kilmoloig in Argyllshire, etc.; and apparently the same name occurs in the HOWE HILL OF HAGGAMALAG, *q.v.*

KNOCKMÒNEY. 'Kirkcolm' (*twice*). *Cnoc monadh* [munney], hill of the moor or peat. *See under* DALMONEY.

KNOCKMONONDAY or KNOCKMUNADY.   'Penninghame.'

KNOCKMÒRE. 'New Luce,' 'Wigtown.' *Cnoc mór*, great hill. Occurs in Ireland, as well as a semi-translation Muchknock, *quasi* Muckle Knock in Wexford; and in a charter by John Lord Maxwell, in 1604, are given two names in the Stewartry, Knokmekill and Knoklytill, where the adjectives retain, after translation, their position as in the Erse form. *Cf.* KNOCK-MUIR.

KNOCKMÒRLAND (*P.* Foirland dycks). 'Kirkcolm.' *Cnoc murlain*, hill of the rough top. *Pont* perpetuates the aspirated form *mhurlán* [vurlan]. *See under* CARRICKAMURLAN.

KNOCKMÒWDIE.   'Kells.'

KNOCKMÒWE. 'Kelton.' *Cnoc m-bo* [moe], hill of the cows. *See under* BIAWN.

KNOCKMÙCK. 'Borgue.' *Cnoc muc*, hill of the swine. Swinedrum is close by. *Cf.* Knocknamuck in Ireland.

KNOCKMÙIR. 'Tungland.' *See under* KNOCKMORE.

KNOCKMÙLLOCH. 'Kirkcowan.' *Cnoc mullaich* [?], hill-top. *See under* MULLOCH.

KNOCKMÙLLIN. 'Stoneykirk.' *Cnoc muilinn*, mill hill. *Cf.* Knockmullin in Ireland.

KNOCKMÙRDOCH. 'Balmaclellan.' *Cnoc Muirchertaigh*, Murtagh's hill (*O'Don. Top. Poems*, xv. 60).

KNOCKMÙRRAY. 'Balmaghie.' *Cnoc Muireadhaich* [Murragh], Murray's or Murdoch's hill. *See under* BALMURRIE.

KNOCKNACÒR.   'Kirkcowan.'

KNOCKNÁIL. 'Kirkpatrick Durham.'

KNOCKNÁIN (*Inq. ad Cap.* 1543, Knoknayne). 'Leswalt.' *Cnoc n-en* [nain], hill of the birds. *Cf.* Birdhill in Tipperary, formerly called *Cnoc-an-ein-fhinn,* hill of the white bird (*O'Don. Suppl.*).

KNOCKNÁIRLING (*Inq. ad Cap.* 1571, Knoknarling ; 1604, Knokmarling ; *P.* Knoknarilin). 'Kells.'

KNOCKNÁLLING. 'Balmaclellan.' *Cnoc n-alluin* [?] [aelun], hill of the hinds. *See under* CRAIGELLAN.

KNOCKNAMOOR. 'Minigaff.' *Cnoc an ammuir* [?], hill of the trough. *See under* BALLOCHANARMOUR.

KNOCKNÁN. 'Balmaclellan.' *See under* KNOCKNAIN.

KNOCKNÁR. 'Mochrum.' *Cnoc an air,* hill of the slaughter or of the ploughing. *Cf.* Knockanare in Ireland. *See under* BARNAER.

KNOCKNÁSH. 'Dalry.' *Cnoc an easa* [assy], hill of the waterfall. *Cf.* Doonass on the Shannon, Caherass in Limerick, Owenass in Queen's County, etc. *See under* ASS OF THE GILL.

KNOCKNÁSSY. 'Kirkcolm.' *See under* KNOCKNASS. *Cf.* Poulanassy in Kilkenny.

KNOCKNAVÁR. 'Kirkmaiden.' *Cnoc na bhfear* [var], hill of the men. *F* is frequently eclipsed by *bh,* which is the equivalent of English *v,* as in Bennaveoch, Craigenveoch ; and, in Carrignavar (*carraig na bhfear*) and Licknavar (*leac na bhfear*), both in Cork. O. ERSE *fer,* a man + W. *gwr,* C. *gûr* + GOTH. *wair* + A.S. *wer* + O.H.G. *wer* + LAT. *uir* + GK. ἥρως (for Fήρως), a hero + SKT. *víra,* a hero + ZEND. *vira,* a hero + LITH. *waira,* a man. All from Aryan type WIRA, a man (*Skeat*).

KNOCKNÁW. 'Minigaff.' *Cnoc an atha* [?] [aha], hill of the ford, or *cnoc n'aithe* [nay], hill of the kiln. *See under* AUCHENHAY and CARSNAW.

KNOCKNÉAN. 'Kirkpatrick Durham.' *See under* KNOCKNAIN.

KNOCKNÉOCH. 'Kells.' *Cnoc n-each* [?]. hill of the horses. *See under* AUCHNESS.

KNOCKNÉVIS. 'Carsphairn.'

KNOCKNIEMÓNEY. 'Leswalt.' *Cnoc na monadh* [munny], hill of the moor or peat. *See under* DALMONEY and KNOCKMONEY. *Cf.* Knocknamona in Ireland.

KNOCKNIEMÒAK. 'Leswalt.' *Cnoc na mboc* [moak], hill of the he-goats. *See under* AUCHNIEBUT.

KNOCKNÌNSHOCK. 'Kirkmabreck.' *Cnoc n-uinnseog* [ninshug], hill of the ash-trees. *See under* DRUMNAMINSHOG.

KNOCKNÌSHIE.   'Whithorn.'

KNOCKNÒN.   'Buittle.'

KNOCKNÙTTY.   'Balmaghie.'

KNOCKÒRR. 'Kirkcudbright.' *Cf.* KNOCKOWER.

KNOCKÒWER. 'Carsphairn.' *Cnoc odhar* [owr], grey hill. *See under* BENOWR.

KNOCKQUHÀSEN [*pron.* Knockhwazen]. 'Port Patrick.' *Cnoc chasain* [?] [hasen], hill of the pathway. *See under* AIRY-HASSEN and CULQUHASEN.

KNOCKRÈOCH (*P.* Knockreochs, Knockreocs). 'Kells.' *Cnoc riabhach* [reeagh], grey hill. *Cf.* Knockreagh in Ireland.

KNOCKRÒBBIN.   'Kelton.'

KNOCKRÒGER.   'Kirkcowan.'

KNOCKRÒID.   'Kirkcowan.'

KNOCKRÒNIE. 'Wigtown.' *Cnoc raithne* [?] [rannie], ferny hill. *See under* BLAWRAINIE.

KNOCKRÒSH. 'Carsphairn.' *See under* KNOCKCROSH.

KNOCKSALLIE. 'Kells.' *Cnoc seileach,* hill of the willows. *See under* BARNSALLIE. *Cf.* Knockersally in Meath.

KNOCKSCADAN. 'Stoneykirk.' *Cnoc scadan,* hill of the herrings ; probably where herrings were sold, or possibly where a fall of herrings took place in a bursting waterspout. *See under* CULSCADDEN.

KNOCKSÈNTICE.   'Balmaclellan.'

KNOCKSHÈEN (*P.* Knocksheen). 'Kells.' *Cnoc sian* [sheen], hill of the foxgloves. *See under* AUCHENSHEEN.

KNOCKSHÌNNIE. 'Kirkcudbright.' *Cnoc sionach,* hill of the foxes. *See under* BLAIRSHINNOCH.

KNOCKSHÌNNOCH (*P.* Knokshinnoch). 'Kirkpatrick Irongray.' *See under* KNOCKSHINNIE.

KNOCKSKÀIG. 'Kells.' *Cnoc sceach,* hill of the hawthorns. *Cf.* Knocknaskeagh in Ireland. *See under* SCAITH.

KNOCKSKÈLLIE. 'Kirkcudbright,' 'Port Patrick.' *Cnoc sceilig,* hill of the rocks. *Sceilec, scillec,* a splinter of stone (*O'Don. Suppl.*), *scillic* (*Cormac*).

KNOCKSKEÒG. 'Wigtown.' *Cnoc sceithióg* [skyoge], hawthorn hill. *Cf.* KNOCKSKAIG. *See under* AUCHENSKEOCH.

KNOCKSTÌNG (*P.* Knocksting).   'Dalry.'

KNOCKSTÒCKS. 'Penninghame.' *Cnoc stuaic* [stook], hill . of the round knobs or lumps. This exactly describes the ground, which is characterised by several round hillocks. O. ERSE "*Stúag,* an arch" (*Windisch*). "*Stuaic,* a little hill, a round promontory; a wall, a pinnacle, a horn; a summit; the highest part of man or beast. *Stuc,* a horn, a pile of sheaves of corn. *Stúchd,* a little hill jutting out from a greater."— *O'Reilly.* Probably akin to E. *stack* (which is also used in the sense of a columnar isolated rock) ; M.E. *stak,* BR. SC. *stook,* a shock of corn — ICEL. *stakkr,* haystack (*stakka,* a stump; *cf.* E. *chimney-stack*) + SWED. *stack,* a rick, heap, stack, DAN. *stak.* The sense is " a pile," that which is set or *stuck* up (*Skeat*). There are several places in Ireland called Stook and Stucan.

KNOCKSTRÀWIE. 'Stoneykirk.' *Cnoc sratha* [?] [sraha], hill of the strath or vale. *See under* STRAMODDIE.

KNOCKTÀGGART. 'Kirkmabreck,' 'Kirkmaiden.' *Cnoc t-sagairt* [taggart], the priest's hill. In each case this name occurs close to the site of an old church, viz. OLD KIRKMABRECK and CHAPELROSSAN respectively. *Cf.* Knocksaggart in Ireland.

KNOCKTÀLL. 'Borgue,' 'Minigaff.' *See under* KNOCKIETOL.

KNOCKTÀLLOW. 'Rerwick.' *Cnoc talaimh* [?] [tallav], hill of the land. *Cf.* Shantallow (*sean talamh,* old land), Tallowroe (*talamh ruadh,* red land), etc., in Ireland. O. ERSE *talam* + LAT. *tellus.*

KNOCKTÀMMOCK. 'Stoneykirk.' *Cnoc tomach,* bushy hill, or *cnoc tuama* [tooma], hill of the tomb or tumulus. ERSE *tuama* + LAT. *tumba* + GK. τύμβα = τύμβος, a burial mound. Probably akin to LAT. *tumulus — tumere,* to swell (*Skeat*). *See under* KNOCKIEDIM.

KNOCKTÈINAN. 'Stoneykirk.' *Cnoc tendhail* [?] [tennal], or *tenneail,* hill of the bonfire. The final consonant is liable to change, as in Ardintenant in Cork, which is mentioned in the *Annals of Lough Key* under the name of *Ard-an-tenneal.* *See under* KNOCKIETINNIE.

KNOCKTÈNTOL. 'Balmaclellan.' *Cnoc tendail*, hill of the bonfire.
Cf. KNOCKTEINAN, of which this is the unaspirated form.

KNOCKTÌM (*Inq. ad Cap.* 1624, Knocktin; *P.* Knoktimm). 'Kirkcolm.' *Cnoc tuim* [?] [tim], hill of the grave or dwelling.
See under KNOCKIEDIM.

KNOCKTÌNKLE. 'Anwoth,' 'Kirkmabreck.' *See under* KNOCK-
TINNEL.

KNOCKTÌNNEL. 'Urr.' *Cnoc tionóil* [tinnol], hill of the assembly
(*cf.* Kkockatinnole in Ireland); or *cnoc tendhal* [tennal], or
tenneail, hill of the bonfire. *See under* DRUMDENNEL.

KNOCKTÒL. 'Balmaclellan.' *See under* KNOCKIETOL and KNOCK-
TALL.

KNOCKTÒMACHIE. 'Kirkmaiden,' 'Stoneykirk.' *Cnoc tomach* [?],
bushy hill. *See under* CAIRNTAMMOCK and KNOCKTAMMOCH.

KNOCKTOÒDEN. 'Stoneykirk.' *Cnoc t-súdaire* [toodery], the
tanner's hill. *Cf.* Knockatudor in Cavan, and Knockeena-
tudor. *See under* BENTUDOR.

KNOCKTÒR. 'Troqueer.' *Cf.* KNOCKIETOR.

KNOCKTÒWER.   'Parton.'

KNOCKVÈNNIE.   'Parton.'

KNOCKVILLE (*P.* Knok Vill). 'Penninghame.' *Cnoc bhile* [villy],
hill of the large tree. *Cf.* Knockavilla and Aghaville in
several parts of Ireland. The well-known Movilla or Moville
was originally *magh bhile*, the plain or field of the great tree
(*Four Masters*, A.D. 649).

KNOCKWÀLKER.   'Kirkpatrick Durham.'

KNOCKWÀLLOCH (*Inq. ad Cap.* 1604, Knokculloch). 'Kirkpatrick
Durham.' *Cnoc uallach* [?], proud hill. This epithet is often
applied to natural features, *e.g.* Uallach, a river in Cork, now
called Proudly. Applied to a hill it means "towering, prominent," *cf.* W. "*Balch*, prominent, towering, superb, proud"
(*Pughe*).

KNOCKWÀR. 'Stoneykirk.' *Cnoc gar*, near hill.

KNOCKWÀRLEY.   'Crossmichael.'

KNOCKWHÀR. 'Girthon.' *See under* KNOCKWAR.

KNOCKWHÀRREN. 'Stoneykirk.' *Cnoc ghearrain* [?], hill of the
grove; or *cnoc ghearran*, hill of the horses. *Cf.* Knockagarran-

baun in Galway, written by the *Four Masters* (A.D. 1600) *cnoc an gearráin báin*, hill of the white horse. ERSE *gearran*, a work horse, survives in BR. SC. "*garron*, a small horse" (*Jamieson*). *See under* GLENGARREN.

KNOCKWHÌLLAN. 'Balmaghie,' 'Rerwick.' *Cnoc chuillinn* [hwillan], hill of the holly. Collin Hill, close by, has the same meaning. *Cf.* Knockacullen in Ireland. *See under* ALWHILLAN.

KNOCKWHÌLLIE. 'Stoneykirk.' *Cnoc choille* [hwilly], wood hill. *See under* KNOCKCULLY and KNOCKHILLY.

KNOCKWHÌRN (a hill of 1633 feet) (*P.* Knokchyrn hill). 'Carsphairn.' *Cnoc chuirn* [hwirn], hill of the cairn.

KNOCKWHÌRR. 'Twynholm.'

KNOCKYCLÈGY. 'Penninghame.' *Cnoc a' claiginn* [?], hill of the skull. "Often applied to a round, hard, dry hill."—*Joyce*, ii. 428. *See under* BARNEYCLAGIE.

KNOITS OF BENTÙDOR, THE. 'Rerwick.' The hillocks of Bentudor. "*Noits*, little rocky hills, also any little rocky rise" (*Mactaggart*) = E. *knop*, *knob*, a protuberance, *knap*, a hilltop ("some high knap or tuft of a mountain," Holland's *Transl. of Pliny*, B. xi., c. 10, ed. 1634) — A.S. *cnæp*, the top of a hill + DU. *knob*, *knoop*, a knob + ICEL. *knappr*, a knot, button + DAN. *knap*, *knop*, a knob, button + SWED. *knopp*, a knob, *knop*, a knot + G. *knopf*, a knob. All probably from Celtic, GAEL. *cnap*, a slight blow, a knob, a little hill, W. *cnap*, a knob, button, ERSE *cnap*, a knob, button, hillock, from *cnapaim*, I strike; as *bump* (subst.) from the verb *to bump*. *See under* NAPPERS.

KNOITS OF LINKENS. 'Kirkcudbright.' *See under* LINKENS.

KNOTTY BURN. 'Carsphairn.'

KNOWEHÀPPLE. 'Kells.' *Cnoc chapul*, hill of the horses (*see under* BARHAPPLE). *Knowe* = E. *knoll* — A.S. *cnol*, for connection of which with Celtic, *see under* KNOCK.

KNÒWLIE. 'Urr.' A.S. *cnol leá*, the hill field, field of the knoll.

KNOX HILL (*P.* Knox). 'Buittle.' *Cnoc*, a hill. *See under* KNOCK.

KNOX'S BURN. 'Carsphairn.'

KÒLPER'S WELL. 'Kirkmaiden.'

LÀBNIE POINT.　　　　　　　　　　　　　　　　'Kirkmaiden, s.c.'

LADY BAY.　'Kirkcolm.'　The farm situated on this bay bears the Erse equivalent in its name, viz. Portencalzie, *q.v.*

LADY BURN.　'Kirkinner,' 'Old Luce.'　This and the four following names are traces of old religious occupation.　BR. SC. *burn*, a stream, E. *bourn*, M. E. *bourne* — A.S. *burna*, *burne* + DU. *born*, a spring — ICEL. *brunnr*, a spring + SWED. *brun*, a spring, a well + DAN. *brönd*, a well + GOTH. *brunna*, a spring, a well + O.H.G. *prunna*, G. *brunnen*, a spring, a well + GK. φρέαρ, a well. The root of *burn, bourn*, is assigned by *Skeat* to A.S. *byrnan*, to burn, just as the root of GOTH. *brunna* is GOTH. *brinnan*, to burn.　The idea is the same as in *well* (*see under* CAIRDIE WIEL), hot, boiling up, and in *torrent, i.e. torrens*, hot, boiling, raging, impetuous (*Skeat*).

LADY CAVE and HILL.　　　　　　　　　　　　　'Kirkcolm.'

LADY RUE.　'Kirkcolm.'　GAEL. "*rudha* [rooa, roo], a point of land in the sea, a promontory."—*Macalpine*.　This word, so common along the west coast of Scotland, does not appear in Ireland.

LADY WELL.　　　　　　　　　　　'Mochrum,' 'Old Luce.'

LAG, THE.　'Glasserton.'　*Lag, log*, a hollow.　Often transferred (as in this case) to the hill beside the hollow.　Common in Irish place-names as *lag, lig, leg*, in the north, and *lug* in the south and west.　ERSE *lag, log* + ICEL. *lágr*, low (whence M.E. *louh, lah, low*, E. *low*) + SWED. *låg*, DAN. *lav* + DU. *laag* — TEUT. base LAG, to lie, to which are akin LAT. *lectus*, a bed (from obsolete base *leg-*, to lie), and GK. λέχος, a bed (from obsolete base λεχ), also appearing in aorist ἔλεξα (*Skeat*).

LAGAGÈELIE.　'Kirkmaiden.'　*Lag a' gile* [?] [gilly], hollow of the whiteness or brightness.　*Cf.* Legilly in Tyrone.

LAGANÀMOUR.　'New Luce.'　*Lag an ammuir*, hollow of the trough.　*Cf.* Lugganammer and Leganamer in Leitrim.　*See under* BALLOCHANAMOUR.

LAGANDÈRRY.　'Penninghame.'　*Lagán doire* [dirry], hollow of the wood.　*See under* DERRY.

LAGBÀES (*P.* Lagbe).　'Minigaff.'　*Lag beith* [bey], hollow of the birches.　*See under* ALLANBAY.

LAGGÀIRY HOWE (*P.* Laggyry). 'Minigaff.' *Lag caera*, hollow of the sheep, with BR. SC. *howe*, a hollow, added pleonastically.

LÀGGAN. 'Glasserton,' ' Kirkcolm.' *Lagán*, dim. of *lag*, a hollow, but not always used in a diminutive sense, *e.g.* LAGGANMORE. *Cf.* in Ireland, Lagan, Legan, Legane, Legaun, Leegane, Liggins.

LAGGANGÀRN. 'New Luce.' *Lagán g-carn*, hollow of the cairns. There are some remarkable remains at this place on the Tarf. The old pack-horse track crosses the river under Kilgallioch (*q. v.*), and there used to be here three standing stones, of which two now remain, each bearing large incised crosses. A story is told of a man who, in rebuilding the now deserted farm-house of Laggangarn, carried off one of the standing stones to form a lintel. Some time afterwards his sheep-dogs went mad and bit him. He also went mad, and his wife and daughters "smoored him atween twa cauf beds" (smothered him between two mattresses filled with chaff), and buried him on the hillside, placing the broken stone over his grave. It is a desolate region.

LAGGANHÀRRIE. 'Glasserton.' *Lagán charrach* [harragh], rough hollow. *See under* BARNHARROW.

LAGGANIMÒRE. 'Glasserton.' Probably the same meaning as LAGANAMOUR, *q.v.*

LAGGANMÒRE. 'Port Patrick.' *Lagán mór*, great hollow. *Cf.* Lugmore in Ireland.

LAGGANMÙLLAN (*Inq. ad Cap.* 1575, Lachinmollan, Laikmullene). 'Anwoth.' *Lag an muilinn*, hollow of the mill. There are still mills here. *Cf.* Lagavoulin in Argyllshire.

LAGGANRÈES. 'Kirkmaiden.' Apparently a hybrid word. The rees or sheepfold of the hollow. "*Ree*, a permanent sheepfold, surrounded with a wall of stone and feal."—*Jamieson*.

LAGGANTÙLLOCH. 'Kirkmaiden.' *Lag an tulaich*, hollow of the hill.

LAGGANÙSK. 'Kirkmaiden.' *Lag an uisce* [isky], hollow of the water. *Cf.* Luganiska in Ireland.

LAGGERAN.   'Carsphairn.'

LAGMÒNEY. 'Stoneykirk.' *Lag monadh* [munny], hollow of the thicket or of the peat. *See under* DALMONEY.

LAGMÙCK. 'Colvend.' *Lag muc*, hollow of the swine. *Cf.* Lagnamuck in Mayo.

LAGNABÀLMER. 'New Luce.'

LAGNABENAE. 'New Luce.'

LAGNAGÀTCHIE. 'Kirkmaiden.'

LAGNAWÌNNIE. 'Port Patrick.' *Lag na mhuine* [vinny], hollow of the thicket. *Cf.* LAGMONEY.

LAGNIEBÒLE. 'New Luce.'

LAGNIEMÀWN. 'Old Luce.' *Lag na m-ban* [maan], hollow of the women. *Cf.* Eilean na mban in Iona. *See under* BARNAMON.

LAGTÙTOR. 'Mochrum.' *Lag t-sudaire* [toodery], hollow of the tanners. *See under* BENTUDOR.

LAGVAG. 'Kirkmaiden.' *Lag bheag* [veg], little hollow.

LAGWÌNE. 'Carsphairn.'

LAGWÒLT. 'Kirkmaiden.'

LAINCHÀLLOCH. 'Inch.' The stream of the *tealach*, or forge. *See under* CHALLOCH and LANE.

LÀIRDLAUGH [*pron.* Lairdlaw] (*P.* Lardlach). 'Kirkpatrick Durham.'

LAIRDMÀNNOCH. 'Tungland.' *Lubhghort* [lort] *manach* [?], garden of the monks. *Lubhghort* is an exact equivalent to the BR. SC. *kale yard*, O.W. *lubgirth*, gardens, sometimes written *luird*, W. *lluarth*.

LÀKENS, THE. 'Anwoth.' *Leacdin* [lackan], a hill-side. *Cf.* Lackan in Sligo, the old residence of the M'Firbis, where the celebrated *Book of Lecan* was written; also Lacken, Lackaun, Leckan, Leckaun, and Lickane, in many other parts of Ireland. "*Leacdin*, the side of a hill, declivity; the cheek."—*O'Reilly.*

LÀKIN. 'Inch,' 'New Luce.' *See under* LAKENS.

LÀMACHAN (a hill of 2200 feet) (*P.* Lommachan). 'Minigaff.'

LÀMFORD (*P.* Lhunfard, Lomphard). 'Carsphairn.'

LÀMLAIR. 'Carsphairn.' *Léim ldira* [?], the mare's leap. *Cf.* Leamlaira in Cork, and Lemnalary in Antrim.

LÀMLOCH (*P.* Lamnoch). 'Carsphairn.'

LAMMASHÌEL, SHEUGH OF (*P.* The Scheel). 'Minigaff.'

LÀNDBERRICK (*P.* Lamberrick). 'Mochrum.'

LANDIS (on which stood formerly the abbot's tower). 'New Abbey.' *Lund*, a word of uncertain origin, appears in the same form in A.S. DU., ICEL., DAN., SWED., GOTH., G., with the meaning "earth, soil, country, district" (*Skeat*). But in Celtic it seems to have acquired the meaning of "an enclosure," hence, specially, a house, a church. W. *llan*, "an area, a clear place, a small enclosure, a church" (*Pughe*). B. *llan*, C. *lan*.

LANEBRÈDDAN, LOOP OF. 'Minigaff.' A hybrid word. BR. SC. *lane*, a stream, ERSE *bradán*, of the salmon.

LANE BURN. 'Kirkinner.' "*Lane*. 1. A brook of which the motion is so slow as to be scarcely perceptible; the hollow course of a large rivulet in meadow-ground. Dumfries. 2. Applied to those parts of a river or rivulet which are so smooth as to answer this description. Galloway."—*Jamieson*. —ICEL. *lón*, an inlet, a sea-loch, *læna*, a hollow place, a vale. The word seems to have been adopted into Celtic speech, just as *Carse*, and other words; perhaps akin to ERSE *leana*, a wet or swampy meadow (*Joyce*, ii. 401).

LANEDRÌPPLE.   'Inch.'

LANEHÙLCHEON POOL (on the Dee).   'Balmaghie.'

LANEMÀNNOCH (a stream). 'Kells.' A hybrid word. BR. SC. *lane*, a stream, ERSE *manach*, of the monks, or *meadhonach* [mennagh], middle.

LANESIDE. 'Troqueer.' = Burnside, side of the stream.

LANGFAULD. 'Kirkmabreck.' BR. SC. the long enclosure. *See under* FALL OF FOURS. In BR. SC. *lang* is preserved the A.S. *lang*, long.

LÀNIEKER.   'Kirkcolm.'

LANIEWÈE. 'Minigaff.' *Leana bhuidhe* [lenna vwee], yellow meadow. *See under* SPITAL LENY.

LANNIGÒRE. 'Old Luce.' *Leana gobhar*, meadow of the goats. *See under* SPITAL LENY.

LARBRAX (*Inq. ad Cap.* 1616, Larbrax Gressie (now Balgracie), Larbrax Stewart, Larbrax M'Quhilzeane (M'William); *P.* Lairgbrecks, Lairgwillia. 'Leswalt.' *Learg bréc* [larg brack], spotted, variegated hill-side. *See under* AUCHABRICK and LARG.

LARG. 'Inch.' *Learg*, the side or slope of a hill. *Cf.* Lerrig in Kerry; but in Ireland the diminutives Largan and Lurgan are more commonly used.

LARGERIE (*Inq. ad Cap.* 1571, Garlarg; 1604, Garlarge). 'Kells.' *Gar learg*, the near hillside.

LARG FELL (a hill of 2150 feet) (*P.* Larg). 'Minigaff.' The Scandinavian *fjall* is here pleonastically added to the ERSE *learg*. *See under* FELL and LARG.

LARGHIE POINT [*pron.* Lurgie]. 'Kirkmaiden.' *Leargaidh* [largie], a hillside; a derivative of *learg*. *Cf.* Largy, a frequent name in Ulster.

LÀRGIE BURN. 'Minigaff.' *See under* LARGHIE POINT.

LÀRGIE HILL. 'Stoneykirk.' *See under* LARGHIE POINT.

LÀRGIES [*pron.* Lurgies]. 'Kirkmaiden.' *See under* LARGHIE POINT.

LARGLANGLÈE (*Charter* 1679, Nether Lag, *alias* Larganglie). 'Urr.' *Leargán liath* [lee], grey hillside. *Cf.* Larganreagh (*leargán riabhach*) in Donegal, with the same meaning.

LARGLÈAR (*P.* Lairglury). 'Parton.' *Learg laira*, hillside of the mare. *See under* AUCHENLARIE.

LARGLÌDDESDALE (*Inq. ad Cap.* 1596, Largliddisdail *vel* Largleviestoun; *P.* Larig). 'Leswalt.' The *learg*, or hillside, of a man named Liddesdale or Livingston.

LARGMÒRE (*P.* Largmoir; MS. 1527, Largmoir). 'Kells.' *Learg mór*, the great hillside.

LARGNÈAN. 'Crossmichael.' *Learg n-en* [nain], hillside of the birds. *See under* BARNEAN.

LÀRGOES. 'Minigaff.' *See under* LARGIES.

LARGS. 'Twynholm.' *See under* LARG.

LARGVÈY (MS. 1527, Largvey). 'Parton.' *Learg bheith* [vey], hillside of the birches. *See under* ALLANBAY.

LARGVÈY HILL. 'Kells.' *See under* LARGVEY.

LARGYWÈE. 'Stoneykirk.' *Leargaidh bhuidhe* [largy vwee], yellow hillside. *See under* BENBUY.

LARIG FELL. 'New Luce.' *See under* LARG FELL.

LAROCHANÈA. 'New Luce.' *Learg an fhiaidh* [ee], hillside of the deer. The initial *f* is often silenced by aspiration. *See under* CRAIGINEE.

LARRANGES.   ' Balmaclellan.'

LÀRROCH (*W. P.* MSS. Laroche ; *Inq. ad Cap.* 1620, Lairoch ; 1681, Larruch). 'Glasserton.' *Láthrach* [laaragh], a place or house-site. There are many places in Ireland called Laragh and Lauragh, *e.g.* Laragh in Sligo, called *Lathrach* in the *Book of Lecan.* O. ERSE, *láthrach*, W. *laur*, a floor, GAEL. *larach*, "stand or site of a building; a building in ruins, a ruin ; a battlefield."—*Macalpine.* A derivative of *lathair*, presence, a spot. +W. *llawr*, a floor + E. *floor.*

LASHANDÀRROCH. 'Leswalt.' *Lios an daraich*, fort of the oak. *Cf.* Lisnadaragh in Wexford. There is a well-preserved fort here. *See under* DRUMLASS.

LAUCHENTȲRE (*P.* Lacchantyre, Laghantyr). 'Anwoth.' *Leacán-t-iar*, west hillside. *See under* BALTIER and LAKIN.

LAUGHENGHÌE (*P.* Lagganghy). 'Girthon.' *Lagan gaeith* [gwee], hollow of the wind, windy hollow. *See under* CURGHIE.

LAURIESTON. 'Balmaghie.' Laurie's place ; formerly called Clauchanpluck.

LÀVICH. 'Parton.' *Leamhach* [lavagh], a place of elms. *Cf.* Lavagh, the name of several places in Ireland. Deriv. of *leamh*, an elm. "In some parts of Ireland Lavagh is understood to mean land of elms, in others land abounding in the herb marsh-mallows."—*Hy Fiachrach,* 269, *note.*

LAWGLÀSS. 'Dalry.' *Lagh glas*, green hill (*cf.* Greenlaw). "*Lagh* [law], a hill, cognate with A.S. *law*, same meaning. It is not given in the dictionaries, but it undoubtedly exists in the Irish language, and has given names to a considerable number of places through the country."—*Joyce,* i. 391.

LEAKIN HILL. 'Whithorn.' *See under* LAKIN.

LEA LARKS (a crag of granite). 'Girthon.' *Liath learg* [?] [lee, larg], grey hillside.

LEATHS [*pron.* Lathes] (*P.* Laiths). 'Buittle.' Barns, sheds. Yorkshire "*Laith, lathe*, shed ; O. NORSE *hlatha* ; SWED. *lada* ; DAN. *lade*, a barn ; GER. and DU. *láde*, a box."—*Lucas.*

LÈAVERLY SPRING.   ' Kirkcolm.'

LECK ROSS. 'Mochrum.' *Leac rois* [lack rosh], stone of the point or promontory ; or, perhaps, as both these words have been adopted in BR. SC. speech, the meaning is "promontory of the stones or tombs." It is a point of land running into Airrieoulland Loch, now drained.

LÈFFNOL (*P.* Lefnol). 'Inch.' "In the western lands . . . the halfpenny becomes Laffen, as in Laffenstrath."—*Celt. Scot.*, iii. 226. Thus this would appear to be *leffen cnol*, the halfpenny hill.

LEIGHT (*Charter* 1355, Lachalpene ; *Inq. ad Cap.* 1600, Mekill Laight, *alias* Laightbeg ; *P.* Laicht). 'Inch.' *Lecht*, a grave. Takes its name from Leight Alpin, a large stone on the borders of Ayrshire which commemorates the burial of Alpin, the last king of Scottish Dalriada. He was killed by an assassin in Glenapp, about A.D. 750, after he had obtained sway over the Picts of Galloway (*Skene: Chron. P. and S.* clxxxv.).

LÈNNANS. 'Kirkmaiden, s.c.' *Cf.* BARLENNAN.

LÈSSONS (*Inq. ad Cap.* 1570, Lessens ; 1625, Lessence). 'Minigaff.'

LEUCARROW.   'Kirkmaiden, s.c.'

LESWALT (a parish in Wigtownshire) (*Inq. ad Cap.* 1607, Lesswoll ; 1617, Leswad ; *P.* Leswalt).

LEWTEMOLE.   'Kirkmaiden.'

LEYS HILL. 'Dalry.' *Leys, leas*, the fields.

LÌBERLANE [*pron.* Libberlan] (*P.* Elricken Libberton). 'Kirkcowan.'

LICK, THE. 'Whithorn, s.c.' *Leac, lic*, or *liag*, a flat stone. *Cf.* Lack, Leck, Lick, Leeg, Leek, in many parts of Ireland. *See under* AIRIELICK.

LÌGGATCHEEK. 'Dalry.' Gate-post. "*Liggat*, a gate so hung that it may shut of itself. Galloway. *Yet chekis*, doorposts. Douglas."—*Jamieson.* A.S. *leag, geat*, field-gate.

LÌGGAT HILL, in many places. *See under* LIGGATCHEEK.

LIGHT BURN.   'Balmaclellan.'

LÌGHTSOME KNOWE.   'Minigaff.'

LILIES LOCH (*P.* Lilly L.).   'Minigaff.'

LINBLÀNE (a salmon pool on the Luce). 'Old Luce.'. *Linn blèan*, the pool of the creek or curve. *See under* BLANYVAIRD. O. ERSE *lind*, ERSE *linn*, "a pool, the sea, water" (*O'Reilly*). W. *llyn*, a lake, a pool ; liquor, juice ; C. *lyn*, B. *lenn*.

LINCLÙDEN. ' Terregles.' The " linn " or pool of the Cluden.

LINCÒM (a salmon pool in the Luce). ' New Luce.' *Linn cam,* crooked pool (the river here turns at a right angle against an opposing rock). *See under* CAMELON.

LINCÙAN (a pool on the Tarf, close to Kirkcowan). ' Kirkcowan.' *Linn Comhghain* [Cowan]. Cowan's pool. *See under* KIRKCOWAN.

LINFÒOT. ' Old Luce.' Foot of the linn.

LINGAN. ' Glenluce.'

LINGDARROCH (a pool in the Bladenoch). ' Wigtown.' *Linn darach,* pool of the oaks.

LINGDÀRROW (a pool in the Urr). ' Crossmichael.' *See under* LINGDARROCH.

LINGDÒWIE BURN. ' Inch.'

LINGHÀR. ' Kirkinner.' *Linn gearr,* short pool, or *linn gar,* near pool.

LINGLÒSKIN. ' Kirkcolm.' *Linn losgann,* pool of the frogs. *Cf.* LINLOSKIN. *See under* DARLOSKINE.

LINGRÈE (a pool in the Cree). ' Penninghame.'

LINKÈLLIE (a pool in the Bladenoch). ' Kirkcowan.' *Linn coille* [killy], pool of the wood.

LÌNKENS (*P.* Lenkinns). ' Kirkcudbright.'

LINKHALL. ' Glasserton.'

LINLÒSKIN (a pool in the Cree) (*P.* Linglhoiskan). ' Penninghame.' *See under* LINGLOSKIN.

LINNCRÒSH (a pool in the Minnick). ' Minigaff.' *Linn crois,* pool of the cross or gallows.

LINNFRÀIG (a pool on the Deuch). ' Carsphairn.'

LOAN BURN. ' Minigaff.' *See under* LOAN HILL. *Cf.* LONG BURN.

LOAN HILL. ' Inch,' ' Minigaff.' " *Loan, lone, loaning,* an opening between fields of corn, for driving the cattle homewards, or milking cows."—*Jamieson.* = E. *lane,* M.E. *lane, lone* — A.S. *láne, lone* + O. FRIES. *lona, lana* + DU. *laan,* a lane.

LOAN KNOWES. ' Inch,' ' Old Luce.' *See under* LOANHILL.

LÒBBACKS. ' Whithorn, s. c.' *Lúbach* [?], crooked, looped, winding. *Cf.* Loobagh, a river in Ireland. *See under* LOOPMABINNIE.

LOCHÀBER LOCH. 'Troqueer.' O. ERSE, ERSE, and GAEL. *loch*, MANX *logh*+W. *llwch*, C. *lo*, B. *louch*+LAT. *lacus·* (whence A.S. *lac*)+GK. λάκκος, a hollow, hole, pit. This name is an example of how completely a place-name loses its significance, even when the original form is retained. To a Lowland Scot of the present day the word Lochaber would not necessarily imply a lake, to indicate which he has to repeat the syllable *loch* in the English position of the predicate.

LOCHANHOÙR. 'Glasserton.' *Lochán odhar* [owr], grey lakelet. Takes its name from a huge grey rock lying along the north shore. *Cf.* Lough Ora (*loch odhartha*) in Fermanagh.

LOCHAN OF VICE (*P. L.* Voyis; *Sibbald* MS., Loch Vuy). 'Tungland.'

LÒCHANS (*Crauf.* MS. 1413, Lochanys). 'Carsphairn,' 'Inch.' *Lochán*, a lakelet, E. plur. added. *Cf.* Loughan, Loughaun, and Loughane in Ireland.

LOCHANSCÀDDAN (a tidal pool). 'Glasserton.' *Lochán sgadan*, lakelet of the herrings. *See under* CULSCADDEN.

LOCH ÀRROW (*P. L.* Amered). 'Minigaff.'

LOCH ÀRTHUR (*P.* Loch Arcturr). 'Kirkgunzeon.'

LOCH BEG. 'Leswalt.' *Loch beag*, little lake. *Cf.* Lough Beg in Ireland.

LOCH BILLY (*P.* Billies). 'Balmaclellan.' *Loch bile* [billy], loch of the big tree. *See under* KNOCKVILLE.

LOCH BRACK. 'Balmaclellan.' *Loch breac*, loch of the trout. *Cf.* LOCHENBRECK.

LOCH BRAIN. (*P. L.* na Brain). 'Mochrum.' *Loch bréan* [brain], foul lakelet. It is a mere puddle in the middle of a quaking bog. *Pont's* rendering suggests *loch na breine*, loch of the stench.

LOCH CHESNEY. 'Mochrum.'

LOCH CONNEL (*P.* Loch Konnel). 'Kirkcolm.' *Loch Connail*, Connal's loch. St. Columba, after whom this parish is named, was one of the *Cinel Connaill*, or Clan Connel.

LOCH DOON. 'Carsphairn,' 'Inch.' *Loch duin*, loch of the fortress.

LOCH DÒRNAL (*P.* Loch Dornell). 'Penninghame.' The prefix is *dobhar, dur*, water. *See under* DARGALGAL.

LOCH DÒUGAN.   'Parton.'

LOCH DOW. 'Minigaff.' *Loch dubh* [dooh], black loch. *Cf.* DOULOCH.

LOCH DUIF (now called Eldrig Loch). 'Mochrum.' *See under* LOCH DOW.

LOCH DÙNGEON.   'Minigaff.'

LOCHENBRÈCK. (*P.* L. na Braik). 'Balmaghie.' *Loch na breac* [brack], lake of the trout. *See under* LOCH BRACK. *Cf.* Lough Nabrack, many times in Ireland.

LOCHENÀLING (now drained). 'Penninghame.' *Loch na fhaio-leann* [?] [ailann], lakelet of the sea-gulls. *Cf.* Loughana-weelaun, the name of several lakes in Ireland. *Faioleann* and *faieleóg* are dimin. of the original word represented by E. *gull*; W. *gwylan*, C. *gullan*, B. *gwelan.*

LOCHENGÒWER. 'Balmaghie.' *Lochán gobhar* [gower], lakelet of the goats. *Cf.* LOCH GOWER.

LOCHENKÌT. 'Kirkpatrick Durham.' *Loch an cuit* [kit], lake of the wild cat. *See under* ALWHAT.

LOCH ÈNOCH (*P.* L. Aengoch).   'Minigaff.'

LOCH FERGUS (*P.* Loch Ferguss). 'Kirkcudbright.' *Loch Fearguis*, Fergus's lake. Named after Fergus, Lord of Galloway in the 12th century, who had a castle here. He was the founder of the Monasteries of Tungland and Saulseat, the Priories of Whithorn and St. Mary's Isle, and the Abbey of Dundrennan. *Cf.* the Fergus River, a tributary of the Shannon, written *Forghas* by the *Four Masters* (A.D. 1573).

LOCH GILL. *Cf.* Lough Gill in Sligo, written by the *Four Masters* (A.D. 1244) *loch gile*, loch of the brightness, clear or bright lake. *Cf.* GILLS LOCH and LOCH GLAR.

LOCH GLAR. 'Balmaclellan.' *Loch gleóir* [?] [glore], loch of the brightness or clearness, or *loch gleordha* [glora], clear lake. *Cf.* Loch Glore, in Westmeath (*Joyce* ii. 70); also *gleoir*, the name given by the *Four Masters* (A.D. 1208) to the Leafony River in Sligo. O. ERSE *gléoir*, probably akin to A.S. *glær*, a pellucid substance, amber (whence M.E. *glaren*, E. *glare*, to shine; "It is not all gold that *glareth*," *Chaucer*, 'House of Fame,' i. 272)+DU. *gloren*, to glimmer+ICEL. *glóra*, to gleam +M.H.G. *glosen*, to shine. These are again connected with E. *glass*, DAN. *glas, glar*, O. SWED. *glær*, ICEL. *gler, glas.* All from the European base GAL to shine— √GHAR, to shine; *cf.* SKT. *ghri*, to shine; E. *glow*, etc. (*Skeat*).

Loch Goich.   ' Tungland.'

Loch Goosie.   ' Kells.'   *Loch giusach* [gusagh], loch of the
     pine-trees.   O. ERSE *gius*, a pine + W. *gwŷd*, trees, wood ;
     C. *gwydh, gûs, gur*, wood ; B. *guida*, wood, *guedhen* and *guezen
     pin*, pine-tree (*Lluyd*).   Akin to E. *wood*, ERSE and GAEL.
     fiodh.   See under AIKET.   *Cf.* Gusachan in Rosshire, etc.

Loch Gower (*P. L.* Gaur).   ' Mochrum.'   *See under* LOCHEN-
     GOWER.

Loch Grannoch.   ' Balmaghie ' (*P. L.* Greenoch).   *See under*
     Loch Grennoch.

Loch Grènnoch (*P. L.* Grenoch).   ' Minigaff.'   *Loch greanach*,
     gravelly loch (*cf.* Greanagh, a stream in Limerick) ; or *loch
     grianach* [greenagh], sunny lake.   *See under* GRAINY FORD.

Loch Hàrrow.   ' Kells.'

Loch Hempton (*P.* Dyrhympen).   ' Mochrum.'   A most decep-
     tive name.   Lying close to the old homestead of Mochrum
     Castle, it appears as if it were loch of the *hame toun*
     (Hampton), but *Pont* shows that the prefix *dobhar* [dour],
     water, originally formed part of the name, of the latter part
     of which the meaning has been lost.

Loch Howie.   ' Balmaclellan.'

Loch Inch-Crindle (*P. L.* Ylen Krindil).   ' Inch.'   *Loch innse
     Crindail*, lake of Crindle's isle.   Crindle and M'Crindle are
     still extant as surnames in Galloway, but there is no record
     to show after whom this island was named ; but it is a large
     " crannog," or lake-dwelling, from which interesting relics
     have been recovered.   *Cf.* Lochnahinch in Tipperary, which
     also takes its name from a crannog (*Joyce*, i. 300).   *See
     under* INCH.

Lochinvàr (*Inq. ad Cap.* 1550, Lochinwar ; *P.* Lochinbarr ;
     Maclellan, Lacus Varii).   ' Dalry.'   *Loch an bharr* [var], lake
     of the hill-top.

Loch Kìnder (*Inq. ad Cap.* 1601, Lochkindeloch).   ' New
     Abbey.'   According to *Mr. Skene* (*Celtic Scotland*, i. 137),
     loch Cendaelaidh [kendelah], Cendaeladh's lake.   Tighernac
     records the death in 580 of Cendaeladh, king of the Picts,
     perhaps of Galloway.   There is a fine crannog in this
     beautiful lake, which may have been Cendaeladh's palace.

Loch Làggan.   ' Glasserton.'   *Loch lagain*, lake of the hollow.
     Cf. Lough Lagan in Roscommon, and Loch Laggan in Perth-
     shire.

LOCH LEE. 'Balmaclellan,' 'Dalry.' *Loch liath* [lee], grey lake. *Cf.* Loughanlea, in Ireland.

LOCH LENNOUS. 'Mochrum.'

LOCH LÙRKIE (*P.* Loch Lurkan). 'Parton.'

LOCH MABÈRRY (*P.* Loch Mackbary). 'Penninghame.'

LOCH MIDDLE (*P. L.* Middil). 'Minigaff.'

LOCH MÌNNOCH. 'Kells.' *Loch meadhonach* [mennagh], middle lake. *See under* BALMINNOCH.

LOCH MOAN. 'Minigaff.'

LOCH MORE. 'Leswalt.' *Loch mór*, large lake.

LOCH MUICK. 'Carsphairn.' *Loch muc*, lake of the swine.

LOCH NÀRROCH (*P. L.* Narrach). 'Minigaff.'

LOCHNATÙMMOCK. 'Penninghame.'

LOCHNÀW (*P.* Lochna). 'Leswalt.' *Loch an atha* [?] [aha, awe], lake of the ford. There is here a submerged causeway leading to a lake-dwelling. *See under* CARSNAW.

LOCH ÒCHILTREE. 'Penninghame.'

LOCH OF CREE (*P.* Loch Kree). 'Minigaff.' *See under* CREE.

LOCH OF THE LOWES. 'Minigaff.' The same name occurs in Selkirkshire. *Cf.* LOWES LOCH ; also Loch of Leys in Aberdeenshire.

LOCH PATRICK. 'Kirkpatrick Durham.' *Loch Pádric*, Patrick's lake. *See under* KIRKPATRICK.

LOCH QUIE. 'Penninghame.' *Loch caeidhe* [quay, kay], lake of the bog. *See under* CULKAE.

LOCH REE. 'Inch.' *Loch riabhach* [reeagh], grey lake. *Cf.* Loughrea in Galway, written *loch riach* by the *Four Masters* (A.M. 3506); and Lough Righe on the Shannon, which they write *loch ríbh* (A.D. 742).

LOCH RÌNNIE (*P.* Lochrenny). 'Dalry.' *Loch roine* [rinnie], lake of the point. *See under* RHINNS.

LOCH ROAN. 'Crossmichael.' *Cf.* CRAIGROAN.

LOCH ROBIN (*P.* Loch Ribben). 'Old Luce.'

LOCH RONALD (*P. L.* Ronald). 'Kirkcowan.' *Loch Raonuill*. Ronald's lake ; *see under* CRAIGRONALD.

LOCH RÒY. 'Borgue.' *Loch ruadh* [rooh], red lake. *Cf.* Loch Dearg in Ireland.

Loch Rutton (gives name to a parish in the Stewartry) (*P.* Loch Ruttan ; Lochryerton, Lochryntoun, Loghroieton, 13th century, quoted by *M‘Kerlie*).

Loch Ryan. *Rerigonium sinus* of Ptolemy. " From Penryn Wleth (Dow Hill in Glasgow, *i.e.* dew hill, *gwleth*, in composition *wleth*, signifying *dew*) to Loch Reon the Cymry are of one mind bold."—*Vita Kentigernœ*, transl., p. 344.

Lochskàe. 'Balmaclellan.' *Loch scé* [skae], lake of the haw-thorns. *See under* Auchenskeoch.

Lochskèrrow (*P. L.* Skarrow). 'Girthon.' *Loch sceireach,* rocky lake. Deriv. of *sceir* (*O'Reilly*).

Lochsmàddy.   ' Crossmichael.'

Loch Spraig.   ' Minigaff.'

Loch Swad.   ' Penninghame.'

Loch Trool (*P.* Loch Truiyll). ' Minigaff.' *See under* Trool.

Loch Twàchton (*P. L.* Twaichtun). 'Minigaff.' The hill beside the loch is written by *Pont* Meal Tuachtain.

Loch Urr (*P.* Loch Orr). ' Urr.' *See under* Urr.

Loch Valley (*P. L.* Vealluy). 'Minigaff.' *Loch bhealaich* [vallagh], lake of the pass. *See under* Balloch.

Loch Wàyoch (*P. L.* Chrauochy). 'Minigaff.' *Loch bheithach* [?] [veyagh, wayagh], lake of the birch-wood (*see under* Beoch). *Cf.* Lough Veagh in Ireland. *Pont's* spelling seems like *loch chraebhach* [hravagh], wooded lake. *Cf.* Lough Crew in Meath, of which the Irish name is *Loch-craeibhe.*

Loch Whin. 'Dalry.' *Loch chuin* [hinn], lake of the dog. *See under* Drumwhin.

Loch Whìnnie (*P.* Loch Wymoch).   ' Dalry.'

Loch Whìnyon. 'Girthon.' *Loch Finain* [St.] Finan's or Winnin's lake. *See under* Kirkgunzeon.

Lòckhart Hill. ' Balmaghie.' *See under* Barlockhart.

Loddanlàw.   ' Port Patrick, s.c.'

Loddanmòre. ' Old Luce.' *Lodán mór,* large pool. This place and the next are rain-pools among the sandhills at the head of Luce Bay. " *Lod,* puddle, mud. *Lodán,* a thin puddle."—*O'Reilly.* Gael. *lod,* a pool, puddle. " *Lodan,* water in the shoe."—*Macalpine.* " *Loddans,* small pools of standing water."—*Mactaggart.* See also *Jamieson.*

LODDANRÈE. 'Old Luce.' *Lodán riahbach* [reeagh], grey pool ; or *lod an fhraeiche* [ree], pool of the heather.

LÒDENS, THE. 'Kirkcowan.' *Lodan*, the pools. E. plur. added.

LODNAGÀPPLE LOCH. 'Old Luce.' *Lod na gcapul*, pool of the horses. *Cf.* Lugnagappul, Pollacappul, and Poulacappul in Ireland.

LÒGAN (*Crauf.* MS. 1413, Logane, Lougan, *P.* Logan). 'Kirkmaiden.' *See under* LAGGAN, of which this is another and frequent form by the ordinary change from *a* to *o*.

LONE HILL. 'Inch.' *See under* LOAN HILL.

LONE STRAND. 'Carsphairn.' The "strand" or stream of the "loan." *See under* LOAN HILL.

LÒNGBERRY HILL. 'Kirkpatrick Durham.'

LONG BURN. 'Dalry.'

LÒNGCASTLE (*Inq. ad Cap.* 1584, Longcaster ; *P.* Wood of Longcastell). 'Kirkinner.' Formerly a parish.

LONG DENNOT. 'Leswalt.'

LONGFORT. 'Old·Luce, s.c.' GAEL. *longphort*, a haven (from *long*, a ship, *port*, a landing-place, a port). This is probably the sense in this case, where there is good landing in Auchenmalg Bay. But in Ireland, the word has a different meaning, "a palace, a royal seat ; a fort, garrison, tent, a camp ; parlour" (*O'Reilly*). Thus the town of Longford is written of old *Longphort Ui Fearghail*, Longford O'Farrell (*Four Masters*, A.D. 1448), O'Farrell's Castle. *Cf.* PORTLONG.

LONG HILL. 'Glasserton.' *Cf.* DRUMFAD.

LONGMAIDEN. 'Glasserton.'

LONG ROW [*pron.* Roo]. 'Mochrum.' *Rudha* [roo], a point, promontory, in this case running into the sea. *See under* RUE.

LONG THANG. 'Old Luce.' *Teanga*, a tongue, strip of land ; or SCAND. *tangi*, a spit of land. *See under* CHANG.

LONGTÒO (*P.* Langtoo). 'Parton.'

LOOPMABÌNNIE (a curve in Grobdale Lane, a stream). 'Balmaghie.' "*Lúb*, a loop, a bow."—*O'Reilly.* From this word is derived E. *loop.*

LORG HILL (a hill of 2100 ft.). 'Carsphairn.' *See under* LARG.

LORRÀIN CROFT. 'Glasserton.'

LOSHES. 'Troqueer.'

LòSKIE, BIG AND LITTLE (two hills of 800 and 900 feet). 'Carsphairn.' *Loisgthe* [luskie], burnt. *Cf.* Ballylusky in Munster, Ballylosky in Donegal, Molosky [*magh loisgthe*] in Clare. *See under* CRAIGLOSK.

LòSSET (*Inq. ad Cap.* 1610, Losset; *P.* Losset). 'Kirkcolm.' *Losaid,* a kneading-trough. "Applied to a well-tilled and productive field, or to good rich land. A farmer will call such a field a *losset,* because he sees it covered with rich produce, like a kneading-trough with dough. In the form of Losset it is the name of a dozen townlands from Donegal to Tipperary."—*Joyce,* ii. 430.

LòTUS HILL. 'Kirkgunzeon.' A modern name.

LoùDON HILL. 'Penninghame.'

LOWES LOCH. 'Balmaclellan.' *Cf.* LOCH OF THE LOWES.

LòWRAN. 'Kells.' *Leamhraidhean* [lavran], a place where elms grow. Deriv. of *leamh. Cf.* Lowery in Fermanagh and Donegal, and Lowerymore, a river in the latter county, from *leamhraidhe. See under* LAVICH.

LòWRING BURN. 'Kells.' *See under* LOWRAN.

LUCE, WATER OF. 'Old Luce.' Though several etymologies have been suggested for this name, none can be considered better than guesses. It is quite possible that in Λυκοπιβια (*Luco*pibia) of Ptolemy, which has been confidently, though unwarrantably, identified with *Candida Casa* or WHITHORN, we have the earliest written form of this name. In Dumfriesshire there was also a parish called Luce, now included in Ecclefechan. *Cf.* Luss on Loch Lomond ; Luce often occurs as *Luss* in old MSS.

LUKE'S STONE. 'Carsphairn.'

LUMAGÀRIE. 'Glasserton.'

LÙNNOCK. 'Kirkmaiden, s.c.'

LURG. 'Whithorn.' *See under* LARG.

LURG HILL. 'Wigtown.' *See under* LARG.

LURGIE. 'Penninghame.' *Leargaidh* [largy, lurgy], a hillside. *See under* LARGHIE POINT.

LÙSKIE. 'Kells.' *See under* LOSKIE.

LÙSKIE HILL. 'Borgue.' *See under* LOSKIE.

LYTHEMEAD. 'Kirkmaiden, s.c.'

Mabie (*P.* Maby).   'Troqueer.'

MABREEDIA. 'New Luce.' *See* HILL MABREEDIA.

MÀCHAR. 'Inch.' A plain. *O'Reilly* gives "*machair*, a battle," "*maghair*, ploughed land." The ERSE *machaire* [maghery], a field, a plain, appears in some names (*see* MACHERMORE), as in the Irish places Maghera and Maghery. Generally Machar may be taken to mean a level plain or field, the idea of "battle" being secondary (*see* BLAIR), from the place chosen for a battle, and of "beach," from its level character, though in modern Gaelic it is "seldom used for anything but a beach."—*Macalpine.* All are derivatives of *mag, magh*, a plain. *See under* MAY.

MACHERÀLLY [*locally pron.* Magherowley]. 'Kirkmaiden.' *Machair Amhalghaidh* [owlhay], Aulay's field. This is the origin assigned by Dr. Reeves to Magherally, the name of a parish in Ireland. M'Aulay is still a common name in the district. *Cf.* TERALLY, in the same parish.

MACHERBRÀKE. 'Kirkcolm.' *Machair brèc*, spotted, variegated field. *See under* AUCHABRICK.

MACHERCRÒFT. 'Minigaff.' *Croft* or farm of the *machair* or plain.

MACHERMÒRE (*P.* Machrymoir ('Old Luce')). 'Minigaff,' 'Old Luce.' *Machaire mór*, great field or plain. *Pont's* spelling retains the original Erse trisyllable, as in Magheramore in Ireland.

MACHERMÒRE STONE.   'Kirkmabreck.'

MACHERSÒIL.   'Mochrum.'

MACHER-STEWART (*Inq. ad Cap.* 1620, Machir Stewart, *alias* Dowellstoun). 'Sorbie.' Stewart's *machair*.

MÀCHERS, THE. The eastern part of lower Wigtownshire. *Machair*, a plain, E. pl. added.

MACKÌLSTON. 'Dalry.' M'Gill's toun or place.

MACMÒIR. 'Kelton.' *Mag mór*, great plain. In Ireland this is softened down to Moymore. *See under* MAY.

MACNÀUGHTEN.   'Kirkpatrick Irongray.'

MÀDLOCH MINES.   'Glasserton.'

MAGÈMPSEY.   'Minigaff.'

MAG FAULD. 'Kirkcowan.' *Mag*, a plain, or field. BR. SC. *fauld*,
an enclosure.

MAGGIE IRELAND'S WA'S.   'Kirkmabreck.'

MAGGOT HILL (850 feet).   'Kells.'

MAHÀAR. 'Kirkcolm.' *See under* MACHAR.

MAHERÈIN.   'Leswalt.'   *Machairín* [maghereen], small plain.
Dimin. of *machaire*. *Cf.* Maghereen in Cork.

MÀHERS HILL. 'Minigaff.' *See under* MACHAR.

MAHÒUL [*pron.* Mahool]. 'Glasserton.' *Maethail* [mwayhill],
soft, spongy land, from *maeth*, soft (*Joyce*, i. 465). *Cf.*
MEEHOOLS; also, in Ireland, Mohill in Leitrim, given in
Irish MSS. *Maothail* (*Four Masters*, A.D. 1331); Mothel, in
Waterford, called *Moethail-Bhrogain* in *O'Clery's* Calendar;
Moyhill in Clare and Meath, etc. *Maeth*, soft+W. *mwyth*,
C. *medal*.

MAIDEN CRAIGS.   'Stoneykirk.'

MAIDENHEAD BAY.   'Kirkmaiden' (*twice*).

MAIDENHOLM.   'Urr.'

MAIDENPAP (a hill of 1030 feet) (*P.* Maidenpape). 'Colvend.'
A common metaphor in hill-names.

MÀIDLAND (*P.* Maidland). 'Wigtown.' Meadow land. *Cf.* LOW
G. *meetland, mädland*, G. *mattland*, a meadow (*Bosworth*). A.S.
méd (whence M.E. *mede*, E. *mead*, and *math* as in aftermath)—
A.S. *máwan*, to mow, which is from a base MA, to mow; whence,
also, LAT. *me-t-ere*, to reap, GK. *ἀ-μά-ω*, I reap.

MÀLLABEY (*P.* Malobey).   'Kirkpatrick Irongray.'

MÀLZIE BURN [*pron.* Mallyie] (*P.* Maille R.).   'Kirkinner.'

MAMMY'S DELPH. 'Port Patrick, s.c.' "*Delf.* A pit: a grave: a
sod."—*Jamieson.* Here applied to a gully in the rocks—A.S.
delfan, to dig, whence E. *delve*. The word *delf* is not now
in use in Galloway, but *Jamieson* mentions that it is used to
express a sod in Lanark and Banff.

MÀNRAP (on Barhullion Fell). 'Glasserton.' Said to have originated from the death of a man who was gored by a bull, and
whose entrails were " wrapped " round the bushes.

MANWHÌLL HILL (1376 feet). 'Dalry.' *Móin chuill* [hwill], hill or moor of the hazel. *See under* BARWHIL and DALMONEY.

MARBRÀCK (*P.* Morbrack, Marbrock). 'Carsphairn.' The prefix *mar*, which occurs in parts of the Stewartry, seems to be of Scandinavian origin (*cf.* FELL), akin to ICEL. *mór*, a moor, peat + O. DU. *moer*, mire + DAN. *mor* + M.H.G. *muor*, G. *moor* + A.S. *mór*, a moor, or bog. The idea seems to be " bog " or " dirt," connected with E. *mire*. If we assign to the prefix *mar* this origin, it may be supposed to have entered Celtic speech like other Scandinavian words; thus MARBRACK would be *mor brec*, brindled, spotted moor. *Mar* may, however, represent a contraction of *machair*, a plain, and in some cases undoubtedly it was originally Mark.

MARBRÒY.   'Colvend.'

MARCÀRTNEY (*Inq. ad Cap.* 1604, Marcartney; *P* Markairtna). 'Kirkpatrick Durham.'

MARE ROCK.   'Leswalt, s.c.'

MARGLÈY (*Inq. ad Cap.* 1604, Margley; *P.* Morgley). 'Kirkpatrick Durham.'

MARGLÒLLY.   'Kirkpatrick Irongray.'

MARGRÈE, GREEN TOP OF.   'Dalry.'

MARGRÈIG (*P.* Markgregg).   'Kirkpatrick Durham.'

MARGRIE (*P.* Margry).   'Borgue.'

MARJORIE HILL.   'Whithorn.'

MARK (in many places). "*Merkland,* a denomination of land, from the duty formerly paid to the sovereign or superior."—*Jamieson.* E. *mark* = 13s. 4d., BR. SC. *merk* — A.S. *marc* + G. *mark* + ICEL. *mörk* + ERSE *marg.* Sometimes it is *mark,* a boundary, a march — A.S. *mearc,* or more probably direct from — ICEL. *mark* + DU. *merc* + SWED. *märke* + DAN. *mœrke* + M.H.G. *marke,* O.H.G. *marcha* + GOTH. *marka* + LAT. *margo* (whence F. and E. *marge,* E. *margin,* ERSE *marghan,* prob. + LITH. *margas,* striped, perhaps + SKT. *márga,* a trace, especially of a hunted animal — √MARG, to rub lightly — MAR, to rub, bruise, pound. " The order of ideas appears to be to rub, rub lightly, leave a trace; hence a trace, mark, line, boundary."—*Skeat.*

MARKBROOM.   'Old Luce.'

MARKDÒW (*P.* Markdow). 'New Luce.' *Marc dubh* [dooh], black Mark.

MARKFAST (*P.* Markfass).   'Urr.'

MARKLACH (*P.* Markolach).   'New Luce.'

MARLINN POOL (on the Ken).   'Kells.'

MARMIE'S DUB. 'New Luce.' A salmon pool on the Luce: Marmaduke's "dub" or pool. *Cf.* Mammy's Delph.

MARNHÒUL.   'Parton.'

MARSCÀLLOCH (*P.* Marskallach). 'Carsphairn.' *Mor* [Scand.] or *marc sceilig,* moor or merkland of the rocks. *See under* BAL-SCALLOCH.

MARSKÀIG (*P.* Markskegg). 'Dalry.' *Mor* [Scand.] or *marc sgeach,* moor or merkland of the hawthorns.

MARSLAUGH (*P.* Murslach; *Inq. ad Cap.* 1608, Marslave; 1661, Marslaugh *vel* Markslave). 'Kirkcolm.' *Marc sliebhe* [slewie], merkland of the moor. *See under* SLACARNACHAN.

MARTHRÒWN OF MABIE.   'Troqueer.'

MARTHRÒWN OF WOODHEAD.   'Troqueer.'

MARTINGIRTH. 'Troqueer.' ICEL. *garδr,* Martin's garth, yard or enclosure. *See under* FRIAR'S YARD.

MARYFIELD (one close to New Abbey, the other to Lincluden Priory). 'New Abbey,' 'Terregles.' Commemorative of the Mother of God.

MARYHOLM (near Lincluden Priory). 'Terregles.' Commemorative of the Mother of God.

MÀRYPORT (*P.* Marypoirt). 'Kirkmaiden, s.c.' Commemorative of the Mother of God.

MARY WILSON'S SLUNK. 'Stoneykirk, s.c.' *See under* BANDOLIER SLUNK.

MAUR'S CRAIG.   'New Luce.'

MAWKINHÒWE. 'Balmaclellan.' The hare's hollow. PROV. E. and BR. SC. *maukin,* a hare; *howe,* BR. SC. *hollow* or *hill.* *See under* HOWE HILL.

MAY. 'Mochrum.' *Magh,* a plain. O. ERSE *mag* + W. *maes,* C. *maes, mêz,* B. *maes.* This word may be traced in many Gaulish names, Cæsaromagus, Drusomagus, Novismagus, etc. It is generally translated *campus* in Latin, and in the Annals of *Tighernach, planities.* In Ireland it becomes Moy, Maw, Moigh, and Muff.

MÀYFIELD [*pron.* Myefield] (*P.* Meefeld).   'Kelton,' 'Terregles.'
A pleonasm ; *magh*, a plain, with E. *field* added.

MEAN HILL. 'Kirkcowan.' "*Min*, a plain, a field."—*O'Reilly.*
"A green spot, comparatively smooth and fertile, producing
grass and rushes, on the face of a mountain, or in the midst
of coarse, rugged, hilly land. There are upwards of 230
townlands (in Ireland) whose names begin with this word, in
the Anglicised form of *meen.*"—*Joyce,* ii. 400.

MEAUL (hills of 2279, 1525, 1591, and 1432 feet). 'Carsphairn'
(*four times*). *Mdel*, bald, bare. A word descriptive of summits or headlands. In Ireland it generally assumes the form
Moyle or Mweel, in Scotland Mull. O. ERSE *mdel*, ERSE and
GAEL. *maol* + W. *moel*, bald. It is used to denote a person
shorn in religious observance, a priest or saint ; and, from
the same connection of shaving with service, retained to this
day in the shaving of soldiers and domestic servants, it was
prefixed to names of saints as a Christian name ; thus Mul-
patrick = servant of St. Patrick ; Mulcolumb, Malcolm, servant
of St. Columba.

MEEHÒOLS. 'Old Luce.' *See under* MAHOUL.

MÈGGERLAND.   'Borgue.'

MÈIKLEWOOD. 'Tungland.' Great wood. *Cf.* CULMORE and
KILLIEMORE.

MEIKLEYETT. 'Tungland.' Great gate (BR. SC.)—A.S. *micel,
mucel ; gæt.*

MELYHODD THORN.   'Penninghame.'

MÈNLOCH. 'Penninghame.' *Min loch*, small lake. *Min*, the
primary meaning of which is "smooth," has also that of
"little.' *Cf.* Meenlagh, on the Blackwater, in Meath, and
Menlough in Galway. The base *min-*, small, appears in LAT.
min-or min-imus + A.S. *min*, small + E. *mean*, moderate,
middling.

MEOUL (*P.* Meald). 'Stoneykirk.' *See under* MEAUL.

MÈRKLAND. 'Parton.' *See under* MARK.

MÈRRICK (a hill of 2750 feet) (*P.* Maerach Hill, Maerack).
'Minigaff.'

MÈRROCK HILL.   'Port Patrick.'

MERSE (*P.* Merss). 'Twynholm.' A.S. *merse*, a marsh, M.E. *mersche.* "Merse. 1. A fertile spot of ground between hills; a hollow. Nithsdale. 2. Alluvial land on the side of a river. Dumfr. 3. Also explained, ground gained from the sea, converted into moss. Dumfr."—*Jamieson.* A.S. *merse* is a contraction of *mer-isc* = mere-ish, full of meres or pools — A.S. *mere*, a mere or pool. It is quite distinct from *morass* (*see Skeat, s.v.*).

MÈRTON [*pron.* Murr-ton] (*P.* Mertoun Makky). 'Penninghame.' A.S. *mór tún,* dwelling or place on the moor.

MID BURN. 'Dalry.' *Cf.* MINNICK RIVER.

MIDTOWN. 'New Abbey.' *Cf.* BALMINNOCH.

MILDRÌGGAN.   'Kirkinner.'

MILKING HOLES.   'Kirkpatrick Irongray.'

MILKY BRAE.   'Kells.'

MILLÀE (a hill of 775 feet). 'Twynholm.' *Cf.* MILLYEA. *Meall*; O. ERSE *mell*; a globe, a lump, a hill. A common name for a hill in Ireland and Scotland, difficult sometimes to distinguish from *maol* in composition. It is perhaps akin to LAT. *moles.*

MILLBÀWN. 'Kirkmaiden,' 'Port Patrick, s.c.' *Meall bán,* white hill.

MILLBÙOY. 'Kirkmaiden, s.c.' *Meall buidhe* [buie], yellow hill. *Cf.* Mullboy in Tyrone.

MILLDÒWN. 'Inch,' 'Leswalt,' 'New Luce,' 'Penninghame.' *Meall don,* brown, dun hill.

MILLÈUR POINT (*P.* Mullawyr). 'Kirkcolm.' *Meall odhar* [owr], grey hill.

MILLFÌRE (a hill of 2350 feet).   'Kells.'

MILLFÒRE (a hill of 2082 feet). 'Dalry.' *Meall mhór* [vore], great hill. *Cf.* MILLMORE.

MILLGRÀIN.   'Penninghame.'

MILLHÀRRY. 'Kirkpatrick Durham.' *Meall gharbh* [harriv], rough hill.

MÌLLHILL. 'Kirkinner,' 'Leswalt,' 'Old Luce,' 'Penninghame.' Sometimes to be referred to E. *mill*, but at others probably from *meall*, a hill, with pleonastic addition, as in Bar Hill, Fell Hill, etc.

MILLÌSLE (*P.* Milnisle). 'Kirkinner,' 'Sorbie.' The "isle" or river-meadow of the mill. —A.S. *mylen, miln* (BR. SC. *miln*) —LAT. *molina.*

MILLKNÒCK. 'Anwoth.' *Maol cnoc,* bare hill. *Cf.* MULLKNOCK.

MILLMÀRK. 'Dalry.'

MILLMÌNNOCH. 'Dalry.' *Meall meadhonach* [mennagh], middle hill.

MILLMÒRE. 'Minigaff.' *Meall mór,* great hill.

MILLQUÀRTER. 'Dalry.'

MILLQUHÌRK [*pron.* -hwirk]. 'Inch.' *Meall cheorce* [?] [hurka], hill of the oats (*see under* AWHIRK), or *meall chearc* [hark], hill of the grouse. *Cearc,* a hen, is the usual word for grouse.

MILLSTÀLK. 'Minigaff.' *Meall stuaic* [?], [stook] stack hill. *See under* KNOCKSTOCKS.

MILLSTONE HILL. 'Port Patrick.' Presumably where mill-stones were quarried. There are several places in Ireland called from *bro,* gen. *brón,* a millstone; *e.g.* Coolnabrone in Kilkenny, the hill-back of the millstones.

MILLTÌM. 'New Luce.' *Meall tuam* [?], hill of the tombs. *See under* KNOCKIEDIM.

MILLYÈA (a hill of 2450 feet). 'Kells.' *Cf.* BRANYEA and MILLAE.

MILMÀIN (*Inq. ad Cap.* 1543, Malvein ; 1610, Malmen, Midmylne-toun, *alias* Balmaunoch ; 1639, Balmannoche). 'Stoneykirk.' *Meall meadhon* [men], middle hill. *Cf.* MILLMINNOCH and MULLMEIN.

MILNTHÌRD (*P.* Millthridt). 'Kelton.' The third part (a division of land) of the mill. *Cf.* "Thrid and tein. A method of letting arable land for the *third* and *tenth* of the produce." —*Jamieson. Cf.* Middlethird in Tipperary, a translation of the ERSE *Trian meadhonach.*

MILTÒNISE or MILTÒNISH (*P.* Multonish). 'New Luce.'

MINDÒRK (*P.* Mondorck). 'Kirkcowan.' *Min dtorc* [?], boars' field.

MINICÀRLIE. 'Glasserton.' *Muine* [minny] *Cerle* [?], Kerlie's thicket. This is on CARLETON FELL, which *M'Kerlie* claims as Cerle's Toun, a proposition which this name certainly tends to strengthen.

MÍNISHTREE. 'Carsphairn.'

MINNÀUL. 'Kells.'

MÌNNICK (a river) (*P.* Meannock). 'Minigaff.' *Meadhonagh* [?] [mennagh], middle, the mid-stream. It occupies the middle position between its tributaries the Cree and Trool, the united stream taking the name of Cree. Minnock or Munnock is the name of lands in Dalry parish, Ayrshire. *See under* BALMINNOCH.

MINNIEBÀY. 'New Luce.' *Muine beith* [minny bey], birch thicket. *Cf.* Monivea, in Gallway.

MINNIEGÀLL. 'Kells.' *Muine geal* [gal], white thicket, or *gall*, of the strangers or of the standing stones. *Cf.* Moneygall in King's County, which *Joyce* interprets the shrubbery of the strangers. *See under* DERGALL.

MINNIEGÌE. 'Kirkcowan.'

MINNIGÀFF, a parish in the Stewartry. Variously written Monegoff, Monigaff, Monigow, Munygoiff, Munygaff, etc. Apparently *muine gobha* [minny gow], the smith's wood or thicket.

MÌNNIN BURN. 'Loch Rutton.' The minnow stream. BR. SC. *minnin*, a minnow; spelt *menoun*, plur. *menounis* in Barbour's *Bruce*, ii. 577. — A.S. *myne*, probably — *min*, small. *Cf.* ERSE *miniasg*, small fish.

MINNIWÌCK (*Inq. ad Cap.* 1602, Muniwick *vel* Mynivick). 'Minigaff.'

MÌNNOCK'S MOUNT. 'Whithorn.'

MINNYDÒW (*Inq. ad Cap.* 1604, Moniedow; *P.* Monydow). 'Kirkpatrick Durham.' *Muine dubh* [dooh], dark thicket. *Cf.* Moanduff in Ireland.

MIRKSIDE. 'Dalry.' Dark hill-side; — A.S. *murc, myrce*, murky + O. SAX. *mirki*, dark + ICEL. *myrkr* + DAN., SWED. *mörk*; from the same root as E. *mark*. *See under* MARK.

MOATS THORN. 'Kelton.'

MÒCHRUM. A parish in the shire, and also a place in Parton. The latter *Pont* writes Mochrumm, the former Machrom, which also appears in *Charter*, 1341, Mochrome, and in a charter of David II., Monchrum. The spelling Motherin, which also is found, is probably a misreading of *t* for *c*. Perhaps it bears the same relation to *magh* as CLACHRUM does to *clach*, and means an open country, champaign. The name occurs in Ayrshire also.

MoÌDOCH HOLE.   'Kirkcolm, s.c.'

MOILE. 'Inch.' *See under* MEAUL.

MÒLLANCE (*Inq. ad Cap.* 1628, Millance ; *P.* Mollens, Mill of Molleins ; 1613, Mollans). 'Crossmichael.' *Muilean,* a mill, or *mullàn,* a hill, dimin. of *mullach.* "It is generally applied to the top of a low, gently-sloping hill. In the forms Mullan, Mullaun, and in the plural Mullans and Mullauns, it is the name of nearly forty townlands (in Ireland)."—*Joyce,* i. 393.

MÒLLAND or MULLAN HILL (*P.* Drummollyin Hill). 'Penninghame.' *Muilean,* a mill ; the prefix *druim* shown by *Pont* has dropped off. *See under* DRUMMILLAN.

MÒNACHAN 'Whithorn, s. c.' *Manachàn,* the little monk, or *manachean,* the monks. It is a sea rock close to the old chapel of St. Ninian, Candida Casa, the earliest stone church in Scotland. Monaghan in Ireland has a different origin, being *muineachàn,* a little brake or thicket (*Four Masters,* A.D. 1462).

MÒNÀNDIE RIG (*P.* Mononduy). 'Kirkcowan.' *Cf.* Knockmononday.

MONEYHÈAD. 'Stoneykirk, s.c.' Headland of the *monadh* [money] or moor.

MÒNEYKNOWE. 'Kirkpatrick Durham.' GAEL. *monadh* [mona], a moor (*see under* DALMONEY) ; BR. SC. *knowe,* a hillock, added.

MÒNEYPOOL BURN.   'Kirkpatrick Durham.'

MONK HILL. 'Wigtown.' *Cf.* DRUMMANOGHAN, close by.

MONRÈITH (variously spelt Murrief, Murith, Menrethe (*Ragman Roll*), etc.). 'Mochrum.' *Moin rialhach* [?] [reeagh], grey moor. *Cf.* Monreagh in Ireland.

MONYBÙIE (a hill of 1050 feet) (*Inq. ad Cap.* 1604, Monyboy ; *P.* Mouybuy). 'Balmaclellan.' *Monadh buidhe* [buie], yellow moor. *Cf.* YELLOW BOGS.

MOORFAD (*P.* Moorefadd). 'Kirkmabreck.' *Mór fada,* long moor. *Cf.* Monfad in Ireland, long moor. *See under* MARBRACK.

MOORTREEKNOWE. 'Troqueer.' Probably a corruption of Bourtree Knowe, the "knowe" or hillock of the elder. *Bourtree, boretree, boartree* "seems," says Jamieson, "to have received its name from its being hollow within, and thence easily bored by thrusting out the pulp." Be that as it may, it was probably used with sand and water for perforating stones in neolithic times.

MÒORYARD HILL. 'Borgue.' *Mòr ard,* high moor. *See under* MARBRACK.

MÒRRACH (*P.* Moroch; *W. P.* MSS. Morache).   'Whithorn.'

MÒRRISON.   'Balmaghie.'

MÒRROCH (*Crauf.* MS. 1468, Morrach).   'Stoneykirk.'   *Cf.* MORRACH.

MORRÒW WELL. 'Kirkmaiden.' *Cf.* BLACKMORROW WELL.

MOSSBROCK GAIRY.   'Carsphairn.'   *Mos broc,* badger's moss. The Scandinavian *mos* seems to have been adopted into Erse speech. " E. *moss,* a cryptogamic plant, M.E. *mos, mosse* — A.S. *meós* + DU. *mos* + ICEL. *mosi,* moss, also a moss, moorland + DAN. *mos* + SWED. *mossa* + G. *moos,* M.G.H. *mos.*"—*Skeat.* Akin to LAT. *muscus.* E. *mire* is related to *moss* through O.H.G. *mios.*

MOSSFEÀTHER. 'Borgue.' *Mos Pheaduir* [?], Peter's moss.

MOSSMÀUL. 'Twynholm.' *Mos maol,* bare moss. *See under* MEAUL.

MOSSNÀE. 'Twynholm.' *Mos n-aithe* [?] [nay], moss of the kiln. *See under* AUCHENHAY.

MOSS RÀPLOCH. 'Kells.' *Cf.* RAPLOCH, a village in Stirlingshire.

MOSS RODDOCK. 'Dalry.' *Mos Rideirch* [?], Roderic's Moss. Perhaps commemorative of Rydderch Hael, the Christian king who defeated the Pagans A.D. 573 at Ardderyd (Arthuret), near Carlisle, and whose name survives in several places; *e.g.* Cloriddrick, a large stone in North Ayrshire. *See under* MUNGO'S WELL.

MOSSTÈRRIE. 'Borgue.' *Mos t-searragh* [?] [terragh], the foal's moss, or *mos Tuire* [terry], Terry's moss. *See under* CRAIGTERRA.

MOSSYARD.   'Girthon.'

MOTHER WATER (a well on Prestrie (Priestery) farm). 'Whithorn.' Probably dedicated to the Mother of God.

MOUNT HILLY. 'Inch.' *Moin choille* [hilly], hill of the wood.

MOUNT SALLIE [*pron.* Salyie]. 'Kirkmaiden.' *Moin seileach,* hill of the willows. *See under* BARSALLOCH and DALMONEY.

MOUNT SKIP.   'Crossmichael.'

MOYLE. 'Borgue,' 'Colvend.' *See under* MEAUL.

MÙCLACH. 'Wigtown.' *Muclach,* "a herd of swine" (*O'Reilly*); a swine-pasture. *Cf.* Mucklagh frequently in Ireland.

MÙDDIOCH ROCK.   'Kirkmaiden, s.c.'

MÙGLOCH. 'Kirkmaiden.' *See under* MUCLACH.

MUIL, THE (*P.* Muil). 'Kirkcowan,' 'New Luce.' *See under* MEAUL.

MUIRDRÒCHWOOD. 'Carsphairn.' *Mór drocheaid*, bridge moor. Between the Bridge of Deugh and the High Bridge of Ken. The adjacent farm is called Bridgemark. *See under* BARD-ROCHWOOD.

MUIRGLÀSS. 'New Luce.' *Mór glas*, green moor. *See under* MARBRACK.

MULDÀDDIE.   'Kirkmaiden.'

MULDÒNACH (*P.* Mealdanach), (a hill of 1800 ft.) 'Minigaff.' *Meall Donnchaidh* [Donhah], Duncan's hill.

MULDÒWN. 'Minigaff.' *See under* MILLDOWN.

MUIGÀRVIE. 'Minigaff.' *Maol garbh* [garve], rough, bare hill.

MULL, THE. 'New Luce.' *See under* MEAUL.

MULLACHGÈNY. 'Minigaff.' *Mullach gaineach*, sandy hill. *See under* GANNOCH.

MULLAN. 'Penninghame.' *Mullán*, a hill. *See under* MOLLANCE.

MÙLLANDÈRRY. 'Kirkmaiden, s.c.' *Mullan dearg*, red hill or headland. *Cf.* Mullachdarrig, Mullachderg, in Ireland.

MULLBÀNE. 'Carsphairn,' 'Girthon.' *Maol* or *meall bán*, white headland or hill. *See under* MILLBAWN. *Cf.* Mweelbane in Fermanagh.

MULLGÌBBON. 'Girthon.' *Maol gobain*, headland of the little snout. *See under* GAB.

MULL HILL OF (1) AIRIEOLLAND, and (2) OF MILTON. 'Mochrum.' *Maol*, a bare hill. *See under* MEAUL.

MULLKNOCK. 'Mochrum.' *See under* MILLKNOCK.

MULLMÈIN (*P.* Mulmein), 'Minigaff.' *Maol* or *meall mín*, smooth or little hill. Or perhaps the same as MILMAIN, *q.v.*

MÙLLOCH. 'Kirkcowan,' 'Penninghame.' *Mullach*, a hill, from *maol*, bare. It takes the form of Mulla and Mullagh in many parts of Ireland.

R

MÙLLOCK (*P*. Mullock, Muloch). 'Rerwick.' *See under* MULLOCH.

MULL OF GALLOWAY, THE [locally pron. Moyle] (*P*. Mull of Gallua). 'Kirkmaiden.' *Maol*, bare, a bare headland. *See under* MEAUL. *Maclellan*, in the article which accompanies *Pont's* map in *Blaeu's* atlas, gives the true etymology :— " *Mula*, id est, glabrum et detonsum ; nam prisci Scoti promontoria appellant *Mula*, metaphora a capite detonso sumpta."

MULL OF LOGAN, THE 'Kirkmaiden.' *See under* MULL OF GALLOWAY and LOGAN.

MULL OF ROSS. 'Borgue.' *See under* MULL OF GALLOWAY and ROSS.

MULLTAGGART.. 'Kirkmabreck.' *Meall t-sagairt* [taggart], priest's hill. *See under* ALTAGGART.

MULNIEGÀRROCH.   'New Luce.'

MULRÈA. 'Kirkmaiden.' *Maol* or *meall reidh* [?] [ray], smooth, bare hill or *raith* [ray], of the " rath " or fort.

MÙNCHES (*Inq. ad Cap.* 1604, Munocheis ; MS. 1527, Muncheiss). 'Buittle.'

MUNCRÀIG (*P*. Monkraig). 'Borgue.' *Moin creag*, moor of the crags.

MUNGO'S WELL. 'Dalry.' This is the only dedication in Galloway, so far as known to the writer, to St. Kentigern or Mungo, the patron saint of Glasgow, who re-converted the Strathclyde Britons. The town well in Peebles is dedicated to him, as well as many other places in Lanark, Dumfries, and Cumberland. He died in A.D. 603. King Riderch, the conqueror of Strathclyde, submitted his crown to him ; and if, as is suggested MOSS RODDOCK in the adjacent parish commemorates that individual, there may be some connection between the names of these two places.

MUNRÒGIE.   'Kirkcowan.'

MUNSACK, FORD OF (*P*. Muinshesh, Monsack).   'Carsphairn.'

MUNSHÀLLOCH. 'Minigaff.' *Moin sealgha* [?] [shalligha], moor of the hunting. *See under* DRUMSHALLOCH.

MÙNTLOCH (*Inq. ad Cap.* 1610, Mulknok). 'Kirkmaiden.' *Cf.* MENLOCH.

MUNWHÀLL. 'Girthon.' *Moin gall*, moor of the strangers or of the standing stones. *See under* DERGALL.

MUNWHÙLL (a hill of 1345 feet) (*P.* Monwhil).　'Minigaff.'
Moin chuill [hwill], moor of the hazels.　*Cf.* Monaquill in
Tipperary.　*See under* BARWHIL.

MÙRCHIE WOOD.　　　　　　　　　　　　　　　　'Minigaff.'

MÙRDOCH HILL.　　　　　　　　　　　　　　　　'Whithorn.'

MURDOCH'S CAVE.　　　　　　　　　　　　　　　'Minigaff.'

MURDÒNACHIE.　'New Luce.'　*Mór Donachaidh* [Donnaghie],
Duncan's moor.　*See under* BARDONACHIE.

MÙRLIN STRAND.　'Whithorn, s.c.'　*Murlán*, a rough top or head.
See under CARRICKAMURLAN.

MUSIC KNOWES.　　　　　　　　　　　　　　　　'Kells.'

MUSSEL CLAUCHAN (rocks on the coast).　'Colvend.'　*Clachan*,
stones, where mussels are collected.　*Cf.* CRAIGNESKET.

MÙTER HILL.　　　　　　　　　　　　　　　　'Borgue.'

MYE.　'Stoneykirk.'　*See under* MAY.

MÝRETON [*pron.* Murrton].　'Mochrum.'　A.S. *mere tún*, the place
or dwelling on the mere or lake.　*Cf.* MERTON.

MÝROCH (*Inq. ad Cap.* 1661, Mairoch; *P.* Maroch).　'Kirkmaiden.'

N ANNIE NAIRD'S HILL.　　　　　　　　　'Kirkmaiden.'

NANNIE WALKER'S WA'S.　　　　　　　　　　　'Kells.'

NAPPERS, THE.　'Minigaff.'　*See under* KNOITS.

NASHÀNTIE HILL.　'Stoneykirk.'　*An sean tigh* [shan teeh], the
old house.　*See under* SHAMBELLY.

NÀSSAN BURN.　'Kirkmaiden.'　*N-easean* [nassan], the waterfalls,
pl. of *eas.*　*See under* ASS OF THE GILL.

NETHERFIELD.　'New Abbey.'　Lower field.

NÈTHERLAW.　'Kerwick.'　Lower hill (antithetically to Overlaw).
—A.S. *neoðra hlœw.*

NÈTHERTHRID (*P.* Netherthridd).　Lower third (a division of land)
—A.S. *neoðra ðridda.*　*See under* MILNTHIRD.

NETHERTOUN.　'New Abbey.'　Lower place —A.S. *neoðra tún.*

NETHERYETT.　'New Abbey.'　Lower gate — A.S. *neoðra geat.*

NEW ABBEY, a parish in the Stewartry, named from the Abbey of Sweetheart (Douzquer, Doxquer, Dux Quer, Douce Cœur, Dulce Cor, etc.), founded in 1275 by Devorgilla, daughter of Alan, Lord of Galloway, wife of John Baliol.

NEWTON STEWART. 'Penninghame.' Formerly Newton Douglas, and still earlier Fordhouse.

NEWHOUSE OF LOCH ARTHUR. 'New Abbey.' The antithesis of SHAMBELLY, *q.v.*

NÈWLAW. 'Rerwick.'

NEW GALLOWAY (*Synod of Galloway*, 1664, Newtowne of Galloway).

NICK OF CLASHNEÀCH. 'Minigaff.' "*Nick*, an opening between the summits of two hills."—*Jamieson.* "*Nick* is an attenuated form of *nock*, the old spelling of *notch ;* so also *tip* from *top.*" —*Skeat.* *Notch*, a weakened form of *nock*, M.E. *nokke*, especially applied to the notch in the end of an arrow — O. DU. *nock* + O. SWED. *nocka*, a notch. *See under* CLASHNEACH.

NICK OF RUSHES. 'Minigaff.'

NÌMBLY (*P.* Nimbelly; *Inq. ad Cap.* 1601, Nunbellie). 'New Abbey.' Probably the *baile* [bally], house or place of the nuns. *Cf.* NUNTON.

NÒGGIE. 'Rerwick.'

NOGNIESCRÈE. 'Leswalt.' *Cnoc na scrath* [scraw], hill of the sods or turf. *See under* SCRABBY.

NORWAY CRAIG. 'Kirkmaiden, s.c.' *Cf.* CARRICKFUNDLE in Addenda.

NÙNLAND. 'Loch Rutton.' The land of the nuns. *Nun*, M.E. *nonna* — A.S. *nunna* — LOW LAT. *nunna, nonna*, a nun, "originally a title of respect, especially used in addressing an old maiden lady, or a widow who has devoted herself to sacred duties. The old sense is 'mother,' answering to LAT. *nonnus*, father, a word of great antiquity + GK. νάννη, νέννα, an aunt, νάννας, νέννος, an uncle + SKT. *nand*, a familiar word for mother used by children, . . . answering to SKT. *tata*, father. Formed by repetition of the syllable *na*, used by children to a father, mother, aunt, or nurse ; just as we have *ma-ma, da-da*, etc."—*Skeat.*

NÙNTON (*P.* Nuntoun). 'Twynholm.' The place or dwelling of the nuns. There are here the ruins of a nunnery.

Nunwood (near Lincluden Priory). 'Terregles.' Wood of the nuns. A sisterhood of Black Nuns was established at Lincluden by Uthred, son of Fergus, founder of the Priory in the twelfth century.

Ochiltree (*P.* Uchiltry). 'Penninghame.' There is a place of this name in Ayrshire.

Ochley Point. 'Kirkcolm, s.c.'

Ochteralìnachan. 'Leswalt.' *Uachdarach lìnachan,* upper flax-field; a derivative of *lìn,* flax. *See under* Port Leen.

Ochtelùre (*P.* Ochtyluer; *Inq. ad Cap.* 1642, Uchtrelmure). 'Inch.' *Uachdarach lobhair* [?] [lour, loor], upper land of the leper or infirm person. *See under* Barlure and Barney-water.

Ochtrimakàin (*P.* Ochtrymackean, Ouchtriemackean; *Inq. ad Cap.* Ucthreid M'Kayne). 'Port Patrick.' *Uachdarach mic Iain,* the upper land of MacEwen or Mackean.

Oldlànd. 'Girthon,' 'Kirkcowan.' *Cf.* Shantallow (*sean talamh*) in Ireland.

Oldman. 'Rerwick.'

Old Tùrie. 'Kirkmaiden, s.c.'

Old Water (a tributary of the Cluden). 'Kirkpatrick Irongray.' *Allt,* a glen or stream, which, being confounded with br. sc. *auld,* has been made genteel and transformed into *Old.* *See under* Aldergowan.

Òrbain Hill. 'Kirkcolm.'

Orchardton (*P.* Orchartoun, Orchardtoun). 'Sorbie.' *Ort-gœrd* or *wort-gœrd tún,* the house with the garden of "worts" or vegetables. The sense of a garden of fruit-trees is a secondary one.

Òrchars. 'Minigaff.'

Òrloge Knowe (close to the ruins of Corsewall Castle). 'Kirkcolm.' Hill of the horologue, or sun-dial. "*Orloge, orlager, orliger,* a clock, a dial."—*Jamieson.* – o.f. *horloge,* horologe (whence m.e. *orologe,* e. *horologe*) – lat. *horologium,* a sun-dial, a water-clock – gk. ὡρολόγιον – ὡρο for ὥρα, a season, hour, and λογιον from λέγειν, to tell.

ORNÒCKENOUGH. 'Anwoth.' *Aridh* [airie] *cnocnach*, hilly pasture.
    See under AIRIE.

ÒRROLAND. 'Rerwick.' Debateable ground. "*Orrow, orra, ora.*
    Unappropriated, not matched."—*Jamieson.* In sorting sheep
    in spring on the hills, those belonging to other flocks are
    put into the "orra bught."

ÒUTON (Chapel, Gallows, and Burgess Outon, and Outon Corwar)
    (*W. P.* MSS. Lytill Owtoun, Owtoun chapell, Owtoun burges,
    Owtown carvar). 'Whithorn.' Out-town, outside the town
    (of Whithorn).

OUTTLE WELL.   'Sorbie.'

ÒVERLAW (antithetic to Netherlaw). 'Rerwick.' M.E. *over law*,
    upper hill, as *Chaucer* writes *over lippe* for *upper lip*, *C. T.* 133.
    A.S. *ofer hlæw; ofer*, prep. (whence M.E. *ouer*, BR. SC. *ower*),
    akin to A.S. prep. *up* + DU. *over* + ICEL. *yfir*, prep., and *ofr*,
    adv., exceedingly (as in E. *over-fond, over-kind*, etc.) + DAN.
    over + SWED. *öfver* + G. *über* + O.H.G. *ubar* + GOTH. *ufar*
    + GK. *ὑπέρ* + LAT. *super* + SKT. *upari*, above. *Over* is the
    comparative form of the root UF (E. *up*), of which the
    superlative survives in *oft.*

ÒVERTOWN. 'New Abbey. A.S. *ufera tún*, upper place; antithetic
    to NETHERTOUN.

OX ROCKS. 'Kirkcolm, s.c.' *Cf.* BO STANE.

OX STAR (a high pasture on the *shoulder* of a hill). 'Minigaff.'
    Probably this is BR. SC. *oxter*, the armpit, figuratively used
    as parts of the human frame so often are to describe parts of
    a hill. The Ordnance Surveyor has made two words of it.
    — A.S. *oxta*, the armpit.

P ADAKIE.   'Kirkmaiden, s.c.'

PADDOCK HALL. 'Rerwick.' This is probably the form of A.S.
    pearroc, a park, alluded to under PARK. The change from
    r to *d*, though not according to rule, undoubtedly took place,
    probably (says *Skeat*) from confusion with *paddock*, a toad.

PALGOWN (on the Minnick) (*P.* Poolgawin). 'Minigaff." *Poll
    gobhain* [gown], the smith's pool. *See under* POLBAE.

PALÌNKUM (*P.* Poolinkum). 'Kirkmaiden.' *Poll linn cam*, stream
    of the crooked linns. *See under* LINCOM.

PAIMÀLLET (*Inq. ad Cap.* 1661, Polmowart; *W. P.* MSS. Polmal-
    lart). 'Sorbie.'

PALNÀCKIE (on the Urr). 'Buittle.' *Poll an achaidh* [aghey], stream of the arable field.

PALNÈE. 'Kirkcudbright.' *Poll na fhiadh* [ee], stream of the deer, or *poll na fhiodhe* [ì] [ee], stream of the wood. *Fidh, fiodh,* O. ERSE *fid* + E. *wood* (see *under* BLAIKET). *See under* CRAIGINNEE.

PALNÙRE (a stream) (*P.* Polnewyir R.). 'Minigaff.' *Poll n-iubhar* [nure], stream of the yew-trees or of the juniper. *Cf.* Terenure, Ballynure, Ahanure, Ardnanure, Gortinure, Killure, Killanure, in Ireland; also Newry and Nure = *an iubhar*, with the agglutinative *n* of the article. O. ERSE *ibar, ibhar, iubar,* ERSE *iubhar,* GAEL. *iubhar, iughar,* W. *yw, ywen,* C. *hivin,* B. *ivin* + A.S. *iw* (whence M.E. *ew,* E. *yew*) + DU. *üf* + ICEL. *yr* + G. *eibe,* O.H.G. *iwa.*

PALWHÌLLIE or POLQUHÌLLIE. 'Penninghame.' *Poll choille* [hwilly], stream of the wood.

PÀPY HA'. 'Minigaff.' Probably equivalent to BALNAB, *q.v.*

PARK (*P.* Parck). 'Old Luce.' *Pairc,* enclosed ground. In Scotland *park* has not the exclusive meaning attached to it in England, but simply means an enclosed field. + W. *park, parwg,* B. *park,* which *Skeat* takes to be borrowed from the Teutonic. E. *park,* ME. *parrok*—A.S. *pearroc* + DU. *perk* + SWED. and DAN. *park* + G. *pferch* + F. *parc,* ITAL. *parco,* SPAN. *parque. Paddock* is another form of ME. *parrok.* The A.S. form is retained in BR. SC. "*Parrock,* a small enclosure in which a ewe is confined to make her take with a lamb."— *Jamieson.* Park is common in Irish place-names.

PARKDÒON. 'Minigaff.' *Pairc duin,* field of the fort.

PARKMACLÙRG (*P.* Parkmaklurg). 'Minigaff.' M'Lurg's enclosure.

PARKRÒBBIN. 'Balmaclellan.' Robert's enclosure.

PARLIAMENT KNOWE.   'Minigaff.'

PÀRROCK STANE. 'Carsphairn.' A.S. *pearroc stan,* stone of the enclosure. *See under* PARK.

PÀRTON (a parish in the Stewartry) (*Inq. ad Cap.* 1607, Partoun ; *P.* Partoun). *Portán,* a landing-place, dimin. of *port.* Sometimes locally aspirated into Farton. "In the eastern part of county Clare *port* is pronounced as if written *páirt,* and this pronunciation is reflected in the names of some places on the Shannon, from Limerick to Killaloe, which are now called Parteen, signifying little landing-place."—*Joyce,* ii. 232.

PASBUERY. 'Leswalt, s.c.'

PAUPLE'S HILL. 'Penninghame.'

PEAKSTÀLLOCH. 'Port Patrick, s.c.' "*Peak* is one of the Celtic words so often met with in English place-names."—*Skeat.* —ERSE *peac*, any sharp-pointed thing + GAEL. *beic*, a point, a bill (whence E. *beak*). In France and Switzerland *Piz* is a common mountain-name.

PEAL HILL. 'Kells.' "*Pele, peyll, peill, peel, paile,* a place of strength, a fortification, properly of earth."—*Jamieson. Cf.* BR. SC. *peel tower*—A.S. *pil*, a pile, a heap; *acervus* (*Bosworth*).

PEAT BURN. 'Carsphairn.' *Peat*, turf cut in boggy places. "The true form is *beat*, as in Devonshire; the change from *b* to *p* is very unusual, but we have it again in *purse* from F. *bourse*. It was so called because used for *beeting*, *i.e.* mending the fire, from M.E. *beten*, to replenish a fire—A.S. *bétan*, to better, amend, repair, to make up a fire."—*Skeat.* —A.S. *bót*, advantage, boot + DU. *boeta*, penitence, *boeten*, to mend, kindle + ICEL. *bót, bati,* advantage, cure, *bæta*, to mend, improve + DAN. *bod*, amendment, *bóde*, to mend + SWED. *bot*, remedy, *bota*, to fine, mulct + GOTH. *bóta*, profit + O.H.G. *puoza, buoza*, G. *busse*, atonement. From the same root as E. *better.* "*Beit, bete, bet, beet*: 1. To help, to supply, to mend by making addition. *To beit the fire or beit the ingle*, to add fuel to the fire."—*Jamieson.*

PEAT HASS. 'Carsphairn.' "*Hass* is used in a general sense to signify any gap or opening."—*Jamieson.* = *Hals, hawse*, a throat, a narrow opening or defile.

PENÈILLY CAIRN. 'Balmaclellan.'

PEN HILL. 'Sorbie.' *See under* PENNY HILL.

PENKILL BURN (*P.* Poolkill b.). 'Minigaff.' *Poll cille* [killy], pool or stream of the church. It flows under the walls of Minigaff church.

PENKÌLN (*P.* Benkiln). 'Sorbie.' Probably the same as PENKILL, as there is a stream beside which stood a church, KILFILLAN.

PÈNNINGHAME (a parish in the shire) (*P.* Pennygham; *Barnbarroch*, 1576, Pennegem; *Synod of Galloway*, 1644, Penygham). A.S. *Peneg ham*, the penny land or holding. "In the western districts (of Scotland) we find the penny land also entering into topography, in the form of Pen or Penny. . . . The two systems of land measurement appear to meet in Galloway, as in Carrick we find the measure by penny lands, which gradually become less frequent as we advance eastward, where we encounter the extent by merks and pounds, with an occasional appearance of a penny land."— *Skene, Celtic Scotland*, iii. 226, 227.

PENNY HILL. 'Kirkinner.' *See under* PENNINGHAME.

PENNYMUIR. 'Borgue.' *See under* PENNINGHAME.

PENNYTOWN. 'Kells.' *See under* PENNINGHAME.

PÈNTICLE. 'Kirkinner.'

PENWHÀILL. 'Girthon.'

PENWHÌRN. 'Inch.' *Cf.* PILWHIRN, of which this is probably a corruption.

PETER'S PAPS. 'Kirkmaiden, s.c.'

PETÌLLERY HILL. 'Carsphairn.' Whatever the prefix *Pet* represents, the latter part of this name is *iolaire* [illery], an eagle. *See under* BENYELLARY.

PHALSHEÙCHAN. 'Kirkinner.' *See* FALSHEUCHAN.

PHALWHÌSTLE. 'Kirkinner.' *See* FALWHISTLE.

PHILBÀINS. 'Mochrum.' *Pholl bán*, white water.

PHILGÒWN. 'Mochrum.' *Pholl gobhain* [gowan], the smith's water. *Cf.* PALGOWN.

PHILHÀR. 'Whithorn.' *See* FALHAR.

PHILSTÀBBIN. 'Inch.'

PHILTÒWL. 'New Luce.' *Pholl tuathail* [towl], north water. *See under* DRUMTOWL.

PHILWHÌNNIE. 'Whithorn.'

PHÝSGILL (*W. P.* MSS. Fischegill). 'Glasserton.' SCAND. *fisk gil* [?], fish stream; ICEL. *fiskr* + DU. *visch* + A.S. *fisc* (whence M.E. *fisch*, E. *fish*) + DAN. and SWED. *fisk* + G. *fisch* + LAT. *piscis* + W. *pysg*, B. *pesk* + ERSE and GAEL. *iasg* (by loss of initial *p*).

PÌBBLE (*P.* Pibbil). 'Kirkmabreck.'

PICKMAW ISLAND (in Loch Doon). 'Carsphairn.' "*Pickmaw*, a bird of the gull tribe."—*Jamieson.* E. *mew*, M.E. *mawe* — A.S. *mæw* + DU. *meeuw* + ICEL. *már* + DAN. *maage* + SWED. *måke* + G. *möwe.* "All words of imitative origin, from the *mew* or cry of the bird."

PÌKEHORN (*P.* Pykhorn). 'Sorbie.' *Cf.* PEAKSTALLOCH.

PILTÀNTON BURN (*P.* Pool Tanton ; *Inq. ad Cap.* 1610, Pontantane). 'Old Luce.' *Poll,* water.

PILWHÌRN BURN. 'New Luce.' *Poll chuirn* [?] [hwirn], pool or water of the cairn. *Cf.* FALWHIRN.

PÌNFOLD. 'Port Patrick.'

PINMÌNNOCH. 'Port Patrick.' Probably corrupted from *beann meadhonach* [mennagh], mid hill. The change from *b* to *p* is contrary to rule, but *see under* PEAT ; and the Erse *beann* seems, in Galloway, to have become assimilated to the Cymric *pen,* prevalent in Strathclyde, although originally a totally different word.

PINWHÌRRIE. 'Inch.' *Beann fhoithrc* [whirry], hill of the copse. *See under* WHERRY CROFT.

PIOT FELL. 'Port Patrick.' *See* CAIRN PAT.

PIPERCROFT. 'Kirkpatrick Durham.' A frequent name near old towns, the town-piper being an ancient and universal institution.

PLAID, THE. 'Kirkmaiden.'

PLAN. 'Crossmichael.'

PLASCOW. 'Kirkgunzeon.' This word has a very Welsh character.

PLEA RIG. 'Balmaclellan.' Land about which there has been a "plea" or litigation.

PLUCKHIM'S CAIRN. 'Tungland.'

PLUMBHOLE. 'Colvend.' "*Plumb,* the noise a stone makes when plunged into a deep pool of water; people guess at a pool's depth by this plumb."—*Mactaggart.* "*Plum, plumb,* a deep pool in a river or stream."—*Jamieson.* From the idea of sounding with a *plumb,* or mass of lead ; M.E. *plumbe, plom*— F. *plumb,* lead—LAT. *plumbum,* probably cognate with GK. μόλυβος, μόλυβδος, lead ; RUSS. *olovo,* pewter, O.H.G. *pli,* G. *blei,* lead.

PLUMJÒRDAN. 'Colvend.'

PLUMJÒRDAN, THE SINKS OF. 'Kirkcowan.' "*Sink,* ground where there is superabundant moisture."—*Jamieson.* *Cf.* SYPLAND. E. *sink,* properly an intransitive verb (we have lost the transitive form *senk, sench* ; *cf. drink,* drench) ; M.E. *sinken*—A.S. *sincan*+ICEL. *sökkva*+DAN. *synke*+SWED. *sjunka* +G. *sinken*+GOTH. *sigkwan.* All from Teutonic base SANKWA, SANK, which seems a nasalised form of Aryan √SAG, to hang down. The sense of immersion is retained in the transitive form A.S. *sencan*, to cause to sink, SWED. *sänka*, DAN. *sœnke*, G. *senken*, to immerse.

PLUMJORDAN BURN.   ' Minigaff.'

PLÙNTON (*P.* Plumtoun, Plumptoun).   'Borgue.'

PÒCHRIE.   ' Mochrum.'

POCHRIEGÀVIN BURN. 'Carsphairn.' *Pochrie* is probably a corruption of the same original as *Poultry*, in Poultrybuie. *See* POLGAVIN.

POINTFOOT. 'Dalry.' Foot of the " point " or hill.

POINT OF THE SNIBE. 'Minigaff.' Another form of Snab. *See under* SNAB HILL.

POLBÀE. 'Kirkcowan.' *Poll beith* [bey], pool or stream of the birches. *Cf.* FALBAE. In Polbeith Burn, a tributary of the Irvine, the silent *th* has been restored. ERSE and GAEL. *poll*, a hole, pit, mire, water either running or stagnant, MANX *poyl*+W. *pwll*, B. *poull*, C. *pol* (whence A.S. *pól*, ME. *pol, pool*)+LAT. *palus*+GK. πηλός. Root uncertain. Enters largely into place-names, in which it indicates either a stream or a pool, in the various forms *fal, fil, ful, phal, phil, pal, pil, pol, pul*, and even *pen*.

POLCHÈSKIE BURN (*P.* Polchesky). 'Carsphairn.' *Cf.* BARCHESKIE.

POLCHÌFFER BURN.   ' Carsphairn.'

POLCÒRROCH BURN. 'Carsphairn.' *Poll carroch*, rough stream.

POLDÒRES BURN. 'Carsphairn.' *Poll doran*, stream of the otters. *Cf.* Puldouran. *See under* ALDOURAN.

POLDÙSTON BURN.   ' Minigaff.'

POLGÀVIN BURN (a tributary of the water of Deuch, near Pochriegavin). 'Carsphairn.' *Poll gamhan* [?], the calves' stream.

POLIFERRIE BURN. 'Carsphairn.' *Poll a' foithre* [?] [fwirrie], stream of the woods. *See under* WHERRY CROFT.

POLJÀRGEN BURN AND HAGS. 'Carsphairn.' *Poll deargán*, red stream.

POLMÈADOW BURN. 'Carsphairn.' *Poll madadh* [?] [madda, maddoo], stream of the dogs or wolves. *Cf.* PULMADDY and PULVADDOCH.

POLQUHÌLLIE. 'Penninghame.' *See* PALWHILLY.

POLRÒBIN BURN. 'Carsphairn.' *Cf.* PARKROBBIN.

POLSHÀG BURN (*P.* Poushaig). 'Carsphairn.' *Poll seobhac* [?] [shock], stream of the hawks. *See under* GARNSHOG.

POLSTON BURN. 'Balmaclellan.'

POLSÙIE BURN. 'Carsphairn.' *Poll subh* [?] [soo], stream of the berries, or *poll samhadh* [soo], stream of the sorrel. *See under* DRUMMIESUE. *Cf.* Inishnasoo in Armagh (written by the *Four Masters,* A.D. 1158, *Innis na subh*), Cornasoo in Monaghan, and Lisnasoo in Antrim. *Cf.* SUIE.

POLTÌE BURN. 'Carsphairn.' *Poll tighe* [?], stream of the house. *See under* DRUMATYE.

POLVÀDDOCH BURN. 'Dalry.' *Poll mhadadh* [vadda], stream of the dog or of the wolf. *Cf.* POLMEADOW and PULMADDY.

POLWÌLLIEMOUNT. 'Kirkmabreck.'

POLYMÒDIE. 'Inch.' *Poll a' madhaidh* [madda], stream of the dog. *Cf.* POLMEADOW and PULMADDY.

POOL NESS. 'Girthon.'

PORTACRÈE. 'Kirkmaiden, s.c.'

PORTACLEÀRYS. 'Kirkcolm, s.c.' *Port a' clérech,* port or landing of the clergy. *See under* BARNEYCLEARY. ERSE *port,* a harbour, fort, bank (*Corm. Tr.,* p. 133); a ferry (*O'Reilly*). Closely akin to, if not derived from, LAT. *portus,* a harbour—*porta,* a gate—GK. πόρος, a ford, a way, from √ PAR, to pass through, ford, which is the root of E. *fare, ford, far, ferry.*

PORT ALLAN. 'Whithorn, s.c.'

PORTAMÀGGIE. 'Port Patrick, s.c.'

PORTANKÌL. 'Kirkmaiden, s.c.' *Portán cille* [killy], the little harbour of the church or cell. *Portán,* dimin. of *port* (*cf.* PARTON). *See under* KILCORMACK.

PORTAVÀDDIE. 'Kirkmaiden' (*twice*), 'Port Patrick, s.c.' *Port a' bhada* [vadda], port of the boat; ERSE *bád* (*O'Reilly*); GAEL. *báta*+W. *bad*+A.S. *bát* (whence M.E. *boot,* E. *boat*)+ICEL. *bátr* +SWED. *båt*+DU. *boot*+RUSS. *bot'.* Probably connected with ERSE and GAEL. *bat, bata,* a staff, cudgel, a *bat.*

PORTBÈG. 'Kirkcolm,' 'Leswalt, s.c.' *Port beag,* little port.

PORTBRÌAR (close to the ruined chapel at the Isle of Whithorn). 'Whithorn, s.c.' *Port brathair* [braher], landing-place or haven of the friars. *See under* ALTIBRAIR.

PORT DONNEL. 'Colvend, s.c.' *Port Domhnuill*, Donnel's port.

PORTDÒWN (*P.* Port Doun). 'Kirkmaiden, s.c.' *Port duin*, port of the fort. *Cf.* Portadown in Ireland.

PORTENCÀLZIE (*Inq. ad Cap.* 1600, Portincalzie, *P.* Portincailly). 'Kirkcolm, s.c.' *Portán cailleach*, port of the nuns. It is a farm situated on Lady Bay, which is a literal translation of Portencalzie.

PORTENCÒRKRIE (*P.* Portinkorkry). 'Kirkmaiden, s.c.' *Portán corcra*, red port. Named from the ruddy granite which crops out here. *See under* BARNCORKRIE.

PÒRTERBELLY. 'Kirkgunzeon.' The latter part of the word is *baile*, a townland. *Cf.* SHAMBELLIE.

PORTERLOOP. 'Balmaclellan.'

PORT GARVÌLLAN (*P.* Port Garvellan). 'Kirkcolm, s.c.' *See under* GARVELLAN. There is a place called Rough Isle close by.

PORT GÒWER. 'Stoneykirk, s.c.' *Port gobhar*, port of the goats or horses. *See under* ALGOWER.

PORT HENRY. 'Whithorn, s.c.' *Port an righ* [?], king's port. *Cf.* PORTREE.

PORT KALE (*P.* Port Kyoch). 'Port Patrick, s.c.' *Port caol* [?] [keel], narrow port. *See under* CARSKEEL.

PORT KÈNAN. 'Kirkmaiden, s.c.' *Port Caenain* [Keenan], Keenan's port [?]. Keenan still survives as a surname in Galloway. It is from *caen* [keen], beautiful.

PORT LEEN. 'Kirkcolm, s.c.' *Port lín* [leen], port of the flax; where flax was landed or steeped. *Cf.* Port Leen in Ireland, also Coolaleen, Crockaleen, and Gortaleen. O. ERSE *lín*, flax. The word is the same in A.S. and M.E. (E. *linen* being the adj. form, as *woollen* from *wool*) — LAT. *linum*, flax + GK. λίνον. To " line " clothes is to put *lin* or *linen* inside them.

PORTLENNIE. 'Kirkmaiden, s.c.'

PORTLÌNG. 'Colvend, s.c.' *Port luing* [ling], port of the ship. *Cf.* Port-na-luing in Tyree. *See under* LONGFORT.

PORTLÒNG. 'Kirkcolm, s.c.' *Port long*, port of the ships. *See under* LONGFORT.

PORTMÀRK.   'Carsphairn.'

PORT MARY. 'Rerwick.' Formerly Nether Rerwick, where Queen Mary embarked in her flight from the battle of Langside.

PORT MONA (*P.* Port-na-mony-a-koane). 'Kirkmaiden.' *Port na monadh a' coin,* port of the dog's moor. *Pont* preserves the full original name. *Cu,* gen. *coin,* a dog + W. *ci,* pl. *cwn* + LAT. *canis* + GK. κυών, gen. κυνός + SKT. *cuan,* from an Aryan base KWAN, dog, whence we have a TEUTONIC type HUN-DA, extended from HUN = HWAN, giving E. *hound* – A.S. *hund* + DU. *hond* + ICEL. *hundr* + DAN. and SWED. *hund* + G. *hund* + GOTH. *hunds.*

PORT MORA (*P.* Moiran's Poirt). 'Port Patrick.' M'Morran is a surname in Galloway formed from *mòr,* great.

PORTMÒRE (*P.* Poirt moir). 'Kirkcolm, s.c.' *Port mór,* great harbour.

PORT MUDDLE.   'Kirkcudbright, s.c.'

PORT MULLIN (*P.* Port Moulin). 'Kirkcolm, s.c.' *Port muileain* [meulan], port of the mill. *Cf.* Millport in Cumbrae.

PORTNÀUGHAN.   'Kirkcolm.'

PORTNÀUCHTRY. 'Kirkcolm, s.c.' *Portán Ochtraidh* [Oughtrie], Uthred's port.

PORTNÈSSOCK (*P.* Port Nustak). 'Kirkmaiden.' *Cf.* CARSE-NESTOCK. In the "Book of the Nativity of Saint Cuthbert, taken and translated from the Irish," a manuscript of the fourteenth century, in the Diocesan Library at York, and printed by the Surtees Club, it is stated that the boy Cuthbert, accompanied by his mother, landed in "Galweia, in that region called Rennii, in the harbour of Rintsnoc." Mr. Skene remarks that this is no doubt Port Patrick, in the Rhinns of Galloway; but it is more likely that it was Port Nessock, an equally good landing-place in those days, farther south on the same coast.

PORTOBEAGLE.   'Colvend, s.c.'

PORTOWÀRREN. 'Colvend, s.c.' *Port a' garrain* [?], port of the horse. *See under* GLENGARREN ; *cf.* PORT WHAPPLE.

PORT PATRICK (a sea-port giving name to a parish in the shire) (*P.* Port Fatrick ; *Inq. ad Cap.* 1646, *Portus olim nuncupatus* Portpatrick, *nunc* Portmontgomerie). 'Port Patrick.' *Port Padric,* (St.) Patrick's port.

PORTREE. ' Port Patrick, s.c.'   *Port righ* [ree], the king's port.

PORT RIG (on Lochinvar).   ' Dalry.'   The " rig " or ridge of the landing-place or haven.

PORT SAND.   ' Kirkcolm, s.c.'

PORTSLÒGAN (*P*. Poirtslogan).   ' Leswalt.'

PORTWHÀPPLE.   ' Mochrum, s.c.', ' Sorbie, s.c.'   *Port chapuil* [hwappill], port of the horse.   *See under* BARHAPPLE.

PORTYÈRROCK (*IV. P.* MSS. Portcarryk, Pottarrak ;   *Inq. ad Cap.* 1647, Porterack).   ' Whithorn, s.c.'   *Port dhearg* [hyarrig], red port.   But the spelling in the Whithorn Priory Rental suggests *port carric*, port of the sea-crag.

POTÒMARAS (a pool in the Minnick).   ' Minigaff.'

POULTRIEBÙIE BURN.   ' Carsphairn.'   *Cf.* POCHRIEGAVIN.

POUNDLAND.   ' Parton.'   Land of the annual value of a pound Scots = 13d. sterling.

POW.   ' New Abbey.'   A sluggish stream.   " Pow, a slow-moving rivulet in flat lands."—*Jamieson.*

POWBRADE.   ' Girthon.'   *Poll braghaid*, stream of the gulley. *See under* BRADOCK.

POWMÒRIN BURN.   ' New Abbey.'

POWTAN.   ' Minigaff.'

PÒWTON (*W. P.* MSS. Powtoun).   ' Sorbie.'   The *tún* or dwelling beside the *pow* or sluggish stream.   *See under* POW.

PREACHING HOWE.   ' Minigaff,' ' Whithorn.'   The hollow of the preaching.   The place of this name in Minigaff is in the hill district, and probably dates from Covenanting times, that in Whithorn is not far from the Priory.

PRESTON (*P*. Prestoun).   ' Colvend.'   A.S. *preost tún*, priest's dwelling.

PRÈSTRIE (*P*. Prestry ;   *IV. P.* MSS. Prestore).   ' Whithorn.' *Priest-ery*, land of the priests.   Part of the old Priory lands of Whithorn.   — A.S. *preóst* (whence M.E. *preost, preest*, E. *priest*—LAT. *presbyter* (whence contracted O.F. *prestre*, F. *prêtre*)) — GK. πρεσβύτερος, comparative of πρέσβυς (akin to LAT. *priscus*, old), DORIC πρέσγος.   The syllable πρις-, *pris-* = *prius*, former, neuter of *prior*, which reappears later as an ecclesiastical title.

PRIESTLANDS.   ' Troqueer.'   The possession of the priests.

PULARÝAN [*pron.* Pullareean] (*P.* Poldenrian ; *Inq. ad Cap.* 1600, Polrean). 'Inch.'

PULBAE (a stream running past Stronbae) (*P.* Phallbe). 'Minigaff.' *See under* FALBAE *and* POLBAE.

PULCÀIGRIE BURN. 'Kells.' *Poll coigriche,* stream of the boundary, or *coigricheach,* of the strangers ; literally those from over the boundary. *See under* DRUMCAGERIE.

PULCÀRDIE BURN. 'Kells.' *Poll cearda* [carda], stream of the forge or workshop. *See under* CAIRDIE WIEL.

PULCRÈE (*Inq. ad Cap.* 1604, Polcrie, Pollincrie ; *P.* Poolkree b.). 'Anwoth.' *Poll crìche* [?] [creeghe], stream of the boundary. *See under* CREE.

PULDÒURAN. 'Glasserton.' *Poll doran,* pool of the otters. *See under* ALDOURAN.

PULDÒW BURN. 'Kells.' *Poll dubh* [dooh], black stream. *Cf.* PULLOW ; also Powduff Burn in Dalry parish, Ayrshire.

PULDRÒIT. 'Kirkcudbright.' *Poll droichit,* bridge pool. Just below Tungland Bridge. *See under* BARDROCHWOOD.

PULFÈRN BURN. 'Girthon.' *Poll fearn* [farn], stream of the alders. *See under* BALFERN.

PULGÀNNY BURN. 'Penninghame.' *Poll gaineach,* sandy stream. *See under* GANNOCH. *Cf.* Pollaginnive in Fermanagh (*poll a' gaineaimh*).

PULGÀP BURN (*P.* Poolghaip b., Biern of Altyghaip). 'Minigaff.' *Cf.* DALNAGAP.

PULGÒWAN BURN. 'Minigaff.' *See under* PALGOWN.

PULHÀRE BURN. 'Kirkmaiden.' *See under* FALHAR.

PULHARROW BURN. 'Kells.' *Poll charrach* [harragh], rough stream.

PULHÀTCHIE BURN (*P.* Poolhatchie).   'New Luce.'

PULHÀY BURN. 'Carsphairn.' *Poll chaedhe* [haye], stream of the swamp. *See under* CULKAE.

PULHÒWAN BURN. 'Minigaff.' *Poll chabhan* [?] [havvan, howan], stream of the hollow (*see under* CAVAN), or perhaps an aspirated form of Pulgowan, *q.v.*

PULLÀUCH BURN.   'Minigaff.'

PULLHAMDÒWN. 'Kirkinner.' *Poll an duin* [?], stream of the fort.

PULLÒSH SIKES. 'Dalry.' "*Sike, syik, syk.* 1. A rill; 2. a marshy bottom with a stream in it."—*Jamieson.* Perhaps the same as A.S. *sic, sich,* a furrow, gutter, watercourse (*Bosworth*), which appears akin to L. *sulcus;* or else it may be connected with *suck* and *soak.*

PULLÒW BURN. 'Minigaff.' *Poll dhubh* [oo, ow], black stream. Aspirated form of Puldow, *q.v.*

PULMÀDDY BURN (*Inq. ad Cap.* 1608, Polvadache ; *P.* Polmady). 'Carsphairn.' *See under* POLMEADOW. The spelling quoted from the *Inquisitions* shows the aspirated form.

PULMULLOCH BURN. 'Dalry.'

PULNABRÌCK. 'Minigaff.' *Poll na breac* [brack], stream of the trouts. *See under* ALTIBRICK.

PULNÀCHIE. 'Balmaghie.' *See under* PALNACKIE.

PULNAGÀSHEL (flows past Craigengashel). 'Minigaff.' *Poll na gcaiseail* [gashel], stream of the fort or castle. *See under* AUCHENGASHEL.

PULNÀSKY BURN or POLNASKIE. 'Mochrum.' *Poll n-easga* [naska], stream of the eels. *Cf.* Pollanaskin in Mayo. Possibly, however, a corruption of Polnisky, *q.v. Easga* or *easgán,* an eel, probably akin to *iasg,* a fish. *See under* PHYSGIL.

PULNÈE (*P.* Poolny). 'Minigaff.' *See under* PALNEE.

PULNÌSKY BURN (*P.* Poolneisky B.). 'Minigaff.' *Poll an uisge* [isky], water hole, stream of water. *Cf.* Poulaniska in Ireland. *Cf.* WHISKEY BURN.

PULRÀN. 'Minigaff.' *Poll rathain* [rahan], stream of the ferny place (*filicetum*). There are many places in Ireland called Rahan, Rahin, and Rahans. Rahin, a parish in King's County, is written *Rathain* by the *Four Masters* (631), and so is Rahan in Donegal (1524). *Cf.* Pollrane in Wexford, Pollranny in Roscommon and Mayo, and Pollnaranny in Donegal. *See under* BLAWRAINIE.

PULSKÀIG. 'Carsphairn.' *Poll sceach,* stream of the hawthorns. *See under* AUCHENSKEOCH.

PULTADÌE [*pron.* Pultadee] BURN (*P.* Poolteduy, Poltaduy). 'New Luce.'

PULTÀRSON. 'Carsphairn,' 'New Abbey.' *Poll tarsuinn,* the cross water. *See under* BALTERSAN.

S

PULTAYÀN BURN.   ' Kirkcowan.'

PULWHÀNITY. ' Carsphairn.' *Cf.* KILQUHANITY.

PULWHÀT.   ' Carsphairn,' ' Kirkmabreck.'   *Poll chat*, pool or
      stream of the wild cats.

PULWHÌNRICK BURN (*P.* Poolwhynrick B.).   ' Kirkmaiden.'

PULWHÌRRAN.   ' Borgue.'

PYATTHORN. ' Crossmichael.' The magpie's thorn.   " *Pyat, pyot.*
      The magpie."—*Jamieson.*

QUAHÈAD [*pron.* Quaw-heed]. ' Kirkgunzeon.' Head of the
      " quaw " or quagmire. " *Quaw* : 1. A quagmire, a name
      given in Galloway to an old pit grown over with earth, grass,
      etc., which yields under one, but in which one does not sink.
      2. A hole whence peats have been dug."—*Jamieson.*

QUAKER NOOK.   ' Kirkcolm.'

QUAKIN' ASH WIEL. ' Minigaff.' A pool in the Minnick, beside
      which grow aspens. BR. SC. *quakin' ash*, aspen.

QUANTAN'S HILL. ' Carsphairn.' *Cointin* [?], a dispute, disputed
      land. *Cf.* Quintinmanus in Ireland. *Cf.* also ACQUAINTANCE
      HILL.

QUARREL END (a stony hill-side). ' Carsphairn.' The quarry-
      like hill-end. " *Quarrel*, a stone quarry."—*Jamieson.* The
      BR. SC. form seems to be a variation of M.E. *quarrere, quarrer*
      — O. F. *quarriere*, F. *carrière* — LOW LAT. *quadraria*, a place for
      getting squared stones — LAT. *quadrare* — LAT. *quadrus*, square.

QUARREL KNOWE. ' Balmaclellan.' The quarry knoll.

QUARTER. ' New Luce,' ' Tungland.' A division of land =
      ERSE *cethramhadh* [carroo]. *Cf.* CARHOWE.

QUARTERCAKE.   ' Rerwick.'

QUÌNTIN. ' Mochrum.' *Cointin*, a dispute.

QUINTINÈSPIE (*Inq. ad Cap.* 1611, Tuncanespeik (*misprint*); *P.*
      Culdanespick ; *Charter* 1690, Cultingspie, Cultcinspie).
      ' Balmaghie.' *Cointin* [?] *espiog* [espig], the bishop's quarrel.
      The present form of the name suggests this explanation,
      which is illustrated by a passage in *Fordun*, in which he
      describes William the Lion leading an army into Galloway
      in 1174 to quell the revolt of Uchtred and Gilbert, sons of
      Fergus ; and " when the Gallwegians came to meet him

under Gilbert, some Scottish bishops and earls stepped in between them, and through their mediation they were reconciled ; the Gallwegians paying a sum of money and giving hostages."—*Annalia*, xi. Owing to mis-spellings in the charters the original name is doubtful, but some forms appear intended for *coillte* [kilty] *an espig*, the bishop's woods. *See under* ERNESPIE.

RAEBERRY. 'Kirkcudbright.' *Cf.* Roeborough in Devonshire.

RÀINTON (*P.* Ramtoun). 'Girthon.'

RAMP HOLES. 'Stoneykirk, s.c.' Boisterous holes, where the sea churns and surges. "*Ramp*, adj. : 1. Riotous. 2. Vehement, violent."—*Jamieson*.

RÀMSEY. 'Whithorn, s.c.' ICEL. *ey*, an island + DAN. and SWED. *ö* + A.S. *íg, ieg*, all from an original Teutonic form AHWIA, belonging to water, or a place in water — AHWA, water, A.S. *ea*, cognate to LAT. *aqua*. *Ey* constantly appears in the end of place-names, *e.g.* Batters-ea, Roms-ey, Aldern-ey, and the A.S. *íg* forms the first syllable of "island" (*Skeat*).

RAMSHÀW WOOD. 'Buittle.' BR. SC. *shaw*, a wood. *See under* SHAW BRAE.

RÀNKIN. 'Kirkinner.'

RASCÀRREL [*pron.* Roscarrel]. 'Rerwick.' *Ros*, a wood or headland.

RÀSHNOCH. 'Mochrum.' *Rósnach*, a place of wild roses.

RÀTTRA (*P.* Rotrow). 'Borgue.' *Rath tóruidhe* [?] [rah tory], fort of the hunter or outlaw, or *rath Tuira* [tirrie], Terry's fort. *Cf.* Ratory in Tyrone. *See under* CRAIGTERRA and DALTORAE.

RÀVENSTONE [*pron.* Raimstun] (*P.* Remistoun ; *IV. P.* MSS. Lochtoun ; *Inq. ad Cap.* 1585, Remistoun, *alias* Lochtoune ; 1620, Clochtoun, *alias* Remistoun). 'Glasserton.' There are considerable ruins on a large crannog here, whence the name Lochtoun.

RAWER HILL. 'Leswalt.' Perhaps the last syllable of STRANRAER, which is not far off, is connected with this name. *Cf.* CLACHRAWER and RINGREER.

REDBANK.   'Troqueer.'

REDBRAE. 'Wigtown,' etc.   *Cf.* BARJARG, BARYERROCK, and DRUMJARGON.

RED BURN, THE. 'Old Luce.'   *Cf.* POLJARGEN.

REDCASTLE (*P.* Ridcastell).   'Urr.'

RED CLEUGH (near POLJARGEN, *q. v.*).   'Carsphairn.'

REDFIELD.   'Twynholm.'

RED GLEN. 'Minigaff.'   *Cf.* GLENJORIE.

RED NICK. 'Twynholm.'   *Cf.* BALLOCHJARGON.

RÈGLAND (*P.* Ruyglann).   'Dalry.'

REIFER PARK.   'Sorbie.'

REPHÀD. 'Inch.' *Réidh* [ray] *fada*, long plain or field. "*Ré*, a field" (*O'Don. Suppl.*), from *réidh*, smooth. *Cf.* Reafadda in Ireland. *Joyce* assigns the meaning of "mountain-flat," but there seems to be no reason for its general limitation to hilly places.

RÈRWICK (a parish in the Stewartry) (*Barnbarroch*, 1562, Rerryk; *Inq. ad Cap.* 1605, Rerik).

RHINNS, THE (the western division of Wigtownshire). *Rinn*, a point, promontory, or headland, E. plur. added. Reference is made in the name to the promontories of Mull of Galloway, Corsewall Point, etc., which, with the long necks connecting them, form this part of the shire. " O'Brien says in his Dictionary :—' It would take up more than a whole sheet to mention all the neck-lands of Ireland whose names begin with this word *Rinn*.' It is found pretty extensively in the forms Rin, Rinn, Reen, Rine, and Ring, and these constitute or begin about 170 townlands."—*Joyce*, i. 40. O. ERSE *rind, rinn*, GAEL. *roinn*, a point, a peninsula ; a share or division, especially of land. The term Run-rig, a primitive mode of agrarian tenure, still surviving in the Highlands and Islands, is a corruption of *roinn-ruith*, or division running. *Ruith* [righ], a running, a course, has taken the form of the Teutonic *rig*, a ridge, and, by a singular accident, *roinn*, a division, has assumed the form of *run*, the English translation of *ruith* (*Report of Crofters' Commission* 1884, Appendix A., p. 451).

RHONE HILL AND PARK (*P.* Ron). 'Crossmichael.' "*Roan*, A congeries of brushwood, Dumfries."—*Jamieson.*

RHÒNEHOUSE (a village). 'Kelton.'

RHONG, THE (a long embankment running out from the Moat of Ballochadee). 'Kirkcowan.' *Rinn* or *roinn*, a point.

RHYNCHEWAIG. 'Kirkcolm.' The name given by *Pont* to the Scaur, a long point of land running into Loch Ryan.

RÌCHORN (*Inq. ad Cap.* 1623, Rithorne; *P.* Richernn; MS. 1527, Raeheren). 'Urr.' A.S. *redd œrn*, red house. *Cf.* WHITHORN.

RIDDING'S HILL. 'Kirkmabreck.'

RIDER'S KNOWE AND RIG. 'Carsphairn.'

RIGG BAY. 'Sorbie.'

RIGGINS HILL. 'Twynholm.' "*Rigging, riggin.* 1. The back. 2. The ridge of a house. 3. A small ridge or rising in ground."—*Jamieson.* Deriv. of *rig* — A.S. *hric*, the back.

RIGMÀY. 'Kirkcowan.'

RIG OF DIVOTS. 'Kells.' Ridge of the sods. *See under* DIVOT HILL.

RIG OF MOAK. 'Carsphairn.'

RIG OF THE JÀRKNESS. 'Minigaff.'

RIG OF WELLEES. 'Kells.' Ridge of the boggy springs. "*Well-ey, wallee*; that part of a quagmire in which there is a spring." —*Jamieson.* The eye of the well.

RING (*P.* Ring). 'Kirkcowan' (*twice*), 'New Luce,' 'Stoneykirk.' *Rinn, roinn*, a point or division of land. *See under* RHINNS.

RÌNGAN. 'Sorbie.' *Rinndn*, small point or division. *Cf.* Rinneen in Galway, Clare, and Kerry.

RINGANWHÈY. 'Crossmichael.' *Rinn an chaeidhe* [hay], point of the quagmire. *See under* CULKAE.

RINGBÀIN. 'Balmaclellan.' *Rinn bán*, white point. *Cf.* Ringbane and Ringbaun in Ireland.

RING BURN. 'Rerwick.'

RINGDÒO. 'Old Luce.' *Rinn dubh* [doo], black point. A point in the sandhills at the head of Luce Bay, where sea-ware collects and makes it darker than the rest. The name also occurs in Mochrum parish.

RINGDÒO POINT. 'Anwoth.' *See under* RINGDOO.

RINGFERSON (a point in Loch Ken). 'Kells.' *Rinn farsaing,* wide point.

RINGHEÈL. 'Mochrum,' 'Penninghame.' *Rinn chael* [heel], narrow point or division. *See under* CARSKEEL.

RINGHILL.　'Mochrum.'

RINGIELÀWN. 'Mochrum.' *Rinn na leamhán* [?] [lavan, lawn], point of the elms. Also called the Soldier's Holm, at the head of Loch Trool, where it is said that Lord Essex's men, slaughtered in combat by Robert the Bruce's forces, were buried.

RINGIEMÒW. 'Kirkmabreck.' *Rinn na mbo* [moe], point of the cows.

RINGKÌLNS.　'Stoneykirk.'

RINGLÈES. 'Inch.' *Rinn liath* [lee], grey point.

RINGÒUR. 'Kells.' *Rinn odhar* [owr], grey point, or *rinn gobhar* [gower], point of the goats.

RINGQUHÌLL [*pron.* -hwill]. 'Kirkcowan.' *Rinn chuill* [hwill], point of the hazel.

RINGRÈEL. 'Kirkcowan.' *Rinn ráil* [?], point of the oaks. *Ráil, rál,* an oak-tree. *O'Reilly ; Joyce,* i. 505.

RINGRÈER. 'Mochrum.' *Rinn reamhar* [rawer], thick, broad point, the antithesis of RINGHEEL. *Cf.* Reenrour, a common name in Cork and Kerry. "*Reamhar,* or in old Irish *remor,* is a word which is very extensively employed in the formation of names. It means literally gross or fat ; and locally it is applied to objects gross or thick in shape, principally hills and rocks. It is pronounced differently in different parts of the country. In the south they sound it *rour.* . . . . As we go north the pronunciation changes ; sometimes it becomes *rawer,* as in Dunbunrawer in Tyrone, the fort of the thick *bun* or hill-base. Elsewhere in the north, as well as in the west, we find the *mh* represented by *v.*"—*Joyce,* ii. 419. GAEL. *ramhar* [raver].

RINGRÈOCH (a point in Loch Dungeon). 'Kells.' *Rinn riabhach* [reeagh], grey point. *Cf.* Ringreagh in Down.

RINGSÀLLOCH (an islet in the Dee). 'Minigaff.' *Rinn saileach,* point of the willows. *See under* BARNSALLIE.

RINGS, THE. 'Mochrum.' *See under* RHINNS.

RINGÙINEA (*P.* Ringeny). 'Stoneykirk.' *Rinn Cinaeidh* [kinny], Kenneth's point or portion of land.

RINGVÌNACHAN. 'Stoneykirk, s.c.'

RINGWHÈRRY. 'Mochrum.' *Rinn fhoithre* [hwirrie], point or division of the copse. *See under* WHERRY CROFT.

RISK. 'Minigaff.' *Riasc* [reesk], a morass (*Cormac Tr.*, p. 147). "There are twenty-two townlands scattered through the four provinces (of Ireland) called Riesk, Reisk, Risk and Reask."— *Joyce*, i. 463. *Cf.* RUSCO. *Riasc*, marsh, rushy ground; perhaps conn. with A.S. *risce*, *resce*, a rush (whence M.E. *rusche*, *rische*, *resche*, E. *rush*) + LOW G. *rusk*, *risch*, DU. and G. *rusch*, rush, reed; perhaps + LAT. *ruscus*, butcher's broom. The word exists in BR. SC. "*Riskish lan*,' land of a wet and boggy nature."—*M'Taggart*. "*Reesk*, . . . A marshy place, Angus."—*Jamieson*.

RÌSPAIN (*P.*Rispin; *Whithorn Priory Rental, circ.* 1550, Respein). 'Whithorn.' The site of the only Roman camp known in Wigtownshire. It is also called ROSS'S BRAE.

ROAN. 'Kirkmabreck.' *See under* RHONE.

ROAN HILL. 'Balmaclellan.' *See under* RHONE.

ROARING CLEUGH. 'Carsphairn.' Named from the sound of the stream in the "cleugh" or ravine.

ROCK M'GIBBON. 'Inch.'

ROLLAND HILL. 'Penninghame.'

RÒSSEN HILL. 'Twynholm.' *Rosán*, dimin. of *ros*, a wood. *Cf.* Rossan and Roshin in Ireland. *See under* ROSS.

ROSS HILL. 'Kells.' *Ros*, a wood. *See under* ROSS.

ROSS, THE (*P.* Ross Yl.). 'Borgue, s.c.' "*Ros*, a wood, a promontory."—*O'Don. Suppl.* In this case it means a promontory, and in others the meaning must be decided according to the nature of the locality.

RÒTCHELL. 'Troqueer.'

RÒUCHAN [*pron.* Rooghan] (*P.* Rouchan; *W. P.* MSS. Rochane; *Inq. ad Cap.* 1600, Rowchan). 'Glasserton.' *Ruadhán* [roohan], ruddiness, reddish land. *Cf.* Rouhan and Rooghaun in several parts of Ireland.

ROUGH GIBB [*g* hard]. 'Kirkcowan,' 'Wigtown.' *See under* GIBB.

ROUGH ISLAND (in Loch Urr). 'Urr.' *Cf.* GARVELLAN.

ROUGH ISLE. 'Kirkcolm,' 'Minigaff.' *Cf.* GARVELLAN.

RÒUGHTREE.   'Kirkpatrick Irongray.'

ROUTING BRIDGE. 'Kirkpatrick Irongray.' Roaring bridge, from
the noise of the water. —"*Rout, rowt.* 1. To bellow. 2.
To make a loud noise. 3. To snore."—*Jamieson.*

ROW OF DOURIE (a point of shingle on the coast). 'Mochrum.'
GAEL. "*Rudha* or *rubha* [rooa], a point of land in the sea, a
promontory."—*Macalpine. Cf.* CRAIGROW. —"*Rubha,* signifying a point of land, is much more frequent in Scottish than
in Irish topography."—*Reeves's Adamnan,* p. 430, *note.*

ROYS (a shoulder of Cairnsgarroch).   'Carsphairn.'

RÒYSTON.   'Twynholm.'

RÙDDOCH HILL. 'Leswalt.' *Cf.* MOSS RODDOCH.

RUE, KNOWES OF THE. 'Kirkcowan.' *See under* ROW.

RUMMLEKIRN. 'Borgue, s.c.' Rumbling churn. —"*Rummlekirns,*
gullets on wild rocky shores, scooped out by the hand of
nature; when the tide flows into them in a storm they make
an awful rumbling noise; in them are the surges churned."—
Mactaggart.

RÙMPLES HILL. 'Parton.' A corruption, probably, of Dalrymple's
Hill; Dalrymple being usually pronounced in the district
D'rumple.

RÙSCO (*P.* Rusko). 'Girthon.' *Riascach,* boggy, marshy. Deriv. of
riasc. See under RISK. *Cf.* Ruscoe in Yorkshire [*pron.* Roosca].

RUSHY HILL. 'Twynholm.' *Cf.* KNOCKGILSIE.

RUSHY PARK. 'Minigaff.' *Cf.* AUCHENGILSHIE.

RYDALE.   'Troqueer.'

RYES.   'Colvend.'

ST. COLUMB'S WELL. 'Kirkcolm.' Probably the original
cross well, now CORSEWALL.

ST. GLASSEN'S WELL. 'Rerwick.' Of St. Glascianus nothing is
known, save that he is commemorated as confessor and bishop.
Kinglassie or Kinglassin parish, near Kirkcaldy, where there
is a St. Glass's Well, and Kilmaglas in Argyllshire, are dedications to the same saint.

ST. JARDAN'S or ST. QUERDON'S WELL.   'Troqueer.'

ST. MARY'S WELL (close to KILMORIE, *q.v.*).　　　'Kirkcolm.'

ST. MEDAN'S CO (*P.* Maidin's Coave).　'Kirkmaiden.'　*See under*
KIRKMAIDEN.

ST. NINIAN'S CAVE.　'Glasserton, s.c.'　The occasional retreat of
St. Ninian in the early part of fifth century.　For a description of the very interesting remains discovered here in
1884, see *Coll. A. G. A. A.*, vol. v.

ST. NINIAN'S WELL.

ST. PATRICK'S WELL.　'Kirkpatrick Durham.'　*See under* KIL-
PATRICK.

ST. RINGAN'S WELL.　'Kelton.'　Another form of St. Ninian's
name.

SÀLQUHARIE [*pron.* Sawlhrie] (*P.* Salachari).　　　'Kirkcolm.'

SALTER'S MOSS.　　　'Rerwick.'

SAMARIA.　　　'Mochrum.'

SANDFORD.　'New Abbey.'　Sandy road or ford.

SANDHEAD.　'Stoneykirk.'　Head or end of the sandhills.　*Cf.*
GENOCH (at the other end).　*See under* GANNOCH.

SANDMILL.　'Stoneykirk.'　A mill among the sandhills.

SANDYMORE CAIRN.　　　'Minigaff.'

SÀNNOCH.　　　'Kells.'

SAUCH GUTTER.　'Carsphairn.'　Marsh of the willows.　BR. SC.
sauch, a willow —A.S. *salh, salig*, a willow.　"*Gutter*, a mire."
—*Jamieson.*　M.E. *gotere* — O. F. *gutiere, goutiere*, a gutter — O. F.
gote, goute (F. *goutte*), a drop — LAT. *gutta*, a drop.

SAULSEAT (*P.* Sauls Seatt).　'Inch.'　Eccles. gloss, *sedes animarum*,
seat of souls, but of doubtful origin.　*Cf.* A.S. "*sawl-sceat*, soul
shot, money paid at death for the good of the deceased's
soul" (*Bosworth*).　"Ærest him to saul sceate he becwæð
into Xr̄es crycan þæt land," *i.e.* "first, for the redemption of
his soul, he bequeaths to Christ's Church that land."—
Alfric's Testament.

SCAB CRAIGS.　　　'Minigaff.'

SCABBY'S LOUP.　　　'Leswalt, s.c.'

SCÀLLOCH (a hill of 800 feet).　'Carsphairn.'　*Sceilig* [skellig], a
rock.　*See under* BALSCALLOCH.

SCAR. 'Kirkpatrick Irongray.' A rock or cliff. M.E. *scarre, skerry*—ICEL. *sker* + DAN. *skiær*, SWED. *skär* + ERSE *sceir* — √SKAR, to cut, to shear, whence A.S. *sceran*, pt. t. *scær* + DU. *scheren* + ICEL. *skera* + DAN. *skære* + G. *scheren* + GK. κείρειν (for σκείρειν) + LAT. *curtus*, E. short. Allied words in E. are *scare, scarf, scarify, scrip, scrap, scrape, share, sheer, sherd, shred, sharp, shore, short, score* (*Skeat*). *Cf.* Scar in many parts of Ireland.

SCAR HILL.   'Anwoth,' 'Rerwick.'

SCAUR, THE. 'Colvend,' 'Kirkcolm.' *See under* SCAR and RHYN-CHEWAIG.

SCAURS, THE (two isolated rocks in Luce Bay). *See under* SCAR.

SCRÀBBA or SCRÀBBIE. 'Glasserton,' 'Mochrum.' *Scrath* [scrah] *bo*, cow's turf, cow's grass. *Cf.* Scrabo in Ireland.

SCRÀNGIE.   'Kirkmaiden, s.c.'

SCRÀNNAGH. 'Old Luce.' Probably another form of STRONACH, *q.v.*

SCREEL, HILL AND GLEN OF (*P.* Hill of Skyill).   'Kelton.'

SCREEN, THE. 'Whithorn.' A reef of rocks protecting the Isle Harbour.

SCROGGIE HALL. 'Balmaclellan.' "*Scrog*, a stunted bush, *scroggie*, abounding with stunted bushes."—*Jamieson.* M.E. *scroggy*, covered with underwood, or straggling bushes (*Skeat*), E. *scraggy*, lean, rough — SWED. dial. *skraka*, a great dry tree, also metaphorically, a long, lean man, *skrokk*, anything wrinkled or deformed + NORWEG. *skrokken*, p. p. of *skrekken*, to shrink, allied to E. *shrink, scrub, shrub.* *Cf.* Scroggs, a valley in the chalk near Basingstoke.

SCROGGIE HILL. 'Buittle.' Scrub-covered hill. *See under* SCROGGIE HALL.

SCUTCHING STOCK. 'Kirkmaiden, s.c.' The frame, post, or anything fixed or "stuck" for scutching flax. *Scutch*, to dress flax = *scotch* + NORW. *skoka, skuku*, a swingle for beating flax +SWED. *skäcka, skäkta*, to beat flax (*Skeat*).

SEAT HILL. 'Inch.' *Cf.* KNOCKENSEE.

SEESIDE (not near the sea). 'Terregles.' *Suidhe* [see], a seat or residence. *Cf.* Seagoe in Armagh (*suidhe gobha*), Seapatrick in Down (*suidhe Padruic*), Seadavog in Cavan, etc. *See under* KNOCKENSEE.

SEG HILL. 'Balmaclellan.' Hill of the flags. "*Seg*, the yellow flower-de-luce."—*Jamieson.* —A.S. *secg*, E. *sedge*. *See under* DERNACISSOCK.

SEGGY NEUK. 'Anwoth.' Flaggy corner.

SÈNWICK (formerly a parish) (*P.* Sannick; *Charter of David II.*, Sanaigh; MS. 1527, Sanak). 'Kirkcudbright.' The sandy bay, or the village on the sand. A.S. "*sand-wic, sond-wic,* Sandwich in Kent."—*Bosworth.*

SÈVERAL. 'Inch,' 'Kirkmaiden,' etc. Separate land. "*Severale,* applied to landed property as possessed distinctly from that of others, or contrasted with a common."—*Jamieson.* —O.F. *several* — LAT. *separalis* — LAT. *se*, apart, *parare*, to provide.

SHÀDDOCK (*P.* Schedack; *Inq. ad Cap.* 1620, Shedzok; *W. P.* MSS. Sedzok). 'Whithorn.' *Cf.* Sheddach in Arran.

SHAKEABÒDIE ROCK. 'Penninghame.'

SHÀLLOCH (*P.* Shelach). 'Kirkpatrick Irongray.' *Sealg* [?] [shallug], the chase or hunting ground. *See under* DRUM-SHALLOCH. Perhaps, however, only a softened form of CHALLOCH, *q.v.*

SHÀLLOCH RIG, 'Carsphairn.' *See under* SHALLOCH and DRUM-SHALLOCH.

SHÀMBELLIE (*Inq. ad Cap.* 1601, Schambellie; *P.* Schanbilby (*a misprint*)). 'New Abbey.' *Sean* [shan] *baillie*, old building. Perhaps here in antithesis to NEW ABBEY and NEW HOUSE of LOCH ARTHUR, both of which are in this parish. *Cf.* SHIN-VALLEY and SHANVOLLEY, showing the aspirated form *bhaile* [valley]; also, in Little Cumbrae, Shanavalley, the name of some cairns, and, in Ireland, Shanvalley, Shanavalley, and Shanballie. O. ERSE *sen*, ERSE and GAEL. *sean* + W. *hen* + LAT. *sen-ex* + O. GK. ἔνος, old + GOTH. *sin-eigs*, old + SKT. *sana*, old. *See under* BAILLIE.

SHANKFOOT. 'Balmaclellan,' 'Kirkgunzeon.'

SHANRÌGGIE. 'Inch.'

SHANVÒLLEY. 'Kirkcowan.' *See under* SHAMBELLIE.

SHAW BRAE. 'Kirkpatrick Durham.' The wood hill. "*Schaw.* 1. A wood, a grove. 2. Shade, covert."—*Jamieson.* —A.S. *scaga,* M.E. *schawe, shawe* + ICEL. *skógr*, a wood + SWED. *skog*, DAN. *skov.* Probably akin to ICEL. *skuggi*, A.S. *scúa*, a shade — √SKU, to cover, as in SKT. *sku* to cover, from which root are E. *sky, scum, hide, shower, obscure (Skeat).* There is a secondary meaning of " *Shaw,* a piece of ground which becomes suddenly flat at the bottom of a hill or steep bank. Thus Birken-shaw, a piece of ground of the description given, covered with short, scraggy birches" (*Jamieson*). It is the same word, the meaning being transferred from the wood to the ground on which it grows.

SHAW FELL.   'Parton.'

SHAW HILL. 'Balmaclellan,' 'Dalry,' 'Girthon,' 'Mochrum,' 'Rerwick.'

SHAW KNOWES.   'Balmaclellan.'

SHAWN HILL.   'Stoneykirk.'

SHAW WOOD.   'Colvend.'

SHEALING HILL. 'Terregles.' The winnowing hill. "*Sheelin-hill,* the eminence near a mill where the kernels of the grain were separated by the wind from the husks."—*Jamieson.* " By every corn-mill, a knoll-top, on which the kernels were winnowed from the husks, was designated the *sheeling-hill.*" —*Agricultural Survey of Peeblesshire.* It is impossible in many cases to distinguish between *shieling,* a hut, and *shealing,* partic. of *to sheal,* to take the husks off seeds. *See under* SHEIL. *To sheal,* E. *to shell* — A.S. *scell, scyll, sceale* + DAN. and SWED. *skal* + GOTH. *skalja,* a tile — Teut. base SKALA — √SKAL (for SKAR), to separate. From this root also come the closely allied words *scale, shelf, skill,* etc. (*Skeat*).

SHEANS [*pron.* Shanes].   'Kirkmaiden.'

SHEEPHANK. 'Stoneykirk, s.c.' A place where sheep may get " hanked " or caught on a steep place.

SHEFFIELD HOLE.   'Kirkmaiden, s.c.'

SHEIL (*P.* Sheel). 'Dalry.' A hut. "*Sheal, schele, sheil, sheald, shield, shielling, sheelin,* a hut for those who have the care of sheep or cattle. A shed for sheltering sheep during the night."—*Jamieson.* ICEL. *skjól,* shelter, *skýli,* a shed + DAN. *skjul,* shelter + SWED. *skjul,* a shed — √SKU, to cover. *See under* SHAW BRAE. Although so similar in meaning and so like in some of the forms assumed, *sheal,* a hut, is quite distinct in origin from *shield* and *shelter.*

SHEILA LINN. 'Dalry.' =*Sheal law,* the hill of the shieling or hut; the pool of the hut hill.

SHEIL BANK. 'Kirkpatrick Durham.' *See under* SHEIL.

SHEIL BURN. 'Minigaff.' *See under* SHEIL.

SHEILHEAD. 'Kirkpatrick Irongray.' The glen-head or hill-head of the shieling.

SHEIL HILL. 'Balmaclellan,' 'Colvend' (*twice*), 'Kirkmabreck,' etc. *See under* SHEIL.

SHEIL HOLM. 'Carsphairn,' 'Minigaff.' *See under* SHEIL.

SHEIL KNEES. 'Carsphairn.' *See under* SHEIL.

SHEILLEYS. 'Kirkgunzeon.' The "leys" or fields of the shieling.

SHEIL RIG. 'Girthon.' *See under* SHEIL.

SHEILS. 'Colvend.' *See under* SHEIL.

SHEILY HILL. 'Buittle.' *See under* SHEILA LINN.

SHELL HILL. 'Kirkinner,' 'Stoneykirk.' *See under* SHEIL HILL.

SHELL HOUSE, THE. 'New Luce.' The hut house (a pleonasm).

SHÈNNAN CREEK (the estuary of a small stream).   'Colvend.'

SHÈNNANTON (*P.* Schinintoun).   'Kirkcowan.'

SHÈNRICK.   'Urr.'

SHEÙCHAN. 'Leswalt.' *Suidheachán* [?] [seehan], a little seat. Dimin. of *suidhe*. *Cf.* Seeghane in Dublin County, Seehanes in Cork, Seeaghandoo and Seeaghanbane in Mayo.

SHEÙCHAN CRAIG. 'Minigaff.' *See under* SHEUCHAN.

SHEUCHANÒWER. 'Minigaff.' *Suidheachán odhar* [seehan ower], grey seat. *See under* BENOUR.

SHEÙCHAN'S CAIRN. 'Minigaff.' *See under* SHEUCHAN.

SHEUGH OF LAMMASHIEL. 'Minigaff.' "*Sheuch*; a furrow, a trench."—*Jamieson.* Applied metaphorically to a cleft in hills or precipitous glens.

SHIELD HILL and RIG (*P.* Scheelhill). 'Kells.' *See under* SHEIL HILL.

SHIELD WILLIE HILL.   'Dalry.'

SHÌGGERLAND.   'Minigaff.'

SHÌLLA HILL. 'Kelton.' *See under* SHEILA LINN.

SHINMOUNT (a hill of 1247 feet). 'Kells.' "*Shin of a hill*, the prominent or ridgy part of the declivity with a hollow on each side."—*Jamieson.* One of the many metaphorical names

taken from the human frame and applied to features of land.
E. *shin* is from the root SKA, to cut, the primary meaning
being " a slice, a form with a sharp edge."

SHÌNNIE BRAE. 'Kirkpatrick Durham.' The fox hill. A hybrid
word — ERSE *sionach* (shinnagh), a fox, and BR. SC. *brae*. *See
under* AUCHENSHINNOCH and BRAE.

SHINNÒCK (*Inq. ad Cap.* 1633, Shanknock). 'Kirkcowan.' *Sean*
[shan] *cnoc*, old hill. "It appears difficult to account for the
application of this word *sean* [shan], old, to certain natural
features ; so far as history or tradition goes, one mountain,
river, or valley cannot be older than another. Yet we have
Shannow, Shanow, and Shanowen (old river), all common
river names, especially in the South ; there are many places
called Shandrum (old ridge), and Shanaknock (old hill), the
former sometimes made Shandrim, and the latter Shancrock,
Shantulla, and Shantullig, old *tulach* or hill."—*Joyce*, ii. 481.
See under SHAMBELLIE.

SHINRÈOCH.   ' Mochrum.'

SHINVÀLLEY. ' Penninghame.' *See under* SHAMBELLIE.

SHIP SLOUCH [*pron.* sloogh]. ' Kirkcolm, s.c.' The gulley of
the ship. *See under* SLOCK.

SHOULDER O' CRAIG.   ' Troqueer.'

SHUTTLEFIELD.   ' New Abbey.'

SILVER CRAIG. ' Minigaff.' *Cf.* CRAIGNARGET.

SÌLVER RIG. ' Minigaff.' *Cf.* CRAIGNARGET.

SÌNNINESS (*Inq. ad Cap.* 1668, Hydder (hither) Synnons ; *P.*
Sunoniss, Sunoness). ' Old Luce.' Southern point. — ICEL.
sunnan nös, southern nose, ness, or point. ICEL. *suðr, sunnr*,
south ; adv. *sunnan*, from the south, southerly + DAN. *syd*,
south, *sönden*, southern + SWED. *syd*, south, *sunnan*, the south
 + O.H.G. *sundan*, G. *süden*, south + A.S. *súð* (whence E. *south*).
All from Teutonic base SUNTHA — SUN, base of Teutonic
type SUNNA, the sun ; "the suffix -*tha* = Aryan *ta*, so that
the literal sense is the sunned quarter."—*Skeat*. *See under*
SOUTHERNESS.

SKAITH (*P.* Skeyith). ' Penninghame.' *Sceach*, the hawthorn,
the place of hawthorns. *Sceach* was originally an adjectival
form from O. ERSE *scé* [skay]. *See under* AUCHENSKEOCH.
Cf. Skagh, Skea, and Skeagh, in Ireland.

SKÀTE (*Inq. ad Cap.* 1582, Skeych ; *P.* Skeych). 'Mochrum.' *See under* SKAITH.

SKATE HILL. 'Kirkinner.' *See under* SKAITH.

SKEENGÀLLIE. 'Kirkinner.'

SKÈLLARIE (*Inq. ad Cap.* 1650, Skellerbie ; *P.* Skellary). 'Kirkinner.'

SKEÒCH. 'Kirkpatrick Irongray.' *See under* SKEOG.

SKEÒG [*pron.* skeōge] (*P.* Skioch ; *W. P.* MSS. Skeoche). 'Whithorn.' *Sceitheóg* [skeōge], a hawthorn bush (*O'Reilly*) ; dim. of *scé. Cf.* Skeoge in Donegal, Fermanagh, and Tyrone.

SKIGLÀE. 'Inch.'

SKIGNIEBÀROCHIE. 'Old Luce.'

SKÌNNEL BURN. 'Kirkcudbright.'

SKINNINGHIDE. 'Kirkinner.'

SKYRE BURN (*P.* Skyir b.). 'Kirkmabreck.' Burn of the cliff. — ICEL. *sker. See under* SCAR.

SLACÀRNACHAN. 'New Luce.' *Sliabh* [slew] *Cearnachain*, Carnachan's moorland. O. ERSE *sliab*, mons, ERSE and GAEL. *sliabh*, generally appears in Irish names as the prefix *Slieve*, although in the names Sleamaine in Wicklow, Slemish in Antrim, it is softened into the vowel termination usual in Galloway, where its use is almost confined to certain parishes chiefly in the west of Wigtownshire. Thus it occurs upwards of thirty-four times in the parishes of Port Patrick, Kirkcolm, Leswalt, Stoneykirk, New Luce, and Kirkmaiden. "The word ꞅⅬⅬⰠⰂⰔ, sliabh, so commonly applied in Ireland to a single mountain, is rarely found in Scotland in that sense ; there it is essentially a heathery tract, and the idea of elevation is more an accident than a property. Thus in an ancient Scotch charter *Scleuemingorne* (sliabh nan gabhran) is interpreted *Mora caprarum* (*Collect. of Aberdeen*, vol. i. p. 172) ; and *Slamannan* (sliabh Mannain), in Stirling, is a moor. O'Brien explains the word : 'any heathland, whether mountain or plain ;' and in his Preface observes : 'the word *sliabh* is made synonymous to *móin* or *muin*, a mountain, though it rather means a heathy ground, whether it be low or flat, or in the shape of a hill.'"—*Reeves's Adamnan*, p. 425, *note. See under* FAULDCARNACHAN.

SLAEHÀRBRIE HILL. 'Kelton.' *Sliabh Chairbre* [harbrie], the moorland of Cairbre. *Cf.* Slieve Carbury in Longford. *See under* DUNHARBERRY.

SLAGNÀW (*P.* Slogna).　　　　　　　　　　　　　　'Kelton.'

SLAMÒNIA. 'Inch.' *Sliabh*, a moorland. *See under* SLACARNACHAN.

SLÀNNAX.　　　　　　　　　　　　　　'Stoneykirk, s.c.'

SLANNIEVÈNNACH. 'Minigaff.' *Sliabh na bhfeannog* [?] [slew na vannog], moorland of the carrion crows. *Cf.* Mullanavannog in Monaghan.

SLATEHEUGH.　　　　　　　　　　　　　　'Glasserton.'

SLEEKIT KNOWES. 'Minigaff.' Smooth hillocks. "*Sleekit*, smooth."—*Jamieson*. Past part. of M.E. *to slecke*, to make smooth ; – ICEL. *slíkr*, smooth, sleek, from the base SLI – Aryan √ SAR, to flow, to glide (whence DU. *slijk*, grease, mud, O. DU. *sleyck*, plain, even, LOW G. *slikk*, G. *schlick*, grease, slime, LOW G. *sliken*, G. *schleichen*, O.H.G. *slîhhan*, to slink, crawl). "*Slik, slike*; slime."—*Jamieson*. The original sense of *sleek* is "greasy," like soft mud (*Skeat*).

SLEWCÀIRN. 'Colvend.' *Sliabh* [slew] *cairn*, moorland of the cairn. *Cf.* Slieve Carna in Ireland. *See under* AUCHENCAIRN.

SLEWCÀRT. 'Kirkcolm.' *Sliabh cearda* [?] [slew carda], moorland of the forge or workshop.

SLEWCRÈEN. 'Kirkmaiden.' *Sliabh críon* [slew creen], withered moorland. *Cf.* Creenkill (*críon coill*) in Kilkenny, and Creenagh and Creeny, written *Críonach* by the *Four Masters* (1086), land where the vegetation is withering. O. ERSE *crín*, whence, probably BR. SC., "*To crine, cryne* ; to shrivel."—*Jamieson*.

SLEWCRÒAN. 'Leswalt.' *Sliabh* [slew] *crón*, brown moorland. *See under* CRAIGCROON.

SLEWDÒNAN. 'Kirkmaiden.' *Sliabh* [slew] *Donnain*, Donnan's moorland. *Donnán*, a brown man, deriv. of *don*, brown, remains as a surname in the district.

SLEWDÒWN. 'Kirkcolm,' 'Kirkmaiden,' 'Stoneykirk.' *Sliabh don*, brown moorland.

SLEWENTÒO. 'Leswalt.' *Sliabhán tuath* [?] [slewan too], north moor.

SLEWFÀD. 'Leswalt.' *Sliabh fada*, long moorland.

SLEWGÀLIE. 'Kirkmaiden.' *Cf.* AUCHENGALIE.

SLEWHÀBBLE. 'Kirkmaiden.' *Sliabh chapul*, moorland of the horses. *See under* BARHAPPLE.

SLEWHÈNRY. 'Leswalt.' *Sliabh fhainre* [slew hainry], sloping moorland. *See under* KNOCKHENRY.

SLEWHÌGH. 'Leswalt.' *Sliabh aithe* [?] [slew aye], moor of the kiln. *See under* AUCHENHAY.

SLEWKÈNNAN. 'Kirkcolm.'

SLEWLÀN. 'Stoneykirk.' *Sliabh leathan* [slew lahan], broad moorland. *Cf.* Ardlahan in Limerick. *See under* AUCHLANE.

SLEWLEÀ. 'Kirkmaiden.' *Sliabh liath* [slew lea], grey moorland.

SLEWMÀG. 'Kirkmaiden.' *Sliabh mbeag* [meg], little moorland.

SLEWMÀLLIE. 'Kirkmaiden.'

SLEWMÈEN. 'Leswalt.' *Sliabh meadhon* [slew mehn], middle moorland; *cf.* Sleamain in Wicklow. Or perhaps *sliabh mín* [meen], smooth moor.

SLEWMÙCK. 'Kirkcolm.' *Sliabh muc*, moorland of the swine. *Cf* Slievenamuck and Slievemuck in Ireland.

SLEWNÀGLE. 'Leswalt.'

SLEWNÀIN. 'Leswalt.' *Sliabh n-én*, moorland of the birds. *See under* BARNEAN.

SLEWNÀRK. 'Port Patrick.' *Sliabh n-arc* [slewnark], moorland of the pigs, or other large beasts. *Arc*, another form of *orc*. *See under* CRAIGGORK. *Cf.* Drumark and Derryork in Derry, Cloonark in Mayo and Roscommon, and Gortnanark in Galway.

SLEWNÀSSIE. 'Port Patrick.' *Sliabh an easa* [slewanassy], moorland of the waterfall. *See under* ASS OF THE GILL.

SLEWSCÌNNIE. 'Leswalt.'

SLEWSMÌRROCH. 'Stoneykirk.' *Sliabh smeurach*, moorland of the brambles or blackberries; adjective from *smeur*. *See under* SMIRLE.

SLEWTÀMMOCK. 'Leswalt.' *Sliabh tomach*, bushy moorland.

SLEWTÒRRAN. 'Kirkmaiden.' *Sliabh torain* [slew toran], moorland of the little tower or little hill, dim. of *tor*.

SLEWTRÀIN. 'Leswalt.' *Sliabh traona* [?] [slew trana], moor of the corncrakes. *Cf.* Cloonatreane in Fermanagh. *See under* CLONE.

T

SLEWWHÀN. 'Kirkmaiden.' *Sliabh bhan* [van], white moorland.

SLICKCÒNERIE. 'New Luce.' *Sliabh Conaire* [slew conary], Conary's moorland. *Conaire* is one of the earliest names in Irish history.

SLIDDER FORD. 'Minigaff.' Slippery ford. "*Slidder, s.* slipperiness."—*Jamieson.* — A.S. *slidor*, slippery. Originally from the base SLI — Aryan √ SAR. *See under* SLEEKIT KNOWES.

SLIDDERICK. 'Kirkmaiden, s.c.' "*Sliddery*, slippery."—*Jamieson.* *See under* SLEEKIT KNOWES.

SLIGGERIE ·KNOWE. 'Leswalt.' Slippery hillock ; = slippery. *See under* SLEEKIT KNOWES.

SLOCHÀBBERT (*P.* Sleuhybbert). 'Kirkinner.' *Sliabh* [slew], a moorland. There is mentioned "the towne and lands of the Habart" among those recorded in the Registry of Clonmacnoise as having been granted by Cairbre Crom to St. Kieran.

SLOCHANÀWN. 'Stoneykirk, s.c.' *Slocán abhann* [?] [avan, awn], gulley of the stream.

SLOCHANGLÀSS. 'Whithorn, s.c.' *Slocán glas*, green gulley.

SLOCHNAGÒUR. 'Kirkmaiden, s.c.' *Sloc na gobhar* [gowr], gulley of the goats.

SLOCK. 'Kirkmaiden.' *Sloc*, a hole or gulley. "*Sloc, slochd*, a pit, hollow, hole, cavity, pitfall, mine."—*O'Reilly.* The farm takes its name from a gulley on the coast. — ERSE *slug*, GAEL. *sluig*, to swallow + W. *llawg*, a gulp + SWED. *sluka* + LOW G. *sluken*, to swallow, G. *schluken*, to swallow, hiccough + GK. λύζειν (for λυγ-γειν), to hiccough. The A.S. *slók* (whence M.E. *slogh*, E. *slough*, BR. SC. *slouch*) is borrowed from CELTIC *sloc* (*Skeat*).

SLOCKGÀRROCH. 'Port Patrick.' *Sloc g-carrach,* rough gulley.

SLOCKNAMÒRROW. 'Kirkcolm, s.c.' *Sloc na mara* [?], gulley of the sea. *Cf.* SLOUCHANAMARS ; also Slog-na-mara, a whirlpool between Rathlin Island and Antrim, *i.e.* the swallow or gullet of the sea. *Muir*, the sea, gen. *mara* + W. *myr*, C. *môr* + ICEL. *marr* + DU. *meer* + A.S. *mere*, a mere, lake + G. *meer*, O.H.G. *mari*, the sea + GOTH. *marei* + RUSS. *moré* + LITH. *mares* + LAT. *mare*. The original sense is "that which is dead," hence a desert, waste, either of land (*moor*) or water ; *cf.* SKT. *maru*, a desert, from *mri*, to die (*Skeat*).

SLOGANABÀA. 'Port Patrick, s.c.' *Slocán na bo* [baw], gulley of the cows.

SLOGANAGLÀSSIN. 'Port Patrick, s.c.' *Slocán na glasin* [?], gulley of the streamlets ; or perhaps *glasain*, of the sea-weed. *See under* CARRICKGLASSIN.

SLOGÀRIE (*P.* Sleugarie ; *Charter* 1611, Sleugarie). 'Balmaghie.' *Sliabh g-caora* [?] [slewgarie], moorland of the sheep ; or *sliabh caithre* [carey], moor of the fort ; gen. of *cathair* or *caithre* [carey], of the standing stones. *See under* CASSENCARIE, in Addenda.

SLONGÀBER. 'Kirkpatrick Durham.' *Sron gabar*, hill (snout) of the goats or horses. *See under* STROAN.

SLOUCHADÒLLOES.   'Port Patrick, s.c.'

SLOUCHÀLKIN.   'Kirkmaiden, s.c.'

SLOUCHANAMÀRS. 'Kirkmaiden, s.c.' *Slochán na mara*, gulley of the sea. *Cf.* SLOCKNAMORROW.

SLOUCHANÀWN. 'Kirkmaiden, s.c.' *See under* SLOCHANAWN.

SLOUCHARÀNGIE.   'Kirkmaiden, s.c.'

SLOUCHATÀLIE.   'Kirkmaiden, s.c.'

SLOUCHAVÀDDIE. 'Kirkmaiden, s.c.' *Slochd a' bhada* [vadda], gulley of the boat. *See under* PORTAVADDIE.

SLOUCHÈEN SLUNK. 'Kirkmaiden, s.c.' *Slochín*, a little gulley, dimin. of *slochd*. *Slunk* is locally used on the sea-coast in the same sense as *sloc*, a gulley, but its original inland meaning, as *Jamieson* says, is a slough, a quagmire. It is from the same root as *sloc*, E. *slough*. *See under* SLOCK.

SLOUCHGÀRIE. 'Kirkmaiden, s.c.' *Sloch gcaora* [garie], gulley of the sheep, or *slochd caithre* [carey], gulley of the fort. *See under* CASSENCARY, in Addenda. *Cf.* SLOUCHNAGARIE.

SLOUCHLAÙRIE.   'Kirkmaiden, s.c.'

SLOUCHLÀW.   'Kirkcolm, s.c.'

SLOUCHNABÀGS.   'Kirkmaiden, s.c.'

SLOUCHNAGÀRY. 'Kirkcolm, s.c.' *See under* SLOUCHGARIE.

SLOUCHNAGLÀSSEN. 'Leswalt, s.c.' *See under* SLOGANAGLASSIN.

SLOUCHNAMÒRROCH. 'Kirkmaiden, s.c.' *See under* SLOCKNA-MORROW.

SLOUCHNÀWEN. 'Leswalt.' *See under* SLOCHANAWN.

SLOUCHSPÌRN.   'Kirkcolm, s.c.'

SLUGNAGLÀSS. 'Port Patrick, s.c.' *Sloc na glais*, gulley of the stream ; or *slocán glas*, green gulley.

SLUNEYHÌGH. 'Leswalt.' *Sliabh na aithe* [haya], moor of the kiln. *Cf.* SLEWHIGH; *see under* AUCHENHAY.

SLUNKRÀINY.   'Stoneykirk, s.c.'

SMÈATON (*P.* Smytoun). 'Carsphairn.' *Cf.* the same name in East Lothian.

SMIRLE. 'Glasserton.' *Smeurlach*, a place of brambles; adj. from *smeur* or *smear*. *Cf.* SLEWSMIRROCH; also Smearlagh, a river in Kerry.

SNAB HILL. 'Kells.' "*Snab*, the projecting part of a rock or hill." —*Jamieson*. This is the same word as E. *neb*, *nib*, a beak, nose, point; the initial *s* (retained in E. *snipe, snap, snaffle, snout*, all from the same Teutonic root SNAP, to snap up) has been dropped. It is retained in DU. *sneb*, a beak; G. *schnabel*, a beak, *scheppe*, a nozzle. The word is applied to pointed hills in the same sense as the Celtic *gob* (*see* GAB HILL) and Scand. *nös* (ness, naze).

SNIBE, POINT OF THE. 'Minigaff.' *See under* SNAB.

SOLE BURN (*P.* Sull; *Sibbald* MS., Solburn; *Lochnaw Entail*, 1756, Swolburn). 'Kirkcolm.' Probably the same syllable that remains in SOLWAY.

SÒLWAY FIRTH. Usually written Sulway and Sullwa in old writings; called by the Celts *Tracht-Romra*, and by *Ptolemy*, *Itunæ Æstuarium*. It is well described in the Irish life of Adamnan. "Adamnan put in at *Tracht-Romra*. The strand is long, and the flood rapid; so rapid that if the best steed in Saxonland ridden by the best horseman were to start from the edge of the tide when the tide begins to flow, he could only bring his rider ashore by swimming, so extensive is the strand, and so impetuous is the tide."—*Celt. Scot.* ii. 171.

SONSY NEB. 'Kirkmaiden.' Pleasant or lucky point. "*Sonsy*; lucky, fortunate, having a pleasant look."—*Jamieson*. Perhaps related to ERSE *sonas*, happiness, good fortune, adj. *sontach, sonadh*, and these to LAT. *sanus*.

SÒRBIE (*P.* Soirbuy). A parish in Wigtownshire. *Cf.* Soroby, a church in Tiree; also Sourby in Ewisdale, and Sourby, a manor in Cumberland, formerly held by the Scottish Kings. There was also a place of this name in Portpatrick parish. —ICEL. *by*, a dwelling, a village.

SOUND CLINT. 'Minigaff.' Smooth rock. "*Soun'*, smooth, level." —*Jamieson*.

SOUNDLY HILL. 'Stoneykirk.' A.S. *sund léah*, M.E. *sound lea*, sound or level, smooth field.

SOUR BRAE. 'Minigaff.' Wet, unfertile hill. "*Sour*; frequently applied to a cold, wet soil."—*Jamieson.*

SOURCROFT. 'Mochrum.' *See under* SOUR BRAE and CROFT.

SOURHILL. 'Buittle,' 'Urr,' 'Whithorn' (*twice*). *See under* SOUR BRAE.

SOURHIP. 'Penninghame.' *See under* SOUR BRAE. "*Hip,* a round eminence situated towards the extremity, or on the lower part of a hill."—*Jamieson.*

SOURSHOT. 'Mochrum.' "*Shot of ground,* plot of land, Lothians. In Fife, *shod.*"—*Jamieson.* A.S. *sceat,* a part, portion, corner.

SOUTHERNESS [*pron.* Sàtterness]. 'Kirkbean.' Southern point. — ICEL. *suðr nös. See under* SINNINESS.

SOUTHWICK [*pron.* Sùthik, Sùddik] (*P.* Suddick, Sudlyick). 'Colvend.' Southern bay. A.S. *suð wic.*

SPEARFORD. 'Crossmichael.' Literally, "Ask-for-the-ford or ferry." BR. SC. *speir,* to inquire — A.S. *spiridn,* to seek, to inquire. *See under* SPIRRY.

SPEAT.   'Kirkmaiden, s.c.'

SPIRN'S CRAIG and MOSS.   'Minigaff.'

SPIRRY. 'Leswalt.' *Sporaidhe* [?] [spurree], the spurs, or pointed rocks. *Cf.* Spurree in Cork county. *Spor,* plur. *sporaidhe,* probably borrowed from E. *spur,* M.E. *spore, spure* — A.S. *spora, spura* + ICEL. *spori* + DU. *spoor,* a spur, a track + DAN. *spore* + SWED. *sporre* + O.H.G. *sporo,* G. *sporn.* All from a TEUT. type SPORA — √SPAR, to quiver, to jerk. The form A.S. *spor,* a footprint + DU. *spoor* + ICEL. *spor* + G. *spur,* is closely allied, and from it comes BR. SC. *speir,* to inquire, to investigate (LAT. *vestigium,* a footprint), E. *spurn,* to kick (*Skeat*).

SPITTAL. 'Penninghame,' 'Stoneykirk.' Hospital; lands formerly owned by the Knights of St. John. M.E. *hospital, hospitalle, hospytal* — O.F. *hospital* — LOW LAT. *hospitale,* a large house, a palace — LAT. *hospit-,* stem of *hospes,* a host or guest. "The base of *hospit-* is usually taken to be *hosti-pit*; where *hosti-* is the crude form of *hostis,* a guest, an enemy. Again, the suffix *-pit* is supposed to be from the Latin *potis,* powerful, the old sense of the word being 'a lord'; *cf.* SKT. *pati,* a master, governor, lord. Thus *hostes*=*hosti-pets,* guest-master, guest-lord, master of a house who receives guests."—*Skeat.* Other forms of this word are *hostel, hôtel*; the French *hôtel* not being limited, as in English, to the meaning of an inn.

SPOTTES (*P.* Bar of Spotts; M.S. 1527, Spottis).   'Urr.'

SPOUT BURN [*pron.* Spoot]. 'Carsphairn.' "*Spout,* a boggy spring in ground."—*Jamieson.* M.E. *spoute*—SWED. *sputa,* an occasional form of *spruta,* to squirt, or subst., a squirt+DAN. *sprude, spröite,* to squirt+DU. *spuit,* a spout, squirt+G. *spritzen, sprudeln,* to squirt; from Teutonic base SPRUT, whence A.S. *spreótan,* to sprout, E. *sprout, spurt.* ERSE and GAEL. *sput,* to spout, squirt, if not borrowed from E., are rather akin to LAT. *sputare,* to spit, than to E. *spout* (*Skeat*).

SPOUTY DÈNNANS (between two forts). 'Rerwick.' The marshy ground of the forts. *See under* DINNANS. "*Spouty*; marshy, springy."—*Jamieson.*

SPYCRAIG. 'Urr.' Crag from which a man may spy, from whence there is a view. *Cf.* LOOK KNOWE.

STABLE ALANE.   'Kirkmaiden, s.c.'

STARRY DAM (on the shore of Mochrum Loch). 'Mochrum.' Rushy bank. "*Starr,* a sedge" (*Jamieson*)—SWED. *starr,* a rush. *Dam* appears here in its original sense of a bank. In the *Prompt. Parvulor.,* p. 113, it is translated by LAT. *agger. Cf.* A.S. *fordemman,* to stop up. The word occurs in O. FRIES. *dam, dom*+DU. *dam*+ICEL. *dammr*+SWED. *damm,* a dam+ GOTH. *faurdammjan,* to stop up+M.H.G. *tam,* G. *damm,* a ditch.

STARRY HEUGH (*P.* Starryheuc). 'Terregles.' Rushy height. (*See under* STARRY DAM). —"*Heuch, heugh, hewch, huwe, hwe, hew*; a steep hill or bank."—*Jamieson.* —A.S. *hou,* a height. In Galloway this form, *heugh,* is usually confined to grass-covered cliffs on the sea-shore. *See under* DRUMACISSOCK.

STARTLING DAM (on the shore of Mochrum Loch).   'Mochrum.'

STARY WELL. 'Kirkmaiden.' *See under* STARRY DAM.

STAY-THE-VOYAGE. 'Kirkcowan.' A resting-place. *Voyage* (—O.F. *veiage, voyage*—LAT. *viaticum,* provision for a journey) is here used in the older and more general sense of a "journey," which is now restricted by modern usage to a "passage by water."

STÈADSTONE. 'Colvend.' Perhaps the anvil-stone, from Norse *städ,* an anvil. *See under* STUDIE KNOWE.

STEÈLSTOP WOOD. 'Kirkpatrick Irongray.' The wood on the cliff or ravine top. —"*Steel.* 1. A wooded cleugh or precipice. 2. The lower part of a ridge projecting from a hill, where the ground declines on either side."—*Jamieson.*

STEIN HEAD. 'Whithorn, s.c.' Headland of the stone. Probably Scandinavian, like many coast names. — ICEL. *steinn.*

STÈLLAGE HILL (close to Gatehouse). 'Girthon.' Market-hill. "*Stellage*; apparently the ground on which a fair or market is held.—*Earl of Galloway's Title-deeds.* From LOW LAT. *stallagium*, the money paid for a stall. *Stallage* in the E. law denotes either the right of erecting stalls in fairs or the price paid for it."—*Jamieson.*

STELLAGE OF BORELAND.   'Minigaff.

STELL HEAD and STELL KNOWE. 'Dalry.' "*Stell.* 1. A covert or shelter. 2. An enclosure for cattle higher than a common fold."—*Jamieson.* — A.S. *steal, stœl* (whence E. *stall*)+DU. *stal* +ICEL. *stallr*+DAN. *stald*+SWED. and G. *stall*; O.H.G *stal*, all meaning a stall or stable+LITH. *stalas*, a table+SKT. *sthala*, firm ground, a terrace+GK. στέλλειν, to set. All with idea of firm standing— √STAL, extended from STA, to stand fast (*Skeat*).

STÈLLOCK (*Inq. ad Cap.* 1620, Stallage; *W. P.* MSS. Stellag). 'Glasserton.' *See under* STELLAGE.

STÈNNOCK (*Charter*, 1595, Stenework; *Inq. ad Cap.* 1620, Stennok M'Connell; *P.* Stinnock; *W. P.* MSS., Stynnok M'Connell, Stynnok Corbett). 'Whithorn.' *Staonag*, sloping ground, from *staon*, oblique (*Reeves's Adamnan*, p. 425). *Cf.* Stenag in Iona.

STEY BRAE and STEY HILL. 'Balmaclellan.' Steep hill. "*Stay*, steep."—*Jamieson.*

STEY FELL (1000 feet). 'Anwoth.' *See under* STEY BRAE and STEY HILL.

STEY GREEN OF KITTERICK. 'Girthon.' Steep green hill.

STINKING BIGHT. 'Stoneykirk, s.c.' Probably named from the collection of decaying sea-weed. *Cf.* DAN. and SWED. *bugt*, used (like *bight*) both for the loop of a rope and for a small bay. From the Aryan √BHUGH, whence E. *to bow*, M.E. *bugen*, *buwen, bogen, bowen*— A.S. *búgan*, to bend + DU. *buigan* + ICEL. *beygja*+SWED. *böja*+DAN. *böie*, to bend (tr. and intr.), *bugne*, to bend (intr.) + GOTH. *biugan* + O.H.G. *piocan*, G. *beugan* + LAT. *fugere*, to turn to flight + GK. φεύγειν, to flee + SKT. *bhuj*, to bend.

STINKING PORT. 'Whithorn, s.c.' *See under* STINKING BIGHT.

STIRNIE BIRNIE BRIDGE.   'Whithorn.'

STÒCKERTON. ‘Kirkcudbright.’

STÒCKING HILL. ‘Old Luce.’ BR. SC. *stoken*, enclosed, past part. of “*steik*, to shut, to close” (*Jamieson*).

STÒNEHOUSE [*locally called* Stane-hoos]. ‘Sorbie,’ ‘Twynholm.’ —A.S. *stan hús*. This name is a relic of the days when houses were built of wood and wattle, or of turf, and houses of stone were remarkable and unusual.

STONEYBÀTTER (a field on Dowies). ‘Glasserton.’ *Joyce* (i. 45) mentions a place of this name in Dublin county as showing a semi-translation of the old name *Bothar-na-gcloch*, or causeway of the stones.

STÒNEYKIRK (*Court of Session Papers*, 1725, Stevenskirk). Steenie’s (St. Stephen’s) Kirk. The change of sound is due to the old pronunciation, *stainie* having been interpreted as *staney*, *i.e.* full of *stanes* or stones.

STRAHÀNNAN. ‘Carsphairn.’

STRAMÒDDIE. ‘Borgue.’ *Srath madadh* [srah madda], strath or meadow-land of the dogs or wolves. *Srath* enters into many Irish names, either alone, as Sra, Srah, Sragh, and Straw, or, in composition, as Strabane in Tyrone (*srath bán*, *Four Masters*, 1583), and Straboe in Queen’s County and Carlow. *Srath*, a strath, probably akin to LAT. *stratum*, that which is laid flat or spread out + GK. στόρνυμι, I spread — √STAR, whence *star, straw, street, strand* (?), etc.

STRANDFOOT. ‘Stoneykirk, s.c.’ The “foot” of land on the beach.

STRANDMAIN. ‘Inch, s.c.’ The “mains” or farm on the beach. “*Mains*, the farm attached to a mansion-house.”—*Jamieson*. Connected with LAT. *mansio*, an abiding, a place of abode — *manere*, to dwell + GK. μένειν, to stay, allied to μόνιμος, staying, steadfast, and to μέμονα, I wish, yearn — √MAN, to think, wish; *cf.* SKT. *man*, to think, wish. Thus akin to LAT. *mens*, mind (*Skeat*).

STRAND OF THE ABYSS. ‘Minigaff.’ “*Strand*, a rivulet.”— *Jamieson*. Probably the same word as E. *strand*, the beach of the sea or of a lake — A.S. *strand* + DU. *strand* + ICEL. *strönd*, margin, edge + DAN., SWED., and G. *strand*. Root unknown; perhaps ultimately due to √STAR, to spread.

STRANFÀSKET (*Inq. ad Cap.* 1607, Stronfaskin; *P.* Stronfaskan; MS. 1527, Stranfaskane). ‘Minigaff.’ *Srón*, a nose, a headland. *See under* STROAN. *Cf.* BARHASKIN.

STRANGÀSSEL (*Inq. ad Cap.* 1607, Strongassil ; *P.* Strongassils). 'Kells.' *Srón g-caiseail* [gashel], headland of the castle. *See under* STROAN.

STRANGER'S KNOWE. 'Minigaff.' *Cf.* DRUMCAGERIE.

STRANNAGÒWER. 'Kirkmaiden.' *Srón na gobhar*, peak or headland of the goats. *See under* ALGOWER and STROAN.

STRÀNOCH. 'New Luce.' *Srónach*, peaked, pointed, adj. of *srón*. *Cf.* SCRANNAGH, STRONACH, and STRONIE.

STRANÒRD (*P.* Schroinord). 'Minigaff.' *Srón ard*, high peak or headland.

STRANRÀER (*Inq. ad Cap.* 1600, Stranraver ; "*Capella*, vel (ut quidam malunt) Stranravera" (*Maclellan*) ; *P.* Stronrawyr). 'Inch.' *Cf.* CLACHRAWER. *Chalmers* derives this name from *srón reamhar* [ravar], thick point, but this meaning appears wholly inappropriate to the place. It has been suggested that it is BR. SC. *strand raw*, the row or street on the strand, but *M'Kerlie* quotes a charter of Robert the Bruce in which the name is written *Stranrerer*. The labial consonant thus appears to be organic.

STRATHMÀDDIE. 'Minigaff.' *See under* STRAMODDIE.

STRAVÈRRAN.   'Kells.'

STRIFE GROUND. 'Mochrum,' 'Troqueer.' This and the five following names may have originated either in combats or lawsuits.

STRIFE HILL.   'Kirkmabreck,' 'Leswalt,' 'Wigtown.'

STRIFE HOLM.   'Minigaff.'

STRIFE KNOWES.   'Port Patrick.'

STRIFE MOAT.   'Carsphairn.'

STRIFE RIG. 'Kirkpatrick Durham,' 'Minigaff.' *See under* DRUMTRODDEN.

STROAN (*P.* Strom). 'Kells,' 'Minigaff.' *Srón*, lit. a nose, a peak, promontory, or headland. *Cf.* Shrone in Ireland. O. ERSE *srón*, a nose + W. *trwyn*, C. *tron, trein*. The insertion of the *t* in the Anglicised form is not uncommon. *See under* STROOL BAY.

STROANFÀSKET. 'Kells.' *See* STRANFASKET.

STROANFRÈGGAN (*P.* Stronchreigan). 'Dalry.' *Srón creagain*, point or headland of the crag.

STROAN HILL. 'Dalry.' *See under* STROAN.

Stroanpàtrick (*P.* Stronpatrick). 'Dalry.' *Srón Patraic,* Patrick's headland.

Stroans (*P.* Strowans). 'Kirkmabreck.' *See under* Stroan.

Strònach Hill. 'Kirkmabreck. *Srónach,* pointed, peaked. *See under* Stranoch.

Stronbàe (*P.* Stronbae). 'Minigaff.' *Srón beith* [bey], headland of the birches. *Cf.* Shronebeha in Cork county.

Stronbèaver.   'Carsphairn.'

Strones Bay. 'Kirkcolm.' *See under* Stroan.

Strònie. 'Port Patrick, s.c.' *Srónach,* pointed. *See under* Stronach.

Strool Bay. 'Kirkcolm.' *Sruthair* [sruhar], a stream. The change of final *r* to *l* is rule-right; so is the insertion of *t* after initial *s*. The word is further disguised when, as sometimes happens, the initial *s* is dropped (*see* Trool). "Struell, near Downpatrick, is written Strohill in the Taxation of 1306, showing that the change from *r* to *l* took place before that early period; but the *r* is retained in a grant of about the year 1178, in which the stream is called Tirestruther, the land of the streamlet."—*Joyce,* i. 457. *Cf.* also Shruel, Shruell, and Sroohill in various parts of Ireland.

Stròquhan's Pool (on the Fleet water).   'Girthon.'

Strumìnoch. 'New Luce.' *Srón meadhonach* [meùnogh], mid hill. *See under* Balminnoch.

Stubliggat.   'Colvend.'

Studie Knowe. 'New Luce.' Hillock of the "stithy" or forge. —"*Crook studie.* Supposed to be a stithy or anvil, with what is called a horn projecting from it, used for twisting, forming horse-shoes."—*Jamieson.* E. *stith,* an anvil, stithy, properly a smithy, but also used with the sense of anvil, M.E. *stith* — ICEL. *steði,* allied to *staðr,* a place, *i.e.* fixed stead, and so named from its firmness. From the same root as E. *stead,* *steady* + SWED. *stüd,* an anvil.

Stùrdie Moss. 'Borgue.' "*Sturdy,* a vertigo; a disease to which black cattle, when young, as well as sheep, are subject."—*Jamieson.* "A plant which grows among corn, which, when eaten, causes giddiness and torpidity."—*Mactaggart.*

Sùie (*P.* Suachtoun hil). 'Minigaff,' 'Rerwick.' *Samhadh* [saua, sawva, sow], sorrel. *Cf.* Sooey in Sligo (sorrel-bearing land); or perhaps *subhach* [sooagh], a place of berries.

Summerhill. 'Balmaghie,' 'Crossmichael,' 'Rerwick.' The village of this name in Meath is also called Drumsawry (*druim samhraidh,* hill of the summer), probably from its being a place of summer pasture.

SÙMMERTON. ‘New Luce.’

SUNKHEAD MOSS. ‘Carsphairn.’

SUNNYBRAES. ‘Mochrum.’ *Cf.* GRENNAN.

SÙRNOCK. ‘Kirkmaiden, s.c.’

SWARE BRAE. ‘Carsphairn.’ — “*Sware, swire, swyre.* 1. The neck. 2. The declination of a mountain or hill near the summit.” —*Jamieson.* —A.S. *swura, sweora, swira, swyra,* the neck (+ O. DU. *swaerde*) — *swer,* a column, pillar. The idea connecting “neck” with “hill” occurs in LAT. *collis,* a hill, *collum,* a neck; *jugum,* a yoke, a hill.

SWAREHEAD. ‘Urr.’ *See under* SWARE BRAE.

SWINEDRUM. ‘Borgue.’ Ridge or “drum” of the swine. KNOCK-MUCK is close by. *See under* DRUMMUCKLOCH.

SWINEFELL. ‘Old Luce.’ The fell or hill of the swine.

SYLLÒDIOCH (*Charter* 1610, Solodzeoche; *P.* Saladyow). ‘Girthon.’

SŸPLAND (*Inq. ad Cap.* 1548, Sypland; *P.* Syipland). ‘Kirkcudbright.’ Wet, sappy land. — A.S. *syp,* a wetting, *sipan,* to soften by soaking, *sæp, sap. Cf.* Sypeland, a large bog on Fountain’s Earth moor in Yorkshire. “*Sipe,* to drip.”—*Lucas.* “*Sipe, sype.* 1. A slight spring of water. Perths. 2. The moisture which comes from any wet substance.” “*Sipe, seipe,* to ooze.”—*Jamieson.*

TACHER BURN. ‘Rerwick.’ *Tachar,* a combat. Perhaps from *tóchar,* a causeway. The change from *o* to *a* is unusual, but *see* TANDOO and TANDRAGEE.

TÀCHER HILL. ‘Sorbie.’ *See under* TACHER BURN.

TAHÀLL. ‘Kirkinner.’

TÀILABOUT LOCH. ‘Stoneykirk.’

TALLOWQUHÀIRN [*pron.* -hwairn]. ‘Kirkbean.’ *Talamh chairu* [talla hairn], land or ground of the cairn. O. ERSE *talam,* allied to LAT. *tellus* (as *tìr* to *terre*)— √TAL, to sustain, GK. τηλία, a flat board.

TALLSLID. ‘Crossmichael.’

TALNÒTRY or DUNNÒTTRIE (*Inq. ad Cap.* 1572, Tonnotrie; *P.* Tonnottry). ‘Minigaff.’ *Dùn Ochtraidh* [?], Uthred’s fort. *See under* KIROUCHTRIE. *Cf.* KILNOTRIE.

TANDÒO (*P.* Tondow). ' Port Patrick, s.c.' *Tón dubh* [doo], black
rump. *Cf.* Tonduff and Toneduff in Ireland. W. *tin.*

TANDRAGÈE. 'Stoneykirk.' *Tón re gaieth* [geu, gwee], backside
to the wind. A descriptive name occurring frequently in both
Scotland and Ireland ; sometimes Tonlegee, with the preposition *le* instead of *re.* *Cf.* TONDERGHIE.

TÀNGART.   'Kirkmaiden, s.c.'

TAN HILL.   ' Kirkpatrick Durham.'

TANNIEFLÙX. 'Kirkcowan.' *Tamhnach* [tawnagh] *fliuch,* wet
meadow. "*Tamhnach,* a fine field in which daisies, sorrel
and sweet grass grow. This word enters into names in mountainous districts in the north and north-west of Ireland, but
rarely in the south. Also, a green arable spot in a mountain."
—*O'Don. Suppl.* It is not in use in Gaelic.

TANNIELÀGGIE (*P.* Tynalagach).   'Kirkcowan.'

TANNIEMÀWS.   'Borgue.'

TANNIERÀGGIE.   'New Luce.'

TANNIERÒACH. 'Old Luce.' *Tamhnach ruadh* [tawnagh rooh],
red meadow. *See under* TANNIEFLUX.

TÀNNOCH (*P.* Tanoch, Tanach). 'Kells.' *Tamhnach* [tawnagh], a
meadow. *See under* TANNIEFLUX. Tunnocks, in Kilbirnie
parish, Ayrshire, is written Tannock by *Pont.*—*Cuninghame,*
p. 376.

TÀNNOCH HILL. 'New Abbey.'   *See under* TANNOCH.

TÀNNOCK. 'Colvend.'   *See under* TANNOCH.

TÀRBET (a neck of land between two seas near the Mull of Galloway) (*P.* Terbart). 'Kirkmaiden.' *Tarbert,* a neck of land
(*O'Reilly*)—*tar* (root of *tarruingim,* I draw, pull) and *bdd,* boatdraught (*cf.* BOATDRAUGHT), a place where boats are drawn
across an isthmus to avoid rough seas at the cape.

TARBRÈOGH (*P.* Torbraoch). 'Kirkpatrick Durham.' *Tìr bréach*
[?], ground of the wolves. *Cf.* DRUMBREACH ; also Caherbreagh in Ireland.

TARDÒW [*pron.* Tardoo]. 'Kirkmaiden.' *Tìr dubh* [doo, dow],
black, dark ground. *Cf.* BLACKGROUND.

TARF (*P.* Tarf R.). A river in Wigtownshire and another in the
Stewartry. There is also a river in Perthshire of this name.

TARKÌRRA.   ' Kirkgunzeon.'

TARLÌLLYAN.   'Colvend.'

TARWÌLKIE (*Inq. ad Cap.* 1604, Tragilhey). 'Balmaclellan.' *Tìr
guilcach,* rushy land. *See under* AUCHENGILSHIE.

TAYLOR'S GAT. 'Whithorn, s.c.' Taylor's gap or opening.
—ICEL. *gat*, an opening. *See under* GATE.

TENNIEWÈE. 'Kirkmabreck.' *Tamhnach bhuidhe* [tawnagh vwee],
yellow meadow. *See under* TANNIEFLUX.

TERÀLLY (*P.* Terally). 'Kirkmaiden.' *Tir Amhalghaidh* [owlhay],
Aulay's land. *Cf.* Tirawley in Mayo. *See under* MACHERALLY.

TERÒY. 'Inch.' *Tighe ruadh* [rooh], red house, or, possibly, *tír
ruadh*, red land ; *cf.* TARDOW and TER ROYE.

TERRÀUCHTIE (*P.* Terachty). 'Terregles.' *Tír uachdar*, upper
land.

TERREGAN. 'Minigaff.' *Tír Eoghain* [?], Egan's land.

TERRÈGLES (*Charter, Alexander II.*, (1214-49) *in Melrose Cartulary*,
treueger ; *Charter, David II.* 1359, Travereglis, Trauereglys ;
P. Toregills), a parish in the Stewartry. *Treamhar eglais*
[traver], church farm. Not from *tir eglais, terra ecclesiæ*, nor
terra regalis—all of which derivations have been offered—
but, as the old spellings show, from *treamhar*, which is interpreted in *John O'Dugan's* " Forus Focail " (quoted by *O'Reilly*),
taobhnocht, i.e. naked side. *Treamhair* [travaer], in Skye means
" houses," and in Erse *treamh* is a plough, *treabh*, a farmed
village (*O'Reilly*). *Cf. treabhair*, resident, *treabhaire*, a
householder, crops, implements, requisites of a farm (*O'Don.
Suppl.*).

TER ROYE. 'Kirkcowan.' *See under* TEROY.

THIRL STANE. 'Kirkbean.' A perforated stone. A.S. *þyrel stan.*
" *Thirl*, to perforate, drill."—*Jamieson.* "Thirlestane grass "
is a rural name for saxifrage. A.S. *þyrlian*, to drill, pierce,
þyrel, pierced + DU. *drillen* (E. *thrill* ; *nostril*, i.e. *nose thrill*) —
√TAR, to pierce, whence also E. *through*, ERSE *tar*, through,
etc.

THORNY HILL. 'Kirkcowan,' 'Kirkpatrick Durham.' *Cf.* DRUM-
SKEOG, DRUMDALLY, etc.

THORNGLÀSS. 'Rerwick.' *Torán glas*, little green hill. Dim. of
tor. See under TOR.

THORN HOUSE. 'Stoneykirk.'

THORNKÌP. 'Colvend.' Thorn hill. *See under* KIPP.

THORNYGRÈNE. 'Parton.'

THÒRTER FELL. 'New Abbey.' Thwart hill. "*Thortour*, cross, transverse."—*Jamieson.* (*Cf.* CRAIGTARSON.) — M.E. *þwertower* (*i.e.* þwert *ower*, transversely over; E. *to thwart, to cross*— þwert). "The word is of Scandinavian origin, as it is only thus that the final *t* can be explained."—*Skeat.* ICEL. *þwert*, across + þwer, the neut. of þrerr, DAN. adj. *tvær*, transverse; adv. *tvært*, across + SWED. adj. *tvär*, cross, unfriendly; adv. *tvärt*, rudely + DU. *dwars*, cross, and (adv.) crossly + A.S. þweorh, perverse, transverse + M.H.G. *dwerch, twerch*, G. *zwerch* (adv.) across, awry + GOTH. *thwairhs*, cross, angry. All from TEUT. type THWERHA — base THARH with which *Skeat* connects LAT. *torquere*, to twist.

THREAVE (*Inq. ad Cap.* 1550, Treifgrange; *P.* Treef Cast, Treve, Treef). 'Balmaghie,' 'Penninghame.' ERSE *treabh* [trave], a farm, "a farmed village" (*O'Reilly*). *See under* TERREGLES.

THREEPNEÙK. 'Kirkpatrick Irongray.' The corner of the scolding, or perhaps of the quarrel. "*Threpe, threap.* 1. A pertinacious affirmation. 2. Expl. "contest;" *Lord Hailes.* 3. Applied to traditionary superstition. Roxb., Dumfr."— *Jamieson.* — A.S. *þreapian, þreagan*, to threap, reprove, afflict (*Bosworth*). *See under* CURATE'S NEUK.

THROWFOOT. 'Minigaff.'

THUNDERY KNOWES. 'Carsphairn.'

TÌBBERT (*P.* Taubyr roy). 'Port Patrick.' *Tiobar*, a well; formerly, as shown by *Pont, tiobar ruadh* [rooh], red well. There is a place called Welton close by. *Cf.* Toberroe in Ireland, Tipper in Kildare and Longford. O. ERSE *topur, tipra*, ERSE *tiobraid, tiobar, tiubruid, tobar* (*O'Reilly*), a well + W. *goffrwd*, a streamlet. This word often appears in composition as *Chipper*. *See under* CHIPPERDINGAN.

TÌEREHAN. 'New Abbey.' *Tir Eoghain* [?], Egan's land. *Cf.* TERREGAN.

TINLÙSKIE. 'New Luce.' *Tìr* or *tòn loisgthe* [lusky], burnt land or burnt bottom. *See under* CRAIGLOSK and TANDOO.

TÌNTOCK. 'Kirkinner.' The same name appears as that of a hill in Lanarkshire, of which it is said,

> "When Tintock tap pits on his cap,
> Criffel wots fu' wiel o' that."

TÌNTUM. 'Parton.'

TÌPPET HILL. 'Rerwick.'

TIREBANK. 'Twynholm.'

TOB-BROUGH. 'Kirkmaiden, s.c.'

TOCHER KNOWES. 'Kirkcowan.' Probably *tachar*, a combat (*cf.* TACHER BURN), as in Carntogher in Derry, which *Colgan* writes *Carn-tachair*, and Cloontogher in Roscommon, which the natives call *Cluain-tachair*. But it may also be *tóchar*, a causeway, a word from which *tachar* is hardly to be distinguished in composition. Thus Ballintogher in Sligo is given by the *Four Masters* (1566) *Baile an tóchair*, the townland of the causeway, but under the year 1266 they write it *Bel an tachair*, the ford mouth of the battle. Again, we may have here a purely BR. SC. name, the knowes of the dowry or marriage portion, *tocher* having that meaning in Scotch — ERSE *tóchar*, a portion, dowry (*O'Reilly*).

TÒDDEN HILL. 'Carsphairn.' Probably an adjectival form from *tod*, a fox.

TÒDDLY. 'Urr.' BR. SC. *tod lea*, the fox field. *Tod*, lit. a bush, a measure of wool — ICEL. *toddi*, a tod of wool. The fox is supposed to be so named from his *bushy* tail (*Skeat*).

TOD RIG. 'Kirkinner.' The fox hill.

TODSTONE. (*P.* Todstoun). 'Dalry.' The farm of a man named Tod.

TONDERGHÌE [*pron.* Tonnergee, *g* hard] (*P.* Toureghe; *W. P.* MSS. Tonerghe). 'Whithorn.' *See* TANDRAGEE.

TONGUE (*P.* Tung). 'Inch,' 'Kirkcudbright,' 'New Luce.' *Teanga*, a tongue or strip of land. *See under* CHANG.

TONNACHRÀE. 'Inch.' *Tamhnach reidh* [?] [tawnagh ray], smooth meadow. *See under* AUCHRAE and TANNIEFLUX.

TOOMCLACK HILL. 'Mochrum.'

TOPMÙLLOCH. 'Leswalt.'

TOR (*Inq. ad Cap.* 1575, Tor). 'Rerwick.' GAEL and ERSE *torr*, a mound, a large heap + ERSE *tor*, lit. a tower, hence a towerlike rock + W. *twr*, a tower + Prov. E. (Devonshire) *tor*, a conical hill + O.F. *tur*, F. *tour* — LAT. *turris*, a tower + GK. $\tau\acute{\nu}\rho\sigma\iota\varsigma$, $\tau\acute{\nu}\rho\rho\iota\varsigma$, a tower, bastion. The A.S. *torr*, a rock, is from the Celtic. "If the GAEL. *torr* be not borrowed from the Latin, it is interesting as seeming to take us back to a more primitive use of the word, viz., a hill suitable for defence."—*Skeat*. The ERSE *tor* has also the meaning of a thicket (*Tor*, id. q. *dumetum—Lhuyd*).

TORBÀE. 'Colvend.' *Torr beith* [bey], hill of the birches.

TORBAIN. 'Parton.' *Torr bán*, white hill.

TORD STANE.   'Stoneykirk, s.c.'

TORFLÀGGAN CRAIG.   'Troqueer.'

TORGLÀSS. 'Twynholm.' *Torr glas*, green hill.

TORHEÙGHIE.   'Balmaclellan.'

TOR HILL. 'Anwoth.' *See under* TOR.

TÒRHOUSE MACKIE [*pron.* Mackèe].   'Wigtown.'

TORHOUSEMÙIR (*P.* Torhouse Moore, Torhouse Mackulloch). 'Wigtown.'

TORKÀTRINE (*Charter* 1677, Tarskatzerine, *vulgo vocatus* Terscrachane ; *Charter* 1743, Tarscrechun). 'Urr.' This was called Torscrachan till quite recently.

TORLÀNE. 'Dalry.' *Torr leathann* [lahan], broad hill. *See under* AUCHLANE.

TORMÒID KNOWE.   'Carsphairn.'

TORMÒLLAN (*Inq. ad Cap.* 1611, Tormellen ; *P.* Tormoulling, Tormoulin). 'Balmaghie.' *Torr muileain*, hill of the mill. *See under* BALLYMELLAN.

TORNAT.   'Buittle.'

TORNIEFÀNE.   'Minigaff.'

TORNÒRROCH (*P.* Tornorroch).   'Tungland.'

TORR. 'Kirkmabreck.' *See under* TOR.

TORRECHAN. 'Buittle.' *Torr Eoghain* [?], Egan's hill. *Cf.* TERREGAN and TIEREHAN.

TORR HILL. 'Anwoth.' *See under* TOR.

TORR KNOWE. 'Kirkmabreck.' *See under* TOR.

TORR LANE. 'Minigaff.' The "lane" or stream of the *torr* or hill.

TÒRRORIE (*P.* Torary). 'Kirkbean.' *Torr a' righ*, the tower or hill of the king. *Cf.* Tornaroy in Antrim.

TORRS (*P.* Torres ; *Inq. ad Cap.* 1698, Hudder (*i.e.* hither) torris). 'Kells,' 'Old Luce.' The sand hills at the head of Luce Bay are so named. GENOCH (*q.v.*) is among them, and GAEL. *torr gainich* means a sand-heap.

TORRWHÌNNOCH (*P.* Torwhinmack). ‘Minigaff.’ *Torr fheannog* [?], hill of the carrion crows. *See under* BARWINNOCK. *Cf.* Tirfinnog in Monaghan.

TÒSKARTON. ‘Stoneykirk.’ This was formerly a parish.

TOULL. ‘Buittle.’ *Tuathal* [tooall], northern (hill or land). *See under* DRUMTOWL.

TOWER. ‘Dalry.’ *See under* TOR.

TOWERS. ‘Dalry.’ *See under* TORRS.

TRÀMOND.   ‘Old Luce.’

TRÀMMOND FORD.   ‘Wigtown.’

TRANASÀLPINE. ‘Buittle.’ A modern name = Transalpine. Formerly called the Court Hill.

TREGÀLLON.   ‘Troqueer.’

TRIP HILL. ‘Balmaclellan.’ Hill of the flock. “*Trip*, a flock.”— *Jamieson.* + E. *troop* – F. *troupe*, O.F. *trope* + SPAN. *tropa*, IT. *truppa* – LOW LAT. *tropus.* “Orig. uncertain, but most likely due to LAT. *turba*, a crowd.”—*Skeat.*

TRIPOLÀRICK.   ‘Inch.’

TROOL BURN (*P.* Truyil R.). ‘Minigaff.’ *Sruthair* [sruhar], a stream. *See under* STROOL BAY.

TRÒNACHAN. ‘Glasserton.’ *Sronachan*, a hilly place; deriv. of *sron*, a nose, a hill. *See under* STROAN.

TROQUÈER (*Charter*, 3 Rob. II., Treqvere; *P.* Troquyir; *Sibbald* MS. Traquire), a parish in the Stewartry. *Treamhar,* a farm. *See under* TERREGLES.

TROQUHÀIN (*P.* Trowhain; *Sibbald* MS. Trouhain). ‘Balmaclellan.’ *Treamhar*, a farm. *See under* TERREGLES.

TRÒSTAN (*P.* Trostan). ‘Carsphairn,’ ‘Dalry,’ ‘Minigaff,’ ‘New Abbey.’ *See under* BARTROSTAN.

TRÒSTRIE MOAT (*Rot. Scaccarii* 1456, Trostaree; MS. 1527, Trostre ; *P.* Trostari; *Sibbald* MS. Trostary). ‘Twynholm.’

TRÒUDALE GLEN (*P.* Draudaill, Traudell). ‘Rerwick.’ The trough dell. – A.S. *troh dœl*, or Scandinavian (Icel.) *trog dalr.* A.S. *troh, trog* (whence M.E. *trogh*, E. *trough*) + DU. and ICEL. *trog* + DAN. *trug* + SWED. *trȧg*, G. *trog*, M.H.G. *troc.* Root uncertain (*Skeat*).

TRÒUGHIEHOUSE (*Rot. Scaccarii Reg. Scot.* A.D. 1264, Turfhous). ‘Kells.’

TRUFF CAVE.   ‘Glasserton.’

U

TRUFF HILL. ' Kirkmaiden.' " *Truff*, corruption of E. *turf.*"—
Jamieson. E. *turf*, M.E. *turf, torf* — A.S. *turf* + DU. *turf*, peat
+ ICEL. *torf* + DAN. *törv* + SWED. *torf* + O.H.G. *zurba* + G.
torf. All from Teut. base TORBA, turf; probably cognate
with SKT. *darbha*, a kind of grass (*Skeat*).

TRYNOCK. 'New Luce.'

TULIG. ' Port Patrick, s.c.' Close by is Catelig, the last syllable
in each being apparently *liag*, a stone.

TÙLMERRICK HILL. ' Old Luce.'

TÙMMOCK FALL. ' Mochrum.' *Fauld* or enclosure of the hillock.
" Tummock, a tuft, or small spot of elevated ground. Ayrsh."
—*Jamieson.* —ERSE " *tom*, a bush, thicket, grove, a shaw ;
a small heap ; *tomach*, bushy, tufted."—*O'Reilly.*

TÙNGLAND (*P.* Tungland). A parish in the Stewartry. *See
under* CHANG *and* TONGUE.

TUNHILL. ' Leswalt,' ' Rerwick.'

TURINDÒOS HILL. ' Leswalt.' *Torrìn dubh* [dooh], black hillock.

TURKEY HILL. ' Kirkinner.'

TURNIEMÌNNOCH. ' Kirkcowan.' *Torrìn meadhonach* [mennogh],
middle hillock. *See under* BALMINNOCH.

TURNOFFYE. ' Colvend.'

TWÌNHOLM (*Inq. ad Cap.* 1605, Twyneme ; *P.* Tuynam ; *Sibbald
MS.* Twinam), a parish in the Stewartry. A.S. *tweon ham* or
tweon holm, the dwelling or the holm land between (the
streams). The exact equivalent of ADDERHALL, *q.v.* " Twin-
ham-burn, *eodem plane sensu quo Italorum* interamna."—
Bosworth. Christchurch in Hampshire was called of old
Tweonea, i.e. between the rivers.

TYDEAVERYS (*P.* Tydauarries). ' Balmaclellan.' The prefix
appears to be *tigh*, a house.

TYPES, THE (a hill of 880 feet). ' Minigaff.' *Cf.* CRAIGTYPE.

ULLOCH CAIRN AND HILL (*P.* Vlioch). ' Balmaghie.'
Uallach, proud, *i.e.* high cairn and hill. *See under* KNOCK-
WALLOCH.

ULPHINTAIL. ' Whithorn.'

ÙMFRA. ' Mochrum.' *Cf.* DRUMHUMPHREY.

URR (a parish in the Stewartry, named from the river) (*Inq.
ad Cap.* 1607, Or ; 1611, Ure, Ur). " The Basque word

for water is *Ur*, and analogy would lead us to recognise it in the rivers called Oure, Urr, Ure, Urie, Orrin, and Ore."—*Skene, Celtic Scot.* i. 216. Perhaps akin to ERSE *dur, dobhar*.

ÙRRAL (*Inq. ad Cap.* 1692, Urle; *P.* Urrull). 'Kirkcowan.

V̀ALLEYFIELD. 'Leswalt.'

VICAR'S ACRES. 'Wigtown.' *Cf.* CURATE'S NEUK and DRUM-MANOCHAN.

VICE, LOCHAN OF (*P. L.* Voyis). 'Tungland.'

WALLTREES. 'Colvend,' 'Twynholm.'

WALLY STANE. 'Kells.'

WATCH KNOWE. 'Kirkcolm.' *Cf.* LOOK KNOWE and SPY CRAIG.

WELLÈES RIG. 'Girthon.' *See* RIG OF WELLEES.

WÈLLTON. 'Port Patrick.' The well-house. *See under* TIBBERT.

WHAUPHILL. 'Kirkinner.' Hill of the curlews. "*Quhaip, quhaup, whaap*, a curlew."—*Jamieson.* The bird is named from its wailing cry — A.S. *hweóp, wop*, a cry (*Bosworth*).

WHEATCROFT. 'Crossmichael.'

WHEEB. 'Minigaff.'

WHEEBS. 'Mochrum.'

WHÈRRY CROFT. 'Mochrum.' *Foithre* [fwirry], copse.

WHÌLLAN HILL. 'Girthon.' *Chuillean* [hwillan], holly. *See under* ALWHILLAN.

WHÌLLEY. 'Kirkinner.' *Choillidh* [hwilly], copse wood.

WHÌLTON. 'Kirkpatrick Irongray.'

WHIMPARK. 'Balmaghie.'

WHINNY LIGGAT. 'Kirkcudbright.' Field-gate of the furze. E. *whin*, M.E. *whynne, guyn* — W. *chwyn*, weeds + B. *chouenna* (gutt.), to weed. *See under* LIGGATCHEEK.

WHÌRSTONE HILL. 'Twynholm.'

WHISKEY BURN. 'Minigaff.' *Uisge*, water. *See under* BENNUSKIE.

WHITECROOK (*P.* Whytcruk; *Inq. ad Cap.* 1610, Quhytcruik). 'Old Luce.' Probably white corner (*Cf.* WHITENEUK).

"*Crukis, crooks.* The windings of a river; hence it came to signify the spaces of ground closed in on one side by these windings."—*Jamieson.*

WHITE HILL, in many places. The meaning is not that of Sierra Nevada, but white, *i.e.* grass or arable land among surrounding moss. *Cf.* DRUMBAWN, KNOCKBANE, etc.

WHITEHILLS (*W. P.* MSS., The Quhytehillis). 'Sorbie.' *See under* WHITEHILL.

WHITELEYS. 'Inch.' White fields, *i.e.* cultivated fields.

WHITENEUK. 'New Abbey.' White corner. *Cf.* WHITECROOK.

WHITEWOOD CAIRN. 'Mochrum.' *Cf.* COLFIN.

WHITEYARD. 'Loch Rutton.' White enclosure; *see under* FRIAR'S YARD and WHITELEYS.

WHITHORN, a burgh and parish in Wigtownshire (*Anglo-Saxon Chronicle*, Hwiterne; Geoffery Gaimar's *Estorie des Engles, c.* 1250, Witernen; afterwards variously Quhiterne, Whitheren, etc., locally pronounced Hwùttren). The place called by Ptolemy Λουκοπιβία [Loucopibia], situated in what is now known as Wigtownshire, has been repeatedly asserted with confidence to be the place afterwards known in Latin as *Candida Casa*, and in Anglo-Saxon speech as *Hwiterne*, or the white house. Now this involves a double assumption: first, that Ptolemy or his transcribers intended to write Leucoicidia instead of Loucopibia; and second, that *Candida Casa* and *Hwiterne* were glosses upon a Greek name which had existed for at least three centuries previously in a remote Celtic country. The possible connection of the ancient name *Loucopibia* with the modern *Luce*, has already been pointed out (*see* p. 42 ; also *see under* LUCE). *Candida Casa*, in Anglo-Saxon *Hwiterne*, would be a descriptive name naturally suggested by the whiteness of a house of stone and lime compared with the mud and wattle prevalent in the district. St. Ninian's church was dedicated to St. Martin ; in the Legend of St. Cairnech it is spoken of as " the house of Martain," and " the monastery of Cairnech " (*Celt. Scot.,* ii. 46). Cairnech was bishop and abbot of the monastery and house of Martin, and in the legend he is credited with the introduction of monachism into Ireland. Probably it is the fact that he first instituted the system of religious orders in Northern Ireland, while St. Finnian took it to Southern Ireland from St. David's in Wales. St. Medana (Monenna, Moduenna, Edana) died at Whithorn (*see under* KIRKMAIDEN) in the days of St. Ninian ; and Chilnacase, a church said to have been founded by her in Galloway, was probably at Whithorn (*cill na casa*, the church or cell of (*Candida*) *Casa*). Perhaps it was the chapel at the Isle of Whithorn, which is called by Irish writers *Iniscais*, or the Isle of Casa, although popular tradition assigns to this ruin the credit of being on the original site of Ninian's Candida Casa. "There can be little question," says Mr. Skene, "that the monastery of Rosnat, called also 'Alba' and 'Candida' and 'Futerna,' and known as the 'Magnum Monasterium,' could have been no other than the monastery of Candida Casa, known to the Angles as Whithern, of which Futerna is the Irish equivalent" (*Celt. Scot.*, ii. 48).

In a paper by the Rev. J. F. Shearman, P.P. (*Irish Hist. and Arch.*, vol. vi. p. 258), the alleged connection of St. Patrick with Glastonbury is discussed and dismissed in favour of Whithorn. Father Shearman holds that the early history of Glastonbury is altogether apocryphal—that the story of St. Patrick having gone there, gathered twelve hermits living in the vicinity into a community, became their abbot and lived with them for thirty-nine years, " is adapted from a genuine but misappropriated record of facts and events appertaining to the Church of Candida Casa. . . . At the time of the consecration of St. Patrick, there was no monastery or school in South Britain. The Saxons under Hengist were warring with the Britons, and all there was in disorder. The west and south coasts of Wales were then held by Irish intruders, established there from the reign of Niall of the Nine Hostages to the middle of the fifth century, when they were expelled by the sons of Cunedda, who had been himself driven away by the Picts and Scots from Manau Guotodin in the north. The excesses and turmoils of war were unfavourable to religious life and literature, which at this time appear to have found a refuge, secluded from rapine and violence, in the monastery of St. Ninian at Candida Casa. . . . 'The Monasterium Magnum' at Candida must have been the cradle in which were nurtured the British youths who became, in course of time, the missionary helpmates of the Apostle of Ireland.

"The ancient chronicle or registry of the monastery of Candida Casa, miscalled the 'Registry of Glastonbury,' either through ignorance, or, more likely, dishonesty, was appropriated to magnify the pretensions to the great antiquity claimed by the church at Glastonbury, or Gleastingaberi, as it was called some time after the year 658, when the Saxons under Kenwalch drove the Britons beyond the river Parret. This venerable document records the decease there of the Abbot Nennius or Gildas, in the year 522. . . . In the year 498, a Bishop Patricianus, flying from the Saxon inroads in North Britain, is stated to have died this year in the 'Isle of Man,' but more probably in the inland region of Manau or Manaan; his relics are said to have been enshrined 'in Ecclesia Glasconiensi,' intended probably for Glasgow, which gave an opportunity to the Glastonbury hagioclept of appropriating that fact to this church. As Patrick junior, son of Deacon Sannan, is said to have retired to Glastonbury after the death of his uncle Patricius Magonius, or Old Patrick, A.D. 463, we are perhaps warranted in regarding North Britain as the scene of his missionary labours and death, which is all transferred to Glastonbury from the accidental resemblance of a name. The Saxon appellation for Candida Casa, a translation of its Latin designation, is Whitherne, or White House, now Whithorn, near which is the Isle of Whithorn, in Irish authorities *Iniscais*, a partial translation of *Insula Casæ*, the Isle of Candida Casa, or Inis Whitherne, which becomes *Inis Vitryn*, and *Bangor Wydryn*, another of the assumed or adopted names of Glastonbury. The latter part of this name is so suggestive of *vitrum*, and its English equivalent *glass*, that we have the Glassy Isle, an *alias* for Glastonbury or Glastonia, rendered *Urbs Vitria*, or Glastown; and in consequence a good deal more of the history of the Galwegian church of St. Ninian is transferred to its southern rival.[1] . . .

" The Arthurian legends, which have their original home in the Lowlands of Scotland, have been transferred between the ninth and twelfth centuries to Glastonbury."—*Irish Hist. and Arch.*, 4th Series, vol. vi. p. 257.

The above extract is given rather as suggesting matter for further inquiry than as settling the points in dispute.

WÌERSTON. 'Kirkcolm.' Wier's house.

WIGG (*Inq. ad Cap.* 1695, Wigne Cairne *alias* Ladywig; *P.* Wijg; *W. P.* MSS. Mekilwig, Midwik, Wygrigarne). 'Whithorn.' A.S. "*wic, wye*, a dwelling-place, village, camp, monastery, fortress."—*Bosworth.*

---

[1] It is noteworthy that Glasserton, the parish adjacent to Whithorn on the west, is locally pronounced Glaiston.

WÌGTOWN (*Act, Ed.* III., A.D. 1296, Wyggeton, Wiggeton ; *P.* Wiigtown).   A.S. *wic, wye* (*see under* WIGG), here used in the sense of a bay ; *wic tún,* the town or fort on the bay.

WÌLCOMBE BRAE.   ' Kirkmaiden.'

WILLIÀNNA (a hill of 1400 feet).   ' Carsphairn.'

WINDY BRAE OF GORDONSTOUN (*P.* Windy Hill).   ' Dalry.'

WINDY SLAP.   'Old Luce.'   Windy gap.   "*Slap,* a narrow pass between two hills."—*Jamieson.*   This name is the exact equivalent of Barnageha and Barnanageeha (*bearna na gaeithe,* pass of the winds), which are of frequent occurrence in Irish hill districts.   *See under* BARNAGEE.

WINDY STANDARD (hills ; that in Balmaclellan is 1250 feet high).   ' Balmaclellan,' ' Carsphairn.'   Windy hill.   *Cf.* DRUMAGEE.

WÌNETREES HILL.   ' Kirkinner.'

WITCH ROCK.   ' Port Patrick, s.c.'

WRAITH.   ' Rerwick.'   *Ráth* or *ráith,* "a circular earthen fort" (*Cormac Transl.*).   The sound of the final *th,* usually silent, is retained in this name, as in Rathmore, Rathdrum, etc., in Ireland.

WREATHS (*Inq. ad Cap.* 1611, Wraithis ; *P.* Cast. of Wraiths).   ' Kirkbean.'   *See under* WRAITH.

YÈLLNOWTE ISLE.   ' Kirkmaiden, s.c.'   BR. SC. *yeld nowte,* cattle that have not borne young.   "*Yeld, yeald, yell, eild.* 1. Barren.   2. A cow, although with calf, is said to *gang yeld,* when her milk dries up."—*Jamieson.*   *Nowte,* pl. of *neat,* an ox, a cow ; M.E. *neet*—A.S. *neát*+ICEL. *naut*+M.H.G. *nóz, nóss,* cattle : "so named from their usefulness and employment—A.S. *neótan, niótan,* to use, to employ."

YELLOW BOGS.   'Minigaff.'   *Cf.* MONEYBUIE.

YELLOW CRAIG.   'Dalry,' 'Kells,' 'Kirkcolm.'   Near Yellow Craig in Kells is DRUMBUIE.

YELLOW HORSE.   ' Terregles, s.c.'

YELLOW ISLE.   ' Port Patrick, s.c.'

YELLOW TOP.   ' Whithorn, s.c.'

YÈTTOWN.   'Sorbie.'   *Yett tún,* gate house or enclosure.

YÒUCHTRIE HEUGH.   'Kirkmaiden, s.c.'   Upper cliff.   ERSE *uachdarach,* and A.S. *howe.*   *See under* BARNEYWATER and STARRY HEUGH.

ADDENDA ET EMENDENDA.

ALLAN FALL. 'Mochrum.' BR. SC. *fauld*, an enclosure.

ALTRY (a hill of 1600 feet) (*P.* Altry). 'Dalry.' *Aill*, a cliff.

ANNAT. "*Annoit—andoit .i. eclais do et in aile as cenn agas is tuiside;* that is, a church which precedes another is a head and is earlier—a parent church."—*O'Don. Suppl.* "The *Annoit* is the parent church or monastery which is presided over by the patron saint, or which contains his relics."—*Celt. Scot.*, ii. 70.

ARBRACK. 'Glasserton.' *Ard borg*, high house or fort. *Cf.* BALLAIRD. This is, in its modern form, a most deceptive name, the last syllable looks so much like *bréc* (*see* AUCHA-BRICK); but the stress on first syllable indicates that as the qualitative, and this is borne out by the ancient spellings Arborg (*Rotuli Scaccarii Regum Scotorum*, A.D. 1476) and Ardborg (1475).

AUCHNABRÀCK. 'Mochrum.' *See under* AUCHABRICK.

AÙCHNESS. This is an exceedingly common name for a field. It occurs on many farms, although not recorded in the Ordnance maps.

BACKROPE. 'Mochrum.' The name of a field.

BÀGBIE. 'Kirkmabreck.'

BÀINLOCH. 'Colvend.' *Bán loch*, white loch.

BALLOCHANÒUR. 'Kirkmabreck.' *Bealach an iobhair* [?] [yure], pass or road of the yew-tree or juniper. *See under* PALNURE.

BALMÀE. 'Kirkcudbright.' *Baile magha* [?], house or land of the plain. *See under* MAY.

BALNÀB. 'Whithorn.' This name seems to be of a high anti-quity, dating from the days when there were abbots of Whithorn, which was not later, at all events, than the close of the succession of Saxon prelates about the year 800 A.D. When the see was restored in the twelfth century Whithorn became a Priory.

BARCHÒCK. 'Kells.'

BARFÀDZEAN. 'Balmaghie.' *See under* BARFADDEN.

BARFRÀGGAN. 'Kelton.' *Cf.* CRANBERRY KNOWE, in Addenda.

BARLÈNNAN. 'Kirkcowan.' "The church of Stornoway, in the island of Lewis, is dedicated to St. Lennan. Dr. Reeves thinks this name to be a corruption of Adamnan."—*Kal. Scot. Saints*, p. 378.

BARNSHÀNGAN. 'Stoneykirk.' There are no fewer than twenty-two persons named or designated *Seanán* [shanuan] in the *Martyrology of Donegal.*

BARWIN. 'Balmaclellan.' A hill adjacent to BARÈWING.

BÈLTON HILL. 'Terregles.' The theory of the prevalence of Baal-worship is so firmly fixed in the minds of sciolists in history and archæology that it will be long ere it is abandoned. Nevertheless it is grounded on pure assumption. A notable instance of the length to which it will carry its supporters is given by *Colonel Robertson* in his work on Celtic topography, when he derives Balgreen from *Baal grían*, the sun of Baal. The name, which commonly occurs near towns and villages, of course signifies the green where games of ball were played, and is pure English. *Dr. Todd* disposes satisfactorily of the false etymology. "This word (Beltine) is supposed to signify 'lucky fire,' or 'the fire of the god Bel' or Baal. The former signification is possible; the Celtic word *bil* is good or lucky, *tene* or *tine*, fire. The other etymology, although more generally received, is untenable (*Petrie* on *Tara*, p. 84). The Irish pagans worshipped the heavenly bodies, hills, pillar-stones, wells, etc. There is no evidence of their having had any personal gods, or any knowledge of the Phœnician *Baal*. This very erroneous etymology of the word Beltine is, nevertheless, the source of all the theories about the Irish Baal-worship."—*Life of St. Patrick*, p. 414.

BENERA. 'Minigaff.' *Beann iarach* [?], west hill. *See under* BLAWWEARY.

BILLIES. 'Kelton.' *Bile* [billy], a large tree. *See under* KNOCKVILLE.

BISHOP'S BURN. 'Penninghame.' Wymond, bishop of Man, resumed his Celtic name Malcolm Mac Eth, and invaded Galloway about A.D. 1135. He demanded tribute from the bishop of that province, and "was encountered by him at the head of his people when attempting to ford the river Cree; and the bishop 'having met him as he was furiously advancing and himself striking the first blow in the battle, by way of animating his party, he threw a small hatchet, and, by God's assistance, he felled his enemy to the earth as he was marching in the van. Gladdened at this event, the people rushed desperately against the marauders, and killing vast numbers of them compelled their ferocious leader shamefully to fly' (*William of Newburgh's History*, B. I. c. xxiv.). The scene of this battle is fixed by local tradition in Galloway, and a stream which flows into Wigtown Bay called Bishop's burn is said to have become crimson with blood."—*Celt. Scot.*, i. p. 464.

BOLT RIG.   'Balmaclellan.'

BÒRETREE HEUGH. 'Rerwick.' Height of the elder trees. *See under* ELDER HOLM and STARRY HEUGH.

BÒRGAN. 'Minigaff.' *Borgán*, a house, or a collection of houses, a hamlet. *See under* BORGUE. *Borgán* accurately corresponds in origin and meaning with E. *hamlet* (M.E. *hamelet*) —O.F. *hamel* (MOD. F. *hameau*). The suffix *-et* is diminutive, so is *-el* (added to O. FRIESIC *ham*, E. *home*), just as *-án* is a diminutive suffix added to *borg*.

BRACKENFALLS. 'Mochrum.' *Faulds* or enclosures of the brackens. *See under* BRECONSIDE.

BRIDGEMARK. 'Kirkpatrick Irongray.' Merkland of the bridge; written by *Pont* Markdrochat, from *drochaid*, a bridge. *See under* MARK and KNOCKDROCHWOOD (in Addenda).

BRÒADLICHENS [*pron.* lèeghens].   'Glasserton.'

BRÒUGHNA. 'Mochrum.' Probably *bruigheanán*, a house. *See under* BRENNAN.

BUITTLE. A.S. *botl*, an abode, a house.

BÙRROW HEAD. 'Whithorn.' Name from the *borg* or fortification which is still distinctly traceable. *Cf.* Burghead, between the Findhorn and the Spey, whereon a *borg* was built by Sigurd, Earl of Orkney, when he invaded Scotland about 895 A.D. (*Celt. Scot.*, i. p. 336).

BUSHABIELD.   'Crossmichael.'

BÙTTERBURN. 'Minigaff.' The bittern's stream. *See under* BUTTER HOLE.

CAIRNBÀSTIE. 'Mochrum.' *Carn blasta*, the beast's or serpent's cairn. *See under* ALTIBEASTIE.

CAIRN MOLLY.   'Balmaclellan.'

CAIRNTÀRRY. 'Mochrum.' *Carn tairbh* [tarriv], the bull's cairn. *Cf.* KNOCKENTARRY.

CARHÀLLOCH. 'Mochrum.' Evidently the same name as CORN-HULLOCH (*q. v.*) which is a different place in the same parish.

CÀRLINGWARK. 'Old Luce.' *See under* the same name in Balmaghie parish.

CARRICKFÙNDLE. 'Kirkcolm, s.c.' *Carraic Finngall*, crag of the Norsemen. *Cf.* NORWAY CRAIG on the same coast. "The two races of the Danes and Norwegians were distinguished by the terms *Dubhgeinte* or *Dubhgall*, that is, black pagans or black strangers, and *Finngeinte* or *Finngall*, white pagans or white strangers. The names Dubhgall and Finngall must not be confounded, as is usually done, with the Christian names Dubhgal and Fingal, which belong to a large class of names ending with the syllable *gal*, signifying valour."—*Celt. Scot.*, iii. 28.

CASSENCÀRIE. 'Kirkmabreck.' There can be little doubt that the derivation from *casan caithre* [caarie], the footpath of the castle, camp, or fort, is the correct one. Castle Carey in Stirlingshire and also in Somersetshire, are named from ancient earthworks near each.

CLACHANDÒW. 'Minigaff.' *Clachan dubh* [doo, dow], black stones or black hamlet. *See under* CLACHAN.

CLAWCRAP. 'Glasserton.' *See under* CLAYCROP.

CLAWYETTS.   'Minigaff.'

CLAYWHÌPPART. This name occurs in Mochrum, on the farm of Barsalloch, as well as in Whithorn.

CLINCHMAHÀFFIE. 'Old Luce.' M'Haffie's *claunch*. *See under* CLAUNCH.

CLÙTAG. 'Kirkinner.' It is possible that this is from the old valuation in pennylands. "A *peighinn*, or pennyland, might be divided into *leth pheighinn*, or half-penny, *feoirlinn*, or farthing, *leth fheoirlinn*, or half-farthing, *cianog*, or quarter-farthing, and *clitag*, equal to one-eighth farthing. . . . In Harris, in 1792, the ancient and still common computation of land was a penny, half-penny, farthing, half-farthing, clitag, etc. . . . The stock or souming for a farthing land was four milk cows, three or four horses, and as many sheep on the common as the tenant had the luck to rear."—*Capt.*

Thomas, R.N., Proc. Soc. Ant. Scot., vol. xx. p. 211. The change in pronunciation from *clitag* to Clutag would be according to a well-known rule.

COLD CRAIG. ' Balmaclellan.'

CORANBÀE (a hill of 1600 feet). 'Dalry.' *Corán beith* [bey], hill of the birches. *See under* CORAN and ALLANBAY.

CÒRSELANDS. 'Kells.' The ordinary vowel change from *carse*. *See under* CARSE.

CÒUNTEM (a hill). 'Dalry.' Probably a corruption of *ceann* [can], a head or hill.

CÒUPLAND. 'Kirkpatrick Durham.' Land that has been *couped*, bartered or exchanged. *See under* CHAPMAN and COPIN KNOWE.

CRAIGALCÀRIE. 'Balmaclellan.' *Creag an caithre* [caarie], crag of the fortress. *Cf.* CASSENCARY.

CRAIGFÀD. 'Carsphairn.' Close to this place occurs the name LANG CRAIG.

CRAIGENFÌNNIE. 'Kirkgunzeon.' *See under* CRAIGFINNIE.

CRAIGENTŸE. 'Glasserton.' *Creag an tighe*, crag of the house. *See under* DRUMATYE.

CRAIGGÀRNEL. ' Minigaff.'

CRAIGMÙIE (*P.* Kraigmuy). 'Balmaclellan.' *Creag m-buie* [?] [muie], yellow craig. *Cf.* CRAIGBUIE. The eclipse of *b* by *m* is very frequent.

CRAIGRÀNGE. ' Rerwick.'

CRAIGSTÈWART. ' Dalry.'

CRAIGTŸPE. ' Balmaghie.'

CRAIGWHÀNNEL. ' Kells.'

CRANBERRY KNOWE. 'Minigaff.' *See under* BARFRAGGAN.

CREE. "The early Latin editions (of *Ptolemy*) have, instead of *Ienæ aestuarium, Fines aestus.* It is possible that this may be the correct reading, and that Wigtown Bay may have marked the utmost limit to which the Roman troops penetrated in Agricola's second campaign."—*Celt. Scot.,* i. 66, note. *Finis*, an end, a limit, may be translated by ERSE *crích*. At all events the Cree seems to have been reckoned immemorially the boundary between East and West Galloway, hence, probably, the name *crích*, a boundary.

CRÙGGLETON. 'Sorbie.' A place called Crogington and Crogelton in Shropshire is mentioned in a roll of Henry VIII., quoted by *Dugdale* (*Monasticon*, iii. 527).

CRÙFFOCK. 'Balmaghie.'

CULRÀVEN. 'Borgue.'

CUTTYSHALLOW. Another form of KITTYSHALLOCH, *q.v.*

DALÀVAN. 'Anwoth.' *Dal abhuinn* [avun], land-portion of the river. It is on the Fleet.

DALÀRRAN. 'Balmaclellan.' *Dal iairn*, land-portion of the iron. *See under* GLENIRON.

DERGÀLL. 'Kirkmabreck.' This is now called the Englishman's Burn, so it is a fair assumption that the meaning of the Celtic is *dobhar* [dour] *gall*, the stranger's or foreigner's stream. There is a reputed site of a battle here, on which is CAIRNEY-WANIE, and there are many sepulchral remains on the hills near.

DERNSCLÒY. 'Kells.'

DRUMATÀGGART. 'Minigaff.' *Druim a' t-sagairt* [taggart], the priest's hill ; or *druim mic t-sagairt*, M'Taggart's or the priest's son's hill. *See under* ALTAGGART.

DRUMBÈG. This name occurs also in Kirkcudbright, alongside of DRUMMORE.

DRUMBLÀIN. 'Parton.' *Druim bléana* [blaney], ridge of the creek or bay. *See under* BLANYVAIRD. *Cf.* LINBLANE.

DRUMKÈESIE. 'Balmaclellan.'

DRUMMIESÙE. 'Old Luce.' The suggested explanation is probably incorrect. It is more likely *druim a' samhadh* [soo], ridge of the sorrel.

DRUMMÒRE. This name occurs also in Kirkcudbright alongside of DRUMBEG.

DRUMSLÈW. 'Kells.' *Druim sliabhe* [slewe], ridge of the moor. *See under* SLACARNACHAN.

DRUMSÙIR. 'Minigaff.'

DRYCOG. 'Kells.' Empty or dry bowl, metaph. of a dry hollow in the land. "*Cog*, a hollow wooden vessel of a circular form for holding milk, etc."—*Jamieson*. *Cf.* ERSE *cog*, a draught.

DUNKÌRK. 'Kells.' *Dun ceorce* [kurkie], hill of the oats, or *dun cearc* [kark], hill or fort of the grouse. *See under* BARNKIRK and MILLQUHIRK.

ÈLDRICK or ÈLDRIG. Places of this name occur in 'Kells' and 'Minigaff.' BR. SC. *yeld* or *eild rig*, barren or fallow ridge. *See under* YELLNOWTE.

ÈRVIE CRAIG. 'Carsphairn.' *Cf.* ERVIE.

FANG OF THE MERRICK. 'Minigaff.' This may not improbably be *fán*, a steep ascent. *See under* FANS.

FANS OF ÀLTRY. 'Dalry.' ERSE "*fán*, a declivity, steep, inclination, descent."—*O'Reilly*.

GALL KNOWE. 'Rerwick.' *Gall*, a standing stone. The next farm to it is called STANDING STONE. *See under* DERGALL.

GALLRÌNNIES. 'Balmaclellan.' *Geal* [gal] *rinn*, white point, hill, or division of land. It is also called WHITE HILL. *See under* CARRICKGILL and RHINNS.

GÀRMEL. 'Minigaff.' *See under* GARMILL.

GLEDE HILL. 'Crossmichael.' *Cf.* BAROLAS and GLEDE BOG.

GÒLDTHORPE KNOWE. 'Kells.' A.S. and M.E. *þorp*, a village or hamlet + DU. *dorp* + ICEL. *þorp* + DAN. *torp*, a hamlet + SWED. *torp*, a little farm, cottage + G. *dorf* + GOTH. *þaurp*, a field. Allied, says *Skeat*, to LITH. *troba*, a building, a house, and perhaps to the Erse *treamh*, a farm, a village round a farm, a tribe, family, clan, GAEL *treabhair*, houses + W. *tref*, a homestead or hamlet, from the verb *treabhaim*, I plough, suggesting the conclusion that *thorp* signifies the houses on the farmed lands. *See under* TERREGLES.

HAGGIS HAUSE (a glen). 'Kells.' *See under* HAUSE BURN. "*Haggis*, a dish commonly made in a sheep's maw, of the lungs, heart, and liver of the same animal, minced with suet, onions, salt and pepper, and mixed up with highly-toasted oatmeal."—*Jamieson*. The use of the word here must be metaphorical.

HÈSTAN ISLE. 'Rerwick.' A.S. *east hólm*, eastern island. This has been identified, with every probability, by *Mr. M'Kerlie* (vol. ii. p. 464) with Eastholm, on which, in 1342, stood the castle of Duncan MacDouall, son of Dungall or Dougall, chief of the family in Galloway. *Mackenzie* refers to Estholm on the coast of Wigtownshire, but he is probably in error. There are traces of buildings on the island ; and it seems to be the island referred to in the *Rotuli Scotiæ* as *insula de Estholm in Scotia* and *Estholm in Galeway.*

HEUGH. 'Colvend.' A height. *See under* STARRY HEUGH.

HIGHLANDMAN'S RIG. 'Minigaff.'

HÌNTON. 'Anwoth.' M.E. *hine's toun*, the dwelling of the *hind* or peasant. *Cf.* CARLETON. — A.S. *hína,* a domestic — A.S. *hiw*, a house (the origin of E. *hive*), from Teutonic base III= √KI, to lie, whence SKT. *çí*, to lie, GK. *κεῖμαι,* L. *civis*, etc.

KENTIE. 'Minigaff.' *Ceann tighe*, hill of the house, or principal house. *See under* DRUMATYE.

KILNÀIR (*P.* Calnair). 'Dalry.' *Cúil n-air*, corner of the slaughter or of the ploughing. *See under* BARNAER.

KILNÒTRIE. 'Crossmichael.' *Cf.* DUNNOTTRIE.

KIRCÀLLA. 'Penninghame.' The church of Gress in the island of Lewis is dedicated to St. Aula, who, says Bishop Forbes, is probably St. Olave, though he may have been the St. Angulus or Aule, who occurs in the Martyrologies at the 7th of February."—*Kal. Scot. Saints*, p. 272.

KNOCKDRÌNAN. 'Parton.' *See under* KNOCKDRONNAN.

KNOCKDRÒCHWOOD. 'Kirkpatrick Irongray.' *Cnoc drochaid*, bridge hill. The next farm is BRIDGEMARK, *q.v. See under* BARDROCHWOOD.

KNOCKENTÀRRY. 'Mochrum.' *Cnoc an tairbh* [tarriv], the bull's hill. *Cf.* CAIRNTARRY.

KNOCKIERÀY. 'Minigaff.' *Cnoc a' ratha* [raa], hill of the fort. *See under* WRAITH.

KNOCKÌMMING. 'Kelton.'

KNOCKLÀE. 'Balmaclellan.' *Cnoc laegh*, hill of the calves. *See under* BARLAE and CAWVIS HILL.

KNOCKMÒWDIE. 'Kells.' *Cnoc madadh* [maddy], hill of the dogs or wolves. *See under* BLAIRMODDIE.

KNOCKNAMÒON. 'Minigaff.' *Cf.* LOCH MOAN. At p. 227 this name is erroneously printed KNOCKNAMOOR.

KNOCKNÀN. 'Balmaclellan.' *Cnoc n-en*, birds' hill. *See under* BARNEAN.

KNOCKNÀW. 'Minigaff.' The first meaning suggested is the correct one ; it is close to a ford on PULLOW BURN.

KNOCKRÒCHER. 'Rerwick.' *Cnoc crochadhair* [crogher], hangman's hill. *See under* AUCHENROCHER.

LESWÀLT (*Barnbarroch*, 1580, Loch Swaid ; *Synod of Galloway* 1664, Lochswalt). *Sympson* says this name was pronounced Lasswade. The first syllable is probably *lis*, a fort. *See under* DRUMLASS.

LOOK KNOW. 'Balmaclellan.' *Cf.* SPY CRAIG.

MAIDENHEAD BAY. 'Kirkmaiden, s.c.' Is it possible that this is, as Maidenhead on the Thames is said to be, from A.S. *meddan hýð*, middle port or landing-place ?

MÈLDENS. 'Minigaff.'

MÙRDOCH CAVE. 'Minigaff.' If not named from Murdoch, the second son of the widow of Craigencallie (*see under* CRAIGEN-CALLIE) to whom King Robert the Bruce granted the lands of CUMLODEN (often referred to as Cumlodden-Murdoch), the cave bears, at all events, the name of some of his successors in the property (*M'Kerlie*, iv. 405).

NICK OF TRÈSTRAN. 'Kirkmabreck.' *See under* BARTROSTRAN.

NÒGGIN. 'Kirkmabreck.' *Cnocín*, a hill, dim. of *cnoc*. *See under* KNOCKEAN.

OLD STRAND. 'Carsphairn.' The *strand* or stream (*see under* STRAND OF THE ABYSS) of the *allt*, glen. *Allt* has become *Old* by the process described under OLD WATER, *q.v.*

ORNÒCKENOCH. 'Anwoth.' This is written by *Pont* Ardkrock-anoc, showing the alternative form *croc* for *cnoc*. *See under* CROCKENCALLY. The first syllable may have been *ard* instead of *aridh*.

PÀPY HA'. 'Minigaff.' Perhaps the Norse *papa*, a preacher. "The Norsemen called these missionaries *Papæ* ; and many of the islands, on which they found some preacher from Iona, still bear the names of Papey and Papeyar."—Innes's *Scotland in the Middle Ages* (1860), p. 101. "The pre-Columban Christianity of Scotland was that of Galloway and Pictland, and if we may credit certain legendary statements, which however have been generally discredited, an earlier infusion direct from the East into Northern Pictland. . . . Pictland, certainly, would be the highway to the northern Islands and to Iceland, and it may be worth consideration whether the Christian monks called Papæ, whom the discoverers of Iceland found there in the ninth century, were not the representatives of some such pre-Columban influence from the Scottish mainland ; for Papa, although it has lingered in the

Breton Church, is certainly not Columban nor Irish, but characteristically Eastern."—Sir S. Ferguson's *Ogham Inscriptions* (1887), p. 137.

PULWHÀNNER BURN.   ' Kirkmabreck.'

RAÈBERRY. ' Kirkcudbright.' A.S. *ráh beorh*, the roe's hill. *Ráh* becomes M.E. *ro*, but *Chaucer* (*C. T.* 4084) gives NORTH E. *ra* +ICEL. *rá*+DAN. *raa*+SWED. *ra*+DU. *ree*+G. *reh*.

RÀMSEY. 'Whithorn.' A.S. *rammes ige*, ram's island. Probably an ancient name for the whole island, though now limited to one point. *Cf.* Ramsey in Huntingdonshire, Romsey and Sheppey (*scéap ige*, sheep island) in Kent, Ramsay in Man, etc.

RÀTTRA. ' Borgue.' There is an old fort here.

RHINNS, THE. ERSE *rinn* is probably akin to GK. ῥίς, gen. ῥινος, a nose, of which the later form is ῥίν.

RÌNGAN. This name occurs also on the farm of CRELLOCH, in Mochrum.

RISK. This name occurs also on the farm of BARWINNOCK in Glasserton.

SÀNDFORD. ' New Abbey,' Places of this name are found in Hants, Berks, Oxfordshire, etc.

SLEWSPÌRN. ' Kirkcolm.' The first syllable is *sliabh* [slew], a moor.

SKEENGÀLLIE. ' Kirkinner.' *Sceithín* [skehin] *gallach*, bush of the standing stones. *See under* KILGALLIOCH, and *cf.* Skehinagan in Ireland, written, in the *Annals of Loch Cé, sceithín na cend*, or bush of the heads.

SOÙTHWICK. ' Colvend.' *Cf.* Southwick in Sussex, Southwyke in Hants and Huntingdonshire, etc.

STÈNNOCK. ' Whithorn.' This is probably not a Celtic name, but A.S. *stan wic*, stone house, like Stanwick in Yorkshire.

WIGG. ' Whithorn.' *Cf.* Uig, a parish now united to Snizort, in Skye, variously written Wig and Vig. The name Uig comes immediately from the Scandinavian (ICEL. *vic*, a bay), but the word is the same as the A.S. *wic*, meaning either a village or a bay.

APPENDIX A.

TRANSLATION of the Article which, in addition to an EXTRACT
from CAMDEN, descriptive of the Province, accompanies
PONT'S MAPS of GALLOWAY in BLAEU'S ATLAS. It was
published in 1662.

DESCRIPTION OF GALLOWAY, BY JOHN MACLELLAN.

Gallovidia takes its name from *Gallovid*, which in the language of
the ancient *Scots* means *Gaulish;* for from the beginning the *Scottish
Brittons* used to call the earliest inhabitants of Britain *Gauls*, implying
that they came from *Gallia*. This ancient dominion of the *Brittons* is
bounded on the south by the *Irish* sea, on the west by the Firth of
Clyde, on the north by *Carrick*, & *Kyle*, on the north-east by the river
Nith; in length it extends from the north-east 70 miles to the south-
west, between the bridge of Dumfries & the extreme promontory of
Mull. In breadth from north to south it reaches in some places 24, in
some 20, in some 16 miles. Six rivers intersect it, *Ur, Dee, Ken, Cree,
Bladna, Luss,* running into the *Irish* sea. The *Ken,* running through
Glenkens, flows into the lake of the same name, and on leaving it loses
its name at its confluence with the *Dee* twelve miles from the sea. There
is also a certain stream, the *Fleet* (about half way between the *Dee* and
the *Cree*), and the *Palnure* (*Palinurus*); but these are not reckoned
among the greater rivers. All are celebrated for salmon-fisheries; but
the *Dee* excels the others. The whole region is most healthy both in
climate and soil; it rarely ascends into mountains, but rises in many
hills. Three mountains of notable height are to be observed therein; one
at the mouth of the *Cree,* commonly called *Carnesmoor,* that is (if you
would interpret it) *Carnesii desertum;* & another, not far from it,
Marocus;[1] & a third, at the mouth of the *Nith, Crefeldius.*[2]

The land lying beyond the *Luce* is called *Rinum,*[3] that is to say the
Beak of *Galloway,* inasmuch as it projects like the beak of a bird; and
its furthest end is called *Novantum Promontorium*—by the natives the
Mule, that is to say, bald & shaven : for the ancient *Scots* used to call
promontories *Mules* (mulls), a metaphor taken from a shaven head. The
estuary of the *Luss,*[4] Ptolemy's *Rerigonius,* on the east, & Loch Rian,
Ptolemy's *Vidogara* on the west, contract the land and make an Isthmus,

---

[1] The Merrick.   [2] Criffel.   [3] The Rhinns.   [4] Luce.

& a Chersonese or peninsula, not unlike *Peloponesus*. The whole of *Galloway* recals the figure of an elephant; the *Rhinns* form the head, the *Mule* the proboscis; the headlands jutting into the sea, the feet; the mountains above named represent the shoulders; rocks & moors (*ericeta*) the spine; the rest of the body consisting of the remainder of the district.

It has the following more important harbours, *Fanum Cudberti*[1] in the estuary of the *Dee*, capable of holding many ships, and a safe shelter, inasmuch as by the protection of the hills and the Isle of *Ross*, it is protected on all sides from the winds; & *Cariovilla*,[2] a safe roadstead for ships, & three in the Chersonese or *Rhinns*, *Nessocus*,[3] Loch *Rian* and Port *Patrick*.

The entire Province is divided into upper and lower *Galloway*; the upper lies between the river *Cree* and the *Mule* promontory, and has as judge of capital affairs the head of the family of *Agnew*,[4] which honour passed to them after the destruction of the family of *Maclellan*. The lower (division) commonly (called) the Stewartry (*præfectura*) of Kirk-cudbright, has as judge the chief of the family of *Maxwell*.

There are there three Presbyteries, that of *Kirkcudbright*, that of *Victon*,[5] and that of *Stranraver*. In the Presbytery of *Kirkcudbright* are reckoned 17 parish Churches, in that of *Victon* nine, in that of *Stranraver* 8: Out of these the Synod is convened twice a year. Whatever Churches there are beyond the *Ur* belong to the Presbytery of *Dumfris*.

It has these towns, Fanum *Cudberti* (commonly *Kirckcubrie*) at the mouth of the *Dee*, celebrated for the harbour of that name; & *Victon*, once a well-known emporium, built (as is believed) by the *Brittons* at the mouth of the *Cree*; *Candida Casa* (commonly *Whithorn*) distinguished by its monastery. *Capella*, or (as some prefer) *Stranraver*, on Loch Rian in the Chersonese. Not so long ago *New Galloway*, on the river *Ken*, was admitted into the list of burghs, but it has almost nothing urban except the name, as there are very few houses built there: forasmuch as *Viscount Kenmure*, who began the construction of the town, being overtaken by death, left the work at its commencement. Weekly markets however are held there, at which the natives assemble in tolerable numbers, some to buy, others to sell produce which is carried thither by merchants from the neighbouring country.

Monasteries in *Galloway* (are), *Candida Casa* sacred to Ninian, who used to be considered a tutelary god in the furthest corner of *Galloway*, whither of old men from distant parts undertook pilgrimages, for the sake of religion, to see the relics & church of *Ninian*, and to carry away a portion of sacred dust, which was in these days considered a signal evidence of sanctity; the Monastery of *Luss*, on the bay of the river *Luss*; *Dundranan*, at the fourth (mile) stone to the east of *Kirk-*

[1] Kirkcudbright.   [2] Carsethorn (?).   [3] Port Nessock.
[4] Agnew of Lochnaw, Hereditary Sheriff of Galloway.   [5] Wigtown.

cudbright ; Glycicardium (commonly New Abbey) on the estuary of the
Nith : Tungland, on the banks of the *Dee ; Marianum,*[1] at the mouth
of the *Dee,* about eight hundred paces below Kirkcudbright ; *Salsidense,*[2]
in the Chersonese, but by whom some of these were founded does not
appear, owing to the absence of Records.

The natives are strong and warlike : assuredly in the late battle of
Neoburn, on the Tine in England, a handful of Galloway knights under
the leadership of *Patrick Mackie*, whose son was killed in that action,
gave a splendid example of their gallantry, for with their long spears
they threw the dense body of the enemy into such confusion as to secure
an easy victory for their comrades. Formerly this race was prone to
maintaining feuds, but it has gradually learnt by more humane culture
and civilised religion to lay aside its ferocity : the gentry, ready alike
with hand and head, are quite equal to any in refinement of person and
of manners. The country-folk are of powerful build, & not deficient in
understanding.

Those who live in the *Mores*, that is to say, in the wastes, make a
living by rearing cattle, and have large flocks of sheep ; the sheep there
are of the best kind both in respect of flavour of mutton & excellence of
fleece. Large quantities of wool are carried hence to foreign parts by
merchants, who derive no small profit thereby.

Those who live in the *Machers*, that is to say the arable ground &
plains, sustain life by agriculture ; nor do they lack fertile pasture, &
flocks, oats of small but well-filled grain is grown there, from which
they make the best of meal.

Galloway produces horses of but small size, but game & strong,
which bring everywhere the highest price.

The most distinguished families here are the *Gordons*, the *Maxwells*,
the *Maclellans, Macdowalls, Mackies, Maccullochs, Stuarts, Agnews,
Adares.* But the *Macdowalls, Maclellans, Mackies* & *Maccullochs* excel
the rest in antiquity, & pristine honour. The others are more recent.
Formerly the clan *Maclellan* flourished there, unquestionably premier
(as Buchanan testifies) in descent and wealth, but when Patrick, chief of
that family, was destroyed by *Duglass*, his kinsmen inspired by vengeance
collected their forces and carried fire and sword among the adherents of
Duglass in *Clydesdale ;* in consequence of which reprehensible deed a
fine was laid upon their possessions, they themselves were outlawed, &
compelled to till the soil, which reduced this wealthy family to such
poverty, that it has never completely recovered from it. But after a
few years the son of Patrick, having been long in hiding, slew the pirate
Moor (pirata *Afro*)[3] who rendered the coasts of *Galloway* dangerous, was
restored to the King's favour, and to part of his ancient patrimony of
Bombie.

Stinceel[4] in *Teviot* was the ancient seat of the *Gordons*, whence two

---

[1] St. Mary's Isle.
　　See under Black Morrow Well in the Glossary.

[2] Saulseat.

[4] Stinchell.

brothers set out, one for *Galloway*, the other for *Bogie*, and founded in either place a prosperous race of *Gordons.* He who came to *Galloway*, having killed a huge boar that was devastating the fields, obtained a grant of *Gordonstoun & Lochinvar* (*Lacus varrii*) from the King, and left a numerous posterity. The Adares are believed to have sprung from the race of princes of Kildare, in *Ireland.*

Among the *Gallovidians* (are these) nobles, *Stuart* earl of *Galloway, Gordon Viscount Kenmure, Maclellan Baron Kirkcudbright*, each the chief of his own people. There are also there many cavaliers natives of the soil.

There are numerous strongholds there, but till lately the strongest of all was *Treve*, in an Island of the river *Dee*, eight miles from *Kirkcudbright.* It was built by *Duglass*, who, in the reign of James the Second caused great disturbance to his country. This place was defended during the late conflicts in our district by the adherents of *Maxwell*, earl of *Nith*(sdale); but, being surrendered at last its vaults were broken down, its roof and floors removed, and it was rendered indefensible. Two towers stronger than the rest appear in the Rhinns, (Castle) *Kennedy*, built by the earl of Casilliss in loch *Inch* (lacu *Insulano*); *Scæodunum* (commonly called *Dunskey*, that is, the winged tower) by the ancestors of *Robert Adare* on a steep cliff by the sea. There are others also, *Crugulton*, for instance, a well-fortified stronghold on the estuary of the Cree, *Glaston*,[1] *Garlice, Clarey, Cudbertana*,[2] *Cardanes & Rusco*, besides many notable mansions.

In lower *Galloway* (there are the following) lakes, *Caloverca*,[3] *Multonius*,[4] *Ritonius*,[5] *Kennus*.[6] In upper (Galloway) *Martonius*,[7] *Macrumius*,[8] *Longocastrius*,[9] *Insulanas*,[10] *Nævius*.[11] The woods which render this region pleasant are those of *Kenmure, Cree, & Garlice.*

Whoever wishes to know about the battles fought in this district should consult the histories of Scottish affairs written by *Buchanan & Boëthius.* To put it in few words (notwithstanding that one may hear it evil spoken of by those unacquainted with the country) *Galloway* is

> A land with native goods content,
> Not craving foreign trade,
> To comforts earned by industry
> Nature here lends her aid.

In no part of Scotland are the fleeces more excellent, nowhere in Scotland are there stouter nags, though (they are) small; they call them *Galloway-nages.* So that Englishmen call all good horses *Gallowas.*

---

[1] Glasserton.   [2] Kirkcudbright.   [3] Carlingwark.
[4] Milton.   [5] Loch Rutton.   [6] Loch Ken.
[7] Myrton Loch.   [8] Mochrum Loch.   [9] Longcastle, *now* Dowalton Loch.
[10] Loch Inch.   [11] Lochnaw.

APPENDIX B.

ERSE AND GAELIC WORDS ENTERING INTO NAMES OF PLACES IN GALLOWAY; WITH A REFERENCE TO THE NAMES UNDER WHICH THE WORDS ARE ANALYSED.

Abb, an abbot,	Balnab.
Abhainn [avan, awen, own], a stream,	Slochanawn.
Achadh [aha], a field,	Achie.
Adhamhnan [ounan, eunan], a man's name,	Kirkennan.
Aedhaire [airie], a shepherd,	Craigary.
Aenach [ennagh], a fair,	Enoch.
Afreca, a woman's name,	Knockefferick.
Aileach [ellagh], a stone fort,	Craiganallie.
Aill, a cliff,	Alhang.
Airgiod [arggid], silver,	Craignarget.
Airidh [airie], a shieling, a hill pasture,	Airie.
Aith [ae], a kiln,	Auchenhay.
Allt, a height, a glen, a stream,	Aldergowan.
Alltán, a little glen,	Altain.
Alltóg, a little glen,	Altogue.
Alluin, a hind,	Craigellan.
Aluin, beautiful,	Craigellan.
Amhalghaidh [owlhay], a man's name, Aulay,	Macherally.
Ammor, a trough,	Ballochanarmour.
Amreidh [amrey], rough,	Carrickcamrie.
Anoid [annud], a church,	Annat Hill.
Aoradh [arra], worship,	Clachanarrie.
Ar, ploughing,	Barnaer.
Ar, slaughter,	Barnaer.
Arbha [arva, arroo], corn,	Arrow.
Ard, high; a height,	Aird.
Ath [ah], a ford,	Carsnaw.
Aula, a man's name,	Kircalla.
Bachall, a stick,	Bachla.
Bachlach, a herdsman,	Bachla.
Bád, a boat,	Portavaddie.
Badhun [bawn], a cattle-pen,	Biawn.

Baile [bally], a farm, a homestead, a town,	Bailie Hill.
Bainne [banny], milk,	Barwhanny.
Bairghín [bareen], a bannock,	Barean.
Bán, white ; *s.* lea-land,	Auchtrievane.
Banbh [bonniv], a young pig,	Auchnabony.
Baoghal [baughal], danger,	Barnbauchle.
Bard, a rhymer,	Barnboard.
Barr, a hill-top,	Bar.
Bathach [ba-ach], a cowhouse,	Buyoch.
Beag [beg], small,	Drumbeg.
Bealach [ballagh], a road, a pass,	Balloch.
Bean [ban], a woman,	Barnamon.
Bean [ban], a man's name,	Kirkbean.
Beann [ben], a hill,	Bennilsa.
Beannach [bennagh], hilly ground,	Craigbennoch.
Beannán [bennan], a hill,	Bennan.
Bearna [barna], a gap, a pass,	Barnagee.
Bearnach, split,	Craigbernoch.
Bearradh [barra], a hill-brow, a precipice,	Barrack Slouch.
Beist, or *béast*, a beast, a serpent,	Ballochabeastie.
Beith [bey], a birch,	Allanbay.
Beithach [beyach], a birch wood,	Barbeth.
Beul [bel], a mouth,	Ballochadee.
Bil, lucky,	{ Beltonhill (in Addenda).
Bile [billy], a large tree,	Knockville.
Blár, a plain ; a battle,	Blair.
Blárach, a level place,	Blairoch.
Blean, the groin ; a creek, a bend,	Blaneyvaird.
Bo, a cow,	Biawn.
Boc, a he-goat,	Auchniebut.
Bodach, a clown,	Drummuddioch.
Bog, soft, miry,	Bogue.
Bogluasgach, boggy, floating,	Anabaglish.
Bogreach, *bogurach*, boggy,	Boggrie.
Bolcan, a man's name,	Barvalgans.
Borgán, a hamlet,	{ Borgan (in Addenda).
Both [bo], a hut, a booth,	Bow.
Bothach [bohach], a marsh,	Buyach.
Bothán [bohan], a hut, a booth,	Barbuchanny.
Bothar [bóhar], a causeway,	Stoneybatter.
Brá, brí, a brae or hillside,	Brae.
Bradán, a salmon,	Lanebreddan.
Braenán, Brennán, a man's name,	Drumabrennan.
Braghadóg [braadog], a throat, a gulley,	Bradock.

Branchu [branhy], a man's name,	Craigmabranchie.
Brathair [braar], a brother, a friar,	Altibrair.
Breac [brack], spotted,	Auchabrick.
Breac [brack], a trout,	Altibrick.
Breacach [brackagh], broken, spotted ground,	Breackoch.
Bréach [bragh], a wolf,	Drumbreach.
Breaclach [bracklagh], broken, spotted ground,	Brecklach.
Breacnach [bracknagh], broken, spotted ground,	Brackenicallie.
Bréan [brain], stinking, foul,	Branyea.
Bréanshcach [branyae], stinking,	Branyea.
Bretan, a man's name; a Welshman,	Culbratten.
Brigid, *Brighde* [breedie], a woman's name, Bridget,	Hillmabreedia.
Brioc [Bric], a man's name,	Kirkmabreck.
Broc, a badger,	Brockloch.
Broclach, a badger-warren,	Brockloch.
Bruach, a brink or border,	Brough.
Bruighedn, a dwelling,	Borgue.
Bruigheanán, a dwelling,	Borgue.
Buachaill [baughil], a herd-boy,	Bowhill.
Buidhe [buie, bwee], yellow,	Benbuy.
Builg, bellows,	Bullet.
Buirg, or *borg*, a fort, a dwelling, a hamlet,	Borgue.
Bun, bottom, end,	Barbunny.
Cabhán [cavven], a hollow,	Cavan.
Caedh [kay], a bog, quagmire,	Culkae.
Caein [keen], beautiful,	Knockeen.
Caer, a berry,	Drumkare.
Caera, a sheep,	Culgarie.
Caerthainn [keerin], a rowan-tree,	Barwhirran.
Cailleach, a nun, a hag,	Barncalzie.
Cainneach, a man's name, Kenny,	Cairn Kennagh.
Caipeal, a chapel,	Chapelrossan.
Cairbre, a man's name,	Dunharbery.
Caiseal, a castle,	Auchengashell.
Caithre [carey], a pillar-stone,	Drumacarie.
Cala, *caladh*, a harbour,	Callie.
Calltuin, hazel,	Caldons.
Cam, crooked,	Camelon.
Camrach, crooked, winding,	Camrie.
Caol [keel], narrow,	Carskeel.
Capall, a horse,	Barhapple.
Carn, a heap, a cairn,	Auchencairn.
Carnachán, a man's name,	Fauldcarnahan.
Carr, a stone,	Cardoon.
Carrach, rough,	Barharrow.

Carraic, a sea-cliff,	Carghidoun.
Carraigán, a cliff,	Cargen.
Casán, a footpath,	Airiehassan.
Cat, a cat,	Alwhat.
Cathag [caag], a jackdaw,	Caggrie.
Cathair [caher],	Kirklauchline.
Ceann [ken], a head,	Cambret Hill.
Ceannach, a bargaining,	Drumcannoch.
Ceannaiche [kennaghie], a pedlar, a merchant,	Barneconahie.
Ceannfhionn [canninn], white-headed, or speckled,	Knockcannon.
Ceapanach, full of stumps,	Capenoch.
Cearc [cark], a hen,	Millquhirk.
Cearda [carda], a workshop, a forge,	Cairdie Wiel.
Ceathramhaidh [carrou], a land-quarter,	Carhowe.
Ceide, ceidach [keady], hill,	Kittyshalloch.
Cennera [kennera], a woman's name,	Kirkinner.
Ceorce, or *coirce* [curky], oats,	Barnkirk.
Ciarán [keeran], a man's name,	Chipperheron.
Cill [kill], a cell, a chapel,	Kildonan.
Cinaedh [kinna], a man's name, Kenneth,	Benniguinea.
Cip [kip], a stump, a tree-trunk,	Ballochakip.
Circ [kirk], a church,	Kirkanders.
Clach, or *cloch*, a stone,	Clachan.
Clacharach, or *cloichreach*, a stony place,	Clauchrie.
Clacherin, a stony place,	Clacherum.
Claddach, a shingly beach,	Claddiochdow.
Cladh [claw, cly], a mound, a bank; a grave,	Cly.
Claen, a slope,	Clamdally.
Claenach, a sloping place,	Clannoch.
Claenrach, a sloping place,	Clanerie.
Claigean [claggan], a skull; a round, dry hill,	Barnyclagy.
Clais [clash], a ditch, a pit; a grave,	Clash.
Clár, a board; flat land,	Clare Hill.
Clérech, a cleric, a priest,	Barneycleary.
Cliabh [cleeve], a basket,	Drumcleigh.
Clitag, one-eighth of a farthing; a land-measure,	Clutag.
Cluain [cloon, clone], a meadow,	Clone.
Cnoc, a hill,	Knock.
Cnocán, a hillock,	Knockan.
Cnocín, a hillock,	Knockean.
Cnoclach, a hilly place,	Knockloch.
Cnocnach, hilly,	Ornockenoch.
Cnuicín [nicken], a hillock,	Knockanickin.
Coigeriche [coggrie], a stranger,	Drumcagerie.
Coill [kill], a wood,	Barnhillie.
Coilleach [killagh], a cock, a grouse,	Drumagilloch.

Coillidh [killy], woodland,	Killibrakes.
Cointin [kintin], a dispute,	Quintinspie.
Coire [kirry], a caldron ; a deep pool ; a narrow glen,	Currafin.
Coll, the hazel,	Barwhil.
Colldean, a hazel wood,	Caldons.
Comgan, a man's name,	Kirkcowan.
Conadh [kunna], firewood,	Knockcunnoch.
Conaire [conary], a man's name,	Slickconerie.
Connal, a man's name,	Loch Connel.
Copán, the dock, docken,	Capenoch.
Cor, a hill,	Coran.
Coradh [corra], a weir,	Corra Pool.
Corán, a hill,	Coran.
Corcra, red,	Barncorkrie.
Corcur, red,	Barncorkrie.
Cormac, a man's name,	Kirkcormack.
Corr, a beak,	Coran.
Corrach, a boat,	Glencurroch.
Cós, a fissure,	Cash Bag.
Cos, a foot,	Cushiemay.
Craebh [crave, crew], a tree,	Castle Creavie.
Craebhach [creavagh], wooded,	Castle Creavie.
Crann, a tree, a pole,	Crancree.
Crannóg, a boat,	Crannoch Isle.
Creag [craig], a crag,	Craig.
Creagán, a crag,	Craigenbay.
Creamh [crav], wild garlic,	Culgruff.
Criathrach [crearagh], waste land,	Creary Hill.
Crindaill, a man's name, Crindle,	Loch Inch-Crindle.
Crioch [creegh], a boundary,	Cree.
Crion [creen], withered,	Slewcreen.
Criosd [crist], Christ,	Kirkchrist.
Crithlach [crillagh], a shaking bog,	Crailloch.
Croc = *cnoc*, a hill,	Crockencally.
Crocán = *cnocán*, a little hill,	Crockencally.
Crochadhair [craugher], a hangman,	Auchenrocher.
Croich, a gallows,	Culcreuchie.
Crom, crooked, sloping,	Crumquhil.
Cromadh [crumma], a hill-side,	Crummie.
Cromóg, a sloping place,	Crammag.
Crón, copper,	Craigcroon.
Crón, brown,	Craigcroon.
Cros, a cross, a gallows,	Balnacross.
Crosra, croissare, cross-roads,	Croshery.
Cruach [croagh], a hill,	Croach.

Cruachach, hilly, uneven,	Craichie.
Cruachán, a hill,	Crochan.
Cruadh [croo], hard,	Crows.
Cruadhas [crouse], hard, dry land,	Crowes.
Cruiteach [cruttagh], lumpy, uneven,	Crotteagh.
Crumóg, a slope,	Crammag.
Cu, a dog,	Drumwhin.
Cudachán, a man's name, Cuthbert,	Killimacuddican.
Cúil, a corner,	Cuil.
Cuileann [cullen], a holly,	Alwhillan.
Cuileannach, or *cuileanóg*, a place of hollies,	Cullenoch.
Cuinneog, a corner,	Cunnoch.
Cul, the back,	Cuil.
Cullach, a boar,	Cornhulloch.
Cultran, a man's name,	Holm Coltran.
Currach, a marsh,	Corra.
Daingean [dangan], a stronghold,	Dian.
Dair, gen. *dara*, an oak,	Arndarroch.
Dal, a portion of land,	Dalmannoch.
Darach, an oak wood, an oak-tree,	Arndarroch.
Dealg [dallig], a thorn,	Clamdally.
Dearg [dyarg], red,	Baryerrock.
Deargail, a red place,	Dalreagle.
Deargán [dyargan], red ; a man's name,	Ballochjargon.
Deisceart [descart], southern,	Barcheskie.
Dess, on the right, south,	Cairntosh.
Dobhar [dour], *dur*, water,	Dargalgal.
Doire [dirry], a wood ; later, an oak wood,	Derry.
Domhnull [donnell], a man's name, Donald,	Cairndonald.
Donachadh [Donaghie], *Donnchadh* [Donngha], a man's name, Duncan,	Bardonachie.
Donn, brown,	Benjohn.
Donnán, a man's name, Donnan,	Cairndonnan.
Dóran, an otter,	Aldouran.
Doub [dub], a gutter,	Blackdubs.
Draighean [drane], blackthorns,	Drangan.
Dréolán [dreelan], a wren,	Drumadryland.
Droichead [droghed], a bridge,	Bardrochwood.
Dromainn, a ridge,	Drummond Hill.
Dronnán, a ridge,	Dronnan.
Druidhe [dreehy], a druid,	Droughandruie.
Druim, the back, a ridge,	Drum.
Drust, a Pictish name of a man,	Bardrestan.
Dubh [dooh], black,	Allandoo.
Dubhaghan [dougan], a man's name, Dougan,	Cairndubbin.

Duine [dinnie], a man, ...	Dindinnie.
Dún,	Doon.
Dúnadh [doonah], } a fort, . . .	Donaldbuie.
Dúnán,	Dinnans.
Dúnagan, hilly, .	Dungeon.
Each, éch, a horse, ...	Auchness.
Eadar, between, ...	Adderball.
Ealtaidhe [eltey], white, ...	Carneltoch.
Eanach [annagh], a bog, ...	Anabaglish.
Earbull [arble], a tail, ...	Darnarbel.
Eas [ass], a torrent, a cascade, ...	Ass of the Gill.
Easbog, a bishop, ...	Ernespie.
Easga, casgán, an eel, ...	Pulnaskie.
Eilean, oilean, an island, ...	Allandoo.
Eilit, elidh, a hind, ...	Carneltoch.
Én [ane], a bird, ...	Barnean.
Eoghagan, a man's name, ...	Barmagachan.
Ernan, a man's name, ...	Knockernan.
Fada, long, far, ...	Auchenfad.
Fadán, a man's name, Fadzean, ...	Barfadden.
Faithche [fahy], green field, ...	Fannygapple.
Faill, a cliff, ...	Fallincherrie.
Fuioleann [feelan], a sea-gull, ...	Lochenaling.
Fán, a slope, ...	Fans of Altry.
Farrach, a trysting-place, ...	Clafaras.
Farsaing, wide, ...	Ringferson.
Feadán [fadden], a streamlet, ...	Barfadden.
Feannóg [fannog], a carrion-crow, ...	Barwinnock.
Fearghus, a man's name, Fergus, ...	Loch Fergus.
Fearn, an alder, ...	Balfern.
Fearnachán, a place of alders, ...	Drumfarnachan.
Fear, a man, ...	Knocknavar.
Feusgán, a mussel, ...	Craignesket.
Fhainre [hanrie], a sloping place, ...	Knockhenries.
Fiach, fithcach [feeagh], a raven, ...	Bennaveoch.
Fiadh [feeh], a deer, ...	Craiginnee.
Fidh [fee], a wood, ...	Palnee.
Fillan, a man's name, ...	Kilfillan.
Finnán, a man's name, ...	Kirkgunzeon.
Finngall, a Norseman, ...	{ Carrickfundle (in Addenda).
Fintan, a man's name, ...	Knockiefountain.
Fionn [fin], white, ...	Blairfin.
Fionnagan, a man's name, Finnigan or Hinnigan, .	Barhinnigans.

Fliuch, wet,	Carrickafliou.
Foithre [firrie], copse,	Wherry Croft.
Fráech, heather,	Freuch.
Francach, a Frenchman,	Auchenfranco.
Fraochán, whortle-berry,	Barfraggan.
Fuinnse, fuinnscán, fuinnseóg [finshie, finshan, fin-shug], ash-tree,	Inshanks.
Gab, gob, a mouth,	Gabarruning.
Gabhail [gowl], a fork,	Adderhall.
Gabhailín [gowlin], a fork,	Goulan Glen.
Gaeth, gaoth [geu, gwee], the wind,	Curghie.
Gaidhel [gael], a Gael,	Galloway.
Gaineach, Gainmhach [gainhach], } sandy,	Gannoch.
Gall, a foreigner ; a standing stone,	Dergall.
Gallach, a standing stone,	Kilgallioch.
Gallnach, a foreigner's or stranger's place,	Galdenoch.
Gamhán [gowan], a calf,	Drumgowan.
Gar, near,	Barwhar.
Gáradh [gaira], *Garrdha* [gairha], } a garden, an enclosure,	Garriefad.
Garán, a wood,	Glengarren.
Garbh, rough,	Kinharvie.
Garrán, a thicket,	Glengarren.
Geal [gal], white,	Carrickgill.
Gearr [gar], short,	Barwhar.
Gearrán, a hack,	Glengarren.
Gile [gilly], whiteness,	Lagageely.
Giolc [guilk], a rush,	Auchengilshie.
Giolcach, rushy,	Auchengilshie.
Giusach, a fir wood,	Loch Goosie.
Glac, the palm of the hand, a narrow glen,	Glaik.
Glaiseachd, verdure,	Glassoch.
Glas, green,	Barglass.
Glasán, a fish, pollack-whiting, or lythe ; also, an edible seaweed,	Carrickglassen.
Glasín, a streamlet,	Airieglassen.
Glasuaine [glassany], green,	Airieglassen.
Gléoir [glore], clearness, *Gléoirdha* [glora], clear, }	Loch Glar.
Gluing, the shoulder, *Glún,* the knee, }	Gloon.
Gobha [gow], *Gobhan* [gown], } a smith,	Aldergowan.
Gorm, blue,	Gormal.

Gort, an enclosure,	Drumgorth.
Graigán, a village,	Greggans.
Gréach, a hill-flat,	Irongray.
Greadadh [graddah], a scorching,	Graddock.
Greallach, dirty, *s.* clay,	Drumgrillie.
Grean [gran], gravel, } *Greanach*, gravelly, }	Grainy Ford.
Greusach, a shoemaker,	Balgracie.
Grian [green], the sun,	Cairnagreen.
Grianan [greenan], a castle,	Grannan.
Gruag, long grass,	Bargrug.
Guillin, a man's name, Gillon,	Craigengillan.
Iain [eean], a man's name, John,	Barewing.
Iar [eer], west,	Balshere.
Iarach [eeragh], } *Iarthach*, } westerly,	Blaw Weary.
Iarn, iron,	Gleniron.
Inbher [inver], the mouth of a stream,	Innermessan.
Inis, an island,	Inch.
Iolaire [illery], an eagle,	Benyellarie.
Iosa [eesa], Jesus,	Allaneasy.
Iseal [eeshal], low,	Corvisel.
Isle [issly], lower,	Drummihislie.
Iubhar [yure], yew or juniper,	Palnure.
Labhair [lour], to speak,	Craiglour.
Lag, } *Lagán*, } a hollow,	Lag, Laggan.
Lagh, a hill,	Lawglass.
Láir, a mare,	Auchenlarie.
Laoch [lee], a calf,	Ballochalee.
Lathrach [laaragh], a place, a house-site,	Larroch.
Leacán [lakan], a stony hill-side,	Lakens.
Leacht, a grave,	Laicht.
Leamh, leamhán [lav, louan], an elm,	Ringielawn.
Leamhach [lavagh], an elm wood,	Lavich.
Leamhchoill [lavhwill, luell], an elm wood,	Barluell.
Leamhraidhean [lavran, lowran], an elm wood,	Lowran.
Learg [larg, lurg], an eminence,	Larg.
Leargaidh [largie, lurgie], a hill-side,	Larghie.
Leathann [lane], broad,	Auchlane.
Léc leac, liag, a flagstone, a tomb,	Airielick.
Lias, a hut,	Drumlass.
Liath [lee], grey,	Barlae.
Lin [leen], flax,	Port Leen.

Linachan, a flax field,	Ochtralinachan.
Linn, a pool,	Linblane.
Lis, *lios*, a fort,	Drumlass.
Lobhar [lour], a leper, an infirm person,	Barlure.
Loch, a lake,	Lochaber.
Lochán, a lakelet,	Lochanhour.
Lochlainn, a man's name, Lachlan,	Barlauchline.
Lod, a pool,	Lodnagapple.
Lodán, a pool,	Loddanmore.
Lois [losh], fire,	Ironlosh.
Loisgthe [lusky], burnt,	Craiglosk.
Long, a ship,	Port Long.
Longphort, a harbour,	Longfort.
Losaid, a kneading-trough,	Losset.
Loscain, or *losgann*, a frog,	Darloskin.
Luachair, a rush,	Drumlockhart.
Luan [loon], a lamb,	Drumalone.
Lúb, a loop, a bend,	Loopmabinnie.
Lúbach, looped, sinuous,	Lobbacks.
Lubhghort [louart], a garden,	Lairdmannoch.
Lughaidh [Lughey], a man's name,	Knockmilauk.
Lus, a herb, a plant,	Auchenlosh.
Ma, *mo*, my,	Hillmabreediu.
Machair, *Machaire* [maghery], } a plain, a field,	Machar.
Machairín [maghereen], a little plain,	Macherein.
Madadh [maddy], a dog,	
Máel [moil], bald,	Meaul.
Maelán, *Máeleoin*, } a man's name,	Clint Maelun.
Maethail [meehill], soft land,	Mahool.
Mág, *magh*, a plain,	May.
Manach, a monk,	Almanack Hill.
Manister, a monastery,	Auchinmanister.
Mantach, a man's name,	Drumawanty.
Maolán, a beacon,	Clint Maelun.
Mart, an ox,	Ardnimort.
Martainn, a man's name, Martin,	Drummartin.
Meadhon [meun], middle,	Barmain.
Meadhonach [meunach], middle,	Balminnoch.
Meadhran [Merran], a man's name,	Kirkmirran.
Meall, a lump; a hill,	Garmeal.
Medran, a man's name,	Kirkmadrine.
Michel, a man's name, Michael,	Blairmichael.
Mín [meen], smooth,	Mean Hill.

Móin, a mountain, moor, or bog, . . .   Dalmoney.
Mór, great, ...   Barmore.
Muc, a pig, ...   Clachanamuck.
Muclach, a swine pasture, . . .   Drummuckloch.
Muilean [mullan], a mill, . . .   Ballymellan.
Muine [minnie], a thicket, . . .   Dalmoney.
Muir, the sea, ...   Slochnamorrow.
Muirchadh [murghie], a man's name, Murphy,   Craigmurchie.
Muirchertach, a man's name, Murdoch, . .   Knockmurdoch.
Muire, a woman's name, Mary, . . .   Kilmorie.
Muireadhach [murragh], a man's name, Murray,   Balmurrie.
Mullach, a hill, ...   Mulloch.
Mullán, a hill, ...   Mollance.
Murlán, a rough top, ...   Carrickamurlan.

Niall [Neel], a man's name, Niel, .   Auchneel.
Niuc, a corner, ...   Curate's Neuk.
Nocht, naked, ...   Castle Naught.

Óchtarach, uachdarach, upper, . . .   Auchnotteroch.
Ochtradh [oughtrie], a man's name, Uchtred, .   Kirouchtrie.
Odhar [owr], grey, ...   Craigower.
Odhartha [owra], grey, ...   Barnhourie.
Oilean [illan], an island, ...   Allandoo.
Orc, a pig, ...   Craiggork.
Ornacht, barley, ...   Knockharnot.

Pádraic, a man's name, Patrick, . .   Kirkpatrick.
Paidin, a form of Patrick, . . .   Kilmacfadzeau.
Pairc, a field, ...   Park.
Peall, a horse, ...   Drumpail.
Petair, a man's name, Peter, . . .   Castle Feather.
Phort, a stronghold, . . .   Campford.
Poll, a hole, a pool ; water of any kind, .   Polbae.
Port,
Portán,   } a harbour or landing-place, .   { Portaclearys.
                                                   { Parton.

Raghnall, Raonull, a man's name, Ronald,   Craigronald.
Raithne [rannie], fern,   }
Raithneach [rannagh], a place of ferns,   }   Blawrainie.
Rál, an oak, ...   Ringreel.
Ras, a shrub, ...   Drumrash.
Rath [raa], a fort, ...Wraith.
Rathad, ród, a road, ...   Drummieraud.
Rathain [rahan], a ferny place, . .   Pulran.
Reamhar [raver, raer], fat, thick, . .   Ringreer.

Y

Réidh [ray], smooth,	Auchrae.
Réidh [ray], a level field,	Rephad.
Ri, righ [ree], a king,	Auchenree.
Riabhach [reengh], grey,	Auchenreoch.
Riasc [risk], a morass, bog,	Risk.
Riascach [riskagh], boggy,	Rusco.
Riderch, a man's name, Roderick,	Mossroddock.
Rinn, *Rinnán,* } a point ; a division of land,	{ Rhinns. { Ringan.
Ród, a road,	Drummieraud.
Ros, a wood ; a promontory,	Ross.
Rós, a rose,	Knockcrosh.
Rosán, a wood ; a promontory,	Rossen-Hill.
Ruadh [rooh, roy], red,	Benroach.
Ruadhán [roohan], red land,	Rouchan.
Rudha [roo], a point of land,	Row.
Saer [seer], a carpenter,	Drumatier.
Sagart, a priest,	Altaggart.
Sail, a willow,	Barnsallie.
Sairach, eastern,	Balsarroch.
Salach, dirty,	Barsalloch.
Samhadh [savva, sooa], sorrel,	Suie.
Samhan [shavun], the first of November,	Drumawan.
Scé, *Sceach,* *Sceath,* } a hawthorn,	Scaith.
Sceilig [skellig], a rock,	Knockskellie.
Sceir, a rock, a scaur,	Scar.
Sceirach, rocky,	Loch Skerrow.
Sceirlach, rocky,	Dunskirloch.
Sceitheóg [skyoge], a hawthorn bush,	Auchenskeog.
Sceithín [skeyin, skeen], a bush,	{ Skeengally (in { Addenda).
Sciath [skey], a shield, a wing, } *Sciathach* [skeyach], winged, }	Dunskey.
Scoloc, a small farmer,	Craigenskulk.
Scrath [scraw], a sod,	Barscraith.
Scabhac [shoke], a hawk,	Garnshog.
Sealg [shallug], the chase,	Drumshalloch.
Seamar, seamróg [shammer, shamrog], clover, shamrock,	Glenchamber.
Sean [shan], old,	Shambelly.
Seangán [shangan], an ant ; a little fellow,	Barnshangan.
Seant [shant], holy, sainted,	Clayshant.
Searrach, [sharragh], a foal,	Barsherrie.

Seiscinn [sheskin], a marsh, ... Barcheskie.
Sgadán, a herring, ... Culscadden.
Sgeallan [sgallan], wild mustard, ... Drumscallan.
Sian [sheen], a foxglove, ... Auchensheen.
Siar [shere], eastern, ... Balshere.
Sidheain [sheehan], a fairy palace, . . . Auchensheen.
Sindach,
Sinnach, } a fox, Auchenshinnoch.
Sionnach [shinnagh], }
Siosg [shisk], a sedge, ... Dernacissock.
Slaod [slade], slaughter, ... Barnsladie.
Sleamhán [slavan, slouan], an elm, . . . Craigslouan.
Sliabh [slew], a hill, ... Slacarnachan.
Slocán, { Slochanawn.
Slochd, } a gulley, · Slock.
Slochín, { Sloucheen Slunk.
Smeurach, { Slewsmirroch.
Smeurlach, } a place of brambles, . Smirle.
Solas, light, fire, ... Barnolas.
Sporaidhe [spurrey], spurs, ... Spirry.
Srath [sraw]. a plain, ... Strammoddie.
Srón, a nose, a headland, ... Stroan.
Srónach, hilly, ... Stronach.
Srónachan, a hilly place, ... Tronachan.
Sruthair [sroor], a stream, ... Strool Bay.
Staonag [stannag], a sloping place, . . . Stannock.
Stuaic [stook], a stack, a hill, ... Knockstocks.
Subh [soo], a berry, ... Polsuie.
Subhach [sooagh], a place of berries, . . Polsuie.
Súdaire [soodery], a tanner, ... Bentudor.
Suidhe [see], a seat, ... Knockensee.
Suidheachin [seehin], a little seat, . . . Sheuchan.

Tachar, a combat, ... Tacher Burn.
Talamh [tallow], land, ... Knocktallow.
Tamhnach [tawnach], a meadow, ... Tannieflux.
Tarsuinn, thwart, across, ... Baltersan.
Teach, tighe, a house, ... Drumatye.
Tealach, a forge, ... Challoch.
Teanga [tanga], a tongue, a strip of land, . . Chang.
Teine [tinny], fire, ... Knockietinnie.
Tendal, { Knocktentol.
Tenneàl, } a bonfire, ... Knockteinan.
Teórann [torran], a boundary, Baltorrens.
Tess, south, ... Cairntosh.
Tiar [tear], westward, . . Baltier.

Tigh, a house,	Drumatye.
Tineol [tinnel], an assembly,	Knocktinnel.
Tiobar [tibber], a well,	Tibbert.
Tiompán [timpan], a hillock,	Dinchimpon.
Tír, land,	Glaisters.
Tóchar, a causeway, a dowry,	Tocher Knowe.
Tom,	Tummock Hill.
Tomach, bushy,	Knocktomachie.
Tón, a rump, a backside,	Tandoo.
Tor, a hill, a tower,	Tor.
Torán, a hillock,	Thornglass.
Torc, a boar,	Mindork.
Toruidhe [toree], a hunter ; an outlaw,	Daltorae.
Traona, tradhnach [trana], a corncrake,	Drumatrane.
Treabh [trave], a farm,	Threave.
Treamhar [traver], a farm,	Terregles.
Túaimm [toom], a village, a grave,	Knockiedim.
Tuas [toosh], upper,	Cairntosh.
Tuath [too], north,	Slewentoo.
Tuathal [tooal], a man's name, Toole,	Drumtowl.
Tuatheal [tooal], northern,	Drumtowl.
Uabhar [ower], pride,	Dunower.
Uachdar [oughter], upper,	Barneywater.
Uachdarach [ouohteragh], upper land,	Auchtrelure.
Uallach, proud,	Knockwalloch.
Uinnse, uinnseann [inshie, insheon], an ash,	Inshanks.
Uisce [isky], water,	Bennuskie.
Ultach, an Ulsterman,	Barnulto.
Umha [oo], a cave,	Bellew.
Urlár, a floor, a flat piece of land,	Airlour.

PRINTED BY T. AND A. CONSTABLE, PRINTERS TO HER MAJESTY,

AT THE EDINBURGH UNIVERSITY PRESS.

www.ingramcontent.com/pod-product-compliance
Lightning Source LLC
Chambersburg PA
CBHW021748110726
47902CB00006B/1448